FLYING MONKEYS

A bullied worker, a broken legal system, and one brave mum's exceptional fight against corruption.

LORI O'KEEFFE

Flying monkey—a popular psychology term—originates from the flying monkeys in *The Wizard of Oz*, who were under the spell of the Wicked Witch and were used to carry out her evil plans. In relation to everyday narcissists, flying monkeys are people who actively participate in a narcissist's smear campaign. As a general rule, flying monkeys are used by narcissists to gaslight, keep tabs on, invalidate, discredit and isolate people that they abuse.

Copyright © 2023 by Lori O'Keeffe

Cover Design by Maricarmen Rubí Baeza

Published by Mouseface Publishing

Paperback ISBN: 978-0-6459026-0-0

Hardback ISBN: 978-0-6459026-1-7

All rights reserved.

No part of this book may be reproduced in any form or by any electronic or mechanical means, including information storage and retrieval systems, without written permission from the author, except for the use of brief quotations in a book review.

This book is dedicated to all those who in good conscience fought for the truth and were punished so the truth could be hidden.

And to those who have had their lives ruined or ended by the scourge of bullying in all its inglorious forms.

Contents

Foreword	vii
1. Me, Myself and I	1
2. Work Woes	12
3. The Nightmare of Injustice	54
4. WorkCover Worries	105
5. Privacy Problems	142
6. Unions Not So Unifying	158
7. Legal Lessons	167
8. Maybe Mediation	181
9. The Compensation Con	185
10. "I Think" to Justify	211
11. Judgement of the Judgement	255
12. The Supreme not so Supreme	278
13. High Appeal not so Appealing	302
14. To Protect and Serve	316
15. Costs Corruption	329
16. Happy Times	346
17. Hard Times	355
18. The Searching Years	369
19. Finding Dan	379
20. Lawyers Not Liable	393
21. I Rest My Case	407
22. Occasional Integrity	431
Epilogue	457

Foreword

Workplace Bullying – 10 Years On
Written by a daughter, October 2010

No parent wants to witness their child being bullied at school. But what happens when it's flipped, and a child watches their mother being systematically destroyed by workplace bullying?

I would never have believed that my mother could be bullied; bullying was something I associated with young or marginalised people. Not Mum. She was mature, kind, attractive, proficient and popular – how could she be a victim of bullying? It didn't make sense. I had never heard of established, professional, successful adults falling victim to bullying.

Over the past ten years, I have become increasingly aware of my mother's complex situation, and workplace bullying in general. I am finding it difficult to accept that my once strong, highly competent, independent mother will never recover from her physical and psychological injury.

While WorkSafe blames inept management for workplace bullying, the potential repercussions of the mess Mum's previous employer made, are colossal. This has meant that my psychologically injured mother has been left with the task of exposing their dysfunction and failures. The hidden costs to the community now exceed $1 million, when early resolution would have cost just a few thousand.

Foreword

The fact that the legislation controlling the Victorian WorkCover Authority has delayed this case from being heard publicly for almost 10 years is sordid. Although they paid for Mum's medical expenses, the lengths gone to deny her a fair hearing or justice are inexcusable, especially considering that Victoria prides itself internationally on its workplace bullying guidelines.

Workplace bullying should be a major concern for all Victorians. In particular, the growing number of middle-aged women victims, who should be able to access the equity and justice they are entitled to.

I know that I cannot be the only daughter, my father the only husband, nor my brother and sisters the only children having to witness and survive their mother's physical and psychological disintegration due to workplace bullying.

I believe that this is a story that needs to be told.

ONE

Me, Myself and I

I have toyed with the idea for many years to write a book on my experiences. Friends have also encouraged me. Now, twenty years on from the major events, I feel the time is right for my story to be told. My experiences are so vast and convoluted that I can only hope by putting them in writing that readers will come to understand how I found myself in such predicaments. I have not included all my experiences – to do so would make my story too long and complex.

I wonder now if I fought too hard. Should I have just given up and returned to the kitchen? Or better yet, take my own life, like many before me? After reading my story I hope you come to a place of understanding of why I did what I did.

When a person experiences a traumatic event, our instinctual trigger of 'flight or fight' kicks in. One can take flight into drugs, alcohol, travel, or suicide, but none of these options were for me. Fight was my drug of choice – but did I really have a choice? We are hard-wired to behave in certain ways when faced with unimaginable terror, and it came to pass that I was a fighter. Whether this was best in the end I really cannot say, but I am alive and that says a lot.

I don't believe we can judge how another responds to trauma – they respond in the manner for which they are destined. Fighting was my destiny; flight may be yours.

Watching current affairs program *Q&A* one night (a favourite weekly ritual for my husband Des and me), a panellist named Andrew Neil (British journalist and Chairman of *The Spectator*) basically answered the question I have been grappling with since I first considered whether to write my story: Should you name and shame your abusers? His response was yes, and he explained his answer this way: for years, all kinds of abuse has been going on, with little done about it. This has largely been because victims (I do not like this word, but will use it here as it puts the story into perspective) will not provide evidence or name those responsible, often out of the fear of reprisal. The #MeToo Movement has changed all that because it started naming names, and that is why it has gathered momentum and at long last abusers are now being held accountable for their actions.

But what of the actions—or more precisely the inactions—of those not directly involved? Do they bear any responsibility? During my journey I have often thought of Kitty Genovese. (I read about her infamous case in my earlier research and I was very moved and saddened by her plight.) In 1964, Kitty Genovese was murdered outside her New York City apartment. Many neighbours were watching from their windows, yet failed to step in to assist or call the police. I know this sounds unthinkable, but it's explained by social psychologists Bibb Latane and John Darley, who popularised the concept of the 'bystander effect' which occurs "when the presence of others discourages an individual from intervening in an emergency situation." Latane and Darley attributed the bystander effect to the diffusion of responsibility (onlookers are less likely to intervene if there are other witnesses who seem likely to do so) and social influence (individuals monitor the behaviour of those around them to determine how to act).

The phenomenon of the bystander effect is what has kept domestic violence in the dark and workplace bullying a bit of a lark. But #silentnomore.

Nevertheless, I still dither. My abuse was not physical per se, but it sure had a physical effect on me and caused a number of physical illnesses. Sometimes I wish that I had been physically assaulted at work or experienced sexual harassment, as this has slowly become an accepted community issue which is on the worldwide agenda. I would've had support and understanding around me from the sisterhood. I was bullied at work, and have referred to my abuse as psychological rape when committed by one to two perpetrators, and psychological gang rape when there are three or more perpetrators.

Rape of the body is a debilitating experience, and so is rape of the mind –

it is very personal, as it is about who you are, your worth, your value. It strips you of feeling that you belong to a tribe; it leaves you to be abandoned, to be alone in a frightening wilderness.

A part of me wishes that my abuse was physical – all these years later I would be recovered and enjoying my retirement years. Scars, bruises and broken bones would be evidence of my abuse, and authorities would take action on my behalf. But when your scars cannot be seen, then no one knows or understands the abuse you have suffered. It is widely understood that overall psychological injuries cost WorkCover more than physical injuries, and there is less chance of a psychologically injured worker ever returning to the workplace. While this is acknowledged by WorkCover, they still too often fight the injured worker to the bitter end with claims of rorting. I can attest that the actions are abhorrent, yet most in the community do not understand this – that injured workers (especially when the injury is not visible) are doomed from the day of injury. There are no lobby groups or anyone with power sincerely helping injured workers – we are on our own, vulnerable, marginalised and taken advantage of by many who make a good living off our 'bones'.

To me, this adds another layer of abuse. An injured worker does not purposely get injured, and in cases of bullying the injured worker is *purposely* injured, and yet the honesty and integrity of the injured worker is questioned and challenged. This has a profound effect on a diligent and conscientious employee and adds 'insult to injury,' further compounding the original injury.

Reading my story, I hope you will understand how important it is to me to get the truth out, to have someone acknowledge the wrong done to me, and to set the story straight. In the words of the wise Dolly Everett, who was taken too soon, "Speak even if your voice shakes." The wonderful Patrick McGorry, Australian of the Year, states that "Telling stories and exposing things that people want to sweep under the carpet is the way to solve the problem – it is the first step." Maya Angelou said, "There is no agony like bearing an untold story inside of you."

I recently read somewhere that courage is not the absence of fear, but rather the judgement that something else is more important than fear. All through my journey I have been fearful, making judgements that I believed were more important than the fear I felt. Whether this turned out to be right or wrong I still do not know.

Writing my story has not in any way been a labour of love but a labour of courage – of places, truths, thoughts, feelings and injustices that have pained me so greatly.

In the words of Benjamin Franklin, "Justice will not be served until those who are unaffected are as outraged as those who are." I hope whilst reading my book you feel a little outrage here and there.

"It must be remembered that abusers don't abuse everyone they come into contact with, so placing doubt on victims based on your own experience with that person is irresponsible and unkind."

Feminist News

Some of my experiences, feelings and thoughts are complex. Over the years I've kept a diary of words I've found inspiring or quotes that explained how I've felt, and I use these throughout this book. On some occasions I recorded the author but on other occasions I did not. I apologise to those whose words I have used without reference, but I feel confident you will not mind.

If you find it difficult to believe or understand my story then be thankful. One of my survival strategies which has assisted greatly is that I have not 'self-attacked.' I believed in myself when I felt sure others doubted. Even though there have been times I've felt lost, I've fought to remain who I am.

My story is 90% truth, 9.9% fair comment and 0.1% hearsay. With any scandal, there has to be a scapegoat, and that scapegoat is me. I read once that "The moment you put a stop to people taking advantage of you and disrespecting you, is when they define you as difficult, selfish or crazy. Manipulators hate boundaries." In my story, there are a number of major manipulators, and hopefully by the end of my story you will know who they are. I will name those who have caused me so much pain, and give lesser players in my story some degree of anonymity.

It took nearly ten years to struggle through the WorkCover process. It does not assist injured workers to regain their health and wellbeing to return to the workforce and a return to the life they once had. The process can and very often does render an injured worker unemployable. With a large County Court and Supreme Court—and on many occasions an empty court—and with many judges, I wonder why the legal process takes so long.

In 1999, Labor came to power. Something that Rob Hulls said in his Ministerial Statement gave me hope: "A fair, accessible and understandable justice system for all."

Also stated was that "The Bracks Government understands that justice is not an abstract concept, but something that affects all our lives in a very real sense. Justice is about openness, transparency and accountability. ... It is about creating courts that are modern and accessible; not only in terms of our court buildings but in the way they dispense justice."

In no way do these statements describe my experiences, which were the exact opposite.

An old quote often cited by judges themselves is that "Justice delayed is justice denied." This pertains to my experience; delay is the major tactic of all players in the game of WorkCover, and sadly this includes the judiciary itself. A common theme among those who have power over us, is them saying words that make us feel valued, and then when it suits them, they seemingly disregard such words.

Around 1992, there were many issues affecting the New South Wales corruption body, the Independent Commission Against Corruption, known as the ICAC, with the then-Premier Greiner asking why the corruption body needed to have exceptional powers. He made a statement that resonated with me: "Corruption is, by its nature, secretive and difficult to elicit. It is a crime of the powerful. It is a consensual crime with no obvious victim willing to complain."

I have survived the consensual crime and I am willing to complain, but unfortunately no one has ever been listening. I have fought alone and my truthful stories are my evidence.

It is my understanding and also my experience that workplace bullying occurs when one or more people commit to destroying a co-worker. This includes the assassination of a worker's reputation, the making of false accusations both professional and personal, and exclusion from accepted workplace activities. The bullies use sabotage, gaslighting, putdowns subtle and not subtle, and unreasonable work demands, all directed to the chosen one. The last item mentioned is how workplaces get rid of workers who complain of this treatment or submit a WorkCover claim. You could have been a competent and conscientious worker for many years without incident, then you follow the organisational procedure for raising concerns about bullying and suddenly you are no longer competent. Everything you do and every decision you make is questioned and challenged, with the ultimate decision that your performance is poor and that is why you are psychologically injured – not by bullying but by so-called reasonable management action taken in a so-called reasonable manner.

When three or more co-workers are involved in the bullying it becomes mobbing, and this is lethal. You cannot fight it alone – you are heavily outnumbered and the psychological injury becomes profound, leading to illness and disease. Emotional abuse is just as bad as physical abuse; at times it can be worse. You can heal broken bones, but healing a broken mind is almost impossible.

I've found it difficult to understand the mindset of these 'mobbers' who bullied me. I knew these women, but I greatly underestimated the group dynamics of ordinary minds. Reading this from C.M. Blow helped me gain some understanding: "One doesn't have to operate with great malice to do great harm. The absence of empathy and understanding are sufficient."

There are many incidents to describe my experiences of 'consensual crime', some long, some short, but all I can give you is an overview, otherwise my story would run to thousands of pages rather than the few hundred here.

Many years ago, I read a quote by Mahatma Gandhi which resonated with me – with my beliefs, how I saw myself, and how I've tried to live my life: "Let our first act every morning be to make the following resolve for the day. I shall not fear anyone on earth, I shall fear only God, I shall not bear ill will toward anyone, I shall not submit to injustice from anyone, I shall conquer untruth by truth, and in resisting untruth I shall put up with all suffering."

I loved school and it was never an effort to go. Pulling a sickie when I was not sick was unheard of, as most of my social life revolved around school and school friends. In those days, life was simpler – there was no technology to lure us away from playing in the street with the neighbourhood kids. There were endless hours playing Monopoly, poison ball, street cricket, hop scotch, skippy, mushrooming, as well as taking walks down to the old aqueduct, playing on the river bank and building a make-believe house in the long grass. Of course, when we got a little older, it was bonfire night, kiss chasey and spin the bottle that took our interest. There were around twenty kids who lived in my little street; ten were around my age, so there was always someone to play with. I do not recall any fights or anyone behaving badly – or any bullying. We treated each other with innocent respect; I say innocent respect because at that age none of us knew what respect really meant and how it is a word and philosophy that should guide your life.

I was happy at school. I had good grades, but not exceptional; sport was my forte. I was tall and possessed a good level of skill. One memory that stands out for me is playing netball, where there were always the same two girls chosen by the teachers to captain each team in Wednesday afternoon sport and they then got to choose their team, one student at a time. Because of my height I was often picked first, while the same student was left to last every time.

I felt for this girl, but I could not do anything about it – this was just the way things were. But one Wednesday the usual captain was away, and I was chosen in her place. With the students all lined up, we two captains started picking the girls we wanted in our team. I can remember standing there knowing which girls I wanted to pick to ensure I won the game.

I looked at the girl who always picked last and something inside me started to stir, and almost without thinking I pointed my finger to her. She beamed with a quizzical look on her face and I knew I had made the right choice.

The game was played and the winning captain came to shake my hand and said, sorry you lost. But did I feel sorry? No way. I believe this is where I started to realise that winning is not as important as how you play the game. There are occasions in life, probably many, where you may lose, but without realising in reality you have actually won.

I was born in the early nineteen-fifties – a time of innocence for most kids born around this time, with stay-at-home mums, and if you were really lucky you may have had a television in your home.

We finally had a TV around 1960, and I remember what fun Friday nights came to be. It was always 'fish and chips night' and 'lolly night', with my father coming home from work with his bag bursting with sweets. These were good times and I remember them fondly.

Friday night was also 'movie night', with the boys wanting cowboy or war movies while my mum and I wanted musicals or love stories. We always eventually compromised, and whoever did not get what they wanted on Friday night got what they wanted on Sunday night after we'd watched *Fathers Know Best*.

One Friday night, my mum and I were watching a movie called *The Diary of Anne Frank*. We were both so sad, crying with the realisation of how innocent people suffered so much during the Holocaust. I remember Mum turning to me and saying "this must never happen again" or words to that effect. I think I realised then that not only is it important how you play the game, but that you must stand against injustice when you see it. These two concepts have encouraged me to live the life I have.

Another time I watched *Gaslight*, an iconic movie made in 1944 with the legendary Charles Boyer and Ingrid Bergman. I did not understand the true message of this film at the time, but by the early years of the 21st century, the abused came to understand this term, and it has now made its way into the vernacular. Gaslighting is serious business and does significant harm to those who find themselves at the mercy of a gaslighter. It is a complicated psychological weapon used to silence victims. Put simply, it is the act of undermining someone's reality by denying facts, the environment around them and/or their feelings. This creates huge personal doubt in the mind of the person subjected to this behaviour, and renders them alone, frightened and in many cases with no ability to fight back or be believed by those who could assist.

When writing about one's self, it is difficult to see how others see you. Insight is a wonderful thing – it is just so scary that others can live a whole life without learning from lessons life throws at them. I'm sure I've been in the classroom of life and sincerely attempted to learn the lessons. During a counselling session with a well-known Melbourne medico, he said to me, "Lori, your problem is you have too much insight." I have struggled to come to terms with this and understand his statement; I feel if I can understand it then I may understand myself.

Normally, having insight is considered a good thing, but not for me and my situation, as I was able to clearly and rationally consider and understand what was happening to me; who did what, where and why. I believe lacking insight can be dangerous for yourself and others, but having too much insight can also be very dangerous. For me this is particularly true, as it led me down paths I should never have travelled.

Communication is so important – it sets the scene, and so I have concentrated on trying to be a good communicator. I am probably much better now than I was back then. Yes, back in the dark days at work I made a few mistakes. Nothing of great significance, but boy did I pay a price for not being perfect. Yet those who judged were far from perfect themselves, and to this day I believe that they still feel they did the right thing. Have any of them learned and gained insight into their behaviour? I sadly doubt it, because to do so would compromise the version of selves that they happily live with.

I have never displayed hostile or threatening body language. I've smiled whenever I could, and have never raised my voice or swore at anyone in the workplace. People (not my former staff) who I worked with over the years often remarked to me about how helpful my interactions with them were, and some of them remain good friends to this day.

⚖

I always tried to have positive interactions in my work life; I am conscious of the fact that I do not know it all, and so I respect others' opinions. If I am wrong, I have no problem admitting this; blaming others was not my usual practice.

I genuinely attempted to operate on a foundational work ethos of Integrity, Respect, Dignity, Compassion and Empathy. Sadly, on one occasion I failed. Sadder yet; I rarely identified any of these values in others.

I have a sensitive soul, which sometimes causes me to become numb on the inside while breathing life into others. It meant being misunderstood, mistreated and even hated at times, which is exemplified in the next chapter. Having a sensitive soul is not a weakness, as some may think, but a strength. Sensitive souls are born warriors, capable of enduring great suffering and heartache. Without them the world would crumble.

In legal proceedings, evidence was given that I was "dynamic," "motivated" and "an intelligent woman" with a "hardy personality". I was called "a resourceful, emotionally strong woman," and it was said that without these qualities "this lady would be in a far worse emotional state." These are qualities and personality traits any employer should appreciate.

Maybe if I was different, I would not have been targeted, or I would have handled it differently. Then my life would be different now. I was too trusting, always thinking the best of people. I blame myself for believing that there was fairness and justice in the WorkCover and legal systems. I came to learn that those supposedly there to help, were really only helping themselves.

My childhood friend Anne rang today and asked how I was going. Anne and I have been friends since kindergarten, and she has also experienced the tragic loss of her only son, so we share a bond that many do not. We talked about my book, the issues that would be included, and how because I still had not come to terms with what had happened, I could still not quite get my head around why I felt the way I did. Anne responded that her belief is that we children of the fifties, having grown up in the working-class town that Geelong was 50 years ago, we developed a social conscience and were fair-minded. We did not live a life of privilege; we lived a life of thinking of others. I appreciated Anne's thoughts – they fit with my own.

I later learned that when I stood up against injustice, matters became worse, and when I did *not* stand up against injustice, matters became worse. This was the oxymoron that afflicted my life over many years.

In my opinion, bullies who use their employers' or shareholders' or taxpayers' money and time to abuse others—and having done so, continue the misuse to hide their misdemeanours or to protect themselves—should be held accountable in a criminal court. Using funds that do not belong to you to defend the indefensible is akin to stealing.

My solicitors breached the confidence and trust I placed in their hands and destroyed the protection of my legal rights – contrary to their legal duty. Any system of justice can only command respect of the community if people can trust justice to be equal, impartial, and transparent – to be a principled system of addressing wrongs. In the Magna Carta, written some 800 years ago, this was recognised: "to no one will we sell, to no one will we deny or defer (or delay) right or justice."

Sadly, today our system of justice is riddled with selling, denying and delaying. How King John must be rolling in his grave.

I feel I am still being subjected to continuous detriment as a result of making qualifying disclosures since 2000. I remember these words I read long ago: "When the world says give up, hope whispers: try it one more time." I did for twenty years, giving hope every available opportunity.

Just because injured souls are functioning does not mean they are not suffering. In the words of Rae Smith, "The enemy doesn't stand a chance when the victim decides to survive." I have chosen to survive, but the enemy is still standing. The law supposedly exists to hold power to account, but through my experiences you will perhaps come to understand when and why the law fails.

It took me many years to understand what had happened to me and many more to come to the realisation that it was not my fault and I did not deserve to be treated in this way.

It is only now I know of narcissists and their flying monkeys. The narcissist is the puppeteer who pulls the strings to do harm, but the flying monkeys carry out the harm to devastating effect. Without these monkeys the narcissist would not be so successful and the target would have some chance. A flying monkey is not to be confused with a by-stander, a by-stander does nothing to help a victim, whereas a flying monkey does everything it can to hurt the narcissists target.

I read somewhere that "A strong person is not one who does not cry. A strong person is the one who cries and sheds tears for a moment, then gets up and fights again." This certainly describes me well – I am a fighter, and I am a woman, so watch me roar!

TWO

Work Woes

I remember quite vividly the evening in mid-1992 when I received the call from Lyn, then the Manager of Children's Services, to inform me that I was successful in my application for the position of Family Day Care Coordinator. Lyn was aware of my past discrimination experience with my previous employer in South Barwon. When I was informed of my successful application, I asked her why this had not gone against me. She responded that "we need someone strong in this position." Recruitment documents show that my rating was "A: Outstanding." Their Family Day Care Scheme had a reputation of being one of the best in the state, and I was looking forward to being part of that.

Given I had been home for three years I thought I may never work again, so this was truly an exciting moment. I'd enjoyed my time at the City of South Barwon immensely until the introduction of a policy initiated by a new supervisor who had arrived in the position while I was on maternity leave. I question why someone new to a role feels it appropriate to make far-reaching decisions and drastic changes before even settling into the job, but this is what Graeme did.

How he convinced management to agree, I do not know, but a new policy was introduced. Staff that were employed in a particular service could no longer also be a user of that service. So, in essence this meant I could not use family day care for my children. I asked for a copy of this policy, but of course it was not written down anywhere – it was just what they thought should happen.

By the time I returned to work from maternity leave the policy was written and ratified by the council. I informed them of my opinion that the policy was discriminatory and in breach of federal government funding guidelines. You can imagine that management did not take kindly to my voiced opinion, or the threat from the Federal Government to withdraw funding for this service for the breaching of their funding guidelines.

To cut a long story short, Graeme was livid, and as a consequence our working relationship was not pleasant. I stood my ground with my opinion that the policy was discriminatory. Even though I was technically in conflict with management, there was little bullying, 'mobbing' or gaslighting like I was to later experience. We may have had a difference of opinion, but essentially mutual respect still remained; we behaved like professionals.

About a year later, the legal arena agreed with me, with the policy being found to be discriminatory and the Council being required to rescind this policy publicly at their next Council meeting. By this time and for a variety of reasons, I had resigned from employment to be a stay-at-home mum for the next three years.

Given my previous experiences and the effect it had on me, I was just so happy to be returning to the workforce in a job I thought was perfect for me. In the first few days of my new employment, everything seemed to be running smoothly, until the culture of the Family Day Care (FDC) staff starting rearing its ugly head.

I felt I had always been a good manager, but sadly not a great leader. I think back to a remark I read somewhere early in my career that it is almost impossible to do a good job and be popular at the same time.

Given the industry in which I worked, doing a good job was more important to me than being popular. Caring for children, their safety and wellbeing is paramount.

I believe it's rare to be a good leader *and* to do a good job, but it does exist, and when it does it's wonderful. The magic ingredient this leader has is typically charisma. I know people who are blessed with being charismatic, and they are such fun to be around. You want to do a good job for them and be part of the leader's world and their success.

On my second day of being on the job, the subject of the end-of-year Care

Provider (I am using the old term from back in my day, with Educator now being the preferred term) Christmas Party came up in conversation.

I was told that the previous Christmas, a picnic had been planned with parents, Care Providers and staff, but unfortunately only staff attended. They thought it was funny – I did not. Approximately 10 staff and their families had had a fun time together, and the staff claimed double time overtime because it was a Sunday. It cost the service around 20 days of staff time, when staff took their two days off owed to them because they had 'worked' on a Sunday.

I felt uneasy about this, and even more so when not one staff member seemed to consider that this may not be ethical. Legal, yes, but morally questionable. This would cause me much pain as the years rolled along.

After a few weeks on the job, I had to complete my first report to our funding body, the Commonwealth Government, who gave the funds to the Council to provide child care for families in their municipality.

I'd been previously told by staff that the number of children in care was around 350. And the Council was being funded for 350 children, but when I came to do the figures for the report I could only find 150 children registered in care. I asked a staff member if I was missing something or calculating incorrectly, and she just smiled. Upon further discussion I found out that there *were* only 150 children in care, but staff were told (by their previous coordinator) to increase the funding number to 350.

I believed this was fraud and definitely dishonest, so I went to see the director of the department. I began to tell him of my findings, and he just smiled at me. It was then I realised he knew about this situation.

The extra funding was used by Council for the purchase of a minivan, shop front and renovations to a community centre, and there may well be other purchases I am not aware of. I believe these two staff—the director and the then-supervisor—were lauded for bringing so much funding into the Council coffers. I do not believe that the Council was aware of this fraud – they thought the funds were legitimately gained because of the hard work of these two particular staff members.

I understood why there appeared to be more staff than what was needed: the Service was staffed for 350 children!

I also noticed at least one staff member was absent every day; a pattern emerging week after week. I could not understand how the staff had so much sick leave and time in lieu. It didn't take long to work out there was no method of recording these leaves of absence from work, and hence leave taken was simply forgotten. I am not convinced this was done purposely, but was symptomatic of poor management practices by previous staff in my role. I developed a recording system and eventually the build-up of sick leave and time in lieu decreased to the actual levels.

Over a period of almost 12 months, I sorted out the funding issues surrounding the number of children in care, and calculated a realistic child–staff ratio. We were overstaffed for a few more years, allowing natural attrition to play its role. In hindsight, maybe I should have left and found a position where I was not so morally confronted, but I loved a challenge and honestly believed I could make a difference. By this time, I loved the Werribee community – it was warm, diverse, interesting and always challenging, and so I made the fateful decision to stay.

The following years were fast and furious, and my position became even more demanding. The State Government had introduced Compulsory Competitive Tendering, which brought no end of additional work for management staff. In 1995, my position, along with all of those in Family Services middle management, were made redundant and I had to reapply for the new Unit Leader position.

The new role replacing my previous position contained all the same areas of responsibility, but included many additional responsibilities, such as contract management, the production of Key Performance Indicators (KPIs), financial management, budget reporting – the list went on. The Service was now to be operated like a business unit. By this time, I loved my job and loved the local community and therefore I applied for the newly developed position, and was deemed to be the best applicant. I was successful in gaining a position in the new structure and became a Unit Leader. There was no recognition of the extra responsibilities in time or remuneration for unit leaders, but what we did get was a new supervisor named Helen. Helen was the previous Maternal Child and Health Nurse Coordinator and gained a position in the restructure to Unit Leader Supervisor.

In early 1996, I began to experience what I believed to be intimidating behaviour by my new supervisor Helen, and this made me feel slightly apprehensive and insecure in my work environment. My first memory of this behaviour occurred in April 1996, when she came into the general office area and motioned to me with a crocked finger to come to her. She appeared secretive, as if she had something she wanted to say in private. I approached her and stood approximately three feet from her. Helen moved closer, very close. I turned my head and looked downwards as Helen spoke softly into my ear. To have not done so would have meant that I would have touched noses with Helen – that is how close she was standing to me. Helen responded by saying, "Will you look at me when I am speaking to you?!" in a tone that I found quite chilling and unnecessary. From memory, whatever Helen had to say to me was of no significance. To justify her behaviour during this incident, she later said she had a hearing impairment and that is why she was so close—to hear what I was saying—but this is incorrect as I had my head bowed and turned because she was speaking to me, I was not speaking to her. I now know that this is referred to as invading someone's personal space.

My employer's goal at this time, as required under their Occupational Health and Safety Plan, was to "Provide a healthy and safe workplace for staff and public." This certainly was not my experience from the years 1999 to 2002.

During these three years, there were many minor incidents of intimidation and undermining. I was able to cope with this behaviour and work within it, though what began to emerge was a pattern of negligence by some senior staff.

Eventually Helen's critical, fault-finding management style became worse. This often left me feeling frustrated, and annoyed that I was being diverted from tasks at hand to justify trivial decisions and actions. Helen micromanaged – she was non-supportive in nature by never or rarely giving any positive feedback, and I doubt a positive word was ever spoken by her to management about any of my accomplishments. Helen did not like helping to fix problems; she wanted to fix perceived problems herself and then be lauded for saving the day. She rarely listened or took the time to understand the demands of the position. Because of this, I started to dread any interaction with her. Helen played the role of the devil's advocate, always found fault, even when the issue was very complex and handled well without further problems or repercussions. Over a period of time, this style of management slowly eroded my confidence.

In mid-1999, the manager John confirmed his position on the taking of time in lieu, and I operated under this position. Sometime later, he changed his position without informing me of the new requirements; I was lambasted for not following his new position.

In August 1999, I sent an email asking Helen if I could take an RDO (Rostered Day Off) owed to me. Given she knew I worked many additional hours without claiming overtime, this wasn't an unreasonable request, but she made a big deal of it because I didn't ask in the correct manner. She responded, "All other unit leaders negotiate their requests in according to management policy. The impact of Unit Leader's changes range from impact on the car pool to inadequate senior coverage of the office at Bridge Street, with many variations in between."

The following November, I read the *Community Services Bulletin*, which highlights the absences of unit leaders and management. Both John and Helen were absent, as were all other unit leaders. I was the most senior officer on duty on this day; I wasn't informed that this was to occur. What about Helen's concerns regarding the impact on the car pool and inadequate senior coverage? Did all other unit leaders negotiate their requests in the manner she required – and if so, why did she and John not know that I was the only Unit Leader attending work that Friday? Apparently, this negotiation with other unit leaders did not occur.

Also in November of 1999, I emailed the Family Services Manager, John, asking why I was the only Unit Leader not to have performed Higher Duties in his absence unlike other unit leaders who had all had a turn, and then another turn. The reason I asked was because my staff had made comments regarding this, and asked me why, as when I was absent all my staff equally had a turn of 'acting up'. I sent John an email asking if we needed to talk, but he never responded to this email or my request. At our next monthly Unit Leader meeting, another member of staff placed Equal Employment Opportunity (EEO) as an agenda item, and I raised the issue of the rotation of the Acting Manager's role when John and Helen were both absent. I asked the rationale behind how this was delegated, and John's response was that he considered the workloads of unit leaders and delegated accordingly. He also stated, "Lori, you are always coming to me, saying how busy you are, therefore you wouldn't be able to take on higher duties." This of course was untrue, and John appeared to be suggesting he was aware of the demands of my job, which were such that I couldn't participate in opportunities all the other unit leaders had – but should be concerning to any fair manager.

I felt the tone in John's voice was condescending. His statement was false, and gave the perception to others at the meeting that I could not cope with my workload. I felt professionally undermined and humiliated in front of those at the meeting. This was not a reasonable approach to take. John should have talked to me in private about any concerns he had.

Later that day I met with John to discuss concerns I was having with my supervisor, Helen. It had taken four years of her management style before I realised the effect it was having on me and my work, and I made the fatal mistake of mentioning it to him. I requested he keep the content of the meeting confidential and did not want him to take any action, just to be aware of the difficulties I was experiencing. John did not offer any support, guidance or strategies, then or subsequently. My concerns were ignored and disregarded, and he informed Helen of our discussion, much to my detriment.

Time flowed by like a raging torrent: so much work and so little time. My team had farewells and hellos, and by the beginning of the year 2000, I thought the team had finally made it – we were cohesive and efficient at last. The only hiccup during these years was Helen, who was never supportive or encouraging, always finding fault.

I make mention now of an issue raised at around the same time, the end of 1999, as it plays a significant part later in my story. As our Service was 24/7, I felt (around 1996) that it was important that care providers had access to support outside of normal business hours, and I discussed with John the importance of this support, to which he agreed. A phone was purchased, and I carried it for the next three years. Towards the end of 1999, I was going on leave for a number of weeks and would be unavailable. I had carried the phone previously during periods of leave, but I was staying local during these periods. I needed another staff member to take the phone, but none would, as there was no 'on-call' allowance.

I was not interested in being paid for being 'on-call,' but understandably the staff believed that an 'on-call' allowance should be paid. I was required to write a report to management arguing that an 'on-call' allowance was necessary and why. This report was accepted by John, and Craig the Manager of Organisational Change, and both agreed an 'on-call' allowance could be paid, as there were funds available in the budget. As it was half-way through the financial year, Craig suggested that the 'on-call' allowance be backdated to the 1st July. I completed a memo to Craig outlining the hours of each staff member who was on-call, and this meant I would be back paid for six months for being 'on-call' at a time I was not claiming for being on-call. Given the above, the largest on-call allowance paid was to me.

Significant Event: The Business Plan

The management of the payment of the Child Care Benefit to care providers on behalf of the Parents and Commonwealth Government was a complex task that needed a dedicated employee. For eight years that employee had been Pauline, and she did a fantastic job – she was one of the best operators I had ever worked with. I enjoyed working with her immensely; she often met stressful times (like meeting a number of deadlines) with good humour, and her laughter was contagious.

In December 1999, Pauline was successful in gaining a temporary position in another Council service; she wanted to expand her experience and skill set and requested a secondment. It was with a heavy heart that I gave her a glowing reference – I wanted her to have this opportunity, but it left me with a vacant position in the team that would be extremely difficult to fill, as this was a specialist role.

Pauline's former position was duly advertised and a team member of mine in another department was successful in gaining the temporary position – and therefore her position was required to be filled.

Around this time, John sent me a memo which stated, "It is unrealistic, and perhaps even inappropriate, to expect that everything we do will have 'correct' process or procedure. You and your staff make many daily decisions without the benefit of a 'procedure' – many of these decisions are far more complex than this issue regarding the proposed secondment."

This secondment caused me much angst because there *was* no procedure, and then I was accused of not following the correct procedure. John refers to this secondment as being of minor complexity compared with the more complex issues that I dealt with on a daily basis. If it was so minor, why did it cause such a fuss? I was lambasted by Helen for not following procedure when there was no procedure. John failed to give due care and attention to this issue, as other staff often went on secondment, including Helen. He should have developed a secondment policy so all staff knew what to do when those occasions arose.

In hindsight, it is here that I should have stopped all this. Pauline could not be easily replaced and I was the only other person that knew and understood the complexities of the role. John later said I should not have let her go and it was a poor decision on my behalf – but what could I do; Pauline badly wanted the position and was successful at the interview. I could not deny her this opportunity, one that other staff enjoyed without hindrance. Imagine if I did deny her this opportunity – the claims would have been that I breached the council's EEO guidelines. John made sure Pauline understood she would be recalled if needed, but she stated to me that she was not happy to be recalled and wanted to concentrate on her new position.

Pauline left in early December, and Louise was successful in gaining the position, so now I had to fill Louise's position as well. But for a variety of reasons, Louise could not start in the Child Care Benefit job until mid-March.

At the beginning of 2000, I worked in my position as Unit Leader and also the vacant Child Care Assistance Officer position for three months. Total weekly hours of both positions was around 68 hours.

This was a period of many important tasks and deadlines, and I worked to full capacity to ensure all was completed without compromising customer service. Time was lost due to public holidays while I coordinated four recruitment processes, covered for other staff on leave, completed a comprehensive Unit Business Plan, and completed the annual Budget which included detailed notes on expenditure items, cash flow accruals, etc. I completed much of this work in my own time, but I was happy to. Pauline had a chance to grow and I was not going to ruin it for her.

John and Helen both failed to recognise the longer hours and effort I was putting in to ensure both jobs were completed successfully and the amount of unpaid work I was completing. Early in January, I spoke to Helen on at least two occasions regarding my workloads and the deadline for a draft of the Business Plan. She assured me that as it was only an update of the previous years, and I would be fine meeting the deadline. It was far from an update of the previous years – it was extremely complex and confusing, as I'd never undertaken a task like it before. Unfortunately, given all the other responsibilities I had on my plate, I did not have the draft of the Business Plan completed by the close of business that Friday; the deadline. The ramifications of this were diabolical and very distressing. I worked in my office all Sunday to finish the Business Plan draft, and subsequently submitted a time in lieu request. John refused TIL for this period and yet claimed if I needed assistance to employ a casual as there was money in the budget – but I knew a casual could not undertake the required tasks. He was happy to employ casual staff to complete these tasks, but refused even TIL to me.

This high-level period of productivity was achieved without appreciation from my management team, and with little support or acknowledgement. I felt a great sense of achievement, but this soon turned to disappointment. In February, I received a memo from John titled 'Business Plan Memo', and it was then that the manager's negative behaviour started to manifest. It appeared to me at this time that John's behaviour was instigated because I was late (by four hours) submitting a draft of the Business Plan. But *was* it this, or my earlier concerns raised with him the previous November? My lateness with the draft resulted in a letter of reprimand being sent to my personnel file. I was disappointed by this – I had never received such a letter before, and felt it to be unfair given the circumstances. I sought help from my union (big mistake). Days later we met the union representative and we resolved the grievance over the Business Plan draft by having the letter removed from my file and replaced with a less offensive letter, and adding a letter of commendation to my file in reference to the high levels of productivity I had achieved earlier in the year.

I found the replacement memo to my file more offensive than the first, and this memo did not fulfil our agreement and John did not follow through on what he stated in this memo – but I did receive a letter of commendation. I didn't find out until 1 September, when I accessed my file, that both negative letters were on file and there was no copy of my letter of commendation. The agreement with the union in mid-February was that he would remove the first memo, replace it with the second and have that one removed after six months. At this time there should have been only the letter of commendation on my file, but instead, there were two negative letters. Interestingly, John states in his sworn statements to WorkCover that he never wrote such a letter of commendation – and yet, I have a copy!

The draft Business Plan was completed on Monday by lunchtime – before other unit leaders had completed theirs, as I later found out. I spoke to two other unit leaders and was surprised to learn they had not submitted their draft by the deadline, or even by this day, yet this was okay because John had granted them extensions of time even though they had not taken on additional duties like me. But John was not happy with me missing the deadline and appeared to not understand I was working in two positions and covering many other duties. It was evident to me that John did not appreciate the predicament I was in, and he was negligent in not recognising this. John mentions in one of his written statements that I acted aggressively by calling in the union. Requesting union assistance is an employee right, it is not aggressive behaviour.

I had previously mentioned to Helen, in January, that I was concerned about the completion of the Business Plan draft, given the priorities of the Child Care Assistance Officer position. She assured me not to be concerned, as the Plan was only an update of the previous year. This was incorrect; it was a totally different document that required many hours of work. The finished document met the organisational deadline of 1 March 2000.

After John made an accusation that I never kept him informed of my work demands, I sent him an urgent email in early March 2000, outlining the demands of my work, as I was still working in the two positions. I was asking for assistance as I had two competing deadlines. A week later he responded to my urgent email (after I'd met both deadlines anyway) and stated, "it is not my job to prioritise what you do on a daily basis." Usually I would agree with this, but given I was working in two demanding positions I felt I needed some guidance. No guidance or support from John, and I was beginning to fear whatever task I prioritised would be the wrong one. I suggested I work a few hours overtime (keeping in mind I worked an extra hour or two nearly every day for the love of the job) to complete all the tasks required. His response was no, so I completed the work in my own time. I was given no approval to work overtime or accrue time in lieu, just a demand that tasks be completed by Friday.

I was working to full capacity covering two demanding positions, as well as attempting to complete the immense workload required by the budget, when John approached me in my office and stated the budget information had to be completed that day or I would have to work on it over the weekend. I emailed him that evening at 8:22pm, and requested approval to work on the budget on the weekend and accrue overtime and to call and let me know. He ignored my request, so I attended the office on the following Sunday and worked from 1:30pm to 8:30pm. John cannot deny he knew I was working many extra hours and I felt he was totally unreasonable in his expectations of me and the pressures I was working under. I felt I had no choice; John was not listening to me. If he was happy to pay an inexperienced casual person to do the job (even if no such casual person existed), why not pay an experienced person to do the job? It made no sense to me.

During this same period, I met with John again concerning workloads. I had a Family Day Care Victoria General Meeting I wished to attend one Thursday. John stated he wanted the Financial Management Reports (FMRs) completed and to him no later than the following day; Friday. I was told to decide whether going to the meeting was necessary. I replied that I felt it was, and would have the completed FMRs to him by Friday. I was the only Unit Leader required to justify my attendance at industry related meetings. Other FDC Co-Coordinators around the state were expected to attend as part of the requirements of their position. My position description stated attendance at these meetings was part of my role. I returned late Friday afternoon from the meeting to complete the FMRs. In passing, I asked the Kindergarten Unit Leader how she was going in meeting the new deadline for the FMRs. She stated that she had not even started her reports. I informed her that John had told me the deadline was today – Friday at 5pm. She responded that John had not said anything to her about this. Other unit leaders were not faced with the same hurdles I was required to jump over – why was I being treated differently to others?

At this time there was a casual worker working part-time in our Service – her name was Narelle. Unbeknownst to me, Narelle had approached both John and Helen regarding her wish to access study leave. John and Helen sent me emails asking me to arrange this for Narelle, but I was concerned because they were not following the Organisation Study Leave Policy which stated that only permanent full-time employees had access to study leave. This left me feeling uncomfortable with this staff member when I reiterated the policy to her, but I suggested to Narelle that a permanent position would be advertised shortly and if she was the successful applicant, she would be eligible to access this benefit. John and Helen should not have put me in this position. Narelle was the successful applicant for the vacant position and immediately accessed study leave, but given the events about to come, it seemed she held a grudge because of my initial refusal to her request.

From December 1999 to March 2000, Pauline's position had been vacant, and because of this there was a significant saving in salaries. Some of this could have been used to pay me overtime, keeping in mind I was regularly working around seven hours per week non-gratis. John did not approve overtime, neither paid or time in lieu, but suggested I employ a casual to assist, surely aware no casual person could complete all the required tasks. His demand was that all tasks be completed by Friday. So back to working in my own time; fortunately, I took my work seriously and was not going to let anyone down, which of course turned out to be a big mistake.

Thankfully, mid-March finally arrived, and Louise could commence in the Child Care Benefit position, though I was still hands-on for a while as Louise found her feet. She turned out to be a real asset, and within a short time I had total confidence in her abilities to get the job done.

It was in late March I received a letter of commendation from John stating, "We have already discussed a range of issues which have led to significant demands on your time. Your draft Business Plan contained sections which were well researched and presented. The section on service profiles received a comment from the general manager indicating 'good work so far'." Strangely, under oath, he denied ever sending such a letter.

It was during this time, unbeknown to me, I began having symptoms of illness. I felt well; this was the insidious nature of Graves' disease.

While still undiagnosed, my workload increased yet again due to the Commonwealth Government's changes to the Child Care Benefit program and implementation of GST. Little information was given to Family Day Care Services (FDC) as the Department of Family and Community Services (who provide the funding to operate FDC) appeared unclear as to the implications of these changes.

The information required to undertake these changes was provided one week before implementation and Services were required to apply these changes within their own programs. Many hours were spent conducting Child Care Benefit analysis, and hundreds of calculations had to be undertaken to determine the best option of implementing additional funding for the benefit of all. Once again, I worked longer hours to ensure completion by 1 July. I later found out that most of the other Family Day Care Services did not meet this timeframe and put off the changes to January of the following year to coincide with their new fee schedule. I felt I could not have done that, as it effectively meant that care providers and Parents would be disadvantaged by this, and I believed —to be fair to them— I needed to apply the changes by the required date. I knew if I did not do this, care providers would be angry, as a number of them were aware of these changes that gave them an increase in their income. I am at a loss to understand how other Services got away without implementing these changes for six extra months.

I knew that without care providers, none of the Coordination Unit staff would have the jobs we liked and enjoyed, and so I was grateful for them. I tried to include the care providers in decisions that affected them. Michelle, a care provider who was proficient in the administration of Child Care Assistance, was assisting staff with the Child Care Benefit analyses to ensure the implementation was agreeable to care providers. She called one morning and spoke to a resource officer, as I was starting late due to working late the previous evening. She was angry: I had not gotten back to her regarding suggestions she had faxed through the previous evening, and was quite derogatory about me to the resource officer, calling me a "moron".

I called her to clarify her concerns, and she stated that she had faxed a number of pages to me and I had not had the courtesy to contact her. I explained that I had just started work and I had not received any faxed documents from her. Michelle apologised for her comment and I accepted the apology. The fax machine she sent the documents to was located in the general office area, so anyone could have taken the pages by mistake – or her fax did not simply come through due to an error on her end? Helen and John quite enjoyed this 'moron' comment and popped it away in their arsenal for future use if needed by keeping a reference to it in the Family Day Care Complaint File. It would be a golden opportunity to use this as a complaint against me when they so chose, but of course once it was known I was unwell it would have been seen as unfair to raise this comment as a complaint made against me, so they must have thought better of it.

Also in June (whilst I was unknowingly quite unwell), the Council was undergoing a SafetyMap Accreditation, during which I was required to be interviewed and assessed as to my and the Service's safety initiatives and compliance with SafetyMap principles. I successfully fulfilled all criteria and the assessor's comments were: "Your introduction of the care provider 'Self-Assessment for Safety' booklet, is on the cutting edge of innovation."

It was in July that I mentioned to Helen, my supervisor, that I was unwell and seeing a specialist the next week. I was beginning to feel tired and a little forgetful and had to work even harder, as I was determined to complete my role satisfactorily and I did so with great effort. I did not know or understand at this time the illness from which I suffered or its symptoms, but the physical symptoms were noticed and acknowledged by my co-workers, including weight loss.

My medical specialist confirmed the diagnosis of an overactive thyroid, with treatment commencing immediately. Within weeks, the symptoms disappeared and I was on the road to recovery.

Graves' disease (GD) is an autoimmune disorder. In GD, the immune system produces thyroid autoantibodies that react with a protein known as the TSH receptor. TSH receptor protein is found on thyroid cells, eye muscle cells and also the dermal cells of skin tissue. This disease is unique to everyone. Some may have only one major symptom; others may have several different symptoms. Predominant symptoms can change over time, and their severity can vary, increasing during times of stress. GD may spontaneously resolve, or follow a lengthy course with variable periods of waxing and waning, or it may progress rapidly.

GD is caused by a combination of genetic and environmental factors. People with GD have a certain combination of genes that make them susceptible to disease development when they're exposed to certain environmental triggers. In some people, this disease may cause an emotional response, but for me —if there was one— it was minor in nature. After diagnosis, I asked family and friends if they thought I displayed any irrational or erratic traits around this time. All said they noticed very little – that maybe I was busier than usual, but this was not unusual for me.

According to the College of American Pathologists, stress is a major trigger for GD. I believe the onset of my GD was triggered by the physical and emotional demands of successfully managing a period of high productivity with little support or acknowledgement. I had felt a sense of personal achievement, that soon turned to disappointment after John's negative behaviour.

It was known I was unwell, but any support or kind word from John or Helen was not to be had. I emailed them regularly when I was required to take sick leave and attend medical appointments.

Around this time, John commenced a trail of emails and memorandums, which created confusion for me. I began to wonder what was going on, and felt that there was a hidden agenda. I was not informed or invited to important meetings relating to the Service.

Significant Event: Dismissal of In-Home Care Provider

In mid-August 2000, Werribee Hospital had made contact with Councils Home Care Service, seeking respite for a mum with young children, to come into the home and provide assistance. The young mum had cancer and did not want her children to be cared for out of the home, as she wanted to spend as much time with them as she could.

Home Care did not have the funding for this to occur, though Family Day Care did – but we did not have a worker who could do this, and Home Care did.

The two Services worked together, and the support worker (who had to apply for registration with Family Day Care and undertake necessary training) was ready to start the next day – a fine example of the efficiency of Family Day Care staff. All were very happy with the outcome, especially Home Care staff and the sick single mum.

However, when the Unit Leader of Home Care returned from leave, she was not happy with this solution – hence a meeting—from which I was initially excluded—was convened.

It was only by chance I attended this meeting – the Home Care Unit Leader mentioned in passing a meeting planned for that afternoon concerning FDC, Home Care and the In-Home Care Program operated by FDC. I knew nothing about any such meeting; I checked my electronic diary and email: no meeting requests. She gave me the time of the meeting and so I attended.

Those in attendance at this meeting were John, Helen, the Home Care Unit Leader and me. The meeting was called by Helen, supposedly to discuss options of utilising new Family Day Care Commonwealth funding for In-Home Childcare. There was no explanation given as to why I was not previously invited to this meeting, and my attendance was not mentioned. A decision was made affecting the operation of the Family Day Care Service, In-Home Care Program, with little consultation with me, involving immediately pulling the home care worker from providing this care. The rationale was that if the worker suffered an injury while in the home, which Service would be liable? I was astounded at the lack of care and compassion for this family, especially given the solution was working so well. It seemed like this decision was made well before this meeting took place.

I tried to explain that Family Day Care, and hence Council, covered Care Providers for WorkCover, as they were deemed workers under the Accident and Compensation Act 1985. I did not see a problem, but they still did. I felt that something was going on, but I didn't know what.

In discussions with John, concerning the rationale for his decision and the consequences of this decision, I was dissatisfied with his response. But he could not be swayed by reason, so my only recourse was to implement a Management's Complaint Procedure, with a written letter of complaint being sent to Bernie, the General Manager of WYNCARE. Over the years, staff were encouraged to use the complaint procedure, but I now realised that while we were encouraged, it was never expected any staff would actually do so. The procedure was just another example of 'window dressing' to give the impression management was progressive and had fair procedures to deal with staff that had concerns.

The general manager responded to me, saying that "my expectation to be included in those discussions and decision making to be a reasonable one." But nothing changed, the worker was effectively sacked, and I have no idea what happened to the sick single mum.

I can remember at this time a staff member mentioning to me that maybe management was planning a restructure of Home Care and Family Day Care into one unit. This thought had also crossed my mind, and she suggested that I might be made redundant, with the Home Care Unit Leader taking on the new combined position, as she and Helen had appeared to be working closely together of late.

Surprise, surprise, around a year later in March 2001 (while conducting research for my WorkCover claim), I came upon a document I had not seen before, titled 'Family Day Care Continuous Improvement Plan', which outlined a possible restructure of Family Day Care and Home Care into one Unit. It made sense to me to combine the two services, but there would be one too many unit leaders and I suddenly became aware of the possible reason I was being treated so strangely.

Still, I was not angry with this – I understood the rationale for merging both Services, and felt the Home Care Unit Leader would be very competent at the task. My concern was more about the covert process that seemed to have been employed to bring this about. I would have accepted redundancy and continued to work on a casual basis within Family Day Care generally if an open and honest redundancy procedure had been followed.

Maybe the rationale was that if I resigned, there would be no need to pay redundancy. In any case, this Improvement Plan did not go ahead. I do not know why, but it could have been that I was on sick leave three months later, after my 'complaint' to the Director.

So began the multiple copies of memorandums from John, some delivered by email with a copy of the same document being left on my chair, and the same one again handed to me by John. On occasion Helen joined in. Again, confusion reigned.

Interestingly, it was around this time that my staff started telling me that when I was absent from work they were individually "grilled" by Helen – about me, my behaviour and my personal life. Staff also informed me they believed Helen had "snooped" in my office. Staff expressed their dissatisfaction with this behaviour. (Though, sadly, less than eight months later, they joined in on the fun and the game of 'let's drive Lori crazy and out of the workplace'.)

I kept my medical reports in my office, stored slightly protruding from behind a bookcase that I would not forget where they were when required for subsequent medical appointments. I saw no harm in this, but was harm to be found? I think so.

In August, Helen was seconded to another position in the Civic Centre – I hoped for maybe at last a break from the torment. Even though Helen was gone from the building in which I worked, John and Helen's micromanagement continued.

The workplace environment was forever changing: John requested I do something when it was already done, and when I did it, that actually it should have been another task. I was being badgered and hauled over the coals for any minor error in my work. He called a two-hour meeting to discuss typographical errors in a letter I had written, one to care providers who I feel sure would not make a big deal out of the fact there was a space before a full stop at the end of a sentence and a small "d" in "Family Day Care".

Up until recently we'd had administration staff to type our correspondence, but now it was another task core staff had to take on. Given this was August, I most likely was still suffering from Graves' disease, which was not yet fully controlled. But did John care? Did he ever ask how I was? Not once, not one iota. He stated under oath in his WorkCover statement that he was unaware I was unwell, even though I'd kept him informed of medical appointments and he signed my sick leave applications. Strange how everyone else in the building knew.

To admit he knew and treated me in such a way would have seen his behaviour classed as discriminatory, so he claimed no knowledge and chose to performance-manage me instead.

John and Helen were both aware of my illness. They decided not to acknowledge it – to do so would have required them to implement a process to assist me in the workplace, but they chose a different path: a paper trail. I was concerned by this, but felt confident that all would be well, as I had not committed any crime and I was competent in my job.

August of the year 2000 was a horrible month for many reasons, all of which I cannot go into here, but glimpses can be found all through my story. Late one evening, a care provider rang to tell me a child to whom she provided weekend respite care had suddenly passed away at his home that morning. The care provider was distressed and she just needed someone to talk to.

The next morning, I informed John that the child had died at home, and other than offering the family as much childcare support as was needed and providing personal support to the care provider, there was not much else the Service needed to do.

Later in the day, staff informed me that both John and Helen had "grilled" each of them about what I had done about this child's death. Helen wrote a detailed memo to the General Manager of WYNCARE concerning the death of this child. I could not understand the need for such a memo.

If John and Helen had any questions, why weren't these questions directed to me, rather than my staff? It was most unusual; their behaviour inferred I had done something wrong, which made me feel I *had* done something wrong, without knowing what.

If a child dies while in the care of the Family Day Care Service, staff would be required to immediately report to management all known information and action taken. In this case, I believed a formal memorandum to the general manager to inform him of the death of a child in their own home, and outlining how Helen had to deal with this distressing event, was not necessary. This had not been the process in the past or since, and a phone call to inform the general manager could have sufficed. What Helen had to deal with I do not know.

On the last day of this horrible month, John requested we meet to discuss work standards. Remember, around this time I was just beginning to recover from my period of ill health. My physical health was improving but my psychological health was deteriorating, and given this I asked the Australian Services Union (ASU) shop steward to join me at this meeting.

The meeting consisted of two hours of me being harassed about current work issues that were complex but adequately handled by me, and over written material that did not meet his standard. (That typographical error in a letter I had written where I placed a space before a full stop and a small "d" in Family Day Care.) If this was all he could come up with after the many months of illness I suffered, he should have been pleased that no major errors had occurred under my management of the Service.

It was in this meeting that I said to John that after 12 weeks of illness he never acknowledged or asked after my health and welfare. John responded that he was unaware that I was ill. This cannot be true.

After the meeting, I asked the ASU shop steward for her opinion as to what she thought was going on. She suggested John was creating a paper trail.

John had stated on two formal occasions that he did not know I was unwell. I am convinced that Helen knew, and it's difficult to believe she never mentioned or discussed my illness with John, especially when signing all my sick leave applications when I had to intermittently leave work for regular blood tests. John has since stated that to ask after my health would have been a breach of my privacy. I was not keeping my illness a secret, and did not formally advise management of my illness because I held the belief the illness was minor in nature and easily treatable. If you're late for work one morning due to period pain you would not be expected to inform your employer of all the details.

When someone is obviously unwell, it shows compassion to ask after their wellbeing. Their response will tell you if they wish to maintain privacy, but you should ask first.

Unit leaders were sent memos concerning staff absences when these absences exceeded organisational standards, and they were expected to discuss and monitor their staff's sick leave. There was never a directive not to raise this issue due to privacy reasons; this would have been in contradiction with the request of the memo sent in the first place. Unit leaders would naturally discuss this in private with staff, not probe and be guided by the staff member's response, so there would be no invasion of privacy. If someone has been absent on sick leave, a natural response on their return to work would be to ask them how they are. Surely this act of compassion cannot be construed as a breach of privacy as John was then claiming.

Gary Namie, a social psychologist and director of the Workplace Bullying Institute, has counselled 4,300 targets of abuse. His research shows that in less than 10% of abuse cases the bullies were punished, transferred or terminated. "Bullying usually stops when the target leaves their job," he said. "Companies will never say they have a problem."

A United States Hostile Workplace Survey concluded that 50% of bully bosses are men, 50% women, with 96% of co-workers being aware of the bullying and 67% of victims reporting no prior history of being bullied. Thirty-one percent of female victims experience post-traumatic stress disorder, with bullies rarely suffering career consequences – in 42% of cases the bully's supervisor helped the bad boss or punished the victim, and 11% of co-workers side with the bully. I do not believe that in Australia the figures would be any different, even though we pride ourselves on the doctrine of the 'fair go'.

Maureen Milford, an American writer who has an interest in this topic and focuses on corporation law and governance matters, states that she believes the victims of workplace bullying include, more often than not, women who do not fight back, who are focused on their work, who are not political animals, who think they can rise above the fray, who are usually not confrontational, who are competent people that become a threat, who are often independent people who are well-liked. I fit into all of these categories bar one; I believe that I'm a textbook case.

The National Prevention of Violence in the Workplace definition of mobbing behaviour includes but is not limited to the following: the withholding of information and resources; public humiliation; arbitrary removal of responsibilities; unrealistic work demands; behaviour consistent over time and designed to humiliate and intimidate the target. This comprises some of what I experienced, but most of my abuse was psychological and therefore harder to recognise. I hope through the reading of my experiences you will learn to recognise the abuse I was subjected to and why I fought so hard to expose this abhorrent behaviour.

In September 2000, John requested I make time to finalise my Performance Development Review before I went on leave. John gave me a copy of the 'signing off' page out of the 1998 Performance Development Review form instead of 1999. On this same day, I had an appointment with my medical specialist, who informed me that in July I was so seriously ill with thyrotoxicosis that she was surprised I was still walking around, let alone competently working with virtually no sick leave taken.

After this medical appointment, I attended the Council Personnel Department to view my Personnel File to see what Performance Development Reviews they had on file, as I felt strongly there was a reason John gave me the 1998 copy rather than the correct 1999 copy. I had with me my own folder of copies of all my staff's previous Performance Development Reviews, including mine. While seeking out my copy of the 1999 PDR documents in my own clearly labelled plastic pocket, I found a Position Description previously unseen by me, with a photocopy of the last page (the signing page) of my 1998 Performance Development Review stapled to this Position Description.

I expressed surprise and confusion, especially when the personnel manager informed me that this Position Description could not relate to the date on the last page, as the style and font of the Position Description has only been in use since the year 2000.

Ian, the personnel manager, copied five Position Descriptions currently held on the Personal Department General File of position descriptions, three of which I had never seen previously, and yet my name appeared on the documents as the incumbent. Why was I not included in this process, which was the usual procedure when updating an employment contract, if the position already had an incumbent? There was something going on, but I was not sure what; it was all buzzing around in my head as I was frantically searching for an answer. Three of these five position descriptions all appeared to have been written in the last couple of months, and it appeared the writer could not make up their mind as to whom the Unit Leader (me) should report to, or their levels of responsibility and authority.

I feel John and Helen were setting in place the scenario of me not fulfilling my position description, with this being discussed at the hurried PDR meeting without me being aware or being too sick to notice the substituted documents. (It was at this time I found the negotiated Union settlement John agreed to in February had not been fulfilled.)

The first letter was still on my file; the second letter which I felt was more offensive than the first was still on my file and no letter of commendation. At this time there should have been only the letter of commendation on my file, but instead, there were two negative letters. I returned to my office wondering what the hell was going on. It had to be John and/or Helen – but were others involved too, possibly Bernie the general manager?

Around 6:15pm I was leaving my office to go home, feeling overwhelmed, when the Maternal and Child Health Unit Leader asked me how I was (she was working late too) – Helen had told her I had thyrotoxicosis.

How did Helen know this, when I myself had only been informed a few hours earlier? Maybe this was a result of the snooping that staff had told me about, and her being a former nurse, she may well have known how to read my x-rays. It's difficult to believe she knew this in August and never told or discussed it with John or any other person from management. It was later in December, during the WorkCover process, that both John and Helen stated in their written and sworn WorkCover statements they did not know I was unwell.

A week later, around early September, John and I met to discuss my Performance and Development Review. I was curious as to why John was hurriedly doing my PDR now, given I was busy with attempting to complete many tasks before I went on leave a few days later. I had completed all my staff PDRs in April and met the organisational deadline, and here it was in September and John was still completing his staff's PDRs. I asked him "why now?" He said, "I want to complete it before you go on leave." This made sense to me at the time, then later in the afternoon during a conversation with the Kindergarten Unit Leader she mentioned that she still had to complete her Performance and Development Review with John. When I returned from my three weeks leave, her PDR and that of another Unit Leader were still not completed.

The achievement of work goals for the PDR year of 1 April 1999 to 31 March 2000 were discussed, despite achieving or exceeding required standards. John still was not convinced, and wanted to rate my performance lower than it had ever been before.

I reiterated that my performance was an outstanding effort when covering the vacant Child Care Benefit position, as well as my own position, during the demanding Christmas holiday season. Especially when coupled with all the other tasks I was required to complete, such as staff recruitment by four, Contract management, financial management reports, OH&S initiatives, SafetyMap Accreditation and implementation of the new Child Care Benefit, to name a few. All these tasks were added to my role since Council amalgamation and I had completed an excessive amount of work over those past 12 months.

My performance did not deteriorate during the period of illness; I worked harder and longer hours to compensate for any time I felt I had lost due to my slower thought processes. There has never been any evidence to prove or even suggest that my work was unacceptable, other than during that August meeting where John highlighted some minor typing errors.

I was at the end of my Banding Level and was not entitled to an annual increment, and hadn't received an increment for five years. If not entitled for an increment in my salary, I would have at least appreciated some recognition through the PDR Process of my achievements.

As usual, John was not to be swayed; his opinion was unchangeable no matter how many hard facts I presented. I requested that this be reviewed by the general manager, but alas my PDR form was filed with the Personnel Department without any further discussion or consultation with me.

Over the next few months, the negative and belligerent behaviour exhibited by John continued, and are far too numerous and on occasion too complex to highlight in this book.

Work Woes

Significant Event: Mediation

In October 2000, the Union and the Human Resource Department were now aware of my difficulties with John, but not with Helen, as she was in another department on secondment, though I believe she was still the puppet master. The Acting HR Manager Marianne requested John and I attend mediation to give us the opportunity to improve our professional relationship. I reluctantly agreed; essentially, I did not have a choice – Emma the ASU shop steward stated that management would not look kindly on a refusal.

I later found out the mediator was known to Marianne, but in what capacity I do not know. I felt continued unease when I saw John and Marianne have three meetings to discuss the mediation session prior to it happening. Why was it necessary for John and Marianne to meet on these occasions to discuss mediation? The fact that I was not involved in these meetings made me feel slightly anxious that John may be receiving coaching as to how he should participate. I had the distinct feeling that this was not to my advantage, but still felt some confidence in the process and that all would be well, as I had not breached any part of the Council Behaviour Code and the standard of my work was acceptable – another mistake on my behalf.

Later in October, the mediation session took place. The first thing I noticed upon entering the room was the layout: a whiteboard, desk for the mediator, two chairs and a side table each for John and me. On each side table was a jug of water and a glass, but the one different item between John and me was that on my table I had a box of tissues, while John's table had no tissues. This alerted me to the possibility that there was an expectation I may cry during the session, with no such expectation of John. Yet I was determined there would be no tears! John appeared overly nervous, and kept clearing his throat and drinking lots of water; this behaviour also made me think that something was going on here – that this was not just a session to assist our professional relationship.

Mediation is a dispute resolution technique, and the mediator's role is to facilitate the process, not the content. Yet during this session, the mediator participated in the content by making a number of remarks that caused me some concern – for example, "Why don't you just leave?" and "I changed careers at fifty."

I participated openly and honestly, hoping this would lead to a successful resolution of whatever John's perceived problems were with me, but now I feel that this mediation session was a set-up and was certainly not a process to better our relationship. This would explain why there were a number of meetings titled "mediation" between Marianne and John prior to the mediation session taking place.

At the meeting's conclusion the mediator stated, "You, John and Council will get my report soon." I asked why Council (meaning Marianne) would get a copy of the mediation minutes, as I was under the impression that this was a confidential process and another person could only have a copy if I agreed. The mediator responded, "Because they are the ones paying me."

I was told that mediation was a technique to help John and me improve our professional relationship, and that was all. However, I have since read in John's statement to WorkCover a number of different reasons as to why mediation was taking place, these being my complaint regarding the situation with mum with cancer, the dispute over the Business Plan draft, and September 2000 PDR process, but of course I was not informed of these three additional reasons. I believe they were a later addition to fit in with WorkCover legislation that if I was in fact being disciplined in a reasonable manner, then no claim can be made.

A few days later the mediator, Winsome, emailed two different sets of minutes from the mediation session to me—the first arrived at 2.04pm and the second at 2.13pm—with the request that I sign and give them to Marianne on the following Monday.

The first lot of minutes were addressed to someone called "Kerrie" but were obviously for me, the second set was re-sent nine minutes later with many additions. The language used was typical HR – for example the word 'fundamentally' was used regularly throughout the document when it was not used during the session. It is disappointing when a professional being paid a large fee cannot manage the simple task of getting the person's name correct. I was held to a much higher standard in my job.

I printed both sets of minutes and took them home that evening to read. The second set of minutes shocked me because they were inaccurate, and many statements attributed to me were not said by me, such as, "I would look for another job within Council or for an external position and take leave while doing so." Statements attributed to John were actually said by the mediator, and quite significant comments the mediator made, such as, "Why don't you just leave?" were not included in her report. I believe someone in HR had access to this document before the mediator sent it to me, and it was this person who had made these many additions to the second lot of minutes, as it couldn't have been done in just nine minutes.

I finally came to the conclusion that the mediation session was another attempt to harass and humiliate me, and showed me the reason why John and Marianne met so often. It was a ploy; one designed to hurt and gaslight me and force me into resignation. I was absolutely gobsmacked that an employer—my employer—could behave in such an abhorrent manner. The symptoms of fear and anxiety start to manifest. I felt agitated, and was awake all that night and felt exhausted the next day. I experienced a tingling sensation all over my body, especially on my scalp, and my hair began to fall out.

It is now recognised that many targets of workplace bullying feel mediation was not fair for them, and it is argued instead that in most cases targets feel further abused and damaged by the process. A representative from the Northern Territory Working Woman's Centre has stated: "The imbalance of power is so profound that she is not able to speak freely . . . I think it would be unsafe and really inappropriate if it required the person who was being bullied to sit face to face with the person who was bullying her . . ."

According to adrresearch.net, bullying is not and cannot be a neutral agenda item. In a typical mediation, the issue to be considered is one that both parties are equally as affected or equally contributed to. But in the context of workplace bullying, the agenda is entirely based on the inappropriate behaviour of the bully in the workplace. A mediator may struggle to frame this issue as an agenda item, and by referring to it as a 'relationship' the target of the bullying may interpret this to mean the mediator does not believe the bullying occurred. At the same time, a bully would view this as a reinforcing their lack of fault. Therefore, in workplace bullying allegations, the person and the issue cannot be separated, and trying to frame it otherwise can be detrimental.

I certainly felt that my mediation was detrimental, and was never planned to be a sincere attempt at resolving issues, and after realising the above I now know why. Issues, it appears, were based on my 'relationship' with John and not his behaviour, and I believe the mediator was clueless that bullying was taking place. I would be glad if workplaces no longer trot out mediation as a supposed cure for bullying.

Researcher Loraleigh Keashly coined the term 'emotional abuse at work' as a synonym for workplace bullying, says the Workplace Bullying Institute (WBI): "All of one's cognitive resources are deployed to cope with the psychological assault. In worst cases there is trauma that must be dealt with. In all cases the target is stigmatised, and social relations with co-workers strained. Bullying triggers distress, the human stress response in reaction to the bully's tactics, the stressors if left unabated, prolonged distress leads to stress related diseases and all sorts of health complications."

All through the year 2000, my health began to deteriorate, so I sought medical attention. I explained to my doctor what was happening and he had no hesitation in stating workplace harassment and intimidation as the cause of my symptoms of anxiety. He strongly recommended time off work. I refused, as I felt that a WorkCover certificate would only increase my problems. I returned to work a week later, worse than before, and I felt I had no choice, so he gave me a WorkCover certificate for two weeks' leave. He also suggested that I get a second opinion to his diagnosis, not due to any doubt he may have had but because he did not want anyone to suggest I was imagining what was happening because of my prior diagnosis of Graves' disease. An appointment was made for me to see Dr Marcus Benjamin.

When I returned to work, I called the in-house WorkCover Officer and explained that I had a WorkCover Certificate of Incapacity from my doctor, and she responded to wait and she would come to my office immediately. She ensured I filled out the forms correctly and took them back to her office.

The last thing I did before I went on sick leave was send Marianne my written response to the mediation minutes, where I highlighted all the inaccuracies in the minutes. I placed it in a large yellow internal mail envelope and addressed it to her, and mailed in the internal mail system. The only person in the building at this time was John, who was in his office, which was unusual as he was usually gone by 5pm. He saw me as I left my office with the large yellow envelope in my hand. I left work thinking I had submitted a WorkCover claim, but Marianne never forwarded it on to the insurer.

Later in November, Marianne visited me at home and issues were vaguely discussed, with a gentle suggestion from Marianne that I drop my WorkCover claim. I was given a few days to think about it, but I was scared that if I dropped my claim things may well return to how they were before. I was under the false impression a WorkCover claim would proffer some protection in the workplace from further harassment, but again I was mistaken.

It appeared Marianne never received my formal written response to the mediation session. She denied ever receiving this correspondence. Was she telling the truth, or did the envelope disappear on its route to the HR Department?

I told Marianne much of the mediation report was inaccurate and false, and I suggested she obtain the original notes from the mediator who had written on butcher's paper what was discussed during the session, and then a comparison could be completed. I don't know if this was done, but I am guessing it was. She also told me a rumour was circulating around the organisation that I was sick, and I do not believe she was referring to Graves' disease. I asked her where that rumour had come from and she responded, "I heard it from Helen."

Marianne changed the date on my WorkCover Certificate to reflect the time she asked me to have a think about the submission of my claim. I often wonder what would have happened if I had done as she asked – that outcome could not have been any worse than what eventuated.

Later in December 2000, I initiated a meeting to clarify issues surrounding the mediation session, but this was not achieved as the focus of the meeting changed, with Marianne stating that the mediation session was now "off the table" and no longer open to discussion. Issues raised by me were never to be discussed! I believed that the mediator's notes were indeed obtained and supported my view of what occurred. The meeting I requested now turned into a Performance Management Session, with performance management the new red herring. I was told I was expected to return to full-time employment in two weeks. If I had just dropped my WorkCover claim and returned to work, would things have worked out better than they did? As per all my reading and research on this topic, the behaviour continued. Once you are targeted, your job is gone no matter what you do, unless there is a sincere and independent investigation – and if proven, the bully is removed, but this rarely if ever occurs.

Marianne also informed me that an internal investigation had been conducted and it had found that there had been no harassment or intimidation. An internal investigation took place and I was not informed of this or involved in the process in any way. This was a sham – a genuine investigation would have included me and given me the opportunity to supply evidence and my account of what had taken place.

After two weeks' leave, I was hoping I could return to full-time work from late December, but my doctor disagreed due to the workplace issues not being resolved and effectively being swept under the carpet. He was concerned that Human Resources had attempted to discredit me with him (effectively trying to destroy the doctor/patient relationship) by writing him a letter suggesting I was mistaken in my beliefs of harassment, but luckily for me, he never doubted what I said to be true. He was such a lovely doctor and a beautiful human being who I continued to see for the next ten years, even when he had moved to the other side of Melbourne.

I desperately wanted to return to work, so I asked my doctor to allow me to return one day a week so I could keep up my relationship with my staff and squash any continued rumours. He didn't think it was a good idea, but acquiesced to my request. In hindsight, he was right – I should've stayed away, as I gave the bullies weekly access to further harass and intimidate me.

On my one-day-a-week of work, John did not let up, making unfounded accusations, and holding me to an even higher standard than before. As I now did not have a car, and travelled by train to Werribee, I requested to use half an hour of my time in lieu from 8am to 8:30am to fit with the train timetable. This request was denied, and in the letter John sent me he stated he expected me in the office at 8am. This was typical of John. Other staff had no difficulties in using TIL for personal reasons or a spread of hours changed to fulfil personal tasks, but an injured worker receives no consideration. It was around this time I read my union newsletter which poignantly stated in its editorial: "In this environment, it is unions that provide service, strength and security for members." I found that through my time of need, there was some service, little strength and no security.

During this period, Justin was elected ASU shop steward, and upon election he sent an email to all staff, stating:

> Obviously, we are mindful that protocol and due process is a right every worker should expect. If, however, you do not have a current union ticket and you find yourself let down through these processes, it may be a harsh call but my concern is really that the same fate does not befall our members.
>
> If you are a woman and have a workplace issue (i.e. discrimination or harassment) that you would like to discuss with the union before approaching HR, or your work area representative, and additionally you would feel more comfortable discussing with another woman, please contact Emma on x776.

Nice sentiment, but this did not reflect my reality. (Justin played an even bigger role later.)

In mid-November, I attended my appointment with a Dr Benjamin, who confirmed my doctor's opinion and wrote his report in mid-December 2000, firstly stating that I presented as someone who was well equipped and well-suited for my job, and that I enjoyed my work and continued to do so. Secondly, he stated in the interview situation that I presented with an appropriate level of stress and anxiety – he believed my diagnosis of Graves' disease was not creating symptoms of paranoia or psychosis. Thirdly, there was no evidence of Graves' disease (hyperthyroidism), in that my major symptoms of weight loss and palpitations had subsided. He went on to say that I had seemed to have coped extremely well with this physical illness, and in his opinion, it was playing no part in my presentation.

Fourthly, he diagnosed me with an acute stress reaction of mild to moderate severity. He believed I was a "stable person who enjoyed her work and her incapacity would be limited." Fifthly, regarding my return to work, he thought it would be dependent on a quite different approach to me from both my supervisor and management, and in his opinion outside organisation monitoring was needed when I did return after a brief period of time away from work. And finally, he stated that at this stage, he felt the important aspect of my medical management was related to an indication that the situation which had caused me difficulty in the workplace was being appropriately addressed.

Dr Benjamin's medical opinion supports workplace harassment as the cause of my anxiety. There was no evidence of mental illness detected and no further psychiatric intervention required. Dr Benjamin stated to me: "Lori, what you think is happening is happening and I do not need to see you again."

An American survey on this topic concluded that workplace harassment resulted in "severe psychological distress and reduced job satisfaction." It also found that many participants in the survey reported having witnessed others being targeted. The study concluded, therefore, that harassment wasn't an illusion of the targets.

Dr Benjamin referred me to Joanne, a Clinical Psychologist experienced in workplace harassment. I saw her for a number of sessions, where I would go through in chronological order what I had experienced during those past 12 months. In her report, she stated my supervisor and manager appeared to have provided little support during this time of recovery, and in fact their behaviour would have clearly added immense pressure. She believed I had endured an enormous amount of subtle put-downs, humiliation and ostracism, particularly by my superiors. She went on to say that my illness may have contributed to some decline in performance, but one would expect an employer to support rather than condemn during recovery. She believed my self-esteem and self-concept had been enormously damaged by this behaviour and if not for my "hardy personality" I would clearly have been in a far worse emotional state than I was.

Joanne's diagnosis was workplace harassment. I was shocked. I thought that it may be something else —that perhaps there was something wrong with me— I could not get my head around the words "workplace harassment". According to research by the Workplace Bullying Institute, around 33% of bullied targets have this experience with the first abuse in their lives. Those people take the longest to recognise the workplace bullying, and this was me. Even workers with prior history doesn't guarantee instant recognition, and when labelling the emotional abuse happening to them (or others), it was the visceral reactions that become the clues to recognition. They have 'been there before' with respect to the emotional negativity; they have known fear, apprehension and anxiety.

I undertook two more medical consultations to attempt to find the answer to my dilemma. My GP wrote his report stating that I had made a reasonable attempt to return to work but that he felt there was no acknowledgement of or any attempt being made to resolve the conflict that had occurred in the workplace, and that a climate of hostility persisted there. He believed exposure to this had had an adverse effect on my mental state, that I had been brave to have withstood this for one day a week, and that there were no delusional or paranoid symptoms. Finally, he stated he was of the opinion that my condition of work-related anxiety arose primarily as a reaction to the unreasonable actions of my employer and was independent of my thyroid illness.

Dr Brendan Holwill was requested to make an assessment of my mental state and causation. In his report, he wrote that on psychiatric review I had persisting symptoms of mild to perhaps moderate anxiety. He received copies of all my relevant thyroid function tests and stated that I was normal in that regard, and that the thyroid disease was not contributing to my current state of mental unrest. My condition of Adjustment Disorder with Anxiety symptoms had arisen entirely as a result of the workplace stress, and a return to work would be dependent on cessation of harassment and discrimination in the workplace.

Five medical specialists all appeared to agree on the causation of my workplace injury. You would feel that would be enough, alas, the 'hired gun' had not yet done his job.

In mid-December, the only medical reports —referred to above— were from my GP and Dr Benjamin. The others came around four to six weeks later, after my WorkCover claim was rejected by my employer and the insurer. The rejection was based on my employer's report of 'no harassment' and the medical report of Dr Dush Shan. His report suggested the symptoms experienced by me may be caused by the diagnosis of Graves' disease, even though two medical professionals had already stated that my Graves' disease was playing no part in my presentation, and blood tests proved this to be true. No notice was taken of these medical reports that supported the cause of my claim. I didn't know the importance of the words 'causation' and 'hired guns' at that time.

I believe that Dr. Shan was biased towards my employer or the insurer (or probably both) at my initial consultation, basing his diagnosis on the false WorkCover statements of Helen the supervisor, John the manager, and Marianne the Acting Manager of Human Resources. I could see that Dr Shan had these statements in his folder. I was surprised when I saw him, as I thought he would want to get to the truth, yet he wouldn't allow me to speak. He just wanted his questions answered, and all his questions related to my various symptoms of Graves' disease and dates when they manifested. When I attempted to explain what was happening, he responded that he was not interested in hearing about anything else. He did not afford me any benefit of the facts already presented, epitomising the term 'hired gun'.

Reading his report, I felt as though I wasn't even *at* this consultation, as so much of what he had written wasn't even discussed. Shan was just a sham, doing what he was paid to do, writing a medical report that fulfilled the needs of my employer and WorkCover: to find no relationship between injury and employment, and therefore no 'causation'.

With my WorkCover claim rejected, I had to access all my sick leave; thankfully, my employer had an unlimited sick leave policy. Against my doctor's advice, in January 2001, I returned to work one day a week. I desperately wanted to return to work and be with my staff, and naively thought the situation would improve.

It was a new year, with the prospect of new beginnings, but sadly not – the harassment continued. I was not allowed to attend mandatory EEO Training, or meetings, and John emailed me stating, "You will not be required to attend any meetings (internal or external), training courses, etc., unless specifically directed by me."

By this time, my emails were being vetted, staff were told not to email me, and my electronic files became inaccessible.

In January 2001, John sent me a letter stating: "I have arranged a 9am appointment with Dr Van Den Berg. As the Council nominated doctor is local, you will have sufficient time to commence your duties at Bridge St and then proceed to the appointment."

I lived in Geelong, 40 minutes from Werribee, and my work starting time was 8am, so I would need to leave work at 8.40am to make the appointment in time in Laverton, which was roughly a 15-minute drive from Werribee. A more reasonable approach would have been to allow me to go directly to the appointment without coming into work first. Still, I attended the appointment with the doctor, who wrote in her report, "It is not my role to adjudicate in these workplace issues which I believe are entirely responsible for her stress reaction."

Now the management-nominated doctor had officially confirmed my position of harassment, three doctors were now in support of my claim, yet management still did not accept any opinion but their own. I've read that truth is always the first casualty of any conflict, and the subsequent years of the truth being tested in a number of different areas proved this to me over and over again.

During this period, I attended a number of counselling sessions with Joanne, Clinical Psychologist. Her diagnosis was that the workplace harassment was the cause of my symptoms of anxiety – the fourth medical professional agreeing that workplace harassment was happening, so why was no one listening? It was no longer just my truth, but the assessment of experts.

HR staff continued with their atrocious handling of my case, and I began to realise they had very little knowledge and skill in these matters, even though they lauded themselves as experts. My doctor was not impressed when they sent him a letter attempting to discredit me and attached a new Position Description never seen by me. He issued another WorkCover Certificate, as it appeared that nothing was being done to address the issues concerning my absence from work.

In February, Wyndham City Council Department WYNCARE won a Premier's Award for continuous improvement. This was based on the development of a checklist for the Home and Community Care Service. Helen (my supervisor) initiated this idea and was subsequently awarded 'Employee of the Year'. It was a familiar theme: in June 2000 the SafetyMap auditor stated the checklist that I had developed and implemented in FDC was "on the cutting-edge of innovation". Helen was aware of this comment, as it was recorded in the Contract Management Meeting Minutes of July 2000. She evidently liked my idea!

February had rolled by and we were in March of 2001, and attending a WorkCover Conciliation Meeting, hopefully to resolve issues and return to work. Even with everything I had gone through, I still wanted to return to my employment. The conciliation meeting was a disaster – human resource representatives would not attend. They positioned themselves in another room and messages were relayed. The conciliator was most apologetic about this arrangement and expressed her dismay. She had not experienced this ever happening before and told me that this was not how WorkCover Conciliation worked. Management was given 23 days to address concerns and settle the matter.

Just after the non-event conciliation session, I had a meeting with John where I was requested to be considerate of Karen's feelings. Karen (then Current Acting Unit Leader) and I met on my one day at work to review Service progress and issues. I told her of John's request to me—to be considerate of her—and apologised if at any time during *my* period of sick leave I had been anything other than considerate. Karen said she was fine. I asked her if John had also made the same comment to her that she was to be considerate of me given the circumstances. Karen responded that John had never asked the same request of her. Karen mentioned that she had found the job demanding and John was unsupportive, due to his lack of skill. She told me she had been crying in the toilets due to the behaviour of the other FDC resource officers and this was significant as you will read later.

This was another example of John's discouraging management style. While I was the one diagnosed with an illness/injury and attempting a return to work, he requested that I be considerate of my staff. However, he did not make the same request to them to be considerate of me in return. Karen was now experiencing some of the same problems that had led to my illness, and shortly after, declined to continue in the role of Acting Unit Leader.

As relayed to me by another staff member, John told resource officers in a staff meeting not to worry; that he "will make sure Lori does not come back."

A new worker attending her first staff meeting was shocked. I did not realise what was brewing and the storm to come. I felt that the reasons for John's continued, systematic, combative and threatening behaviour was beginning to make sense – I had to be left alone and unsupported in the workplace so I would either resign, or prove he was not guilty of bullying and that the real problem, simply, was me. As long as my WorkCover claim remained unaccepted, he was innocent and I was guilty.

From this time on, my staff appeared to avoid any contact with me. This isolation was obviously encouraged and allowed by HR and John.

A significant event around this time was the re-registration of all of the care providers, and it came to light that a number were working without current police checks. It was the role of one of my staff, Christine, to check and coordinate police checks, but somewhere, something had gone wrong.

I was very concerned that this opened the Service and the Council to a possible negligence claim if something had happened. It is a legal requirement that all home-based childcare workers have a current police check. Resource officers were responsible to ensure these were up to date at re-registration time by viewing each police check and ticking the box verifying that they had personally viewed the document. I had to prepare a report on this issue for John, and in this report, I had to be honest. I gave a number of possibilities of how this occurred – one being staff did not follow up on this requirement and may have ticked the box without actually seeing the completed police check.

This is where I made another mistake. I should have given my staff the benefit of the doubt and made up some other reasons for the problem before us. I now believe this was the final issue that turned my staff against me, as they didn't want to accept responsibility for this problem (and it was easier to blame someone off on sick leave). John knew the difficulties my staff sometimes presented, and would often ask me about their behaviour, and I now believe he covertly used this knowledge to create disharmony within my staff.

The 23-day Accident Compensation Conciliation Service deadline was up, and I called them to ask what was happening with my case. The conciliator was surprised that my employer (management) had ignored her directive to attempt settlement. I informed her I had heard nothing since the 1 March meeting and the conciliator said she would contact them.

At the end of March, I asked John to send me a copy of council policies and procedures regarding Grievance and Complaint Resolution procedure, Behavioural Code of Conduct, Harassment and Equal Employment Opportunity documents. Upon reading them, I knew I had not breached any of these standards, and I continued to follow these guides in my future activities.

On a number of occasions, my privacy was seriously breached when I found my medical certificates lying about around the reception area. There was an account from my treating doctor which outlined the date, cost and details of my medical condition. This account was loose and not secured in an envelope, so information was freely available to all in the reception office. I informed HR of this and raised issues of confidentiality. It was suggested that I make a formal complaint as it was also viewed by HR as a serious breach. I chose not to do so, as I was learning that any complaint from me would be viewed negatively. It happened again, but I never did find out whether this was just an oversight or was done purposely.

After doing my job for two months (and having her own position backfilled), Karen was nominated by John for 'Employee of the Quarter'. The Unit Leader for kindergarten and I never received a nomination, and this was expected, as any recognition we felt would not be supported by our supervisor, Helen. Overall, we both received very little or no recognition for anything, unlike others who were recognised for minor achievements (e.g. learning basic computer skills). But we both enjoyed the work we did and had self-satisfaction, knowing we had done a good job.

According to EndWorkplaceAbuse.com, "challenging a narcissist's carefully constructed delusional world of power with the truth you possess about their character sets you up to be a target of a massive smear campaign where you will be fought against with a psychopathy you did not know existed."

I certainly never expected this degree of psychopathy to be directed at me as I had not done anything to justify such an attack, but that is simply not relevant when the 'mob' is on the job.

In early April 2001, I asked my doctor to clear me for a gradual return to work – firstly two days a week, then three days per week, and in four weeks I would return to full-time employment. He was not convinced I should return to work as nothing had taken place to address the issues, but I felt that nothing was ever going to be done and I would return and just hope things would calm down. I should have taken my doctor's advice.

Also in early April, the WorkCover conciliator issued a 'Genuine Notice of Dispute'. I was now able to pursue my claim through the legal channels, which also turned out to be a huge mistake. With this the 'mobbing' began.

"Mobbing can be understood as the stressor to beat all stressors," says Dr.

Kenneth Westhaus of the University of Waterloo, author of *Eliminating Professors*. According to him, "the typical mob victim is a good-to-high achiever personally invested in a formally secure job who somehow threatens or shames co-workers or managers who then decide to get rid of him or her." I agree with most of Dr Westaus's quote, except the shame co-workers part – I disagree with this because victims rarely have the power to shame anyone. They are the ones in the end who are shamed out of their job and in some cases shamed out of their lives.

On 19 April 2001, two weeks after the WorkCover Conciliator issued a 'Genuine Notice of Dispute', I was informed that Council had received serious allegations of harassment and breaches of Equal Employment Opportunity regulations against me from a number of the staff in my team.

According to the Workplace Bullying Institute, it's no surprise that bosses are more likely to bully at work than co-workers or subordinates, but what may be surprising is that bosses alone aren't most likely to bully. About 47% of respondents to a 2012 poll said a mix of people were responsible for their bullying (mobbing), while only 34% of respondents said they only had one bully with a higher ranking than theirs.

The Institute goes on to say: "bullying always begins with a single instigator who nearly immediately recruits the assistance of others. Those who did aid and abet the bully do either through a direct and explicit appeal or through implied coercion. Thus, bullying becomes mobbing (involving multiple perpetrators who gang up on a single target). In other words, it's an abuse of power that leads targets to isolation. Fear prevents the reverse from happening. Subordinates rarely join together to go against a boss out of fear of losing their jobs or becoming targets themselves." I feel this describes precisely happened to me, but with one digression: the resource officers did not feel fear or concern that they may lose their jobs. I believe this was purely an opportunity to gain some sense of power and control they had not had before – an opportunity for them to satisfy their grudges, a chance to bring down the tall poppy. They became an angry mob baying for blood; my blood.

Days later, I was alarmed to see John's diary sheet for the week displayed outside his office, and scheduled in at 3:45pm to 6pm was a meeting with him and the Acting Manager of Human Resources, the WorkCover Coordinator, Rhonda (Council's EAP counsellor), and Steve (an occupational rehabilitation consultant), convening to discuss "L. O'Keeffe."

I was going to be discussed and other employees could see it, I was never informed of this meeting and was never informed of any outcomes.

Around this time, Karen (Acting Unit Leader) was keen to find fault with me. I found this strange given her earlier admissions to me about the resource officers' behaviour towards her. I felt her confidence and her opinion of herself was increasing, because even though she had earlier given me her thoughts on John, he was now recruiting her in his plan to gaslight me.

On 11 April—also unknown to me—Karen and the resource officers attended a 'debriefing session' with Council's Employee Assistance program counsellor, to set in motion the wheels that would cause the derailment of my efforts to return to my normal position. I find it incredulous that a counsellor would recommend the action they took against me without any care towards me as a staff member on sick leave and attempting a return to work. In my opinion, the counsellor compromised her role – she joined 'the mob' without a thought about the damage she was helping to create, and all without ever meeting me.

Was I not the one with a WorkCover claim alleging workplace harassment as the cause of injury, with three medical experts agreeing with this, a claim made in November 2000 with it now being April 2001? What about the perpetrators? They were to be protected, with the victim thrown under the bus.

I was later told by another staff member (who could barely believe these shenanigans) that she observed Karen, Andrea and Narelle entering the private upstairs lounge with Helen (who was no longer their supervisor and worked in another building). They met for approximately 45 minutes. Immediately after the meeting, Narelle was heard to remark to Jenny "we now know what to do."

My gut instinct was correct: Helen was still playing the game and strenuously pulling strings.

This is the background to my attempted return to work, one which was spectacularly halted on the 19 April by my suspension from employment.

This was to be my second full day at work, leading back into full-time employment within a month. I excitedly attended work, looking forward to seeing everyone, but unbeknown to me the resource officers were meeting with Marianne at the Civic Centre and all agreed that I be suspended. I was wondering where they were, and on their return to the office I attempted to talk to them but was ignored.

Earlier that morning, I had received an email requesting I attend a meeting at midday with Marianne and Michael M, the latter who was Acting Manager of WYNCARE, to discuss a 'staff issue'.

I naively believed it was to be about one of my staff, but soon my gut started to churn, my heart was thumping in my chest and I began to feel panic. My physical reaction was telling me something bad was going to happen. I didn't know what; just that it was bad. And I was right.

Kerry, the WorkCover Officer, called me to inform me they were running late for the meeting and would be arriving at 12:30pm. I asked who else would be attending this meeting – she responded that it would be the Acting Manager of WYNCARE and Marianne. I'd received no notice of this formal meeting and felt I may have needed support. I called the union shop steward Justin, but he was not available until after 5pm. I rang Emma, member of the Union Shop Committee, but she was not at work that day. I also rang John M, another member of Union Shop Committee, but he was also not in.

I rang Union Headquarters to speak to Danny, my Union Industrial Officer. Danny was not in the office, so I asked to speak to Neil and he was not in. My feelings of panic increased as no one was available for me to gain advice and/or support. The union receptionist tried to assist further and checked Danny's diary. She said Danny was in fact already at Wyndham City Council and to ring him on his mobile. I rang Danny on his mobile number, but the phone rang a number of times and then the line went dead. I rang again and the line went to an answering service.

I rang Kerry concerning the need for a Union presence at this meeting. Kerry spoke to Marianne who was still in her office; Marianne responded, "Will not need it this time." What an outrageous statement from a supposed human resource specialist who, knowing what was to come, believed that an injured worker did not need support.

The meeting commenced one hour late, with no one available to attend with me, but I thought it would be okay – I had done nothing wrong; the 'staff issue' must be regarding one of my staff. But if so, why did I feel so physically unwell? How strange this all was, coupled with the fact there were a number of other staff absences on this day, including the department manager John, Helen the supervisor and Bernie the WYNCARE Director, which is why Michael M was acting in his position and tasked with this very unpleasant job.

This was either one mighty coincidence, or a planned strategic event to protect these staff from any fall-out from me. It was cowardly – gutless behaviour from so-called professionals being paid sizeable salaries to deal with such issues. They all ran and hid until the coast was clear.

The meeting was held to inform me that serious allegations of harassment and breaches of Equal Employment Opportunity regulations had been reported to management from a number of staff in my team, and due to their seriousness, management had no option than to suspend my employment.

I found this really difficult to get my head around. A decision was made to suspend me, a staff member who was on sick leave and attempting a return to work, a person who was citing workplace harassment as the cause of her injury and illness (which was supported by three medical experts). Now, without any investigation or any discussion with the subject concerned, action is taken to cause further harm and damage to this injured worker.

I was heartlessly escorted from the building and left dumbfounded on the street, wondering what to do (as I had no car at this time). Kerry (the Work-Cover officer) walked past the building. I found this strange, as she worked at the Civic Centre, not in the Bridge Street Office, and it was way past lunchtime. Was she coming to gloat, to witness my despair? Or was she the spy on the street observing my behaviour?

I was suspended within 24 hours of a complaint being made about me, a complaint that was—conveniently—anonymous. I felt that this complaint was somehow contrived to thwart my pending WorkCover claim.

Given that my employer was aware of my health issues as stated on my WorkCover certificates, ones provided by three different medical practitioners who were in consensus as to their diagnosis and causation, I felt my employer's behaviour was unconscionable. I was not afforded natural justice or procedural fairness in this process. Given the knowledge my employer had at this time regarding my health issues, they should have conducted a thorough investigation before taking such drastic action.

There was no assistance given to ensure my welfare, and no offer to see me home safely, which had been past practice when a staff member was ill at work.

Up to this time I held Bernie, the General Manager of WYNCARE, in high regard. We had previously enjoyed an amicable working relationship and shared a mutual respect for one another. It was disappointing for me to come to the realisation that he was a party to this behaviour by not participating in any resolution and without ever speaking to me.

At no time did Bernie make any attempt to meet or discuss issues with me, which would have been an initial task for a General Manager to diffuse a difficult situation. He appeared to handball the problem straight to the Human Resource Department. He ultimately lacked the professionalism and skill to handle what was becoming a very difficult and sensitive situation. He often did a 'walk and talk' around his departments, as did the CEO Ian, but disappointingly, neither actually demonstrated good leadership during this period.

A few days later, after the shock had settled a little, I rang my union for advice. I spoke to Neil and explained the situation regarding the FDC resource officers, but of course I believed the union already knew. Neil responded in a sarcastic tone, "Yeah, a real nice bunch of ladies." He suggested I submit a complaint against my supervisor Helen and manager John for harassment and breaches of Council Policies and Procedures. This would be a separate action to my WorkCover claim.

I requested Marianne provide details of complaints against me, including incidents and dates, with each incident signed by the aggrieved party. This should have been done prior to any suspension with an investigation – very poorly handled by the Human Resource Department and senior management. Human Resources subsequently wrote to me and explained they had engaged an external investigator, Garside Consulting, to complete an investigation of the complaints against me. Once again this should obviously have been done prior to suspension.

The letter states: "The choice of Margaret Winson is based on her having no previous knowledge regarding this case and that she had not previously been engaged by Council."

It later became known to me that Margaret Winson was married to Phillip Garside, the principal of Garside Consulting, who had been engaged by my employer on numerous occasions to provide Harassment and EEO Training to all employees. This was the training that John would not allow me to attend. I am not convinced Ms Winson was ever truly independent.

On the last day of April, I attended my office and met with Marianne. She gave me the written and signed complaints by various resource officers. I told Marianne the union informed me that I should have participated in the selection of the investigator so as to add to my belief of independence. Marianne was quite concerned, as she then realised she should have done this and I was asking about this now – the investigator had been working on the case for a couple of days when she was made aware of her error. Marianne contacted

Margaret Winson, who was in the building interviewing the complaining staff, and requested she come and talk to me immediately.

I met with Margaret and I felt physically calm in her presence. We had a chat and she explained to me the process she planned to undertake. I felt quite confident that she would be impartial and I agreed to continue with her as the investigator. (Remember: it was not known to me until much later the connection between Margaret and Garside Consulting.) Were they independent? On balance I believe they were.

After perusal of these staff complaints by me, along with the Union Industrial Officer and Craig the Director of Corporate and Community Services, the consensus was that the complaints were a number of years old, rather minor, insignificant or related to expected work practices of a supervisor. As these allegations were unsubstantiated why didn't someone—anyone—pull the brake right then and there?

Through my reading on this topic, I came to learn that when a 'bully' personality is present and a 'target' selected, quite often by-standers will join in on the abuse or do nothing to prevent the abuse from occurring. This is what can happen to a team with a diverse range of personalities, when strong leadership is absent, and there is coercion from the bully/bullies. While I was the Unit Leader I did empower staff, but at times it was necessary to have some degree of control. The Service was well run and staff efficient in their roles, but when I was removed, the stronger personalities of staff members—Narelle and Andrea—joined forces and became informal leaders, which resulted in long term negative impacts on themselves, myself and Service stakeholders.

THREE

The Nightmare of Injustice

This Chapter opens with text taken from a website referencing an Australian Mobbing Conference. It will prepare you for what you will read later.

NATURAL JUSTICE

This section provides an overview of natural justice principles, including the Dream as well as an overview as to what can be expected in practice, ie. the Nightmare.

The Dream

These principles are commonly understood in the process of providing natural justice. These form the basis of training of employers by the Human Rights and Equal Opportunity Commission (HREOC) into the provision of natural justice in the handling of grievances in the discrimination jurisdiction.

The principles include:

- Informing the respondent (or in the case of workplace mobbing, the target) as to who has made the complaint.

- Providing the respondent (or in the case of workplace mobbing, the target) with the specific incidents, dates, and context including any witnesses, in writing.
- It is a denial of natural justice when the target or the accused is not given the incidents or information as to who has made complaints against them.
- The respondent must have the full opportunity to respond to each of the incidents before penalties or disciplinary actions are imposed. For example, 'ejecting' those accused from their employment on the basis of vague accusations by unidentified persons is a fundamental breach of natural justice.
- The penalties imposed, should the incidents be proven, must not outweigh the crime. That is: ask, does the punishment fit the crime?
- All parties to the complaint have the right to be heard.
- All relevant submissions and evidence are to be considered.
- The employer does not take into account matters that are not relevant.
- The person who lays the charge must not determine the charge.
- The decision-maker must be fair and just.

Terms of reference must not favour any party to a complaint. For example, gathering evidence to support the claims of the accusers denies natural justice to the respondent.

The Nightmare

Often grievance processes have spurious definitions of natural justice that mean that an accused person does not have the right to fair treatment.

Despite common perceptions that 'an accused' has basic rights, this is not guaranteed and often not required by grievance policies.

Despite commonly accepted assurances about fairness and equity, the following is a summary of employee experiences, particularly in public sector agencies, when complaints have been made against them.

1. An accusation or complaint is made without any substantiating evidence or witnesses. There is no requirement to advise the person who has been complained about as to the details of the complaint.

There is no requirement on the complainant/s to formalise their complaint before punishing actions are taken against the person complained about. The 'accused' can be effectively 'dismissed' by being transferred to another work area without consultation. Complainants are often guaranteed that they need not be identified when making a complaint. Consultants are appointed to construct a case for the complainant/s against the accused person. There is no requirement to similarly construct a case for 'the defendant'

2. The case against the accused can focus on the perceptions and emotions of the complainant/s rather than the facts or incidents. The final recommendations are those that support actions already taken against the accused

3. The punishing actions taken against the person complained against are not legally defined as disciplinary actions. There is no requirement on complainant/s to be accountable for trivial, vexatious or false accusations. The accused is not provided the opportunity to question the grievance process. There is no requirement to provide redress to those who are falsely accused.

Unfortunately, I experienced the nightmare.

Little did I know, that over the presiding years the staff I had interviewed and deemed the best for their jobs were the ones who betrayed and caused me so much harm. My self-esteem was so low that it could barely sustain life, but the human spirit can still be strong at these times when it is needed the most.

A week after the anonymous staff complaints of April, the appointed independent investigator stated in a letter to Marianne (the Acting Human Resource Manager) the following: "The group nature of the complaint as it currently stands causes two problems. Firstly, there is a lack of fair process to the respondent, in that she cannot tell from reading the document who is alleging what against her, and she has the right to know, as the identities may be relevant to her defence. Secondly, this is also a practical problem if the allegations are found to be fabricated – individual complainants would have to be held accountable for making a false complaint." So, allegations were found to be fabricated, but no one other than me was held accountable, as you will shortly discover.

I had an appointment in early May to meet with Margaret Winson to answer the allegations and any queries she may have had. The day prior to my appointment, Craig informed me that Garside Consulting did not need to interview me. A few days later he received the Garside Consulting report written by Margaret Winson recommending that the investigation cease at once. There were no questions or allegations to answer or clarify? I knew the truth and I now knew that Margaret did too; I had no case to answer.

I asked Craig if this meant the suspension was lifted, and Craig responded, "I suppose it does." He advised that a letter from him would be couriered to my home that day. That letter took another 11 days to arrive and resolved nothing.

Around this time, I became aware that on or about 19 April (suspension day), Pauline—an ex-Family Day Care staff member, the one whose job I did for three months so she could go on secondment—was contacting ex-Family Day Care staff to encourage them to also make complaints, and inviting them to Andrea's home for a get-together the following weekend to discuss what-I-do-not-know. But the three ex-staff (from my understanding) did not have any complaints to make nor did they want to participate in the 'mobbing'. They showed the integrity sadly lacking in everyone else around me.

If this get-together did indeed take place, it was highly likely that the events concerning me would have been freely discussed. These staff were informed in writing that this situation was to remain confidential, as I was informed of the same. Because of this confidentiality rule I had no staff group providing support nor staff I could talk to, confide in or debrief with. I had no one I could trust for support, yet they were inviting others to join the mob. Staff therefore would have breached Council's 'Code of Behaviour' which can result in instant dismissal, but of course this would not occur as their misconduct played to management's full advantage.

I later met with one of these former staff members – I was interested in her opinion as she was present when a number of the resource officers' allegations were supposed to have taken place.

I asked her if she was aware of what was going on. She said that Pauline did tell her about it, but she hadn't heard anything for a long time, and that she didn't see any of these people other than Pauline.

I outlined a few of the staff members' allegations to her, such as verbal abuse of staff, having a dictatorial style, and not caring about their needs.

She responded, "Lori, you were the one verbally abused. There are occasions when a manager may need to be dictatorial, especially with that lot – they never wanted to do any work.

I do not know how you have put up with it all this time. That's why I had to get out of there.

You never seemed really aware of what was going on. You always wanted to think the best of people. I spoke to them one day and asked them if they believed the Service operated better now than it did before you. They seemed to agree the Service was operating better, but did not appear to give you any credit for this. Lori, this was not necessarily just against you, they would have done the same to anyone. They just wanted to do what they wanted to do, which was nothing, except sit at their desks and work on little projects of their own."

I knew what she was saying was true, but she was wrong in one aspect: I did know and was fully aware of what was going on, and developed many strategies in an attempt to create some team efficiency, effectiveness and cohesiveness. I knew that on occasion team dynamics were fragile and there was potential for conflict, but I never expected this potential to go to the depths of depravity it did.

The resource officers often complained they were overworked, but they never provided evidence of such. I regularly measured the work they were required to undertake with the hours they were employed, and it was a fair distribution. The only time the Service was short-staffed was when the Child Care Benefit administration officer went on secondment in December 1999 and I took over this role. The FDC Resources Officer did not undertake additional work due to this. It was completed solely by me, with some assistance from a casual worker when she was available, which was not often. When I was on leave due to my WorkCover claim, my position was initially filled by Karen, a resource officer who had her position backfilled.

Previous to this, the manager John often asked me in our meetings, "How are they going?" and he meant how was *I* going, managing them, as he was aware they were a difficult lot. Individually they all had a good opinion of themselves and how great they were at the job. They were all adequate in their positions, and on some occasions very good, but ultimately, it wasn't their inability to get the job done that was of concern – it was their group dynamics, which would be proven. Individually, on the surface, all were lovely women, but in a group they were lethal – they all backed each other up and demanded they get what they wanted. Their group dynamics exhibited psychopathic traits.

Just what the doctor ordered; John had his 'mob' to attack and falsely accuse me, thereby giving some victimhood status to him and Helen, and my submission of a WorkCover claim—citing John and Helen for harassment and intimidation—was clearly false in their view. The 'mob', combined with the bullies, were truly great manipulators. They were able to lie, defame and lambast me, and somehow managed to make it all seem like it was entirely my fault or that I deserved it. I have learned that this tactic is called 'gaslighting,' which is a form of psychological manipulation that seeks to sow seeds of doubt in a targeted individual making them question their own memory, perception and sanity.

In my later years of attempting to understand this phenomenon of gaslighting, I developed more interest in bullying and mobbing, which has resulted in much research into the topic. This paragraph in a research paper resonated with me: "It's not a target problem, research shows there is zero evidence to support targets brought on the abuse through weakness. In fact, evidence shows the opposite. Targets are often high performing, highly ethical employees whose competence poses a threat to their low performing, low ethical bosses. The bully's motivation is to keep the upper hand, an ego-driven control move that's about abuse of power. The bullies are often deceptive managers who trick others into thinking the target is the problem, setting the stage for mobbing." This, I believe, is what happened to me.

In May 2001, I met with Craig and he reinstated his comments from a few days earlier. He gave me a copy of the report from Garside Consulting, which recommended terminating the investigation immediately.

The second paragraph of the report stated that it had become apparent that the complainants were uncomfortable with having their concerns dealt with in a formal investigation process, as they felt it was unnecessarily adversarial. I was amazed that they felt uncomfortable. They made their complaints and by doing so initiated this process, and they agreed to my suspension from employment. I presume that they were held accountable to prove their allegations and they could not. I doubt the resource officers would have considered it "unnecessarily adversarial" if the outcome was appearing to be favourable to them.

They all stated that they would prefer to work through the issues with me in order to reach a satisfactory outcome, and mediation was recommended for this to occur – and then they refused to participate in the mediation. When mediation was recommended for John and me, I had no desire to participate in this process, but was warned that if I did not participate management would not look kindly on my refusal, and yet the resource officers refused to participate and it appeared that no such warning was given to them. I feel that management and, in particular, John and Helen did not want the resource officers and me settling this issue – they wanted the issue to remain unresolved because it suited and protected them.

The investigator said that hopefully the parties could negotiate an agreement over how things would work in the future, in which case there would be no need for the investigation to be completed. There was no negotiated agreement and no completed investigation. The investigation was left in limbo because the complaints against me were not panning out and so they could not be substantiated. I felt that a completed investigation would have exonerated me, and that this was known, and was why it was left in limbo. I requested that the formal external investigation continue to conclusion, as no mediation or negotiated agreements were reached. My request was ignored, and an internal investigation appears to have been conducted – an internal process that could be more contrived and controlled than an independent external investigation. The outcome could be whatever management wanted without any accountability for decisions made.

One complaint was that my management style needed to become more inclusive, but there were no examples provided that supported their complaint, so I found it difficult to respond. I feel that my management style was one of inclusion, empowerment and support, but the many examples of this that I provided were disregarded.

It was alleged that I made decisions arbitrarily and inconsistently rather than in accordance with the national standards. Individual resource officers each gave care providers different answers concerning the provision of care, and that they felt embarrassed when they were wrong and blamed this on me.

The 1995 National Standards for Family Day Care had an additional section added to the Standards in 1997. This section was titled 'The Victorian Perspective'. I wrote this document because I felt the National Standards did not go far enough and our Service was already exceeding the Standards. For me, there were still too many grey areas that needed to be addressed, explained and implemented, hence the Victorian Standards. To make a complaint that I did not understand the standards was ridiculous – I knew them inside out and upside down; I wrote them and was fully conversant with the standards for the provision of home-based childcare.

It was the resource officers who didn't understand the Standards, and if necessary, how to interpret them. It was due to their own lack of knowledge that they gave incorrect and conflicting information to care providers. I regularly reminded them that if they didn't know the answer to a question, to seek information and clarification before answering. Any embarrassment they felt was of their own doing. For example, through the early years of my employment I had many complaints from care providers regarding how resource officers assessed home safety. There was no consistency; one staff member would tell a care provider that they must do something while another staff would say to another care provider you do not need to do the same thing. How staff assessed a home appeared to be based on their own beliefs, values and judgments.

In 1998, I initiated, developed and implemented the care provider 'Self-Assessment for Safety Checklist'. This booklet provided information and a consistent approach to home safety. There were few complaints regarding this issue from then on. It was such a wonderful initiative that the Mayor personally thanked me for it, and later in June, during the Services assessment for SafetyMap Accreditation, the assessor remarked that this OH&S initiative was "on the cutting edge of innovation." This was the very idea Helen used to create her Home Care Checklist, for which she won an award.

It was claimed my approaches were inconsistent, but again no examples were provided, thus I couldn't address the allegation. I did provide information I believed may have shown this allegation was unfounded, but this was again ignored. What the resource officers may have been interpreting as inconsistency may have in fact been a supervisor using their expertise and discretion to problem-solve and make sound decisions. Given the nature of Family Day Care, not everything was black or white; there was still a lot of grey even with the Standards.

While I was working at the Civic Centre in early 2002, I read a letter on the FDC File Network from Caitlyn, an agency worker who was temporarily the Acting Unit Leader. This letter gave approval to a care provider to breach her contract by having more than the contractual number of children receiving care in her home. I'd never heard of any Co-ordination Unit putting such a proposal in writing before. My employer could have been deemed negligent if an injury occurred, and therefore liable, and the care provider's own insurance cover would be void. Caitlyn had her employment agency contract extended a number of times; it was originally for two weeks, but she was in the position for nine months. I couldn't understand an agency employee taking such a risk; it appeared to me she was not as experienced in the role as she portrayed and did not understand the National Standards for Family Day Care and the Victorian Perspective, as she was being inconsistent. I wonder if the resource officers made a complaint about her inconsistency.

The resource officers claimed they needed better communication and information systems and yet there were no examples provided, which meant I again wasn't able to respond to the allegation. I did provide information I believed may have shown this allegation was unfounded, but this too was ignored.

The resource officers alleged that there was "occasional, perceived" intimidatory behaviour from me, including speaking over staff in monthly staff meetings, banging files on the table and not leaving time for agenda items nominated by staff. There was the odd occasion where I had to raise my voice slightly to get their attention because they had a tendency to all talk at the same time. There was one occasion where I had a large number of files required for the meeting and I attempted to carry them in all in one go and by the time I reached the meeting room they had started to slip. I quickly put them down on the table as they concertinaed down. An innocent occurrence turned into a formal complaint – just one example of how the resource officers' perception was clouded by 'mob thinking'.

There was always a full meeting agenda, and prior to being under a contract of Service due to the introduction of CCT in 1996, meetings primarily consisted of whatever the staff wanted to talk about. Over the years this changed and the focus of the agenda consisted of the bigger picture items that had to be discussed, such as QA Accreditation, OH&S, Contract requirements, Strategic Direction, Policy Development, and Business Plan objectives and targets. The resource officers resented not getting their airplay on minor issues and the validation of other officers. These issues could have been discussed with another officer or me if advice, direction or debriefing was required. They did not need to be 'stored up' for a formal meeting. There was always someone in the office to talk to and they sat in close proximity to me and each other. Rather than have eight staff sitting around spending valuable time on what was on most occasions a minor operational issue was not the most effective use of our short meeting time.

A few years into the job I realised that I did not know where staff were if not in the office and what they were doing. I had heard rumours that some staff were going home during the day to bring in their washing or cooking their dinner, or going shopping. I didn't know if this was true. I set up a whiteboard for staff to write when they were out of the office and what time they would return. I believe that any person responsible for staff needs to know roughly where they are – this is just good management practice. I could just imagine John or Helen coming to me asking where so and so is and me having to say that I didn't know.

On leaving work one evening around 10pm after a care provider meeting, I went to the whiteboard to put 'late start' against my name. As I had just worked a 14-hour day I was permitted to start later in the morning. I noticed on the whiteboard that there were no resource officers in the office the next morning until 10:30am. All were absent for various reasons, and as Andrea was the designated 'office duty' person for that morning I felt I had no choice but to call her. I asked if she had organised another staff member to cover for her. She had not and wasn't prepared to come in, so after having just worked a 14-hour day myself I was the one in the office first thing the next morning. I was peeved, but not angry.

I understand from Andrea's complaint that she was angry with me for calling at 10pm, after she had previously told me this was alright. She made the choice not to come to do office duty and I covered the office.

Words used by Andrea to describe how she felt about this phone call are: confused, upset, visibly upset, unsure, sleepless night, angry, disappointment, emotional, extremely nervous, and anxious. She wanted to meet the next day to discuss her feelings and I arranged the glass conference room to be available. Andrea responded that she did not want to meet in this room as she did not feel comfortable, and as she was feeling emotional we moved to a small private lounge area.

Andrea wanted this meeting and the only time I had available was my lunch break. Andrea made mention in her complaint that I'd brought an apple and yoghurt to the meeting and "Lori continued to eat her yoghurt/apple and lounged back on the couch." This was not a formal meeting, but a chat about last night's phone call and in my lunch break. As Andrea mentions this in her complaint, I can only deduce eating my lunch was a complaint as well, because why would she feel this even needed to be mentioned?

Other issues she raised were: equality between staff; coordinator not readily accessible for communication and respect; and feeling harassed. I feel very sorry that a phone call had caused Andrea so much distress that she needed to seek counselling. Now reading her response I feel justifiably quite distressed.

Here I will quote Narelle's full complaint because it is blatantly wrong:

"Lori always intimidates when leave applications are made and claiming that it would not be her fault if the application was not accepted as management made the final decision. She never consults or plans our annual leave and leaves us frustrated and stranded in terms of our applications regardless of how early we put in our requests. She always has her leave as she wants it and our needs come last – always." And Karen stated in her complaint regarding the same issue, "Applying for annual leave around Christmas has always been a frustrating experience. I have observed that Lori has always taken leave when she likes. It <u>appears</u> as if 'I'm the boss, so I get first pickings' regardless of other people's needs or expression of interest."

This allegation was nonsense, and management knew it. I never referred to myself as 'the boss' and always considered the needs of my staff. Documents regarding leave requests are evidenced in the existing Service files that proved this allegation to be false. When staff were on leave, I often had to pick up additional tasks which I didn't mind, as I wanted them to have the leave they wanted and I often took my leave around their leave. I did inform staff that I signed "recommended" on all leave applications and management gives the final approval – this was their role. I always consulted staff concerning their plans for annual leave, with this being a regular agenda item from October onwards as all staff want leave around Christmas. (One only needs to read the meeting minutes to know this is true.) Some resource officers occasionally submitted an application for leave very early, believing it would be first in, best dressed. I had always explained to them that I would attempt to ensure that everybody got the leave they requested, but I couldn't guarantee it as I was required to consider the needs of the Service as well.

There was not one single occasion when I rejected a staff member's annual leave application, and the final comment that "She always has her leave as she wants it and our needs come last" – "always" cannot be supported by any evidence. These two complaints are very similar, so it appears that there may have been some collusion at play. I provided as evidence four memos outlining the annual leave process that I had written over the past few years, and suggested that Unit Meeting Minutes would also show this allegation as being untrue. I can say, categorically, there has never been an occasion where a staff member did not have the leave they requested. This is why I found this allegation particularly hurtful and even more so when management ignored the evidence.

I was accused of invading a resource officer's personal space. As there were no examples provided it was impossible to completely answer this allegation, but I think this may relate to staff member, Elda. She states that I used physical intimidation with her because I had apparently leaned on her desk and moved slightly forward, right into her personal space, and badgered her until she became very frustrated regarding a very unrealistic workload issue (which I intend to clarify directly). She claimed this was in a public setting and another team member witnessed this event; she claims it was very humiliating and intimidating and that she had to ask me to stop and get off her desk twice before I stopped badgering her. Elda claimed I did not respect staff privacy when there were issues to be discussed and that I just did it anywhere.

Now the alternate view of the same story: Elda was refusing to participate in the 3+Activity Group, a requirement of her position description. Resource officers generally disliked working in the Activity Group. I didn't understand this, because it released them from other duties and allowed them to play with a delightful bunch of children for two hours per week with four hours of prep time—very generous—because I did not want any excuses that they did not have time to plan their group.

This is why, in February 1999, I wrote a long-term program plan that allocated two resource officers to Activity Group each year for the next three years, so that they would have time to adjust. It meant once every three years they would have to do this task. It was Elda's year and she flatly refused and notified the union that she was being treated unfairly. I knew that senior management did not look favourably on staff contacting the union, as I was told very early on by the personnel department not to make waves. I didn't want Elda to back herself into a corner, as I knew the union could not help her, as this was part of her contract of employment and that is why I went to her desk – to have a quiet word. As she was sitting, I didn't want to stand over her, so I leant casually on the open side of her desk and leaned slightly forward. I actually did this so not to appear to be intimidating and immediately removed myself upon her request. This occurred in our office, which is not a public space or venue, and there were few staff around. I was trying to keep it informal and for her not to make a big issue out of something she would lose. I used a quiet voice to talk to her and was hopeful she would accept this task as her responsibility as there was no possibility of any other resource officer taking on this role when it was not their turn. I went on sick leave at the end of that year, and from memory I think it was a short time later that Activity Group was scrapped.

Another allegation of invading personal space was made by Narelle. She stated that she was at her work station and was walking to and from the filing cabinets located in the office area. Andrea, who sat beside her, was on the phone to her husband. I entered the area and stood behind Andrea, indicating that I needed her to speak to me. When Andrea did not respond, I then positioned myself closer to Andrea (entering personal space) looking down at her and listening to her phone call. I persisted with this strategy until Andrea ended her phone call and attended to my request.

Now the alternate view of the same story, and I have a good recollection of this incident: Andrea was on her phone when a call for her diverted through to my phone. It was a parent or care provider who required urgent information regarding a child's care for the next day and they did not want to leave a message. I couldn't help as I didn't have the required information, but Andrea did (as she had coordinated this care). I asked them to hold, and went to Andrea's desk. She was sitting slightly to the side, and upon seeing me, she turned her back and ignored me and continued with her call. I was concerned about the person on the phone on hold, therefore I persisted in my position, though I did not move closer – I just stood where I was. I was not intently listening to the details of her call but knew it was her husband.

I believe that any senior professional would be concerned if a subordinate ignored them because they were on a personal call, and then continued the personal call in defiance. Even a co-worker would find this behaviour disrespectful. The expectation would surely be that the person terminates the call and attends to business, or at the very least asks the husband to hold for a moment.

The next allegation is complex, and I'm not sure what it means: "Frequency of requests and demands to perform tasks, and the manner in which the requests and demands are made." As usual, there were no *examples*, so it wasn't possible to answer the allegation, but I did supply some information to show this allegation was unfounded (that was unsurprisingly ignored). One of the reasons I had so much work to complete during the year 2000 was that I attempted to do it all myself. I made very few requests, and never placed any demands on my staff – I shouldered the burden of a heavy workload to spare my staff from becoming overworked, as I felt I had become. According to my role's position description, I had the authority to direct and to delegate, but — aware of the attitudes of my staff— knew that any delegation would be viewed

The Nightmare of Injustice

as me offloading my work to them, and I feel this allegation to be proof of exactly that.

I had a few concerns with the Garside report because of the false assurance I was given that the investigator was independent without any potential conflict of interest. There was of course potential bias by the author, given her relationship with Phillip Garside of Garside Consulting, who had a lucrative contract with my employer and the potential for more. I was not given the opportunity of being interviewed to answer these allegations and therefore a balanced report was not possible. I believe it was realised by Garside Consulting that these complaints were misconceived, and that is why my scheduled interview did not take place. Given this, a report should not have been written at all. The report was basically a statement of some of the allegations, and if I had been interviewed then the allegations, no doubt, would have been found to be false, and I feel that this is precisely the reason I was not interviewed.

I will not go into a lot of detail—except some minor detail of the complaints not covered in the Garside report—as they are so vast that they are out of this world, but I will give you a snapshot. In my view, the reason they weren't included in the report because they were just so frivolous, vexatious and completely untrue.

Resource officer, Narelle, made an allegation in her complaint that I had sent her an undeserved reprimanding email. I reprimanded Narelle because she opened a controversial letter not addressed to her and distributed this letter to other staff before I had seen it. I informed her, in a neutral tone of voice, that it was not right to open mail not addressed to her, and distribute it. She alleged in her statement that, "Lori responded by email, reprimanding me. She was the boss and she would decide if we were to participate and reminded me to follow correct procedure. What was the correct procedure? I felt I was being punished for using my initiative." In this instance, Narelle's initiative was misplaced. I never sent a reprimanding email to Narelle and once again never referred to myself as 'the boss'. This allegation could be easily proven by the production of this email. I knew that no such email existed so I requested a copy. It was never provided, not even during later legal proceedings.

From Andrea, another resource officer: "Just yesterday, Lori received an email from the Director re contributions to the WYNCARE Newsletter – we were all sent an email from Lori that was so demeaning and accusing in tone. Rather than asking us to assist with contributions, we felt we were to blame for not attending to something we were not even aware of and that was essentially her responsibility."

I don't believe my email was demeaning or accusatory; I was simply enquiring as to which staff member had 'marketing' as part of their Workplan. I did use the word 'surely' in my email so presume this is what was interpreted as "accusing in tone." I was conscious that I wouldn't be able to fulfil this request because of my absence on sick leave, and didn't want to miss the opportunity if there was something newsworthy happening in the Service that I was unaware of due to my absence. Of course, it turned out that Andrea did have marketing in her Workplan, and suspect if I'd gone ahead fulfilling the Director's request myself, staff would have complained that I didn't include them in media opportunities. Andrea had a half day a fortnight in her roster to pursue media opportunities; her grievance proved her misunderstanding of both her own role, and my role of delegation.

I mentioned earlier some of the allegations of Andrea and Narelle, who I believe were the main instigators of the mob forming. Others also made allegations which were of a minor nature but nonetheless added to the tally of my wrongdoings.

Christine, one of the resource officers, wished to change her part-time days of employment from Friday to Monday, and was annoyed when this request was denied; she stated this left her feeling frustrated and unsupported. In my role as Unit Leader, I had to ensure staffing hours were fairly spread to ensure adequate staff coverage. At this time, I believed that Mondays were less demanding than other days of the week, with Fridays being the most demanding, with many an emergency occurring on Friday afternoons. I wasn't convinced this change desired by Christine would increase her ability to complete her role. Nearly a year later, when Christine's position description no longer contained the tasks that she said required her to change her day from Friday to Monday, she again requested the change in days, and the Acting Unit Leader (Karen) approved. I accepted Karen's decision based on what she told me; that, by then, Mondays were busier than Fridays.

In 1997, late one afternoon Karen requested she leave work early as her father needed her to help look for her mother who had not returned home from shopping. I said, "Go, just put on the board that you are on leave." Karen's mum had sadly passed and Karen took two weeks' leave. On the day she returned, staff met for afternoon tea to welcome her back, but unfortunately, I couldn't attend as I had a pressing deadline. In passing, as the staff were all

The Nightmare of Injustice

together, I flippantly said, "Don't forget timesheets tomorrow." I feel I have paid dearly for this moment of thoughtlessness.

In her complaint, Karen said that I came out of my office and asked her—in front of everyone—if she had completed a timesheet for the 40 minutes she left early on the day she left with her father. I made the comment it was timesheet week, but absolutely no comment regarding a timesheet for those 40 minutes. I checked the Staff Leave Record Sheet and I hadn't even recorded Karen's two weeks leave, let alone any 40 minutes. I didn't remember Karen leaving 40 minutes early at all until her complaint, and if her allegation is true, where was her completed timesheet for these 40 minutes?

When I went on sick leave and returned to work one day a week, I would meet with Karen—who was acting in my position—for about 30 minutes in the morning to discuss Service issues she needed to tell me about. Karen mentioned to me during these meetings how she was feeling and made the following comments: that she found the job demanding and couldn't wait to get out of there, that she was looking for another job, that she found John the manager unsupportive due to his lack of skills, and that she had spent time crying in the toilets because the other staff treated her badly. I asked why the other resource officers were treating her badly and she said that they didn't want her in the Acting Unit Leader position – that they had wanted Andrea. I counselled her as best I could under the circumstances and let her know she could contact me at any time.

I really liked Karen, both personally and professionally, and we had gotten along well (at least I thought we had) in our working relationship, up until her allegations where she had also stated that during this period (on advice from Helen the supervisor) she had sought counselling from the Employee Assistance Program due to my behaviour. When her mindset changed, and why, are questions I cannot answer.

Another resource officer named Jenny made an allegation against me that she felt unsupported, when back in 1997 John the manager issued a 'First Official Warning' for her use of bad language in the office more than once, and where members of the public may hear. At the time I supported John's action, but now in hindsight I regret that we did not handle it differently. In her complaint, Jenny states: "I am not raising this incident now as allegations of harassment, but as core reasons for my dissatisfaction and distrust of management."

That does not appear to be a complaint about me, but apparently Jenny joined in the mobbing anyway.

Team spirit was something alien to these women. I was damned if I did and damned if I didn't; I couldn't win no matter how hard I tried. And I did try hard, but I was apparently never good enough for them.

When staff didn't get what they wanted I was accused of being unsupportive, yet they didn't appear to recognise the times I was supportive. I understand and supported the ethos of maternity leave, study leave, family leave, secondment, change of hour's request – and coupled with this the administration of annual leave, sick leave and long service leave. These accepted workplace practices need someone to coordinate, and on many occasions, I was the one to pick up the slack. There was only one occasion when I did not support a change of hours request, and that was with Christine, as outlined earlier.

As I look back at these allegations, years later, I can see how these staff were initially manipulated by John, Helen and Marianne, but I don't believe this manipulation was itself the sole cause of their behaviour. Good people would just walk away from this kind of manipulation, maybe becoming bystanders. But these staff had a collection of grudges and petty jealousies that were bursting to get out, and Marianne gave them licence to mob, having invited vicious allegations in her first meeting with them. There was never any evidence to back up their claims, no evidence to back up even *one* allegation, and this was Marianne's undoing. She needed to solve the problem of me if she was to have any chance at the permanent position of Manager of Human Resources. But she failed, and left not long after.

I have read somewhere that whenever pretend crimes are treated as crimes, such unjust treatment constitutes a crime in itself, and I feel that is what has happened to me. By this time, management knew the allegations against me were pretend crimes, and their inaction constituted a crime of epic moral proportions. My feelings and rights were ignored; I was sacrificed for the greater good of the organisation – or should I say the lesser good. I believe all the players in this drama kept repeating the lies, because if you repeat a lie enough, it becomes believable.

With the Garside report, Craig also provided an outline of the mediation session he planned to instigate with the resource officers. He stated that some of the staff were reluctant to participate. I responded that even though I'd had a bad experience with mediation I was prepared to follow Garside's recommendation, but the resource officers refused, much to the delight of management no doubt.

I asked Craig if the suspension was lifted, as no official letter from him had been received, and he said the suspension was lifted. I asked that if the suspension has been lifted, what kind of leave was I to be on while he works out with staff the process to resolve our differences. I suggested compassionate leave would be appropriate and Craig agreed. He stated I would receive a letter the next day confirming these arrangements.

I explained to Craig that this has been the most horrendous experience of my life and that I was having great difficulty dealing with the issues, and he informed me that I was entitled to have my counselling sessions paid for under the Employee Assistance Scheme. I asked if this would be paid retrospectively, as I had already paid $500 and owed another $500. He explained that it would be from then on, so I asked how many sessions would be paid for, and Craig responded, "as many as you need." He told me to have the accounts sent to him. I informed Joanne, the counsellor, of this arrangement. She called Craig, and he confirmed that the accounts be sent to him and that there was no limit on the number of sessions I could attend.

Much later I learnt the counselling accounts had not been paid, and when I raised this with Craig his response was, "Lori, as you have now taken action against Council, we will not be paying the counsellor's account."

The counsellor notified management she was commencing legal action over the unpaid accounts and they were then swiftly paid.

I provided my written complaints concerning John and Helen, as per my union's advice, to human resources in May and July. These were detailed, and contained evidence to support my allegations, however neither were suspended as a result of my allegations, or even investigated, to my knowledge.

I followed management's Grievance and Complaint Resolution Policy Statement, and even though this process wasn't followed in regards to the allegations against me, I still held the belief that this process would be adhered to. Later it was revealed that this policy was once again not followed in regards to the concerns I had raised.

Around the end of May, I received a confidential memo from Craig regarding the FDC investigation and the manager John's complaint outlining process to be followed: "Unfortunately we have been unable to progress enquiries on this matter any further due to Marianne's absence due to ill health." And: "four days has been allowed for John's response."

I never received any further information, or a copy of John's response within four days. He wasn't suspended, didn't suffer any detriment in his employment and there was no external investigation. Process was not followed, and it became clear that there were different rules for different folks.

Marianne's absence due to ill health stalled the investigation – how very convenient. I can just imagine how a citizen needing police assistance would feel when told something like, "Sorry, the officer for your area is away sick today – can you wait till tomorrow?" Or a CEO being told his document cannot be typed today as the typist is away ill. The absence of one staff member should not prejudice any complaint; senior management should have been able to continue with the process. But this was just another delay tactic, and an example of their inefficiency. This was a tactic I would come to know very well over the coming years; a tactic that changes truth to myth, veracity to lies and the innocent party becoming the guilty one.

Around this time, I interestingly read the 'Staff Relations Consultative Committee' (SRCC) Meeting Minutes EEO Sections relating to such complaints:

May 2001: "It was believed that the normal process would not be appropriate and this complaint was referred to an external investigation process."

June 2001: "It was determined that an external investigation would not be appropriate and this complaint is being handled by an internal process."

July 2001: "No new complaints were received since the last meeting."

The external investigation process did not go as planned; as it appears the investigator found nothing to substantiate the resource officers' complaints. Therefore, it had to become an internal process where management could manipulate the outcome.

My formal complaints in regards to John and Helen were submitted in May and July respectively, but were *not* counted as 'complaints', so it seemed that complaints made about general staff were taken to the SRCC, but complaints against more senior management were not.

I felt this committee failed in their role to ensure a discrimination- and harassment-free workplace; only my 'issues' were to become known, but not those relating to Helen and John.

I don't believe that this committee was truly set up for the purposes as stated; a more relevant purpose would have been the dissemination of information management wanted staff to know. In my situation, I felt that I was discredited through the release of information via this group, and that's why I wasn't offered support by others in the workplace. Conversely, Helen and John's credibility was not so affected.

In May the complaint investigation is to be external and Garside Consulting is to conduct the process. The Garside report didn't support the finding that I had harassed my staff, or that I breached Council's Equal Employment Opportunities Policy. Not the response management anticipated, so the investigation then became internal. If any internal investigation did take place, I was not informed of the details or requested to supply witnesses who could verify my complaints concerning John and Helen's behaviour.

Around June, Marianne (the Acting Human Resource Manager) resigned from her position supposedly due to ill health; this appeared to be an unusual action given that our employer had an unlimited sick leave policy; if you were unwell you could have extended periods of absence from the workplace on full salary. This policy was used to pay for my absence from work and gave management time to stall any decision regarding my future; to not be paid would have led to union intervention. Even though the union was doing nothing to help me, they would've been required to take action if I wasn't being paid.

The ASU Industrial Officer John H informed me that Marianne "got into trouble" over her involvement in my suspension. John H made the comment that "the CEO was not happy" and he "hit the roof." I figured the CEO had read my written response to the complaints against me and I can understand why he hit the roof. He would have been acutely aware that I was not guilty of the allegations made against me; that they were frivolous, vexatious and without substance.

On the balance of probabilities, keeping the staff complaint against me active and unresolved compromised my WorkCover claim and legal representation; it was used to recreate doubt in the minds of those who may have been able to assist me. It was not until years later that I became fully aware the damage the anonymous staff complaint document dated 19 April 2001 would be and how it would become WorkCover's 'silver bullet'.

Words fail to explain how it feels to be accused of a crime, be found innocent, and be punished anyway. I was guilty of being innocent. I had to be guilty of something to justify all that had been done to me. I love this quote from the Deep South: "The ones doin' the accusin' are usually the ones doin' the doin'."

Around mid-June I called Robert, the new Manager of Organisational

Change, to ask him what was happening to the complaint I'd made concerning John around five weeks prior, as I hadn't received a response. I also told him I'd completed my complaint concerning Helen and it would be sent shortly. Robert informed me Helen was on long service leave and little could or would be done until her return. This was again convenient; nothing could be done because she was on leave – what about a preliminary investigation?

I still trusted management to follow correct employment procedure in dealing with complaints, but I was perturbed there hadn't been any response to my detailed complaint concerning the manager John. The pain of my suspension was still with me – even now, writing this, it's still with me: I feel pain in my chest and churning in my stomach. The allegations made against me were unreasonable, unsubstantiated and untrue. My complaint against Helen and John contained much documental evidence but did not solicit the same action. No action was taken against John and my complaint was never resolved.

A few weeks later I was informed by Craig that the decision was to remove me from my position, the position I had held for nearly nine years. I wrote to him and simply asked why, but I didn't get a response. My correspondence was again ignored. By early July, Management had both of my complaints concerning John and Helen. Unsurprisingly, for my complaint a different process was followed, one that didn't include an investigation by external investigators and I received a letter stating: "It will not be possible to properly deal with this complaint until Helen returns from long service leave. I have checked with Payroll and confirm she is scheduled to return to work at the end of August. Once Helen has returned, we will be in a position to process your complaint in accordance with our procedures and we will keep you apprised of progress through Craig."

Helen returned from leave and I heard nothing. My complaint was not processed in accordance with the organisation's procedure, and I also wasn't kept appraised of any progress or any outcome of my complaint. In Helen's statement for WorkCover she said she wasn't informed of the complaint against her for many months, but this is most unlikely. My submitted complaints regarding John and Helen were treated differently to the complaint made against me, and this was a mistake. The union gave me bad advice about submitting these two complaints – it only made matters worse and my employment untenable, especially given the union was providing little to no support.

The complaints against me were baseless allegations without evidence; my allegations were not baseless and contained evidence. My complaints against

Helen and John were ignored: no outcome, no resolution, no staff suspended, no staff held to account, no one lost their job – except me.

A woman named Helene had become the new Child Care Officer (permanently replacing Pauline) and had refused to join the mob. I was abiding by the confidentiality demanded by management when Helene, a rather new FDC Staff member asked if the reason I was absent from work was due to harassment, as she had been a victim since the day she started. She had witnessed certain behaviours and comments from FDC staff concerning me, and these had led her to believe I was a victim, that these staff were not victims themselves but were putting on an act. Helene was quite distressed and considered resigning. I could not comment on my situation due to confidentiality, so just verbally supported her as best I could. I knew these resource officers did not want Helene, a former care provider, in the position; they did not view her as their equal. But Helene had applied and was the best applicant at interview. The person they'd actually wanted had done the job casually for a short time here and there, and fitted their mould, but she performed poorly at interview. Helene was terrific in the position.

Prior to the Garside investigation decision, whenever I attended my office, I was required to let Craig know so he could organise someone to be with me – someone to 'guard' me. This is the tenor of John's memos to staff when I come near the building: "I have just been informed that Lori may be visiting Bridge Street sometime today. If she does, she will be accompanied at all times by Robert K . . ."

This form of correspondence to the resource officers would have added to their sense of importance, with John's desire to have it be seen that he was looking after their welfare, and thus their 'bond' strengthened. I felt continually demeaned and humiliated by these kinds of actions.

Around the end of May, after my suspension was lifted, I visited my former office in the morning to conduct some research into my complaint against my supervisor Helen. No resource officers were present in the FDC general office area. I was later informed by Helene (the new CCA administrative Officer) they were 'hiding' in the small conference room because they felt threatened by me; from her observation she believed that it all appeared to be a bit of an act. In my view, it was all rather childish and pathetic.

A few minutes later, Craig Kenny arrived and requested I leave the premises. He apologised for the misunderstanding that led me to believe I was permitted to visit my office unguarded. Many general staff could see what was going on and I felt totally humiliated. I responded that management knew of my visit and if the resource officers were not informed that this was not my error. I informed Craig that I would leave when I had completed my research in about one hour's time. He agreed and left. I left the office around midday, after not attacking anyone, without destroying anything and without speaking, yelling, swearing, or raising my voice at any time.

Helene later informed me that my unguarded visit prompted resource officers to walk "off the job" in the afternoon and go to the hotel. Resource officers then went on strike and did not attend work the next morning, children's programs were cancelled, and home-based care providers were left without support, resourcing and monitoring. A witness who observed these events informed me that the new union shop steward Justin told the staff to strike.

I have mentioned this shop steward earlier, the one who upon election stated, "Obviously we are mindful that protocol and due process is a right every worker should expect. If, however, you do not have a current union ticket and you find yourself let down through these processes, it may be a harsh call, but my concern is really that the same fate does not befall our members."

I was the worker denied the right of protocol and due process, yet I was the one let down, and a harsh fate did befall me, yet he did the unthinkable. Not one of the allegations against me was substantiated, and yet these staff were allowed to run wild because John and Helen needed them onside.

The strike action was not 'protected action' under Industrial Relations Law, as three days' notice to the AIRC was required. The only occasion where this was not applicable was when there was an immediate threat to safety. What was the immediate threat to these staff? I was 50 kilometres away. More a case of sour grapes or pay back, as they didn't get their own way the day before by having Craig eject me from the premises.

At the end of the day, John sent a memo to all Family Day Care Staff, basically apologising to them for me being in the building unguarded and without their prior knowledge.

The memo states: "Apparently there was a mix-up in Lori's understanding of the arrangement that was negotiated between her and the Human Resources Department."

The mix-up was due to a misunderstanding between Robert K (new Manager of Organisational Change) and Craig – not me. Craig later apologised to me for his error, but the damage was done.

The Nightmare of Injustice

John sent a memo of apology to resource officers, but not a memo regarding their absence from the workplace without just cause. I was later told by a staff member not involved in my very poorly managed saga of harassment, discrimination, intimidation, bullying, victimisation, gaslighting and mobbing that the resource officers attended a meeting with Craig and they were given what appeared to be a letter which they had to sign. I believe this letter was probably a disciplinary warning letter for their personnel file concerning their behaviour of the previous days. This behaviour would be in breach of many Council policies, as well as the Commonwealth's funding agreement with Council, as well as Industrial Relations law. None of them were suspended or removed from their positions when they were in breach of Council's Behaviour Code, but I was when I had not breached any code, policy or law. My continuing sense of injustice increased and I felt that a soft approach had been taken because management needed the mob onside.

Craig and I had a number of useless meetings—that didn't go anywhere—where we discussed various issues. Significantly, Craig said to me, "If the FDC issue did not exist then we would normally bias our decision towards the complainant . . ." – oh, that's me! So the staff complaint about me *was* management's 'silver bullet', despite the fact that all allegations were found to be unsubstantiated.

The comment made by Craig confirmed my opinion that the resource officer complaint against me was kept alive and active by management. This in effect meant I couldn't return to my position; subsequently, dealing with the complaints against John and Helen could be avoided, and added doubt to the veracity of my WorkCover claim.

Also around this time, management began using staff from an external agency to fill my position. It is unknown to me why Karen didn't continue in the role, but I figured she'd been finding the work a little more difficult than she previously believed, and managing the staff at that time wouldn't have been easy.

It was the beginning of winter in 2001, when Helene finally met with Robert K, Manager of Organisational Change, and the Acting Direct Services Co-Coordinator to lodge a formal verbal complaint of harassment against Karen, Jenny, Andrea, Narelle, Christine and Elda, all resource officers, all the same staff who made false allegations against me.

Unsurprisingly, many months later, Helene told me that she'd asked another Acting Manager of Organisational Change (as Robert left in July) for a copy of the notes taken when she gave her verbal complaint. She was told that her complaint was not officially recorded, nor were there any notes.

The Garside investigation and my response to the staff complaint basically cleared me of any wrongdoing, but remember: the investigation was no longer external, but internal. This was the point of no return – the CEO now understood the gravity of what was done to me and who played a role, but the train still throttled down the hill. I was still guilty of being innocent, this is known, but no one had the courage to eat a few crumbs of humble pie, even when I'd had the whole pie thrust in my face. All I wanted was to return to work and all would be forgiven.

As with the Acting Manager of Human Resources, the ASU shop steward Justin left his employment suddenly and unexpectedly; both these players disappeared from the workplace. I saw this as a consequence of their awful behaviour and extremely poor decision-making. I had never met Justin, but I reckon he rues the day he ever met the mob at Family Day Care.

All the meetings over the following months, with Craig trying to attempt some sort of resolution, appeared to me to be a waste of time. The staff complaint (even having been disproven) was still given great credence, while mine were ignored. I believed it was possible that Craig was skirting around the OH&S Act: "Section 76: prohibiting an employer from dismissing or prejudicially altering an employee's employment because the employee has complained about a matter concerning the health, safety or welfare of employees at work."

The mob complaint justifies Craig taking the action he did, which he should know would have been extremely distressing to me and with the added value of compromising my WorkCover claim, which may have been the true intent all along.

By the end of July 2001, the new Manager of Organisational Change, Robert K, appeared to be attempting some resolution and organised an appointment for me with Donnelly Ayres Vocational Assessment. In his letter to me he states: "As indicated, our intention of going down this path is to effectively separate the past from the future and thereby allow them to be dealt with separately, and at the same time work towards getting you back to work in the most effective manner."

I was left wondering how sincere this was, or if it was just another attempt to orchestrate a report that will be used against me. The report from Donnelly Ayres was favourable to me and highlighted my many skills and experience. There was nothing stated that I did not agree with, and after my assessment, the subsequent report from them states in part, "The assessment will then be used to assist in the formulation of a Return to Work (RTW) plan within the Council structure." No Return to Work Plan ever eventuated and management took no further action regarding the recommendations in this report.

I felt relieved that at least it was an honest process by Donnelly Ayres, but unsurprisingly nothing came of this report, as I believed management were hoping they could use the report in a manner that supported their agenda, which was not to be so. When discussing the assessment with Craig, he commented, "Bloody consultants, you pay them a lot of money to tell you what you already know."

I became aware the mob was not respecting the confidentiality requirements placed on all of us by the process, and heard they were making derogatory remarks about me where others not involved could hear. But what could I do – by this time I was well aware that management would no doubt be agreeable with this as it suited their apparent purpose.

Again and again, I was defamed, and yet I was directed not to discuss the issues with anyone – that to do so would result in disciplinary action for breach of confidentially. I had no choice but to follow this directive, as I knew if I breached the 'confidentiality clause' it would be used to dismiss me.

By this stage, I had been home on sick leave, compassionate leave, special leave or whatever leave, for four months on full salary. Some workers may enjoy four months off work with full pay, but for me, given the circumstances, there was nothing to enjoy. This time was spent researching and writing, trying to sort this matter out, but there was to be no sorting the matter out as that didn't suit management's agenda.

Towards the end of August 2001, I finally returned to work two days per week in a temporary project officer position at the Civic Centre. My role was to update the Municipal Emergency Recovery Plan. Craig advised me of my duties and stated that a position description would be made available shortly. Unsurprisingly, a position description was never provided. Given the offer of this position, I presume special leave/suspension had been cancelled, though I wasn't informed of this (or any information regarding my future).

My temporary office was situated in the Organisational Change Department, away from my usual office building. In discussions with the new Manager of Organisational Change he stated, "Lori, you have been through enough shit." He counselled me to help me understand what was happening, and purchased a book for me to read; *The Abilene Paradox*.

The book was helpful, exploring how, in the author's opinion, "the phenomenon is explained by social psychology theories of social conformity and social influence, which suggests human beings are often very averse to acting contrary to the trend of the group. The phenomenon may occur when individuals experience action–anxiety–stress concerning the group potentially expressing negative attitudes towards them if they do not go along. This action–anxiety arises from the author termed 'negative fantasies – unpleasant visualisations of what the group might say or do if individuals are honest about their opinions – when there is 'real risk of displeasure and negative consequences for not going along. The individual may experience 'separation anxiety', feeling exclusion from the group."

I could really see how that paradox would work in the mobbing group, as some of the staff I felt were rather nice people in their daily life, but some held grudges and led the others on the road to Abilene; a trip they may not have wanted to take, but went along with to be accepted as part of the group – more important than sticking to their own values. There's nothing more effective in bringing a disgruntled group together than a common enemy or foe, and the safety the group offers is powerful. I believe the power John, Helen, Craig and Marianne gave this group cemented their belief they were collectively doing the right thing, when in my opinion they were actually doing the wrong thing.

This is the only occasion that anyone in the organisation affirmed I had been treated badly. Robert was such a nice person, and I feel sure had it been left to him to sort out it would have been sorted out fairly.

Over the next few months of my return to work (two days per week), working in the Council Civic Centre, I was moved many times. I was moved to the Engineering Department, Assets and Projects Department, Resident Access Department, Assets and Projects Department, Organisational Change Department, Engineering Department, Council Chambers, Records Department, Finance Department, and the IT Training Room. OH&S Meeting Records for this period show concerns regarding the safety of this last room, and yet I am directed to work there. I did have a couple of trips over cables while working in this room, but even though I was aware of my responsibilities under the OH&S Act I didn't report them, as I was of the belief it was pointless.

I'd been moved so many times I began to lose count – more than 10 times.

I carried my office supplies and belongings in a cardboard box I took with me from office to office. On one occasion I hurt my arm carrying this box and required medical treatment, but I dared not submit a WorkCover claim and paid all the medical expenses myself. Eventually, I decided I was no longer prepared to assist in my own humiliation. Over the preceding nine months many positions had been advertised (approximately 50), with these new staff placed somewhere. Given the circumstances, my needs should have been considered a higher priority than new employees, contractors, casuals and consultants. But I knew they were trying to break me; this knowledge made me stronger.

Due to the lack of progress with my WorkCover claim and my return to work in my former position, I sought legal advice. The advice was to give it "one more try, be definite about what you want, ask for it all, then negotiate." All I wanted was to return to my former position; I would consider dropping my WorkCover claim, as it was not assisting me in addressing any of the issues anyway. In mid-September, following the legal advice to give it one more go, at an internal resolution, I requested a meeting with Craig to discuss issues relating to my previous correspondence, the treatment I'd experienced and the ongoing impact on my health and wellbeing. I offered my desired outcomes to gain resolution of the now major dispute; I wished to return to my original position, would drop my WorkCover claim, medical expenses of around $3,000 be paid and $1,000 in recognition for the pain and suffering I experienced.

Craig requested that he be given six weeks to consider the settlement requirements as proposed by me, and I agreed. Though I agreed, I couldn't understand why another six weeks was needed for a decision to be made when this issue had already been running for nearly a year, was costing a lot of money and causing a lot of misery. I felt they were stalling for time, but for what reason I did not know.

A further meeting was scheduled for 25 October to discuss and hopefully finalise the dispute. On leaving this meeting the ASU Industrial Officer commented to me that he could get me an attractive redundancy payout if I wanted to leave, but this wasn't what I wanted. I didn't want to leave; I just wanted my job back and the opportunity to work. In hindsight, this would have been a viable option, but I couldn't see that at the time. I later requested a copy of the minutes of this meeting, but they were never supplied.

Four weeks into the six weeks sought by Craig, he requested we meet. I was given a letter dated 2 October 2001 concerning 'Return to Work Arrangements'. At long last, something was happening! Nope. The letter basically stated, "There is no job for you here", so the 'Return to Work' heading was just a charade. Craig also asked if we could meet again on Thursday after 3pm. I met with him at 3:30pm on 11 October and he stated that my position was to be advertised on Saturday 13 October. I protested, and asked if the advertisement was for a temporary position or permanent position. Craig commented, "There is no such thing as a permanent job." I felt if the position was advertised as a temporary position then this would allow time for the dispute to be determined without my losing my job permanently.

Council's Manual of Personnel Management states, "The Organisation of Council support structure is presented diagrammatically. The Organisation Diagram includes all approved Permanent Full-Time and Permanent Part-Time positions."

I have seen many Council "personnel advertisements" that state a permanent position is available. In reality, it is realised that no job is really permanent due to a variety of factors that face workplaces today, but none of these were relevant in my situation. Staff are categorised by their employment status: permanent full-time, permanent part-time, and casual. Many of Council's personnel/HR forms relate to the employee's status.

Craig's comment, "There is no such thing as a permanent job" appeared at odds with the practice of the organisation. So I guessed from Craig's behaviour my 'offer' was rejected and this was their 'counter-offer,' and there would not be any sincere attempt at internal resolution.

Words such as malfeasance, malpractice, misadministration, and breach of fiduciary duty in public office spring to mind. The direct costs to the public purse at this time would have been $4,000, but ultimately around $1,000,000 was wasted to save $4,000. All this because an injured worker wanted to return to work and someone didn't have the courage to acknowledge that maybe a mistake had been made, or that the processes could have been handled better or differently – fairly, according to law, or more expeditiously. The outcome could have been so very different.

Previous legal advice was that I may have been discriminated against and I should submit a claim to the Equal Opportunity Commission Victoria (EOCV). This action by Craig was the deciding factor in my making a complaint to the EOCV. The next morning, I attended the office of the EOCV in Melbourne and was assisted in making a complaint, but this was Friday and the job was being advertised the next day. Their advice was to take it to the Victorian Civil and Administrative Tribunal (VCAT). I immediately started to prepare a case for an interim order to prohibit management from advertising the position.

With the assistance of the Equal Opportunity Commission staff, a submission and legal requirements were completed in time for a 3pm hearing before VCAT's Anti-Discrimination Tribunal, and given this I contacted the union seeking support and advice and eventually got to speak to John H. I informed him I was about to go into the tribunal to apply for an interim order against the advertising of my position. I asked if he could attend, but he responded, "No, I am in Bendigo." I asked for assistance next week and he stated, "This issue is outside the jurisdiction of the union."

Unbelievable! I was left to fend for myself. How can trying to save a job and being a target of workplace harassment be out of the union's jurisdiction?

The tribunal granted a 28-day interim order, but the advertisement had already gone to print in *The Age* (3pm Thursday print time) and couldn't be cancelled. The interim order stated that no action can be taken on any applications received due to this advertisement. I believed it was no coincidence that Craig wanted to meet with me on the Thursday after 3pm, when he would have known the advertisement would have already gone to print. Had it not been for the wonderful and caring support of the staff at the EOCV and at VCAT, I would never have achieved this hearing deadline.

Ten days later another letter from Craig stating the meeting scheduled for 25 October had been cancelled due to the complaint to the Equal Opportunity Commission. He stated, "A range of matters that were to be discussed and potentially settled at this meeting have not been able to be progressed due to the hearing relating to the interim order at VCAT."

I received a copy of Craig's response to my complaint to the EOCV in part relevantly stating, "It is conceded that a range of complex factors including administrative delays have caused these complaints to linger, but it had been Council's intention to resolve these along with other matters in good faith at the 25 October 2001 meeting which was deferred subject to the outcomes of the EOCV complaint process."

Craig proposed there was the intention of "good faith" – that my outstanding issues were to be discussed and potentially settled at the meeting scheduled for 25 October 2001. I dispute this "good faith" due to Craig advertising my position on October 13 and informing me of such *after* the advertising deadline. This did not show "good faith." Coupled with the letter of 2

October, it appeared decisions concerning the issues were already made prior to the scheduled meeting date; had this meeting gone ahead it would have been a farce and certainly not in my favour.

It was the underhanded manner of advertising my position which precipitated the submission of my complaint to the EOCV. How much longer could I trust management? They could have at any time approached me to settle the dispute, as I was willing to participate in any alternate dispute resolution process, but my external notification to the EOCV just led to further victimisation.

By this time, some Councillors must have known something was going on, as they would have had to be informed of the pending discrimination claim to be heard at VCAT in April 2002. I am only guessing, but I felt all players believed that the settlement of this claim prior to hearing should have been enough to compensate me for what they had done. Of course, they were wrong – this was not about financial compensation, but about validation and vindication. A few dollars doesn't return you to the position you've had taken from you. Ask any bullied worker what they want; it is not dollars – money is just the icing on the cake. What is wanted and needed is the recognition of what has happened to them, vindication of their reputation—as they are always a victim of gaslighting—and accountability from the guilty parties.

I didn't want anyone to lose their job or go through the horror I had endured – I just wanted some accountability, and a small crumb of an apology would have been acceptable.

I believed that I was in effect unfairly dismissed, and should have approached the Industrial Commission, but as my complaint was at EOCV I didn't know that I could have approached both Tribunals, which in hindsight was a mistake on my part. I had no one assisting me; the union had already said "this issue is outside the jurisdiction of the union" so I was alone on my journey to justice.

Later, in November 2001, the union's industrial officer wrote to me stating they were aware of the unfair and discriminatory treatment I had experienced and that I had not been afforded natural justice in the process, but that it appeared there was little else they could do, and so they did nothing more – unlike a month or so earlier, when a union-backed strike was called at the depot because a staff member had been caught stealing and was dismissed. His mates went out on strike with union support and he was paid off. Or the occasion that a female member of staff was touched on the breast by a male coworker, the latter who was instantly dismissed.

What does this behaviour tell us – that your union rights depended on how much support you had from your workmates?

I have previously said that it is almost impossible to do a good job and be popular at the same time. I did not care about popularity; I cared about doing a good job and keeping 700 children safe and healthy. I now see the folly of my ways – had I concentrated on being popular, the bullying would still have occurred, but maybe not the mobbing, and it was the mobbing that sealed my fate. For many years I struggled with this concept of not being popular, and being in fact disliked, and felt my personality was flawed, until a young woman came to me for advice. She was young, attractive, smart and charismatic—everything I wasn't—and she was also being bullied in her job!

The VCAT injunction was extended on three occasions, giving time for management to participate in a dispute resolution process. I was still working two days per week and felt the workplace was becoming more hostile with each passing day. You're probably thinking by this time, why didn't I just leave? Because I had done nothing wrong. I exercised my legal and human rights and was punished for doing so, and those ignoring my legal and human rights suffered no consequence.

I cannot understand what my employer was thinking. I believed the councillors knew nothing up to this time as it was purely a staff management issue, one for the CEO and his management team to work out. The CEO and the director of my department often came to our workplace and gave a pep talk, a 'walk and talk', but unfortunately in my opinion they failed to work the talk. Management only needed to follow their policies and procedures and the issue could well have been resolved.

As the matter was now with VCAT, I believed the Council must have been told what I can only guess was a very one-sided story which would protect their failings and their egos. Interestingly, around this time another Family Services Unit Leader informed me she had lodged a complaint with the Manager of Organisational Change against Helen the supervisor for unprofessional conduct and bullying.

In early January 2002, I met with Craig concerning my project management role. During our conversation Craig asked me if I found working at the Civic Centre okay. Not wanting to let on to Craig his behaviour was having a very detrimental effect on me, I responded it was okay. In response to this

Craig stated, "So you haven't found it too bad around here? If you continue with your legal action, it may not be as pleasant."

Pleasant! This unveiled threat caused me concern. How could he, on any level, believe it had been pleasant for me – he had read of my experiences, participated negatively in many of them, and yet did not understand the psychological impact on me. How was this being an effective Director of Organisational Change? These days, it would be criminal.

In early 2002, the VCAT Anti-Discrimination Tribunal directions hearing decision was handed down. The decision was that the Council had a *prima facie* case to answer for direct and indirect discrimination based on impairment. A day later, I was denied access to all my and general Family Day Care computer files.

I moved into the New Year with hope still in my heart. In January 2002, I visited Bridge Street and I was introduced to a new FDC staff member. I asked her how she was enjoying the job. She stated that she was considering resigning. I asked how long she had been employed in the position, and she stated two weeks. Naturally I asked why she was considering resigning and she responded, "Those resource officers are just horrible."

Helene later told me she asked this new resource officer if she knew who I was when she met me the other day. She responded, "She seems very nice, didn't she used to be the boss here? But with all that I have heard . . ." I would really like to know exactly what she had heard and what had happened to confidentiality as requested by management. This new staff member could only have heard it from the resource officers who made the original complaint, and it appeared they were intent on continuing to defame me. I believe they felt they needed to convince everyone that they were the innocent victims. (It is quite a common phenomenon for bullies to feign victimhood once their behaviour is questioned, or they are held to account, and this is what the Garside report had done.)

I was visiting my former office to speak to the Acting Unit Leader concerning her accessing and removing some of my computer files. I suggested to her that, as I was still an employee, it would have been appropriate for her to inform me before accessing my private file records. Many of those files contained sensitive information concerning my issues with management, and for reasons of confidentiality, I would have removed them myself if I had been given the opportunity. This person would've had to read each file to decipher between a service record that could be moved and what was personal to me. After speaking to Craig, these files were restored under his direction.

Also during this visit, I spoke to the Unit Leader of Kindergarten Services, who informed me that each time I visited the Bridge Street office Helen the supervisor called the Manager of Organisational Change. On my previous visit, he arrived at the office just after I had left. The staff member stated, "She's not going to be happy until she gets you out of here."

Later that day I read what personal files were left under my name and I discovered two highly sensitive documents, one titled 'Mediation Minutes' dated October 2000, and a Return to Work letter sent to my doctor on 5 December 2000, which due to their sensitivity I stored in my password-protected email records only, never in the FDC General File. I wondered who had moved them there and why. They were complete documents emailed to me, with no reason for them to be stored as Word files.

The only explanation that I could come to was that someone had placed a copy in the FDC General File, compromising my privacy with all resource officers being able to read these documents.

Sometime later I realised the staff complaint matched information contained in these two documents, with words, terms and phrases used which were not part of these staff's normal dialogue.

Around this time, I attended the FDC Launch of the National Quality Accreditation Program held at the Civic Centre with management, FDC staff and care providers in attendance. From memory I probably was not specifically invited to this event but attended anyway, because (very strangely, in hindsight) I still believed I would return to my job eventually. Upon my arrival, a care provider enthusiastically jumped up to hug me; this felt so very good, and I was very thankful for her show of support. Many care providers that day talked to me and showed concern for my welfare – they were a major reason I wanted to return to my position. I viewed care providers as my colleagues, but resource officers viewed them differently – to them they were subordinates. Even when there was a service dinner with food and drinks provided, the resource officers refused to attend unless they were paid. They refused to attend, but I didn't want the care providers to know the reason why, so I would acquiesce to their demands for payment.

Heaven only knows what the care providers were told, but it certainly couldn't have been the truth. I'd heard from a reliable source that the complaining resource officers (mob) covertly discredited me when on home visits to care providers. It was believed that this was an attempt to confuse care providers and get them onside. If they thought I'd done something wrong, they'd be less inclined to risk being supportive. This would supposedly work in management's favour, as care providers were also ratepayers and could be a powerful lobby group for me if the truth was known. It also abdicated the staff's sense of responsibility if they could convince others of their victimhood.

Upon my arrival at this event, a resource officer (one of the mob) was heard remarking to another mob member, "Here's Lori – she looks sick, isn't that good." The person who heard this comment informed me of this a few days later. This person felt that I needed to be aware of the depth of the depravity of these staff members so I could protect myself. Protect myself – that was all I had been trying to do for nearly two years.

In February 2002, Worksafe Victoria's draft document 'Proposed Code of Practice for the Prevention of Bullying and Violence in the Workplace' was released. Through tears I read with great interest and great sadness; at last someone—or several someones—knew what I had been going through. Reading this document, I finally understood what had been happening to me – behaviours expressed in this document were only too familiar to me.

Even though my general practitioner, two psychiatrists and a clinical psychologist had all diagnosed harassment, intimidation and discrimination as the cause of my symptoms, it was not until reading this document that the realisation finally hit home: it was 'workplace bullying.'

The VCAT proceeding was still progressing, and around the end of April 2002, a mediation was held with a settlement agreement being reached. Everyone in the 'chain of harm' had made a decision not to assist me, from the CEO down, and including the union. As a result, the work environment was intolerably toxic, further damaging my health.

I felt I had little choice but to settle, as medical and legal advice was that the pattern of abuse I experienced in the workplace would continue until I had a breakdown. I was never going to be allowed to return to work – the only options were to: resign; continue to work and be harassed into a breakdown; or wait to be unfairly dismissed. I only ever wanted to return to work; under duress I agreed to resign, even though my feelings of injustice were skyrocketing.

I had no choice but to settle at VCAT, as the offer was more generous than I would receive if successful at hearing, though—as I have stated earlier—this

The Nightmare of Injustice

was not about money. I wanted a hearing so my story of abuse could be told. I was informed by lawyers that if I did not settle when the amount was more than VCAT could award, then the tribunal would not look kindly on this. In many cases, settlements higher than the jurisdictional limit are used to stop public scrutiny, and in VCAT it only had to be more than the statutory amount of six months' wages. This is how many public servants and probably others avoid being held accountable. I felt all those present at the mediation, especially John, Helen and Craig, were feeling elated as they got off scott-free, with ratepayers probably footing the bill.

All the Acts, Codes, Polices and Laws then did not protect me, and I feel confident the 'Protection Act or the Code of the Prevention of Bullying and Violence in the Workplace' (as it was known then and implemented after I had left the workplace) wouldn't have helped either. I'm still not sure what helps 20 years later, but today people generally have a better understanding of bullying in all its forms. Workplaces now recognise bullying, and there are various forms of litigation available that was difficult to access in 2002.

The terms of settlement needed to get approval at that evening's council meeting. Council minutes record that this section of the meeting was closed to members of the public as a confidential personnel matter was to be discussed. Many of my co-workers are listed as attendees at this council meeting, and it is unknown if they stayed in attendance during the discussion of this personnel matter. I was later informed by some staff that weren't at the council meeting that the rumour going around the organisation was that I had "lost" my discrimination claim. Management were still spinning the story; even when they'd had a great result, I still had to be vilified. From that time on, I wasn't required to attend work and was paid to the end of the financial year, on top of the settlement amount. I estimate that up to this time about $300,000 of ratepayers' funds were used to hide the incompetence of senior management – and these are dollar figures of 20 years ago.

A few days after the VCAT mediation, I attended the offices of ATB Lawyers to sign the Deed of Release. I pointed out many errors in the document, especially dates. The lawyer responded, "It's not important." I disagreed, and requested correct dates be used. The lawyer appeared agitated, and I let go the many other errors which went uncorrected. This is the first time I realised how laissez-faire some lawyers could be – even when information which may not be that important at the time could be very important down the track.

I noticed this scenario also played out in independent medical reports written on behalf of WorkCover, with dates being incorrect, critical facts being omitted and some information being just plain wrong. These reports are full of inaccuracies, and eventually these reports are given to future independent medical assessors who repeat these errors in their reports, and before long, an untruth becomes a truth.

Senior management were able to write a letter or report that was false but sounded very legitimate. For example, in 2002 a letter was written to GIO, my WorkCover insurer, regarding the hearing of my claim in the Magistrates' Court. Information in this letter regarding my discrimination claim was blatantly false. The letter stated: "The Tribunal originally dismissed the complaint, the worker lodged an appeal and an out-of-court settlement was recently reached." This is not correct: VCAT did not dismiss my complaint. I did not lodge an appeal; a directions hearing was held where it was determined that my employer had a *prima facie* case to answer for direct and indirect discrimination based on impairment. It was then, that an out-of-court settlement was reached. I am not sure if they were attempting to convince the insurer that they had acted fairly and reasonably when they hadn't, and were trying to cover their tracks.

Around the end of May 2002, I was getting ready to permanently leave the job I loved and the organisation of which I was once a proud member. It was a difficult time, but was made easier by some staff who obviously were not buying into the rumours they must have heard. Nic, Glen and Helen H were three home-care staff who were situated right outside my office door for a number of years and who would have been privy to my manner and behaviour over a long period of time and would have been witness to my interactions with my staff, including the resource officers. Upon hearing of my leaving, they expressed their sentiments in emails to me regarding my departure in the following terms:

"Lori, How shocked we both are to read that you will be leaving after all this time, the place is not going to be the same. We have really missed your beautiful infectious laughter and immaculate dress sense since you have left Bridge Street. We must catch up in the last few weeks before your departure. We are really really really really really going to miss you. Love Nic and Glen"

"Lori, for once in my life words fail me. Everything I go to write seems inadequate. I too have been blessed in the crossing of our paths. Isn't it interesting that fleeting moments can make an impact on our lives. I wish you every happiness for what your future brings. Love always, Helen H"

I recite these emails in their entirety because of their positivity. Their genuinely kind words appear to be at odds with the comments made by resource officers in their complaints and Helen the supervisor in her statement to the insurance investigator regarding my 'angry demeanour'.

I am again in awe as I read a letter dated May 2002 to GIO, the WorkCover insurer, from Kerry the Injury Management Co-ordinator (a recently invented new title). My awe is related to how something misleading can be written in a way that sounds totally accurate and true, when it is not: "Council has provided alternate duties to the worker within the guidelines set by her doctor." Given all that had happened, this statement was taking the insurer down the garden path, as my doctor played no part in setting any guidelines. It should have said, "We took unwarranted disciplinary action when it was not justified, and we acted before we ascertained the facts."

The letter goes on to state: "The worker commenced discrimination/harassment action against Council shortly after her WorkCover claim was rejected in December 2000." The comment is misleading the insurer into believing the discrimination claim was related to the WorkCover claim.

The discrimination claim was lodged on 12 October 2001, after I became aware that my former position was being advertised that coming weekend. That was nearly a year after my WorkCover claim was lodged, and its intent was to convince the insurer that my discrimination claim was the result of the rejection of my WorkCover claim, which it was not. I do not believe the duration of a nearly a year would fit within the definition of "shortly."

In February 2003, my WorkCover claim was finally accepted, as it met the legislative requirements, with the respondent to pay costs. My claim for weekly payments was dismissed, as it was determined that I had a current work capacity. This was not surprising given how determined I was to return to work and not make a 'big deal' of how this experience had affected me. I remember an occasion where I had a medical assessment for Return to Work in Melbourne at 9am one morning, so wanting to be found fit for work I stayed in a motel a few doors down so I could arrive at the appointment presenting well – as cool, calm and collected. Many injured workers are accused of overplaying their injuries, but I was the opposite – I was downplaying mine because I wanted to return to work and not be found incapacitated.

Management's spin took flight again with an email to staff who were witnesses on my behalf at the Magistrates' Court. The hearing email states, "The worker's (L. O'Keeffe) weekly payments complaint has now been dismissed with no order that any weekly payments of compensation be paid to the worker." I guess this is technically correct, but the main goal of having the claim accepted was achieved; weekly payments was secondary. Once again management needed the rumour mill to do its job so as to make them look like they had done nothing wrong and that I was at fault again.

I feel sure many injured workers have found the same scenarios happening to them. Misinformation about the worker is spread throughout the organisation as well as through the channels of the workers compensation system. Injured workers are maligned as 'rorters' and yet it is not they who are rorting but their employers who don't want to accept claims and ruin their image. Even truer if bullying is alleged against senior management.

By this time, it was 12 months since I'd left my employment and I felt it was time to get back into the workforce, but management didn't want this, and attempted to thwart any return to work.

I signed up with an agency to do casual work in the childcare field, but needed a letter from human resources to fulfil the 1996 Child Care Regulations, which required evidence that I had worked directly with children within the past three years.

I contacted Ian, the Personnel Officer, regarding the provision of a letter fulfilling the agency's request. He rang me and stated he was happy to do so and had written the required letter, however he felt he should refer it to the Manager of Human Resources. This new manager directed him not to provide me with this letter and stated that it was against management policy to provide any information other than a Statement of Employment. He said they weren't to provide written references or other written information as requested by staff. Now, I knew this wasn't accurate because when I was in my role I often gave requested information in letter form, or on occasion a written reference.

By this time, I believe Craig had left the organisation. I was told by a former colleague she believed he left because he knew his time was over and he would never be made CEO, so he had taken a sideways move to another council, and stayed sideways for another 12 years until he retired.

Steve was now the new Director of Corporate and Community Services. I knew Steve, and knew he was a good person not involved in any of my previous issues with management. I wrote him a letter outlining what had occurred in my efforts to get the required statement. Steve was very supportive of my request and I received the letter I needed.

Another attempt to thwart me from gaining employment was about a month later. I attended an interview at another council for the position of part-time temporary Children's Services Officer. Prior to my interview, I discussed this with Rhona (who would have been my supervisor); we already knew each other well. We both agreed that we could work together as we had worked successfully in the past and had always enjoyed a very positive professional relationship during those 20 years. This would have been a golden opportunity for me to get on with my life and rebuild. But no, the bullies wouldn't allow it; you have to fail and remain failed to prove that they were right. I felt I was being subjected to blacklisting and further discrimination. I was quite confident that all players—the employer, the insurer and WorkCover—all wished that I had been given that chance.

The hour interview went very well, and during the interview I received very positive feedback. Later, I was informed that I was the preferred applicant and all that was needed was a reference from my former manager, John. I was hopeful he would feel charitable as he really had gotten away with bad behaviour, and my actual work was acceptable, because if it wasn't that would have been used to dismiss me – they never did dismiss me because they could not prove poor performance or poor behaviour. I relied on the 'Deed of Release' which was written in the settlement of the discrimination claim. This deed states: "Obligations of the Council: the Council must not make any statement denigrating publicly or otherwise, including to current staff of the Council or to prospective employers."

Reluctantly, I gave his phone number to the interview panel and I said I would ring him to let him know, but unfortunately, I couldn't get hold of him. That evening I was contacted by a member of the interview panel and informed my application was unsuccessful. Later that same evening another member of the interview panel rang me to explain what had taken place. She said I was the most outstanding applicant, all panel members agreed. One stated "I could have listened to her all day, she is so knowledgeable," and that all panel members were incensed that I did not get the position.

This particular council had a policy which was part of the recruitment process which stated a potential employee must provide a reference from their most current former manager. I was told John was contacted and his response was, "No comment, get your CEO to call my CEO." The issue was taken to senior management, and due to my being unable to fulfil this part of their requirement, I was unsuccessful. The successful applicant had no qualifications and no previous experience, whereas I had 25 years' experience and was appropriately qualified.

This would have been a wonderful opportunity to recover some of what I'd lost, and it would have been in everyone's best interests for me to gain useful employment. I felt they were being vindictive and I'd in effect been 'blacklisted' or was suffering from 'blackballing'. I didn't know at the time exactly what those phrases meant, but I sure learned. In my opinion, John breached his obligations under the 'Deed of Release', but what could I do? I was beyond powerless.

I came to believe that settling my discrimination claim for a nominal amount, without any players other than myself being held accountable for their bad behaviour, should have been enough for the perpetrators. The behaviour around my attempting to return to work proved to me that they had acted in bad faith during the settlement negotiations and planned all along to stymie my career by indirect denigration. Therefore, the 'Terms of Settlement' were null and void and no longer had my respect nor likely any legal force.

At Christmas 2003, I received a card from my former personnel officer with the message, "My Xmas to you is to inform you that Helen has finally fallen on her sword. She leaves in Jan 04." So someone after me had also had to pay a price, with Helen now being the organisational scapegoat.

Around this time, another employee working under the supervision of John and Helen had a WorkCover claim accepted by the insurer for workplace bullying and harassment. It's my understanding upon intervention from WorkSafe that Helen was asked to leave. She said to staff that they will know why she had left after she had gone. This tells me that there may have been something afoot, but it appears nothing came from this, probably because no one wanted to give my WorkCover claim any legitimacy. Surprisingly, a short time later she successfully gained new employment with the Shire of Macedon, and it appears management must have provided an excellent reference for this ex-employee who had two successful WorkCover claims against her for workplace bullying. I later heard she left this new employment for reasons I will not state because what I heard was in effect a rumour and therefore hearsay.

Another survivor of workplace abuse sums it up well: "The financial and legal cost that organisations incur to protect them is wasteful and unconscionable. And the hiring costs to replace good workers who resign is significant. Everyone loses when bullies are not held accountable. They impact the reputation and culture, fostering a toxic and hostile workplace. Employees need and deserve to feel safe respected and treated with dignity." I could not have said it more concisely – thank you, Jane Nash.

Knowing what I know now and what I have learnt over the years, my estimate of the cost of this debacle in direct and indirect costs to the ratepayers would be conservatively in the vicinity of $300,000 (of 20 years ago). Not that I believe Council would have been aware of this. I feel confident much of the direct costs would have been hidden even deeper, and indirect costs can be even more hidden unless you undertake the task of Activity Based Costing. The emotional cost to me and others involved is incalculable, and lives were left ruined.

Another bullied worker, Jen De Luca, once said, 'Workplace mobbing is an attack on the spirit and soul by those who have none left." The trauma of my experiences shocks all of my systems, and I am in full agreement with Dr Odelya Gertel Kraybill who says that trauma affects your cognitive ability to process thoughts and make good decisions. Emotionally it causes ongoing loops of fear, anger, pain, shame, guilt and moral injury.

Furthermore, she says that such bullying affects your muscles, joints, metabolism, stamina, libido, temperature, sleep and your immune system. Most of the illnesses I suffered fit exactly into these categories, and were accepted by the insurer as being work-related, so there is some validation there. I must say overall that insurance companies have been kind to me.

Dr Kraybill further states there can be a shift in your worldview – the lens we view the world (or aspects of it) becomes unsafe, as does our meaning of life, society, and the world. My belief in the world and people has certainly changed. But I felt I have done a significant amount of learning through this process and have not let it totally destroy my faith.

And finally, Kraybill says that there will be massive "shifts in relationships with spouses, family, friends and any potential colleagues." She also believes it changes your interactions with strangers, which doesn't resonate with me because my experiences have taught me to be more tolerant of the world and those around me. My family have suffered because they have witnessed my suffering, even though I tried with every fibre in my body to hide it and have our family life continue as successfully as it had in the past. (Did my late son Dan know the depth of my suffering? Did it impact on his own suffering? These are questions I will never have the answers to.)

The Family Day Care service did not appear to flourish after I was gone – for the six years from 2001 to 2006 there were approximately 12 unit leaders who either acted in the position, were on contract from an employment agency, or who were employed permanently but stayed only for a short time (on average six months). Interestingly, no resource officer was considered suitable for the position; some of these staff had worked in the Service from eight to 20 years; it would have been a natural career progression for all of them. They appeared not to have the ability or desire to undertake this role, and yet were instrumental in my being removed from the position, partly due to their perception of my perceived lack of skills. I do not know why there was such a high turnover, but I can only guess: the direct and indirect recruitment costs alone would have been significant, but so what: "not my money!"

I believe John had to deal with a number of complaints over those years six years from government agencies, families, care providers and staff. There were no complaints during my eight years in this role until the resource officers' complaint of April 2001 while I was attempting a return to work.

As stated to me by a number of care providers: "It just hasn't been the same since you left" and "No-one can manage the Service as well as you did."

In August 2006, my former employer announced that they would cease operating the Family Care Service from July 2007 due to government changes that would open up the Child Care Service to the private sector under new Federal Government rules starting the following June. The Federal Government expected the new system to generate about 25,000 extra places across Australia by 2009. From my knowledge, it may have generated extra places, but how many extra 'ghost children' did it in fact produce? Less support and scrutiny by coordination units; and I believe the quality of care in most private services would be lessened.

Fees charged for the service would also be deregulated and decided by individual providers, and providers would still need to meet quality and licensing requirements. And how is that working out? The then-Mayor said they were disappointed local governments were not consulted before the changes were announced, and stated, "We wouldn't have changed it if we'd had the choice" and "The bottom line is that we don't want it to go backwards and are very committed to continuing the Service." Hold on a minute: they *did* have a choice, and chose not to continue with the Service, and since then the Service had gone backwards. Listen to the spin. The Mayor said no jobs would be lost as a result of the changes, but there were losses – not all resource officers were redeployed, and to their no-doubt-delight they would have received generous redundancy payouts, which some had been sweating on for many years after missing out during the 1995 CTT process.

There are many care providers who are still providing care, which is an excellent choice for parents, but they must do their due diligence. Good home-based care is a great option for children, especially those under three years of age, but bad family day care or any form of bad childcare is damaging.

The funding for the Service was given back to the Commonwealth, and the reasons given for me do not stack up. None of these changes necessitated Council ceasing to provide this Service; it appears at this time that no other local government operator had followed the same course of action (though later many did). I rang a staff member at the Government Department, someone I had come to know over my years in the role, and asked him why. He responded that any changes to the funding agreement didn't encourage or justify why Council would be dumping the funding, and we all know what has occurred since the Service was effectively privatised: millions of dollars rorted by those involved in private Family Day Care Services, huge amount of fees to 'ghost' children and claiming costs of care for each other's children. We have gone full-circle.

The CEO, to my knowledge, appeared to be an experienced and competent CEO, so why he did not take control, I find difficult to understand. A quote by Gloria Steinem is relevant: "Whenever one person stands up and says 'Wait a minute – this is wrong' it helps other people to do the same." This could have been senior management's position, but through these years they failed, and not just as a senior management team – in my opinion they failed as decent human beings.

I wonder if the CEO did pay a price, because eventually he left his position, a job he appeared to enjoy, just three days before my County Court hearing in April 2008, with the proverbial excuse of wanting to spend more time with his family. This may well be true, but for me, the timing says it all.

Then, Bernie had been in a director role for around 11 years—this should have been his opportunity to be CEO—yet although he acted in the position until it was filled, it wasn't he who filled it. That successful applicant came, but didn't last long, and the hunt was soon on again for another CEO, with Bernie acting in the position, and again he wasn't the one to fill it. My belief is that Council knew Bernie couldn't deal with sensitive employment issues, and as CEO, this would be a major component of the role. These issues and the cost to Council had been extraordinary – if I'd gone to the media, there'd have been the bad PR as well.

Had my situation not arisen I feel confident that Bernie would have made CEO, and after him, Craig; both were technically outstanding in their positions but unfortunately were bad decision makers. They only used their head to solve a problem when you really need to use your head *and* your heart. In the words of Sir Francis Bacon, "truth can never be reached by just listening to the voice of authority."

In late 2005, in preparation for my legal action, I was assessed by a human resource expert consultant by the name of Baily Shaw, and spent nearly a day telling them of my experiences in the workplace. On leaving he took my hand and said to me, "You have really had a bad time." Jim provided a comprehensive report which stated in part, "it seems clear that Mrs O'Keeffe's employer failed to protect her in her workplace from ongoing harassment and discrimination, practised over a lengthy period of years by her supervisor and also her boss at the next level of management." The report went on to explain what good management practice is and included 15 areas of such practice.

The report examined the issue around workplace bullying according to the 'Prevention of Workplace Bullying and Violence at Work, Guidance Note' put out by WorkSafe in 2003.

The report noted that "the management and supervisory team at Wyndham, over a long period of time, breached every one of the above listed practices, many on more than one occasion. It seems clear that at least two levels of supervision/management were well aware of the continuing working practices situation which Ms O'Keeffe was subjected to."

And: "Even had the employer's actions been procedurally sound, which it appears they were not over a long period of time, they appear to have been conducted with significant lack of consideration and compassion."

And: "It seems that these actions could reasonably have been anticipated to produce significant stress in someone of Ms O'Keeffe's workplace performance, proven commitment and personal situation and from the medical and other reports provided, it seems clear that they did."

And finally: "From the information available to me, it is my clear view that Ms O'Keeffe's employer, Wyndham City Council, could have taken a significant number of actions in terms of policies, procedures and behaviour, to provide her with a healthy workplace, rather than one in which she was subjected to repeated bullying/harassment and discrimination. It seems extremely clear that this organisation and its management could have prevented her from being damaged by these events and that they were negligent in not doing so."

The Wyndham City Council per se is not responsible for the behaviour I was subjected to – I feel quite sure they would not know much or anything about what was going on, and if they did, it would've been a much-sanitised version from the senior management team.

By now you may be wondering, even more, why I put up with this behaviour and why I didn't just leave. I liken it to asking the same question of a domestic violence victim. Leaving isn't always easy; there are many facets that keep you there, nowhere else to go, including financial reasons and fear. I had done nothing wrong, so why should I be the one to pay the price and leave? When you value yourself and the work you do, it's very hard to accept what's been done to you. The unfairness racked at my soul, and being a fair person myself I believed and hoped someone would stop the abuse and save me, but it turned out there was no one. The mental abuse of 'gaslighting' makes it difficult and confusing, but I never doubted my own memory, perception and sanity. The support of medical professionals who believed me kept me firmly grounded in reality. If not for my hardy personality I may have well disappeared into obscurity, but now in hindsight I feel that maybe this would have been a better option, since more abuse was yet to come.

I still believed that all the behaviour I was subjected to was because management were skirting around the OH&S Act, which states: "Section 76 prohibits an employer from dismissing or prejudicially altering an employee's employment because the employee has complained about a matter concerning the health, safety or welfare of employees at work." They were attempting to show that the action they took wasn't because they had breached this section of the Act, but because the staff complaint justified management taking the action they did.

I felt that in the end, they couldn't justify their behaviour and they knew it, so the only strategy left was to attack my character, and coupled with the attacks on my integrity they followed a typical recipe of action (as according to the EndWorkplaceAbuse.com), the abuse recipe of repeatedly reprimanding an above-average target (tick), convincing others the target is incompetent (tick), driving the target to report the problem (tick), making tactics outrageous and unbelievable (tick) and making sure the target is alone and vulnerable (final tick).

The last legal hoop to jump through in the WorkCover process is the compensation hearing where you need to prove your employer was negligent and this negligence caused you injury. You must be able to show your employer failed to give due care and attention, through thoughtlessness or carelessness, and ignored or disregarded facts they should know, and that this behaviour resulted in injury to the worker.

In preparation for the compensation hearing, I came to access a number of documents that the defendant had placed in its court Book. Even though the defendant is cited as Wyndham City Council, they are not in reality the true defendant – the true defendant is the Victorian WorkCover Authority, a statutory government department.

I will just outline a few such documents. In an April staff meeting to discuss my suspension, it was written in a joint staff diary that "MG advised that the organisation have a 'duty of care' to the FDC Team members, and to act on these serious issues." The very next day I was suspended with no thought to any "duty of care" the organisation may have owed to an injured worker attempting a return to work after a period of sick leave. Also recorded: "LO informed of suspension and escorted out of Bridge St."

Also in the joint staff diary around early May there were four different types of handwriting, with comments obviously written after the event, squished into vacant lines above and below another entry and written around the edge of the page. One item stated, "Investigators advised Council to stop the process and take it back internally, wasn't enough evidence to proceed."

Sometime in mid-2001, at a staff meeting to discuss the issues of the day, it was recorded that, "Experiences they have encountered with Caitlyn, staff maybe feeling that she is at times overstepping the role of temporary and what support staff are requiring."

Another one in May, "Spoke about and discussed yesterday's situation with Lori. Lori will get another memo in regards to her entry into the building and contact with staff and if it occurs again quite possible that a suspension will be put in place again." This was mentioned earlier in regards to coming to the office to prepare my response to the staff complaint.

Further: "Discussed staff's attendance at work yesterday and this morning – confirmed that pay will not be deducted." This is in regards to my visit when the staff went off work and went to the pub and did not turn up to work the next morning.

And further: "Discussed staff's feelings of lack of support from JC, he is not hearing us and therefore are feeling over worked, highly stressed. Memo to JC, level of support, lack of support, workload."

One staff member made a diary entry which said, "Concerns with Garside passing on emails to Lori. I expressed my disappointment and trust broken." I do not know who wrote this as I cannot recognise the writing, but obviously this person does not understand the rules or ethics of natural justice.

In June 2002, there was a record of a FDC Mediation Meeting which states, "Discussion then commenced and the following matters were raised as issues of concern between the FDC team and management (Helen Rowe & John Circosta) and Bernie Cronin. The team has an issue with the current style of leadership as depicted in Dolores's behaviour. For example, the team felt that some questions asked of them appeared to have hidden motives. In view of this, they have requested to have an input into the selection of their next Unit Leader."

Dolores was the Unit Leader, and she was not at this meeting. No doubt she would be devastated to learn there was a Mediation Meeting taking place which was discussing her, complaining about her, without her knowledge. It does not surprise me that she left not long later.

And: "Suggestions put forward by the team included either being involved in the shortlisting process, or even having a staff representative on the interview panel." This is not the usual procedure, management has this prerogative, but I do not necessarily disagree to this suggestion. But as an experienced unit leader I would feel that staff would use this opportunity to power play.

I do not know if management involved the resource officers in the selection of the next four unit leaders after Dolores left, which were Gaye, Marlene, Gayle and then Chinzia. In between Gayle and Chinzia three in-house Family Services staff also managed the Unit Leader role.

Gaye became Unit Leader after Dolores, and from the little bits I heard she experienced a number of problems with the resource officers. Gaye was amazing, showing great integrity, more than any other person in that workplace, when she came forward to testify on my behalf in the Magistrates' hearing in February of 2003. Gaye left not long after, and was replaced by Marlene.

The word 'support' is used twice in the above-quoted particular paragraph in regards to management providing more of it. Further, it is stated that "the issue of trust was also raised"; it appears staff were wanting to attend a conference and resented being questioned about their attendance, stating "Or, if questioning was to occur, they would prefer it in a direct open management style.

... In general they felt that trust had been shattered and that questions that were being asked more than likely had hidden motives. ... The topic of QA was also raised with considerable concern. The team feels totally unsupported and leaderless on this project."

Remember this meeting occurred more than a year since my departure from the role, yet the words used are very familiar:

> "The team feels that many items in the agenda are 'token' and that decisions have already been made, even before the team meetings. They feel that they do not have a real opportunity to discuss matters and put their ideas forward. They also had concerns about the way the agenda is formatted. They felt that the items that are of importance to management are placed high up, to ensure that they are covered, however items that relate to the team are often left to the bottom and time runs out, with issues being left to drop off. The team would prefer that team meetings were chaired in a more equitable way, with equal time being allocated to agenda items."

The team was still making the same complaints even after I have gone – they still did not understand the role of team meetings.

They had issues around staff bonuses, stating that they had all put in a considerable amount of extra work but only one staff member was singled out for a bonus. Their concerns were around a lack of "direct acknowledgment" by management and a comment from Bernie (the department Director) for the work they had put in to keep the service running. How wonderful that they worked to keep the service running when that was exactly what they were employed and paid to do!

I probably shouldn't revel in the next statement, but I feel a little validation here: "The FDC team used the term 'police tape' around our work space. This was how they felt that they had been treated for the past 18 months, feeling very isolated and ostracised from the rest of the office, John 'hanging out' and chatting with other areas, but not with them." I was gone by this time, so John no longer needed them onside. Other Family Services staff by this time must have known about their behaviour and chose not to associate with them, and I totally understand why.

Also, part of this same statement: "They did note that their relationship with Helen and John may have been fragmented because of the last coordinator, and indicated a real desire to re-build a *trusting, professional working rela-*

The Nightmare of Injustice

tionship." (Italics are mine). Problems with "the last coordinator" is not in reference to me, as during that time both Helen and John were supporting these staff immensely to keep them onside. I feel it must be a reference to two of the unit leaders who came after me; Caitlyn and Dolores.

Also recorded: "The team has asked for clarification of Bernie's role and some acknowledgment of what has happened." Bernie had been the Director of WYNCARE (a council business unit, which included FDC) for the previous six years and they still did not understand his role. What kind of "acknowledgment" are they after – more support, maybe?

A common complaint the resource officers mentioned many times was the lack of support. These staff had good working conditions and good salaries, but with all the level of support they required, this tends to tell me they sadly lacked the necessary skills and temperament to get the job done. This takes me back to when I first gained the position, when the then-supervisor told me she needed someone strong in the position – but strong was obviously the opposite of what these staff wanted or needed. They had 'strong' for eight years, and when the strong was gone, it all fell to pieces.

Finally: "They understand that dispute had been transferred for management through Corporate & Community Services, however, they would like some contact from Bernie and an opportunity to talk."

Another dispute, and the director of a huge department of course has time to let these ladies continue with their 'whining' about the lack of acknowledgement and support. Bernie never said a word to me during my two years of hell in his department. After five years of letting the genie out of the bottle there was no way of putting it back, and coupled with problems and complaints to government on how the Service was operated, a decision was made to smash the bottle and cease the Service and pay the genie to disappear.

I feel I've included more detail in this chapter than you wish to have read, but psychological workplace bullying is all about the detail, and as the saying goes 'the devil is in the detail'. This was such a complex period of time that I have included dates here and there to help with chronological understanding.

As you are now hopefully aware, in order to succeed against an employer in an action at common law for damages, it is necessary to prove the employer failed to take reasonable action to prevent the risk of a reasonably foreseeable injury. Did my employer take reasonable action? Do you believe it was reasonable action? If you do, maybe it is best you leave my story here.

Given all the allegations, including those made by John and Helen with the intention of thwarting my WorkCover claim, it was with surprise John admitted in evidence in the Magistrate's hearing "there was no requirement for any disciplinary action." He had no choice but to admit this, because if he said there was a "requirement" he would have had to give evidence as to what this was, and there was no way this requirement could be justified. WorkCover must have known the truth by this time and yet they did nothing, so I am of the belief that WorkCover is not primarily for the benefit of injured workers but for the benefit of all those who feed off the system and the carcasses of injured workers.

I will leave this chapter with the words of a wonderful human being, Audrey Hepburn: "Nothing is more important than empathy for another human being's suffering. Nothing. Not career, not wealth, not intelligence, certainly not status. We have to feel for one another if we are going to survive with dignity."

FOUR

WorkCover Worries

I was bullied until I broke, mobbed until I was shattered, then pulverised by the WorkCover legal system. Why? Who knows! I was a dedicated, competent and committed employee, but that wasn't enough – or was it too much?

It's quite interesting when you submit a WorkCover claim, especially one for the reasons I had, as it would appear you suddenly, according to management, become a different person. You are no longer a competent, conscientious, dedicated employee, but now someone who is bureaucratic, rigid, angry and a poor performer. It is these false allegations that produce the second layer of injury. You are now attacked because you must be wrong and they are right – you are now entering the territory of 'when wrong is right'.

It was not until I was reading the sworn statements given by John, Helen and Marianne again in order to write this book, that I really came to understand these statements were frivolous in the extreme, or blatantly untrue. I can see that now, but at the time I was so hurt that I could not see the truth through my pain. Was I the person they were desperately trying to depict in their statements? There was no evidence at all to support the claims made, but the fact they made them was enough for WorkCover to deny my claim. Evidence and truth in this system comes secondary to someone who is prepared to sign a sworn statement full of untruths. This is what WorkCover wants, and it is why when statements are proven to be untrue that nothing is done.

Through their statements to WorkCover, especially John's, there are references to attached or enclosed documents, but these documents were not provided to me when their statements were, therefore it was difficult to fully respond to the unknown. But I question why these documents were not provided, and the only answer I can come to is that they did not support their case and were no doubt flighty in nature.

Some issues are repeated in their individual sworn statements, and for clarity I may write about some of John's comments in Marianne's statement, or Helen's in John's, or John's in Helen; hopefully you will get the gist of what was going on that caused me so much grief.

In Marianne's statement, she says that the mediation held between John and me in October of 2000 was related to work performance. I was not informed of this; I was told that it was designed for John and me to gain a better understanding of how we may work together successfully given our differences over the previous months. In my belief, Marianne was setting the scene for the use of Section 82 (2A) of the Accident Compensation Act 1985, which states, "if a condition has arisen wholly or predominantly from either reasonable action taken by my employer in a reasonable manner to discipline or my expectation that the employer would take action to discipline and that consequently, you are not entitled to compensation by virtue of this section." I believe this is purposely written this way to give employers an out by suggesting to them that any claims of stress, bullying or psychological abuse can be thwarted by putting injured employees under more stress by taking unjustified disciplinary action. Rarely in this situation can an injured worker get the truth out that the unjustified disciplinary action was taken after they made a complaint about their working conditions, and this appears to me something WorkCover just do not want to know about once a claim is submitted.

I requested a meeting with Marianne to discuss my response to the mediation minutes, and I asked her to retrieve from the mediator the notes she had made on butchers paper during the session which could confirm my stated position. Whether this occurred or not I do not know, but no one ever referred to this again.

This meeting commenced with Marianne stating management's position, which was: "Mediation is now off the table and not open for discussion" and that "the matter was satisfactorily resolved." For me it remained unresolved because the record of this mediation session was inaccurate and false. I felt that the mediator was not independent, as she had recorded conversations that never occurred. The mediator recorded that I would seek another position, but this was not discussed and I never stated I would seek an external position. I remember the mediator saying she had changed careers at 50, and yet this statement is not in the minutes. We have a situation where things not said were recorded as said, and things said were not recorded.

Nor was there any discussion that John had an option to progress to a full and formalised full performance management procedure. This contradicts the proposition that John was going to respond to my request for a "more supportive management approach" while simultaneously putting me under "full performance management."

John said in his statement that it was in mediation when he first learnt I had Graves' disease. All my staff knew in July 2000, the general manager's PA knew in August 2000, Helen the supervisor knew prior to September 2000, and yet John claimed he did not know until late October. He must have been working in a bubble or under the 'cone of silence' not to have known. In the previous August, during a special meeting with the union delegate present who told me the meeting was the start of John setting up a "paper trail", I said to John that I had been sick for six months and he had not even asked how I was.

A direct quote from John in his statement: "Lori made claims that I knew she was unwell in August 2000, however as indicated previously I knew nothing of Lori being ill until 25/10/00 at the Mediation Meeting." Given my emails informing John and Helen of absences due to medical appointments, given that he signed my sick leave applications and given that it was common knowledge in the Family Services Department that I was unwell, I refute that John did not know until 25 October 2000 that I was unwell, and later in the Magistrates' Court given the evidence I provided, the Magistrate's decision was that John knew from August that I had an illness.

Back in October 2001 I was asked to sign the Mediation Minutes as being true and accurate, I refused – I would never sign a document attesting to its truth and accuracy if I knew it was not true or accurate. In his statement, John attempted to make a big deal about my refusal to sign the mediation minutes, even though my written response to the mediation minutes to clarify the inaccuracies was ignored; I never received a response.

In another statement of John's, taken two years later in preparation for the Magistrates' Court hearing; he made sweeping and undefined allegations. Most of the documents he referred to as proof were not attached to the copy of his statement given to me. Why this was so remains unknown, but the only scenario I can think of is that it was considered that the documents were not proof of anything.

In his statement, John had ignored some facts and had altered other facts to suit, but you cannot change facts, facts are just facts. Once again, mention was made of an attached position description and once again the PD was not attached. I was interested to see such a position description as so many were turning up, left, right and centre, yet none were my then position description.

John and Helen both complained and stated under oath that I had been selective with workplace training. I attended all training that was required of me, and the records of such training give no doubt that they both were not telling the truth. I cannot understand making such a complaint about a staff member when you must have known that records existed which would prove otherwise. In response to their statements, I provided 48 diary printouts or certificates that show training and workshops I attended between 9 February 1999 and 6 October 2000. These facts prove on average I attended two training sessions per week, as per a requirement of my position – but these facts do not support John's allegation, so it would appear he just made up his own. A few years before this, I had set up an extensive training calendar for care providers which proved to be very successful, with care providers happily attending a huge amount of training to improve their skills. All staff, including myself, had completed the 'Train the Trainer' course in anticipation of providing this training in-house. To state I was selective with my own training cannot be supported by any evidence.

In November 2000, management was providing EEO and Harassment Training to all staff; you were required to go, but on the day I was too ill to attend because I was suffering from symptoms of my then-unknown illness. It was on this same day that my doctor told me he believed I was being harassed and discriminated against by my management team of John and Helen; he gave me a WorkCover Certificate of Capacity. I rebooked to attend a later session of this EEO and Harassment Training, but John would not allow me to attend. After I had submitted my WorkCover claim, I was denied the right to attend training, and yet both John and Helen previously had the gall to state that I was selective.

John claims he was concerned by my overall performance and that Helen was speaking to him on a regular basis, but I was not informed of this and this was not highlighted in any of my professional development reviews prior to

2000. I believe these conversations didn't start until after November 1999, when I had a private chat with John concerning Helen's management style and the effect it was having on me. It was at this time they became a team. Myself and other staff believed John was struggling in his role and that he needed Helen – if he only knew at the time how often Helen denigrated him to staff, but we ignored this, because at the time we liked John, and wanted to make him look good at his job.

In his statement regarding this November 1999 meeting, John says he indicated to me that he would talk to Helen and that he would share some of Helen's supervision responsibilities with me and to give me an alternate supervisor to work with. He stated that I appeared happy with this response. This whole statement is a fabrication – John never said anything of this nature. I specifically requested that John keep our conversation confidential, as I didn't want any action taken at the time.

I feel that this statement was a reconstruction to protect John from liability from the fact that he took no action that equated to support or assistance – in fact he took an alternate course.

In his statement, John said that from August 2000 he supplied all his directions and requests in written form to minimise any confusion I may have felt. These directions and requests were sent by email, as well as a copy being hand-delivered, as well as a copy being left on my desk or on the seat of my chair. On some occasions I would receive the same document three times by each of the different methods described above. This did not minimise my confusion – it added to it.

John stated that he often had to intervene to address actual or potential poor practices and poor decision-making on numerous occasions prior to the year 2000. I do not know of an occasion where I have made a bad decision, because if I did, I would certainly have been made aware of it. I made a number of decisions every day; they were sound decisions. There was one in July 2000 where I had written a report which included a recommendation. Helen didn't follow my recommendation; she made her own decision (which was her prerogative) and it blew up in her face, but I was blamed for it nonetheless.

John stated that he had to constantly remind me to produce a contingency plan for Pauline's secondment from Child Care Benefit Officer to Meals on Wheels Coordinator, and that he and Helen had an enormous amount of work to do in regards to this. Yet I know that I had responded four days after their request with a plan – once again the facts do not support this allegation.

I don't know of the enormous amount of work Helen and John were required to do; the work fell to me. All that was required from them was to sign a couple of letters and the secondment approval document. I carried out all the recruitment tasks to fill this position, and then a second recruitment process was required because the successful applicant worked in my team in another position. Her position had to be filled before she could move to the Pauline's vacant position.

For a variety of reasons, this position was not filled until mid-March 2000. In the intervening three months, I completed the role and duties of this job, as well as fulfilling the requirements of my own position.

I had never been privately or publicly aggressive towards John, but he made that allegation. He was my manager, and as such, he was accorded my due respect at all times. John made the allegation that I was consistently reacting inappropriately, but provided no further details, as is the case all through his so-called evidence. He could not describe what behaviour he considered inappropriate, because there was none. John consistently stated his perception of my inappropriate behaviour without ever defining it.

Any public display of aggressiveness surely must have been witnessed by the public. John didn't provide any date, place, times or detail who was present when this public aggressiveness occurred. He didn't provide any detail because the allegation was false. John also accused me of poor time management when completing the work of two staff and meeting all deadlines; bar missing one by four hours, I cannot recall any other occasion where I missed a deadline.

A factor which caused John and my relationship to falter was in the beginning of 2000, when John formally reprimanded me for missing the deadline for the Unit Business Plan draft by four hours. This initial deadline was extended by four days due to the fact that many unit leaders were experiencing difficulty meeting this deadline. I was completing two roles at this time and was very conscious of the demands of both, but I did approach Helen with my concerns on two occasions and her response was that it wouldn't take long to complete the Unit Business Plan draft as it was only an update of the previous year's. When I read the outline of what was required, I realised Helen was clearly incorrect, as it was a whole new complex document requiring a huge amount of information.

John approached me one week prior to the deadline to ask how it was going. He did send emails reminding unit leaders of the deadline for the draft Unit Business Plan, but as I was swamped with many conflicting deadlines for the CCA Pay run and staff recruitment processes, I may not have given it the attention it deserved.

It should be noted that other unit leaders did not meet the new extended deadline and had still not provided their drafts after I had provided mine. After the deadline had passed, I asked another unit leader how they went completing their draft, and they said that they had not even started it. They were not reprimanded, but I was. And they had not taken on an additional position, coupled with their usual role. Had I forgone my duties to meet the CCA payroll deadline to concentrate on an internal deadline, which if not met would not cause anyone an adverse reaction, there would have been a huge uproar from care providers if their child care reimbursement was late; for many this was their salary.

Any worker would be miffed or even angry if they did not receive their pay because their boss had other priorities. Care providers relied on getting paid each fortnight; I don't feel that Council or I would have enjoyed explaining to them that an internal management requirement was more important than their salary. John wrote in his statement this was an example of poor prioritising on my behalf, but I stand by my decision as the correct one and thoroughly believe if I had chosen the other way around and care providers made complaints about not being paid then he would have said an external customer need would take preference over an internal management requirement that was obviously flexible. I felt, especially during 2000-2001, that no matter the decision I made it would be the wrong one.

My completed Unit Business Plan did meet the organisational deadline, and interestingly once it was submitted there was little organisational feedback. Our director Bernie stated in the last line of a memo sent to unit leaders regarding the Business Plan that "In 2000, we will also be reviewing progress against Business Plan targets on a quarterly basis."

This did not occur – I never received any feedback regarding the completed Unit Business Plan, it was not reviewed on a quarterly basis, and it was never mentioned to me again. All the grief this had caused me appeared to be not that important after all; I believe John and Helen caused me this grief on purpose, that this was the beginning of their 2000 bullying rampage.

All through his statement, John attempted to paint me in a bad light to encourage WorkCover to believe I had a laissez-faire attitude to my work. Anyone who knows me, particularly my former colleagues at various workplaces, would know this to be untrue. If anything, I was the total opposite: I cared too much.

On the young mum who was battling cancer and required childcare in her own home, John stated, "Lori had participated in relevant discussions." The only discussion that I was ever involved in regarding this issue was in mid-August 2000 for approximately five minutes. It centred on general WorkCover issues for home-based childcare workers. John was now attempting to set the scene again, to try and show appropriate discussions and considerations regarding this mum included me when they did not.

In this five-minute discussion, there was no mention of dismissing the FDC worker providing in-home care for this terminally-ill mother the next morning. I was very concerned about this action, believing it was thoughtless and that the WorkCover issues were not the only agenda item here. This was the occasion I outlined my concerns in a memo to the general manager and in his response to my written concerns regarding the internal decision-making process he stated, "Your expectation of being included in discussions is reasonable . . .."

It was not until much later I came to realise the significance of Section 82 (2A) of the Accident Compensation Act 1985 – that the "reasonable action taken by my employer in a reasonable manner to discipline" curtailed any WorkCover Claim and was an easy out for bullies and employers.

Just know that all this behaviour fuelled my feeling that something very amiss was going on, but at this time I had no understanding of 'gaslighting'.

It is illegal to be retaliated against in the workplace for reporting harassment. One of the most difficult aspects of domestic violence to understand is that every time an abusive event happens, there is a chemical reaction in the brain that bonds the couple together, even when one is the perpetrator and one is the victim. This is called 'trauma bonding' – what is called Stockholm syndrome can also occur in abusive relationships. This is when a victim feels empathy toward an abuser. Trauma bonding and Stockholm syndrome are two reasons that people who are victims in abusive relationships find it so difficult to leave.

One of the hallmarks of gaslighters is their lack of empathy; if you dare cross them, or even make your needs known, they will come after you with a vengeance. Gaslighters in power usually show nothing but contempt for educated people as the educated are the people most likely to speak out against a gaslighter's behaviour. Why? Because these people have facts to back up their criticisms and gaslighters don't like to be challenged by facts.

Pay attention to your body language when you are talking, as you want to communicate that you are open. Arms folded across your chest gives the message 'I'm not interested in what you are saying' or 'I'm fed up'. I wish I knew about this before I engaged gaslighters to represent me in court – some barristers in the civil division, especially in the personal injury jurisdiction, are expert at this form of manipulation.

Given all that had occurred up to this time, particularly the reprimanding letter to my personnel file for being four hours late with my Unit Business Plan draft, when others hadn't even started to write theirs until after the deadline, the lack of support, the paper trail John appeared to be setting up, the dismissal of a care provider from providing in-home care, the curious Performance Development Review, and finally the mediation session that was appearing to complete whatever process management was undertaking.

Helen made a statement towards the end of 2002 in preparation for the hearing in the Magistrates' Court. She stated that I came under her coordination as one of three unit leaders, but this is incorrect; there were four units under Helen's supervision from 1995 until Child Care Services were tendered out under Compulsory Competitive Tendering (CCT.) They were: Family Day Care/Occasional Care, Kindergarten Services, Child Care Centres and Maternal and Child Health. Three out of the four unit leaders of the above programs experienced difficulties with Helen's behaviour, and three unit leaders made a number of complaints regarding this behaviour to the manager, John. I was the last to speak to John regarding Helen's managerial style and the negative effect it was having on me, but I was the one to pay the price. I requested in my meeting with John in November of 1999 that I wished to keep the details of my concerns confidential. I requested that no action be taken, but simply wanted John to be aware of the difficulties I was experiencing. I was keeping him informed.

As mentioned, I felt this was because at this time John was struggling in his position and Helen seemed to be helping him out – or so he thought. He didn't know Helen was undermining him at every opportunity. It appeared to some of us that Helen may have been after the manager's job, but we Children's Services unit leaders personally liked John and worked hard and smart so this would reflect on him being a good manager.

In her statement, Helen referred to an attached position description which was not attached. An estimated guess on my behalf is it was not attached because of all the different position descriptions I had come across, the one in my private file that arrived there by magic and the four I found on Councils file of position descriptions. There may have been a generic PD for all Band 6 unit leaders in Family Services, but at no time was I informed that my current PD was not really my current position description. The latest position description I had was dated 1995, and related to the new structure of Family Day Care and Occasional Care after CTT was implemented.

All through her statement, Helen made outlandish allegations, even suggesting I didn't have a full understanding as to my role of Unit Leader. She provided no proof to support any of her statements. I didn't know of any occasions where I failed to take responsibility for some tasks that were part of my job. Helen also stated that she was required to spend more time than she should have assisting me, yet her role was to assist unit leaders in their role, and her salary came out of our budgets. No doubt there were occasions where Helen was required to participate in some duties listed in my unit, as this was her role, but her participation as stated is highly exaggerated. Prior to the year 2000, my abilities in the role weren't questioned and I wasn't informed of any major managerial, interpersonal or behavioural problems.

At no time did Helen ever say to me that she was spending too much time assisting me and picking up after me. My budget paid one third of her salary, therefore a third of her time should have been spent in assisting the services I managed. I didn't need or want Helen's assistance, and definitely didn't want her spending the majority of her time with me; working with Helen was challenging, and my work was already hard enough.

Helen claimed I was unapproachable because of the position of my desk; I positioned my desk in the right-hand corner of my corner office. I chose to have my desk positioned as I did because it allowed me to turn my swivel chair and face the person who came into my office without the desk creating a barrier. I felt that this made me more approachable. I was never informed that the position of my desk caused anyone to feel that I was unapproachable. On occasion over the years, both John and Helen had placed their desks in the exact same position as I had mine; she failed to mention this in her statement.

Unit leaders met with our supervisors about once per week, with a number of informal chats held over the period as well. I never felt or believed that my meetings with Helen were an intrusion, but she "sensed" they were. I find it strange that if giving a sworn statement to WorkCover, you would even bother including such a silly remark. Sensing something doesn't make it true, and it's definitely not important or proof of anything.

Helen wrote that I behaved in an aggressive manner towards her during many of our meetings, but this is grossly untrue. There had never been an occasion of such behaviour displayed by me – if anything, I was meek, as I felt intimidated by Helen. I have never seen any documents reprimanding me for this behaviour, because if it was as bad as Helen alleged there should be at least one note or an email or a formal chat with John. But there are none, of course, because this didn't happen.

The Family Services Department offices were open-plan, with thin partitions dividing rooms and offices of unit leaders, therefore any aggression would have been witnessed or heard by others. I was never informed, counselled or disciplined regarding aggressive behaviour towards Helen or anyone else. If she sincerely felt this way, I'm surprised that no complaint was made at the time to her manager John. As she stated earlier, she was in regular contact with him regarding her concerns about me.

When my resignation became known, three Home Care Staff who sat directly outside my door for a number of years sent me emails that would refute Helen's assertion that I had an aggressive nature. The walls of our offices were thin partitions, so loud, angry, aggressive behaviour would be hard to hide.

Helen alleged she found me difficult to manage, but once again I was not informed of this; if I was hard to manage on occasions (which I refute) this was due to the fact Helen made bad decisions and she occasionally made mistakes. These mistakes usually caused me a headache while I tried to sort them out. I consistently achieved departmental objectives without assistance from Helen.

In all my years in my position I undertook many training opportunities. One which was quite memorable was around 1998, when unit leaders participated in a 360-Degree Human Synergistic Workshop. Helen comments that she undertook the same training and this assisted with her management and leadership skills. After the Human Synergistic course, I didn't feel there was any improvement in Helen's leadership skills – if anything, her manner became more critical and fault-finding in nature.

I felt that this may have been due to the fact that during the Human Synergistic course we were required to break into groups to discuss our results.

Helen did not join a discussion group but instead was taken by the facilitator to another room for a private one-on-one session. I remember feeling empathy for Helen at this time, but also hopeful that she could use the feedback given in her assessment to improve her interactions with others.

In my eight years in the position, there were numerous delicate and/or problematic situations to deal with, and they were dealt with successfully by me without Helen's assistance. But Helen alleged that a number of these situations escalated to become confrontational and personalised, yet I can only remember one occasion where this may have occurred to a slight degree and that is when home-based child care provided for the mum dying of cancer was terminated by the Home Care Unit Leader alongside John and Helen. I stood up for this mum, but it was never confrontational. Once again, Helen provided little in the way of proof or facts.

One example of Helen's 'assistance' was in April 1999, when I wrote a memo to her regarding the behaviour of a care provider. I included a number of recommendations, and as Helen didn't respond I let the matter go. The behaviour didn't relate to poor quality or unsafe child care practices. It wasn't surprising that Helen did not respond, but that this memo turned up on my desk a year and a half later in mid-2000, with a post-it note attached that now caused concern.

Dialogue of Post-it Notes Stuck to Memo:

On 16 August 2000, a post-it note from John stating: "Lori, is any more action required re this? John."

On 17 August 2000 I responded by post-it note: "John, I feel it is now too late to respond to my memo. There was no response from Helen at the time, so I just let it go. I now of course regret this decision. Thanks, Lori." I put this on John's desk.

On 21 August 2000 I was looking in the FDC Complaints Folder (not staff complaints, but a folder of complaints made to us by Service users) and I found the same memo with another post-it note attached, dated 16 August, stating: "Examples of giving problem/responsibility away."

Apparently informing and asking your supervisor for an opinion was now considered giving the problem or responsibility away. I was informing my supervisor of a situation, only because I felt this may escalate at another time. This note was dated 16 August and was in John's handwriting. This notation may be dated 16 August, but on this date the memo was in my possession until 17 August when I placed it back on John's desk.

I wrote this comment on the same post-it note: "The above comment is dated 16 August. Did not appear in complaints folder stuck to this until after I wrote my sticky note on 17 August 2000." I do not know why it secretly turned up in the complaints folder or why anyone would feel that it belonged there, as it wasn't a complaint. By this time, mid-2000, strange things were happening which left me confused and unsure.

In my opinion, the purpose of all this was that in early August, Helen had a loud phone conversation (heard by many in the office, but not me) with the care provider referred to in my memo and Helen then realised what I had meant by my memo, but now she had experienced this for herself and realised she hadn't responded to my memo regarding the behaviour of this care provider. I would even go on to say that the phone call must have been quite confrontational for Helen to seek out the old memo from me 18 months earlier. Helen couldn't deal with difficult situations; her manner often escalated problems. A minor issue would require the writing of an unnecessary report; she had this ability to make whatever you did appear wrong.

As mentioned, I always kept John and Helen informed of my movements and was completely accountable in this regard, but again Helen alleged that I did not. Remember when in September 1999, I wished to take a Rostered Day Off that was owed to me, and emailed Helen with my plans. Her response was most unwarranted. She stated: "All other unit leaders negotiate their requests in this manner. The impact of unit leaders changes range from impact on the car pool to inadequate senior coverage of the office at Bridge Street, with many variations in between."

Never in the past had I been required to negotiate when I took an RDO. RDOs were always planned well with the needs of the Service considered. Other unit leaders were not required to negotiate their RDOs.

As previously stated given Helen's response to my request, you can imagine how I felt when I read the Daily Bulletin Sheet for 1 November and saw that all unit leaders were absent on various sorts of leave with Council cars, and no senior staff coverage in the building other than me. John and Helen were also absent for the day, and I was not informed of any of this, or of anyone else's absence. I was the highest-ranking staff member, and this was clearly in contradiction to Helen's email (re the taking of RDOs). Obviously, no one else in the department had read Helen's email, not even John or Helen herself.

Not keeping Helen informed was another Helen gripe, but I provided numerous emails and memos to prove this to be untrue. Remembering back to a time when there were no records of staff absences, I kept a 'Time in Lieu Record' and a 'Staff Leave Record' sheet in my office so it could be seen by all staff that we were all accountable for recording any leave of any nature we took. No other unit leader at this time kept such records. Sometime later, a time in lieu record was introduced for all unit leaders and was centrally located in John's PA's office. I was ahead of my time; my innovative idea became departmental procedure.

Around the years 1999/2000 I had three full-time staff on maternity leave, with all of them returning at around the same time, and all wanting particular hours and days that suited them. All wanted to go from full-time to part-time, and as any manager can attest this is quite a lot of work, logistically. Helen claimed I worked outside my authority by working out a plan that suited these returning staff and the needs of the Service.

It was not my final decision to accommodate all the requests from staff returning from maternity leave – the requests related to the number of days they would work per week as well as what days per week they would work. The final decision to approve the staff requests for part-time work was made together with Helen and John, but in her statement, this is one example Helen used to attempt to prove I worked outside my level of authority by approving these changes, which is ludicrous. I well knew that I didn't have the authority to approve such requests. I informed both John and Helen of what the staff wanted and their position. That position was that if they didn't get what they wanted, they would resign.

In Helen's statement to WorkCover, she said that she didn't know I was ill. This statement by her is simply untrue. I verbally informed Helen on 3 July of 2000 that I was unwell and that I was seeing a specialist the next week. During July and August 2000, I often left work for short periods to attend a variety of medical appointments, and I always informed Helen or John of my absence for medical reasons by email.

I also submitted a sick leave application for each absence, and sick leave was approved on each occasion by John or Helen, and this is proved by records held in my personnel file. This was an extremely important statement to make, because if I hadn't informed Helen of my illness, then there would be no legal foreseeability – this was the lie she and management were desperate to make true.

It was common knowledge among staff that I was unwell – many staff asked after my health; I never kept it secret. I chatted about it to the personal assistant of the director that I was ill with Graves' disease after she enquired after my health. It was obvious to everyone that I was ill, as I had lost a considerable amount of weight, and my appearance was tired and drawn.

Furthermore, in September 2000, I was leaving the office late to go home and on my way out, Sue the Maternal and Child Health Unit Leader called out to me – she was still in her office. She asked how I was, and I responded that I had "thyro… thyro…" – I could not pronounce the word. Sue said "thyrotoxicosis." I was surprised that Sue knew, as my specialist had only said this word to me two hours earlier during my 4pm appointment. I asked Sue how she knew and she said Helen had told her even before I was told by my specialist – therefore Helen did know of my illness from at least August 2000.

Other than on 3 July 2000, I didn't inform Helen directly that I was suffering from an illness, as she apparently already knew, and my belief that the illness was minor negated a formal notice to management that I was unwell, I didn't think it necessary. Helen never asked after my welfare or enquired if I needed any assistance in my role. Given the above, it is preposterous that Helen would then claim she didn't have any knowledge of my illness until October. In this statement, I believe she was setting the scene for her and John to be able to argue the denial of liability for the legal concept of foreseeability.

My WorkCover claim was dated November 2000, and my formal complaint, including my rebuttal to her first statement (December 2000) to the WorkCover investigator were provided to Council in July 2001.

It is inconceivable that Helen wasn't informed of my written complaint until the time of providing a statement to WorkCover in November 2002, where she swore she wasn't aware of any complaint by me. I was sent a letter in July 2001 acknowledging my complaint and the intended process. Obviously, this process didn't occur and it would appear from Helen's statement that she wasn't even informed of my complaint, but I seriously doubt this.

Over the years, a number of staff complained to me about Helen's behaviour, which included her calling a staff member the night before her wedding and telling her that she wouldn't have a job when she got back from her honeymoon (as told to me by the bride) and then turning up to the wedding ceremony the next morning uninvited. Back at work the following Monday I was surprised to see that Helen had a copy of the wedding booklet displayed on her desk.

Elda, a resource officer, was concerned when she attended the staff kitchen and saw Helen and another staff member toasting with champagne the success of getting rid of another staff member. Elda told me she thought this was totally unacceptable. I attended the staff kitchen and was offered a glass—or should I say a plastic cup—of champagne to celebrate. I thought to myself that this was totally unacceptable.

Two of my staff told me Helen would go snooping in my office whenever I was absent from work. A number of staff told me that when I was on leave Helen would "grill" them about my personal life and my marriage.

Even though I had requested John to keep our chat of November 1999 confidential, he obviously informed Helen of the concerns I raised with him. I can only wonder if he also informed her of the complaints made by other staff – why I was the one targeted and not the other staff, I do not know. Generally, staff were reluctant to formally complain about Helen to management, as it was accepted that management routinely supported the more senior officer. This proved even more so with my formal written complaint, as it was not acted upon at all and Council's Complaint Handling policy was not followed. Very different treatment to the resource officer complaint made about me (but I had a WorkCover claim so had to be the one who was wrong). It was difficult to respond to the broadness of Helen's formal statement to WorkCover, as her allegations weren't true, weren't evidence-based, and documents referred to in the statement weren't included.

Helen repeated similar claims in both her statements to WorkCover, but she never gave particulars as to what behaviour she had observed that equated to aggressiveness or poor behaviour. She never cautioned or warned me of this alleged behaviour – there were no records relating to anything like this prior to the year 2000. It would have been her duty to report all of this offensive behaviour and poor performance to our manager, John. Surely if she had he would have spoken to me or counselled or disciplined me, yet he never raised such an issue with me over the preceding five years.

I was never formally or informally reprimanded regarding any deficiencies in the programs I administered; nothing was raised during the annual PDR process except for the issues surrounding my PDR in September 2000. Each month during my Financial Management Report Meeting with the Director, he expressed approval of my financial management skills. Over the CCT Contract period, the supervisor of the contract never stated any concerns regarding the management of the contract or the attaining of the Key Performance Indictors. Services I administered made healthy surpluses. In the last year of my management, the 1999/2000 financial year had a surplus of many thousands of dollars.

In the busy period at the end of 1999 and beginning of 2000, I co-ordinated five recruitment processes with such expertise the personnel manager said I held the record for the most efficient recruitment procedure. He said the manager of IT had had employment applications sitting on his desk for more than six months.

In my response to Helen's two statements, I provided evidence that either proved my position or supported the response I made, while her allegations were untrue and not supported by factual evidence. I believe that all through my response it can be seen that Helen's style of 'guidance and support' had a very negative effect on me. She'd provided me with more 'support' than other unit leaders, but all this 'support' actually made me ill.

Given the evidence I provided, how could Helen's allegations be sustained or be given any credibility? And yet, they were, by a system that ignored rather than accepted the truth. She created problems where there were none; this caused frustration for a number of staff.

I was in a state of confusion as I knew something was going on, but had no idea what; I visited my doctor who suggested I submit a WorkCover claim and go on leave. I didn't accept his suggestion, as I knew anyone on WorkCover was viewed in a poor light, and I thought I could sort it out. But after my request to discuss mediation, and the incorrect minutes of this session, and management's behaviour around this, I knew I actually couldn't sort it out; this was bigger than me. I was beginning to experience severe symptoms of illness, and again visited my doctor, who stated his belief I was being harassed and intimidated and strongly recommend I leave the workplace, submit a Work-Cover claim and give my employer time to sort out whatever was happening.

Around three weeks later, I met with Marianne, the Acting Manager of Organisational Change (this was a meeting I requested to see how we could move forward) and she informed me that an investigation had been carried out and the determination was that I hadn't been harassed or discriminated against. I was unaware that an investigation was taking place; I was not interviewed, nor was I asked to supply any evidence to substantiate the allegations on my WorkCover Certificate. She informed me that arrangements would be put in place for me to be under performance management when I returned to work and that I would be expected to return to full-time employment from 3 January 2001. As always, the record of this meeting was not accurate, but by this time I was getting used to the spin human resources put on their meetings, or any activity for that matter, so that they always appeared in the right and me in the wrong.

I discussed with my treating doctor the expectation that I resume full-time employment on 3 January 2001. His medical advice was that I was incapacitated to resume full-time work. I did not attend my doctor claiming harassment or discrimination; I simply explained to him what was happening at work and the physical and emotional effects on me. It was his diagnosis that my symptoms related to my being harassed, intimidated and discriminated against at work.

At the VCAT hearing in January 2002 (action brought after my job was advertised without telling me), the Deputy President determined the following:

> Is there then a *prima facie* case, a case to answer in respect to the claim of impairment discrimination?
> **In my view there is.**
> The Respondents have **not satisfied me that there is no case to answer** here. I now turn to possible advantage or detriment to the public interest in making the order.
> I now deal with detriment to the complainant's case. Wyndham submits that there will be no detriment if the order is not made. They submit that since there is no prima facie case, orders cannot be made. I have already said that I am **satisfied there is a case to answer with relation to impairment discrimination**. Ms O'Keeffe seeks reinstatement to her unit leader position as her ultimate relief.

My doctor and many after him also came to the view I was harassed, intimidated and discriminated against, but management didn't take any of this on board. I was still wrong and they were right – even more right than the medical professionals and the VCAT Deputy President.

After a number of weeks on leave, I asked my doctor to clear me to work one day a week, as I feared losing contact with my staff and my absence being linked to the rumour Helen was obviously spreading around the workplace. He reluctantly agreed, but in hindsight this was an error on my behalf. I should have never returned – or only when there were convincing efforts on behalf of my employer to sort this matter out. I threw myself out of the frying pan and into the fire of hell.

John in his statement attempted to convince that he was abiding by the Return to Work Program as defined in the OH&S Act. I don't believe that I actually received what could be defined as an "ongoing Return to Work Plan" – all I ever received was a memo stating what my duties would be for the one day I worked each week. To my knowledge, my treating doctor was never consulted concerning any structured Return to Work program – the only written advice he provided was the WorkCover Certificate of Capacity.

I was with my doctor on an occasion when he rang Craig, the Director of Corporate Services, to discuss my return to work. Craig was not available and so my doctor left a message for him to call – it is my understanding that Craig did not return his call.

John appeared to be attempting to give the impression that he accorded reasonable management action and support for my return to work, but in reality, his behaviour was in no way supportive of my return to work. The incidences of this are many and varied and examples are all through the current and previous chapters.

By and large, I wondered if the major perpetrator (John) of the offences committed against me, which led to my ill-health and the submission of a WorkCover claim, should be the person to supervise my return to work. It was bound to fail, and it did, because he made sure it would, no doubt with a little help from Helen.

In August 2001, I was requested to attend a Vocational Assessment conducted by Donnelly Ayres Consulting, around three months after my suspension, and from memory I was very happy to do so as I looked at it as a positive action for me to return to work. The third paragraph of the Donnelly Ayres report states: "The assessment will then be used to assist in the formulation of a Return to Work plan within the Council structure." And also: "There was no discussion about external options as this was not a consideration for the worker or the employer."

No 'Return to Work Plan' ever eventuated, and this I felt was just an exercise formulated by Craig to once again give the impression management were attempting to have it seen that they were taking reasonable management action in a reasonable manner. The comment regarding 'external options' was astonishing, considering Craig organised the advertising of my substantive position without my knowledge some eight weeks later. I attended this assessment in good faith, with the honest belief that my employer was genuinely seeking an alternate position for me, and that until such time I could return to my Unit Leader position in Family Day Care.

The last page of report states: "For any new employment to be successful and sustainable, a training schedule should be established to allow Ms O'Keeffe to develop into a new role." No training schedule was developed. After I received a copy of this report I had a meeting with Craig, and this is when he stated to me, "Bloody consultants, you pay them a lot of money to tell you what you already know."

Nothing more was said regarding this report or implementing any of the recommendations. It was as if the assessment never took place, and I can't help but think that it was because the Assessment placed my skill level as high, which didn't support John and Helen's view of my performance being poor.

As mentioned, John denied in VCAT proceedings to knowing I was ill in August, in the face of three particular emails I sent him informing him of such. In Council's 'Particulars of Defence' in response to the allegations I made in my 'Particulars of Complaint' filed in March 2002, they state as follows: "On the basis of information provided to them by the Complainant (me) since 31 August 2000 it is admitted at times since March 2000, the Complainant suffered from Thyrotoxicosis." This didn't quite feel like an admission; they accepted I was unwell from March but made no mention of the fact that they knew at this time, and the *knowing* is vitally important for 'foreseeability' and hence 'negligence'.

Management submitted my WorkCover claim dated 9 November 2000 eleven days after I submitted it to them, and after a few weeks I was informed my claim wasn't accepted and the usual excuse was paraded before me. My WorkCover claim was denied principally on the grounds that my condition "had arisen wholly or predominantly from either reasonable action taken by my employer in a reasonable manner to discipline me, or my expectation that the employer would take action to discipline me, and that consequently, I am not entitled to compensation by virtue of section 82(2A) of the Accident Compensation Act."

This section of the Act is routinely used to thwart claims relating to workplace bullying, and I believe it is purposely written to give an employer an out so that they can use it as the blueprint to cover any claims of bullying. Part and parcel of the actual bullying is to unfairly discipline the worker or have them expect that this may be done. Hopefully you can understand through reading the preceding chapter how unreasonable action taken in an unreasonable manner is turned into reasonable action taken in a reasonable manner by the perpetrators of workplace abuse, and how the law is used to this end.

No disciplinary action was required against me, and the accusation was a fabrication after the submission of my WorkCover claim to deny liability and circumvent the Act. I believed I had proven that action taken by my employer wasn't reasonable, or taken in a reasonable manner. I don't believe that advertising an employee's position without telling them can in any way be seen as a reasonable action.

After a two-day hearing in the Magistrates' Court, my WorkCover claim was finally accepted in February 2003 as being work-related – too little, too late. I found the Magistrate to be fair, and was happy with his adjudication.

In the hearing, my ex-manager John admitted in evidence that there was "no requirement for any disciplinary action." I had no expectation that my employer would take action to discipline me, no expectation that they would follow accepted industry practice for this process, as I knew there were no grounds on which this could be relied upon. My employer didn't have any substantial and quantifiable evidence on which to base any disciplinary action. I was fearful that the harassment/bullying/intimidation/discrimination would continue 'under the radar' until I was too ill to continue working, and this is exactly what happened. As WorkCover had rejected the claim, management allowed the previously mentioned behaviour to continue and I had no protection under the law or conscience to a safe working environment.

John attempted to distance himself from responsibility, and stated under oath that he was on annual leave in April 2001 when everything was happening and thus wasn't aware of the resource officer complaint and the action taken against me. He stated that he had no knowledge until his return from leave at the end of April, after Easter. Except the thing is; if he had taken leave and returned after Easter, he would've been at work during the suspension process – a small detail he failed to realise. It is inconceivable that Helen did not tell him, Craig or Marianne that she had organised for the resource officers to go to the Employee Assistance Program Counsellor to bolster the authenticity of their combined allegations against me. I find it ludicrous that John gave evidence he was not involved in the process and knew nothing about it at the time.

John's diary sheet for the week commencing Monday 9 April was displayed outside his office, and it stated that he had a meeting scheduled with the EAP Counsellor. He sent me a memo dated 10 April regarding a report about police check Procedure in Family Day Care which I completed and gave to him by the end of the day. I believe this report was the last nail in my coffin.

On 11 April, resource officers called for a debriefing session with Employee Assistance Program Counsellor concerning 'fears' they had with me returning to my normal position. Interesting that John stated he had no knowledge about the staff complaint, and yet it's recorded that he met with the counsellor two days before the resource officers met with her. John wrote a letter to me on this day outlining RTW Arrangements – it stated: "I will advise you of the outcome of rehabilitation assessment once the review has been completed." This did not occur, but it does show he was at work on this day.

The 12 April 'Staff Relations Consultative Committee Meeting Minutes' record John's presence at this meeting. The next day was 13 April (Good Friday) and the 16 April (Easter Monday). My last day at work at this time was 17 April and he was at work on this date, but he certainly was not at work on 19 April, and whether he was at work on 18 April I do not know. Given the dates, how could he have not known what was happening? If he did indeed take annual leave, it could only have been from the 18 April, and therefore he was certainly at work during the period my suspension was being arranged and this was certainly in conflict with his sworn evidence given in the Magistrates' Court.

John had also written a memorandum to the resource officers dated 23 April 2000 – this document shows he was at work on this date. Given Easter that year, the only period of leave possible was from Wednesday 18 April to Friday 20 April 2000, and this doesn't equate to the timeframe he testified to in court, which was early April. From the evidence I have, John was at work on 9, 10, 11, 12, (Easter the 13 and 16) 17 and 23 April, so when exactly did he take annual leave? I was suspended on 19 April, so my belief is he was absent on this day because he knew what was happening – it was no coincidence.

I was gobsmacked by his evidence, as I knew it to be untrue, but I've since learnt that many people don't tell the truth under oath, and the courts and the police know it but rarely do anything about it. That is unless you're a celebrity, serious criminal, politician or have bucketloads of money. And then, and only then, will there be those who will fight and argue perjury. But generally speaking, ordinary everyday people do not get charged with perjury because we the victims just aren't important enough. WorkCover appeared to take no interest in the fact testimony and written statements made by John were false.

In the previous chapter, I mentioned the Independent Medical Examiner Dr Dush Shan and how his report supported the non-acceptance of my Work-Cover claim. I was sent to see him again in 2002 in preparation for the Magistrates' Court hearing, and this time his report gave a much more balanced opinion. He was called as a witness for the defendant, but overall, his testimony was of little value. The Magistrate said that Dr Shan's report had reached a conclusion that he "was not able to perceive any harassment." The Magistrate believed that Dr Shan expressed that opinion as a matter of fact, which gives the perception of bias in favour of those who employed him. Dr Shan also expressed an opinion of law regarding the Accident Compensation Act 1985; an opinion he was not required to share.

Towards the end of the hearing, when talking about "medical and like expenses", the barrister for the defendant made what I believe to be an inappropriate statement to the Magistrate – he said (or words very close to): "as Mrs O'Keeffe drives a Mercedes, she is obviously not financially embarrassed." Was he suggesting that I wasn't entitled to a legal right because of the kind of car I drove? The Magistrate rightly shut him down, but what was his purpose for making the statement in the first place? I have found that in legal proceedings barristers covertly or overtly make statements in court to diminish your worth.

By this time, I was intrigued by everything WorkCover, and read their website with interest as I needed to get my head around what had happened to me and attempt to understand it. I read WorkCover's stated vision, mission, and values on their website, which was listed as following:

Commitment – Drives us to improve Victoria's workplace health and safety system
Integrity – Compels us to be honest fair and objective
Cooperation – Motivates us to work in an open and supportive way
Accountability – Demands we are professional in the delivery of high-quality services and
Care – Is what we try to show in everything we do.

I'll leave it to the reader to decide for themselves if the stated vision, mission and values were being met, but for me it was a resounding no.

In September 2003, I contacted WorkCover concerning the victimisation I had experienced since the submission of my WorkCover claim, and what I believed were offences committed under the Accident Compensation Act 1985 by my former employer. Being unemployed meant I had much time on my hands – time to raise these matters and hopefully create change.

The offences consisted of breaches of the Occupational Health and Safety Act and included the failure to provide a 'Return To Work Plan', a Return to Work coordinator, and that an employer must not dismiss a worker from employment because the worker has given the employer notice of an injury, taken steps to pursue a claim for compensation and given or attempted to give a claim for compensation to the employer.

In my opinion, my former employer was guilty of this, and so had breached the Act. I prepared my list outlining each breach which supported my claim of constructive dismissal. Helen and John had written statements for WorkCover which were clearly false and my rebuttal proved this, but no action was taken.

WorkCover's decision in relation to these breaches appeared to rely solely on the following two assertions: that as my claim wasn't accepted, my employer wasn't obliged to provide me with a Return to Work plan in accordance with the Act, and that the information provided by management showed at the time of my employment that they did have an Occupational Health and Safety program and a number of Return to Work coordinators to implement the RTW programs.

These facts were uncontested, and indeed I had never asserted that my employer did not have an Occupational Health and Safety program or any Return to Work coordinators. The issue was that, in my case, they didn't fulfil these duties. The implication seemed to be that as long as people are employed in these roles, an employer was adhering to the Act, regardless of whether these roles were performed or not.

It is a fact that stress claims are often initially rejected, and a claim for harassment and intimidation would seemingly fall into the same category. A WorkCover claim is not finalised until all relevant procedures are completed, including conciliation and court proceedings. It would appear contradictory under the Act to say a WorkCover claim is finalised at the first point of rejection. This is especially true when it is the prerogative of the employer, supported by the insurer and WorkCover, to reject the claim.

My WorkCover claim was a genuine claim, and a live claim, for more than two years. It wasn't in my control to resolve this claim earlier, even though I did attempt resolution. I believe that it is prudent that employers continue to follow the Act until such time that a final decision is made.

Management was aware of my illnesses. Employers have an obligation under Occupational Health and Safety to assist an ill/injured worker, even if the illness or injury isn't work-related. In addition, the employee should be treated in a manner that supports and encourages them back into employment when they are able. There would also be an expectation that the worker would be provided with a healthy and safe work environment, not an environment that exacerbates their injury or illness. But predictably, WorkCover's decision was that my employer had not breached certain sections of the Act – which I of course found quite troubling, given the information I had provided that essentially proved the opposite.

WorkCover's explanation was these areas come under the jurisdiction of WorkSafe, and were referred there, it once again placed me in a state of confusion. I wondered if WorkSafe was a separate entity to the Victorian WorkCover Authority.

After waiting five months and after 17 different WorkSafe staff dealt with my concerns, (yes 17) I found their response disappointing. I was told if I had an issue with this to ring the Complaint Hotline, I had travelled from the top of the tree (Hulls) to the bottom with nothing achieved. I was surprised that given the lapse of time and the complexities of my concerns, that (other than giving an additional statement in October of 2003) I had not been approached regarding further information or clarification, or to supply any documentary evidence to support my claims.

After 12 months, the decision appeared to be that my employer did not breach the Acts because I wasn't entitled to a Return to Work Plan because I had no claim, as it had been rejected. My employer had all the policies and procedures required by the Act. I informed WorkSafe that they would have, but they simply chose not to follow them – this was my point of concern. In the next chapter, you will read my Privacy action, where my employer claimed that as I had a claim, my private life was open to the scrutiny of surveillance.

WorkSafe conducted an inspection at my workplace, not an investigation – they did not access files that would have assisted in the investigation, nor did they interview anyone. In the end, the whole complaint process was flawed and white-washed. WorkCover didn't address the hard questions, and I feel it was because there was a conflict of interest: they are mandated by law as the industry regulator, *but* they are also the defendant in any legal proceedings – even if they hide behind your employer, they are the true defendant, hell-bent on ensuring most injured workers don't get fair compensation. The Model Litigant Guidelines are totally ignored, so why have them in the first place? These guidelines are window dressing to give the impression to the minions that government understands the inequities in the judicial system and have developed guidelines to level the playing field, but this is false as these guidelines are continually disregarded by the players in the system, without recourse.

The Occupational Health and Safety Act states:

> "If a company knew there was an issue and did nothing to prevent further damage, any further bullying or lack of response to your stressors is a clear breach of their duty of care. For legal reasons, it is important to notify your employer of the bullying and your depression – and let them know that it is caused by the stresses at work. All complaints about the cause of the depression (bullying) should also be made in writing, preferably using the grievance procedures for legal reasons (whether you know at this stage that it will go legal or not). From this point, they are now on notice that should they fail to make suitable changes to your work environment or carry out a risk assessment, they are breaking health and safety laws. In most cases, employers are only liable from the time they are made aware of the situation. Because stress is so prevalent and therefore an inherent risk of workplaces, employers should have the onus put back on them to provide evidence as to why they should not be liable for employees' welfare all the time."

I notified my employer verbally, in writing and by the submission of a WorkCover claim of the issues, and their response created further damage by allowing the bullying to escalate.

They clearly breached their duty of care as per the Occupational Health and Safety Act, and they were liable for the breach of their duty, yet nothing happened. I believe this was because of the conflict in WorkCover – any action by them against my former employer for these breaches would have added legitimacy to my claim and this is something that was simply not going to happen.

For many citizens in a democracy, we believe that we can call on our government representatives and that they will help us. Sadly, it seems for most this does not occur, and further adds to the confusion surrounding their plight – they know they are right, but no one in a position of power will assist. Even with this in mind, in October of 2003 I wrote a letter to the then-Minister for WorkCover, Rob Hulls, outlining my concerns with the manner my issues have been dealt with by both my former employer and WorkCover. I was surprised at his response – I was expecting the typical 'thank you for writing...', but his response was in fact, "This is a serious matter and I will comment further when a full investigation has taken place." At long last; recognition! It appeared that he had come to this decision after contacting WorkCover and reviewing my concerns, and found some merit to my claims.

On the Sunday evening following Minister Hulls' letter, I received a phone call from a staff member in his office. He stated he needed to see me to discuss my concerns as soon as possible, as he was under a ministerial direction to see me immediately and had to have a report to the minister by Wednesday of this week. We met a few days later.

Three weeks after that, I was informed that my former supervisor Helen has been asked to resign, and that she had reluctantly done so, making the comment to staff: "You will know why I have left after I do so" or words to that effect. Remember my Christmas card from the Personnel Officer, which stated, "You will be happy to know that Helen has fallen on her sword."

A number of months later, two WorkCover Inspectors visited me at home and took a statement, and in a phone conversation with the Inspector, he said to me "Helen is definitely a bully and she has now gone." He also told me that in their inspection, Wyndham had not breached the Act, as they had the policies and procedures in place to address workplace bullying; I stated that I knew this, but that my concerns were that they did not implement them. His response was that this was not a breach of the Act; the Act required them to have these policies and procedures, but doesn't state they had to be implemented. My head was hurting; I couldn't comprehend this anomaly.

In effect, there was really no investigative process, just an inspection about whether I had been bullied, though this was just a small part of my concern – it was what happened after the submission of my WorkCover claim that was even more concerning. The victimisation I experienced when pursuing a legal right was horrendous.

During the inspectors' visit, I gave them information and the particulars of the victimisation I had experienced, which obviously contained a component of bullying, but this wasn't the sole basis of my concerns. The area of my original concerns that came under their jurisdiction were offences committed against the Occupational Health and Safety Act 1985.

WorkCover's final letter to me with their outcomes did not satisfy me that a fair and reasonable investigation had happened.

In the letter it was said: "The alleged incidents of bullying occurred prior to the year 2000." I asked why this mattered, and in my response at the time I said that if they read the documents in their possession then it was clear that most of the bullying incidents occurred in 2000 and 2001 (not prior to 2000), and did not cease until I left the workplace in April 2002.

The WorkSafe Inspector stated: "Helen no longer works for the Council." I asked how that was relevant, as she didn't bully in a vacuum. My former employer was still vicariously liable for her actions, and it was my understanding that Helen left her employment due to another successful WorkCover claim citing her for harassment.

He also stated: "John, who was also named, is currently overseas" but he had returned. John appeared to take leave at times when something dramatic was going down; he was supposedly on leave when I was suspended, along with all members of my management team and in-house union representatives.

Furthermore, he stated: "Human Resources personnel who were involved at the time are no longer employed at the workplace." I said at the time of the submission of my WorkCover claim that Marianne was the Acting Manager of Organisational Change, which included responsibility for the Human Resource Department. She denied my claims of bullying and didn't follow accepted procedures for investigating my concerns that were relayed to her on a number of occasions. She denied my right to natural justice and procedural fairness when instigating suspension. After my response to the resource officers' allegations were provided, Marianne went on sick leave and resigned from her position – *resigned*, when our employer had an unlimited sick leave policy. It is my understanding that she didn't resign to take up another position elsewhere.

I briefly mentioned earlier how I was told by the ASU Industrial Officer that Marianne had "got into trouble" over her involvement in my suspension. He stated: "The CEO was not happy." Now that should have been the time for the CEO to show true leadership and tell his leadership team (who were plainly in the wrong) to eat a crumb of humble pie, to apologise and get me back to work. A chance to walk his talk. Why he failed to do this is unknown, though I feel now he wishes he had.

My employer was still vicariously liable for the actions of their staff; just because they were no longer employees doesn't afford them protection under the law, especially when senior management would have had to approve those illegal actions. Included in their response they state, 'Copies of the Human Resources Bullying Policy, Grievance and Complaint Resolution and Discrimination and Harassment were provided and reviewed,' and I said I had also been provided with these documents and reviewed their content. I never stated that my employer was guilty of not having these written policies; they simply chose not to follow them. If they had, the situation we subsequently found ourselves in may not have occurred. I asked if they were implying in their letter that as long as an employer had these policies when required for inspection, that they were fulfilling the objectives of the Act, and it was irrelevant whether they were followed in workplace disputes. There was no response to my question – they just chose not answer.

When the WorkCover Inspector visited me in April 2004, he made reference to how accidents happen at work and part of his role with WorkSafe was to assist in the prevention of workplace accidents, and to educate employers. I stated that if my injury had been the result of an accident we would not be talking today. I can accept that accidents happen, but this wasn't an accident, these were intentional acts to create further distress; distress so severe I was unable to continue working. It wasn't possible to dismiss me as there were no grounds on which my employer could have relied. This was a very clear case of workplace bullying.

When the inspector visited my workplace, I was under the impression that this was in the manner of an investigation, not a review of policies and procedures. During his visit to my home, I gave him a confidential file number where he could find many documents that could be used in evidence. I also showed him information in my possession that could assist in an investigation. During a phone conversation in mid-April between the inspector and myself, I gave him the names of staff he would need to speak to who would be aware of the situation. It is my understanding that he only spoke to a temporary junior human resource consultant, someone who would know nothing about the case he was investigating (or, not investigating).

The inspector made comment concerning timeframes, which I believed were irrelevant, and a comment regarding the lack of available corroborative evidence, which again was incorrect. The evidence is available; the Victorian WorkCover Authority (VWA), the insurer and I all possessed a vast array of evidence – the inspector only needed to ask for the evidence he required, but it seemed he didn't actually want the evidence. And just not him – all the players. They had done wrong, but were to be protected, even with giving false evidence under oath. All the evidence in the world is useless if you have nowhere to take it, and this is the situation for many injured workers, and especially so for workers injured by workplace bullying.

The final outcome: "not warranting further investigation." My belief is that my concerns were considered and found to be correct, so they decided they must do nothing, for they couldn't legitimise this claim, no matter how genuine.

I read with interest the 'Application of Public Interest Criteria to Eligible Offences' on WorkCover's website which states having met the criteria for commencing a comprehensive investigation (as set out in part 11 of the Guidelines), an offence will be regarded as serious enough to prosecute where sufficient evidence exists. However, when consideration is given to the public interest criteria in part 14 of the Guidelines, such as the nature, type, and impact of the offence and the level of public concern relating to it, WorkSafe may determine that an eligible offence is a 'relatively minor' offence.

Examples of public interest factors that may be of particular relevance to determining whether an eligible offence is relatively minor include: the seriousness of the alleged offence; the extent of the risk; the actual or potential consequence of the alleged offence (e.g. extent of injury to a person); the prevalence of the alleged offence; whether the nature of the alleged offence is of considerable public concern; and the impact of the alleged offence, in particular, the impact on any person who was injured or exposed to risk and on any other relevant persons (e.g. witnesses to the offence).

Upon application of such criteria, WorkSafe may determine that, in all the circumstances, the offence is relatively minor, and I guess this is where my concerns laid for reasons already explained. The effect the bullying has had on my life is massive to me, minor to them, and I was nobody, not important enough to invoke the public interest, and coupled with the fact that my former employer is a customer of WorkCover and the WorkCover conflict, my former employer was never going to be held accountable. But I say, given the costs expended to defeat my claim by all parties, to deny any compensation, the appalling treatment many injured workers are subjected to, is actually in the public interest.

It is disappointing given the level of public interest in workplace bullying and the maladministration of public funds, that my concerns were considered not warranting further investigation. I do note that changes to both the Accident Compensation Act 1985 and the OH&S Act 2005 assist future injured workers not to fall through the same cracks as I experienced. From 1 July 2002, the law in Victoria changed regarding returning injured workers to work. Further changes were made to employers' obligations effective from 1 March 2004. If my plight helped in any way to contribute to these changes then I have achieved something.

A few years after the Guidance Note on the Prevention of Workplace Bullying was released, there was a review that stated in the section under the heading "Role of Inspectors" that investigations on bullying incidents can last up to six months. Investigating cases are resource- and time-intensive. Along with the emotive content of bullying, a most difficult role for inspectors is to substantiate a bullying claim. The note states that evidence is the key. I provided much evidence, evidence which in my opinion proved the bullying, much of which I have included in this chapter and the previous, and yet it still took years for my case to reach the courts. I say again: all the evidence in the world is useless when you have nowhere to take it, simply because it is not wanted. In my opinion, inspectors don't want to find that a worker has been bullied if they have a current WorkCover claim – if no claim exists and the perpetrator is not a government body there is the possibility of prosecution. I am guessing their position is that the second tier of government prosecuting the third tier is rarely going to happen, because once again the injured worker isn't important enough. It was also stated that the biggest problem for inspectors is dealing with victims' distress, pain and injury. If it's difficult for the inspectors to deal with, just imagine how it is for the victims to deal with it, without support.

It appears the problem lies where an inspector's role is to investigate a potential breach of the OH&S Act while the victim wants resolution, validation and vindication. The duality of the inspector's role lies in their responsibilities to monitor breaches of the OH&S Act and potential prosecution, against their role in assisting organisations in controlling the risk of bullying. The review stated that inspectors were happy with the scope of their role, but quite frustrated by the lack of real power that they perceive it to have. The burden of proof required by the OH&S Act makes it difficult for them to obtain a prosecution. Some of the main criticism about the effectiveness of the Guidance Note has been levelled at WorkSafe inspectors, and this, at least on the surface, is fuelling some of the debate for moving to a Code of Practice.

Stakeholders recognise that there are some WorkSafe staff and inspectors who see bullying as a legitimate OH&S issue. However, there is a perception that there are still some parts of WorkSafe and some inspectors who do not recognise bullying as a Health and Safety issue, and therein lies the problem. Unions feel that the WorkSafe Inspectors would not adequately address workplace bullying until there was a Code of Practice. It was asserted that the Code of Practice would send a message to all of the inspectors that this was an important OH&S issue that warranted real addressing as any other OH&S hazard.

Unions are dissatisfied with how WorkSafe has implemented the Guidance Note, and argue that to fix this the next step needs to be upgrading the Guidance Note to a Code of Practice. On the other hand, an employer group mentioned that as this issue is outside the norm for WorkSafe inspectors; raising the legal status of the document may only make it more difficult for WorkSafe inspectors to enforce. Now it is over a number of years since this was discussed, and there appears to still be no Code of Practice.

When a WorkCover claim is submitted and accepted, either by the employer/insurer or successful action in the Magistrates' Court, the injured worker after many years of waiting can make a claim for compensation for their injury. However, employer 'negligence' has to be shown as the cause of injury for a compensation claim to be successful. It is at this time when 'foreseeability' is of major importance.

If the employer can prove there was no possible way they could have been aware of the danger of whatever caused the injury, then a claim of no foreseeability can defeat a claim of negligence, but if it can be proved the employer knew of the danger then there is foreseeability and negligence which can lead to a successful compensation claim. This is the precise reason why John denied he knew I was ill, because if he knew and then behaved the way he did then this proves both foreseeability and negligence and this usually leads to a successful compensation hearing.

In effect, my claim was never about being unable to work because of physical illness, but because of the psychological illness caused by the bullying. How can an injured bullied worker inform their employer prior breakdown that they are breaking down because of bullying? Why would they give the abusers a 'heads up' that their behaviour is working and having a negative impact on the worker? The workers informing occurs when the breakdown occurs, or with the submission of a WorkCover claim, which is after the fact. This then makes it difficult to prove foreseeability because the employer is never going to admit they bullied the worker into breakdown or admit they knew this behaviour was detrimental to the worker's mental health, because to do so once again enlivens foreseeability. This point was lost by my lawyers, but more on that later.

I'm not sure if WorkCover believed my evidence in response to the allegations against me, but in hindsight their main criteria at that time was to deny liability, as to admit it would have given my claim authenticity and possible recourse at a hearing for compensation. But the possibility that Helen was asked to leave certainly supports my view that they did. In my view, I was suffering from the suppression of dissent; an attempt to stop or penalise a person who makes a public statement or does something that is seen as a threat to a powerful interest group, such as a government, corporation or profession. Typical actions include ostracism, harassment, censorship, forced job transfer, reprimands and dismissal. Suppression is action against dissent that doesn't involve physical violence. I was to suffer because of my dissent for the next 20 years, especially during my legal years.

I believe without doubt there is a strong need for an organisation such as WorkCover, one that does valuable work in ensuring workplaces are physically safe. Unfortunately for me and many other injured workers, they also create a lot of suffering and add to an injured workers already severe sense of despair. As my experience was many years ago, I can only hope that things are different today.

I should say here that many complaints are made by injured workers about the WorkCover insurers, and also the independent medical examiners, and I have little doubt they're valid, but thankfully for me—since Dush Shan—I have been treated well over the years, with care and compassion on most occasions. In nearly all written reports the examiners believed me, and to me that is validation.

By mid-2005, I was still feeling unwell. Bullying as we now know is a very personal attack on your life, and that's why we all get so damn ill because of it. I knew and understood my physical injuries, but my emotional injuries were more complicated. I had to do more reading to understand what it was, and finally I had an answer: Post-Traumatic Stress Disorder (though I prefer to call it Post-Traumatic Distress Disorder). The insurer accepted liability for my physical injuries and for my PTSD, and has been contributing to my medical and like expenses for many years now.

I was hopeful that after my experience and with the passage of time Work-Cover would improve how they operate, but sadly after reading Ombudsman Glass's 2016 report 'Investigation into the Management of Complex Workers Compensation Claims', very little has improved for the majority of serious and long-term injured worker claims. The current system fails some particularly vulnerable people.

The investigation examined complex and often extended claims across different industries, roles and injuries (both mental and physical) to assess whether agents unreasonably denied liability or terminated claims, whether agents took such actions in order to obtain financial rewards available under the contract with WorkSafe, and if WorkSafe provides effective oversight of the agents and their claims management processes. The report stated that Victoria's workers' compensation scheme must be recalibrated to ensure that complex claims are resolved in a fair and timely manner. My experience was definitely not one of being fair and timely, and I was disappointed to see that 15 years later nothing had changed.

Ms Glass, the Victorian Ombudsman, said "The overall system is not broken, but the problems we identified in complex cases—some 20 per cent of the overall claims—go beyond a few isolated examples of bad behaviour. They cannot simply be explained away as a few bad apples spoiling the barrel." I agree the system works well in minor or catastrophic claims, but is broken for serious injury complex claims, which may become more complex with the passage of time and unsupportive behaviour of both WorkCover and the employer.

The report found agents were cherry-picking evidence to support a decision to reject or terminate a claim—as little as one line in a medical report—while disregarding overwhelming evidence to the contrary. It was found that the Independent Medical Examiners (IMEs), whose opinions agents use to support their decision making on compensation, received selective, incomplete or inaccurate information. There was also evidence of decisions being influenced by financial incentives to terminate claims.

"In effect, we found cases in which agents were working the system to delay and deny seriously injured workers the financial compensation to which they were entitled – and which they eventually received if they had the support, stamina and means to pursue their cases through the dispute process," said Ms Glass.

The report went on to say that action must be taken to address the complex end of the system where terminations are rewarded. WorkSafe needs to examine its incentives and the use of IMEs to ensure the system rewards sustainable decisions and to target its oversights accordingly. The process for resolving disputes also demands careful reconsideration, as it is in the interests of workers, employers and the public at large that the resolution of claims should be both timely and fair. My 'timely' was 10 years and my 'fair' never eventuated, as you'll read in the following chapters.

In the second report of December 2019, as a follow-up to her first, and after receiving roughly 800 complaints the previous year, Ombudsman Glass states the following: "Many of the decisions and actions we saw were not only unjust, unreasonable and wrong. Some were downright immoral and unethical."

In a 2019 ABC Radio interview on the topic of her reports, she said, "Fairness has gone out the window."

Ms Glass also said, "The cases we investigated are not merely files, numbers or claims; they involved people's lives, and the human cost should never be forgotten." From my experience, WorkCover often fails to consider the human cost: we are just a means to someone's end.

This ombudsman is really 'worth her salt' and isn't just the usual window dressing – Glass is the real deal: she investigates without fear or favour. If we had more like her in our state's statutory positions and in the judiciary, what a wonderful, fairer world it would be.

I have set out below some comments I came across after reading a newspaper article regarding workplace bullying to give you another perspective rather than just my own. I repeat them here without their knowledge, but as they were made in a public forum, I am hopeful this is agreeable to them. I have removed surnames.

Karen of Bendigo *Posted at 11:05 PM April 08, 2011*
My greatest concern about Brodie's Law is – who will administer it? I understand the Gatekeeper will be WorkSafe. If this is so, there will be no prosecutions, no convictions, no jail sentences, as WorkSafe, who appear to be above the law, will use their powerful position to make

sure no case of workplace bullying ever gets classified as "Serious Bullying" unless (perhaps) the victim dies or suicides – then it is too late for the victim. Just try getting a workplace bullying injury claim past their 'Serious Injury Certificate' blockade. The way I see it, if the injury is not determined as Serious, the cause – bullying – will never get air space. It is my opinion that the planned enquiry should have gone ahead to allow public contributions from both professional groups and private individuals with well thought out submissions open to public scrutiny. Instead we have a law rushed through which may well end up being totally useless to victims of serious bullying. Bullying is an insidious behaviour practised by the lowest scum of our society. No manners, no conscience, no compassion, no accountability for their actions. Will this change? I have serious doubts.

Zee Posted at 11:09 PM April 08, 2011
It isn't surprising that bullying is out of control in Australia, when you see it at a federal and state level weekly with politicians bullying one another. And I doubt anything will change as many Australians think of bullying as "just a part of growing up."

Stuart of Sydney Posted at 11:40 PM April 08, 2011
Too little, always beyond 'too late.' too late. Too cowardly. Too typical. Go away, die.

Stuart of Sydney Posted at 12:05 AM April 09, 2011
It's not 'BULLYING.' To continue to call it that, is denying that brutal assault, whether mental or physical, has been foundationally denied, ignored, and, by action, and inaction, fostered and promoted the 'bullies,' 'hunt' their victims/targets. The Authorities are scared of them, nothing concrete is done, no results achieved. That's all.

Quiche of Western Suburbs Posted at 1:18 AM April 09, 2011
What kind of society are we becoming when a little boy loses his mum and brother and then is bullied and needs to move away. Shame on them and their parents, where has human compassion gone? Blake stay strong, you are better than them And let us not forget all victims/survivors of this horrid behaviour. We all deserve respect and dignity,

whether at school or at work "We will never walk away from taking on workplace bullies where it can be proved they've destroyed someone's life at work," Mr Birt said. Now Mr Birt you know this is not true! Had Brody submitted a WorkCover claim, WorkSafe would never have prosecuted the offenders; she would have been the one to have her character assassinated, by those funded to help. Ask a bullied worker and they will tell you that WorkCover spins it around and the injured worker becomes the offender and the bully becomes the victim just read a few court cases to enlighten understanding. This system does not provide justice, but protects the bullies, because we must ensure the viability of WorkCover who pay fair compensation NOT. This is a cash cow for government, read annual reports and see who the real winners are and it is not injured workers.

Dr Doug of Heathcote *Posted at 9:34 AM April 09, 2011*
The proposed new bullying law is a sickening joke for psychological bullying victims. We are told WorkSafe will make the decision whether bullying has occurred before they refer it to the police. In the past 10 years WorkSafe has never recommended even one case of psychological bullying for prosecution. In the same 10 years they have only sent a handful of cases for prosecution and they all have been for physical bullying cases. If there is not blood on the floor WorkSafe is just not interested enough to even bother. If WorkSafe does not see the blood and the bruises, then in their eyes, there is no injury. You have to die before WorkSafe or the Government takes any notice. There are many, many, many victims walking around with their lives in ruins.

I have tried to get politicians and WorkSafe involved, but they're just not interested. It isn't even possible to get the media interested in WorkSafe's failures. As I write my story in 2020, I ponder whether or not things have changed. At least mainstream media is starting to sit up and take notice because of the Victorian Ombudsman, Deborah Glass, and we the survivors, thank you.

FIVE

Privacy Problems

I read with interest the public lecture by then-Victorian Privacy Commissioner, Mr Paul Chadwick, and agreed with it wholeheartedly. The lecture was held at Melbourne University in 2002. Briefly, what most appealed to me was the following:

> "Privacy is essential to our sense of self. Privacy has several dimensions, including privacy of the body. This dimension is critical to dignity: don't touch me unless I say so; respect my physical person. Privacy of the home; the home is special in privacy law. It is a sanctuary where we are free from the world's scrutiny, where we can relax our public faces and 'be ourselves'. It is a place of intimacy and security. It reflects us through the ways we organise it and decorate it. We like to control who enters and who communicates with us there. Privacy from surveillance; not being spied on is perhaps the best understood dimension of privacy, and finally; information privacy is about personal information. Control over who knows what about us, for what purposes, and to whom it is disclosed, is the main concern of this dimension of privacy.
> Privacy is for natural persons, not governments. Privacy – it's real. It's a right. It's the law."

Privacy Problems

And with this, I began my search to understand what 'privacy' really meant.

The Magistrates' Court hearing that accepted my WorkCover claim was held in February 2003, and my main memories of this were how much I disagreed with my former manager's testimony. But over the years I have learnt that lying under oath is very common, and there are very few occasions where, even if it can be proved, action is taken against those providing false testimony.

My belief has always been that perjury is a serious matter, but apparently not so if you are an ordinary person. Politicians may be held to account as there are many vested interests attempting to bring them down, and any hint of impropriety is strongly scrutinised, but we ordinary folk and the legal profession are usually exempt.

I recall a barrister making a comment to the magistrate regarding the car I drove. I felt the question was quite strange and irrelevant, and wondered how they knew what kind of car I drove. I pondered this for some time, and wondered if I had ever been under surveillance; was I being watched by my former employer, their insurer or WorkCover, or was I simply becoming paranoid? As it turned out, it was most likely all three, as my employer and the insurer who works for WorkCover all had a vested interest, because when I submitted a WorkCover claim they were in effect one organisation trying to thwart my claim and any financial benefit I might've been entitled to receive.

According to the insurer's Claim Manual, it is permitted to have injured workers under surveillance if it is believed the worker is committing fraud, or if there is no other way you can acquire information you need to monitor the claim.

If an injured worker is in receipt of weekly payments and is found to be participating in activities that are in conflict with the said injuries, such as working or taking part in sports, then the claim may be a rort. Surveillance in this instant may be justified, but I was not in receipt of weekly payments and up to this time had not received any financial benefits, so there was no fraud. The second ambit of "there is no other way you can acquire information you need to monitor the claim" was also not relevant to me, as I had never been requested to provide information they sought, nor had I refused to provide such information. So technically they had no legal right to have me under surveillance.

During 2002, I really had no choice but to resign my position, as my former employer had made no or very little attempts to resolve our dispute. My medical advice was to resign; if I had stayed, I would have been harassed into a total breakdown. I was told on two occasions I was not required to attend work, and yet in defence of my 'privacy complaint' my former management team stated that surveillance was necessary to ensure that I was not working.

Negligent employers or employees are not placed under the same scrutiny or suffer the loss of their basic rights to privacy. The perpetrators' rights are not rescinded, nor are they subjected to surveillance to check the validity of their aspersions regarding the injured worker.

While legislation restricts exploration of the victim's past in rape and sexual assault cases, an injured worker's past is explored, and their personal history and psychiatric evaluations are made public, including to their employers. If the events in the workplace are not regarded as sufficient to have caused the injury it seems reasonable to investigate the potential contribution of the worker's past. To investigate the worker and publicise their personal details in advance of investigating the facts of a claim is, in my opinion, a violation of privacy.

A related issue is that these disclosures may prejudice the claimant's future employment prospects when in some circumstances it would be more appropriate to label the claimant a victim of crime than with psychiatric diagnoses. A legal response which focuses on the facts of a claim is needed for this reason, and the injuring party should suffer social consequence, not the injured party.

Under common law, an employer is under a duty to protect workers from workplace bullying. This duty exists in tort law – for example, negligence: failure to provide a safe workplace, and as an implied term in the employment contract that "the employer would not, without reasonable cause, destroy or seriously damage the relationship of trust and confidence between employer and worker."

On occasions, I believe the use of surveillance is for more sinister purposes, as in my case, for I had never committed a crime, always been honest at work, never pilfered and everything I had stated through the process was true. But remember: I was guilty of being innocent, and so something was needed to find me guilty of something. Having that 'something' turn up on surveillance would be a godsend to them.

I read of a case where an injured worker under surveillance was recorded going into a motel room with a woman who was not his wife. Infidelity is not a

Privacy Problems

crime, but would you want your spouse to know this? This activity did not alone suggest any rorting, but these are 'silver bullets' for the insurer, who while negotiating any financial settlement will make sure you know they have this video and will use it in court, so you would be silly not to settle, and for an amount less than is fair. The gentleman concerned did take his compensation claim to court and the motel video was used, and from memory he was unsuccessful. No compensation, and probably no wife.

After the comment in the Magistrates' Court, I decided I wanted to follow up on whether I was indeed under surveillance, and so I made a Freedom of Information request to the insurer for a copy of any surveillance reports, videos, etc. I wanted to ensure all the surveillance undertaken during the years 2002 and 2003 was legal and carried out according to law.

In discussions with the Privacy Officer of Cambridge Integrated Services I was told, "No surveillance carried out by our Agency or any request from our Panel of Solicitors for this date and month. No report and no record of payment for surveillance."

Later I requested confirmation that this information was indeed correct. Surprisingly, they wrote to me stating I could not have access to these documents and then proceeded to list all the documents denied to me. That was very helpful, as I now had dates and types of documents in their possession and it meant that their statement was clearly untrue. I then specifically requested under the Freedom of Information Act a copy of the listed documents. This was denied me, and on appeal to WorkCover it was denied again. I was still not working and had too much time on my hands and decided to follow this up.

In early 2004, I referred my Freedom of Information request to VCAT for judicial review of WorkCover's refusal, and a directions hearing was set for April. At this directions hearing, a Tribunal hearing date was set for the 15 June.

Two weeks later, on 31 May, it was a busy day for me – it was my son Dan's 17th birthday and I was organising a family dinner and shopping for his gifts. As I turned the corner of our street, I could see a large parcel at my front door, and thought it must be a gift for Dan. Upon arriving at my front door, I noticed the parcel was addressed to me and the sender was the insurer. I opened the express post parcel and the contents revealed numerous surveillance reports, photographs and videos. I was surprised and quite shocked. I believed my FOI request was reasonable and fair and within the law, but a Tribunal might well have decided to award costs if it was of the opinion it was fair to do so. I put in a request for 'costs' and this was successful. I donated the payment to charity, as I was never after money, only validation.

I was under surveillance on various days from my resignation date of June 2002 to the following January by an investigations firm named MPOL. An investigator must have travelled from Melbourne for these 19 occasions.

In many of the reports of these dates the investigator wrote "Subject not observed," "Subject at St Vincent's Hospital," "Subject at IMA appointment," "Subject picks up car," "Watched through window" "Subject seen inside home," "Subject at front door." "Subject gets son from school," "Subject at supermarket for 32 mins," and in one Surveillance report it is stated, "Subject walked across the road to a business premises at 224 Clarendon St, with the signage specialising in business analysis. She entered the building and remained inside out of view for just over an hour" and "She visited two medical clinics and a business analysis premises."

The video for this date also shows the ABS building in Clarendon Street, and I believe that part of the reason for continued surveillance was due to the fact that it was reported that I was visiting a business analysis specialist, when in actuality I was having a coffee at the café next door.

And another: "She shows no sign of stress in peak hour traffic, nor did she show any sign throughout the day." I did not know the investigator was in the car with me; he must have been hiding in the back seat, for how else does another driver make an assessment that another driver is not stressed? Is it because the stressed driver is driving safely and obeying road rules, and not driving erratically or speeding? If I had been driving in a dangerous manner I feel confident that this would have been used against me. Injured workers cannot win; I could lose my claim because I drove responsibly. As a matter of fact, I took three attempts to park my car because I felt stressed, but no mention is made of this in his report.

And another: "She is in a shop looking around."

On my way home from Melbourne I dropped into an optometrist in Werribee, as the glasses I had bought there had an arm which was crooked which made them uncomfortable to wear. There were a few people in a queue waiting for service and I joined this queue. I was not looking around the shop as if wanting to make a purchase – I stood quietly in the queue looking ahead. I feel his report was to make it appear that I was 'shopping', and that me shopping would imply nothing was wrong with me, and thus grounds to deny the claim. But strangely, he had taken video of this that showed me quietly standing in a queue with no 'looking around'.

How riveting my life was! Not. The investigator sat outside my home, up the street or around the corner, and I was surprised I never suspected I was being followed. He must have been good at this job, or I was just not paranoid enough. I know it was a 'he' as I could see some of him in the videos. He wore the tiny camera either on his cap or on his glasses and it was quite strange to see yourself 'shopping.' Lucky I didn't hide a can of baked beans or a tube of toothpaste under my coat, as this would've been a silver bullet for them and blackmail for me.

There were days he sat outside my home for up to 11 hours. How boring for him – if I had known I would have offered him to come in and have a cup of tea. No 'sinister' activities to be seen, nothing devious to be used against my credibility, just the usual activities of an injured worker.

The only information gained from surveillance used in the Magistrates' Court was that I purchased a new car – not totally correct, as the car was four years old when I bought it. They said that I renovated my bathroom, but this is also incorrect: the tiles and flooring were replaced due to water damage. The cost of replacing the flooring was covered by our household insurance policy with GIO Insurance, who also happened to be the insurer managing my Work-Cover claim.

Given the stated activities in the surveillance reports, it could be seen early on that my lifestyle reflected the actual injuries stated in my rejected Work-Cover claim. I believed surveillance was instigated not to prove fraud, as at all material times I was not in receipt of any funds, but to invade my privacy in an attempt to find an activity—any activity would do—that would discredit my integrity and be used to attack my character. The insurer and WorkCover had enough evidence to support the validity of my claim prior to surveillance taking place, or soon after the first periods of surveillance took place. However, the surveillance had continued.

When I had appointments with Independent Medical Assessors arranged by the insurer, I was followed from my home to various Melbourne locations for medical assessment and treatment. In one Investigation Summary report covering a three-day period of surveillance, the investigator makes a suggestion of entrapment: "During the period of surveillance, the subject was quite inactive and left home on only one occasion when she drove to pick up a child from school. It is recommended that a medical appointment be arranged in order to observe the subject away from her home. Due to the subject's inactivity, no video coverage was obtained."

In regards to this statement, WorkCover responded the comment was unsolicited and that the suggestion was not acted upon. The surveillance that I was subjected to raises a number of issues in relation to privacy – in particular, for the WorkCover system to remain viable there must be a full investigation of the authenticity of claims before payments are made for such claims. However, such an investigation should never entail the total loss of privacy, particularly when other evidence substantiates the claim and the surveillance is providing no evidence of a false claim.

Loss of privacy should not be an additional price the worker must pay for being injured at work. The worst of criminals appear to have a greater right to privacy than law-abiding citizens who through no fault of their own find themselves having to exercise their legal and human rights by accessing the judicial system.

By doing so, it is required that the most intimate details of their lives are aired in court in an attempt to discredit the injured worker. These details are included in the judgement which is displayed on the court's website. Past practice of archiving court files meant interested parties had to apply and travel to the court for access, but now with the internet, court files are only four clicks away in the comfort of your own home from anywhere on the globe. This is lauded as 'open justice', but for the injured it is very different – it can amount to open injustice. It is accepted that the law must be seen to be done, but I see no benefit in not respecting the privacy of innocent workers.

This legal form of defamation may have long-lasting repercussions for the injured worker. If the title fits, as it would in bullying, it may be more appropriate to label the injured worker a victim of crime. In the past, a period in the stocks was shortly over and confined to your local village, but now once you pursue your legal rights you are in the stocks forever, not just in your local village but throughout the world.

I believe in order to publish a judgement on the internet, certain criteria should be met, such as informing the injured worker that the judgement will be published online, and giving them the choice of anonymity. This way, the law is seen to be effective, others learn from the rationalisations of judges, the common law evolves and the brave individual can heal. Once you initiate action to protect your legal and human rights, you actually have more taken from you. It is a very strange feeling to be under 'legal' surveillance through the windows of your home in Australia; a democratic society.

It is my understanding and hope that all citizens have some rights to privacy. It would appear that due to my submission of a WorkCover claim, my rights to privacy were completely rescinded. I would also contend that the surveillance directed at me was excessive and that this surveillance was undertaken at the bequest of either WorkCover or my former employer under the guise of being necessary for the management of my WorkCover claim. By this time my former employer must have known that everything I said had happened did happen – that I was bullied, harassed, mobbed, victimised, intimidated, and discriminated against, and they had no evidence to prove I 'deserved' this. They needed something to justify their behaviour, and so surveillance was their only hope, their 'holy grail' that may expose something which could be used in court to discredit me or something that could be used to encourage a settlement. Of course, there was nothing that they could use to this end, and surveillance was never raised in any court proceedings. That says it all.

Once again I needed answers, and so started reading other court cases that involved insurers carrying out video surveillance on injured workers. Of some of the cases I read where surveillance was carried out, they all related directly or indirectly to the continuance of weekly payments and medical and like expenses. At all of my relevant times I was not receiving any payments under the WorkCover system, as my claim had been rejected. I briefly scanned 27 reported cases and found 26 had been subjected to less surveillance than me; my case attracted more scrutiny than others, and I now believe this was because my claim was genuine, because I was genuine.

My husband was a member of the Australian CPA and received monthly magazines, and I flipped through them on occasion. I did find an article of interest regarding workplace relations, that stated, "Commission reinstates workers spied on by employer. The Commission also ruled that the use of video surveillance may have been an improper use of public money and that the employer's conduct in carrying out this investigation should be referred to the Health Administration Corporation and the Attorney-General's department."

Yet it seems that when the employer is technically a government department and in concert with another government department, it is okay to spy on employees or former employees under the Accident Compensation Act. Even at the cost of thousands of dollars—and in my case $15,000—for evidence of nothing which would enable WorkCover to deny my claim.

I have never breached any Act or any employer Code of Conduct, Policy or Procedure. I have never committed an illegal act or any act of dishonesty, nor have I ever behaved in an unethical or unprofessional manner. There was no evidence of any wrongdoing that could be used to discredit me. Surveillance was used as a costly fishing expedition, simply because I was guilty of being innocent and this would be evident in the Magistrates' Court hearing.

After receipt of all these photos, written reports and videos, I submitted my concerns to Privacy Victoria regarding a breach of the Information Privacy Act. In the Claims Manual used by the Agents of WorkCover it states that "Surveillance should only be used if other less intrusive methods of investigation have been considered and have been assessed to be ineffective and inadequate or have been tried and found to be inconclusive." And that "surveillance should only be used if there is adequate evidence to suggest the worker may be misrepresenting their disability, claiming excessive disabilities, malingering or involved in the commission of a fraud." I do not believe there was any evidence that suggested that I might have been guilty of any one of these categories.

Additionally, "The use of video film must be authorised by supervisors of the agent, and restricted to cases if there is clear evidence that it is justified and necessary." At no time have I been informed of what the 'clear evidence' was that proved in my case that surveillance was justified and necessary. And finally, "Determining the necessity for conducting surveillance, surveillance should only be used: where the benefits arising from obtaining relevant information by surveillance are considered to outweigh to a substantial degree the intrusion on the privacy of the claimant." In theory, this sounds ethical and respectful, but in actuality I feel it is ignored when it suits.

There were no benefits arising from the surveillance I was subjected to that were meaningful in any way. Except for the 'new car' and 'bathroom renovations', the information gained was not used in the Magistrates' Court proceedings, which basically proves the evidence collected by surveillance did not outweigh the intrusion of my privacy. Early in the surveillance period it should have been evident that the benefits arising out of using surveillance were minor or non-existent.

My WorkCover claim was submitted in November 2000 and rejected in December 2000. WorkCover confirmed in February 2004 that as my claim was

Privacy Problems

rejected, I was not entitled to the usual provisions provided to accepted claims – for example a Return to Work Plan, an occupational rehabilitation program and the support of a Return to Work co-ordinator.

As my claim was rejected, I therefore did not have a claim, and if I did not have a claim how could surveillance be legally sanctioned? As stated in the Claims Manual Section, "Surveillance investigations are a claims management tool."

I assert that given WorkCover's response outlined above, there was no claim to manage, therefore no right to surveillance.

Amazingly, WorkCover state that it is unlikely that I would have been aware of surveillance at the time it was carried out, because I had said that I first became aware of the surveillance during the course of the Magistrates' Court hearing, and I did not complain to WorkCover about surveillance at any time prior to the hearing. I find this comment quite interesting – does it imply that because I was unaware of surveillance, my privacy was not compromised? How could I raise my concerns prior to knowing I had them?

I first became aware of the possibility that someone had been watching me during the course of the Magistrates' Court hearing, due to the irrelevant nature of some of the questions put to me while on the stand. This is when I first became suspicious about surveillance and I didn't know I was under surveillance, or the extent of it until May 2004; I did not complain to Work-Cover about surveillance prior to the hearing, simply because I had no knowledge of it at this time. As WorkCover used some information (the 'new' car) gathered by surveillance at the Magistrates' Court hearing, they were under an obligation to disclose this during discovery, but they did not.

What surprised me the most was the surveillance conducted through my kitchen window, and WorkCover's response was enlightening. They noted that no surveillance was conducted or surveillance footage collected on the relevant date. The MPOL agent apparently only conducted a 'spot check', noting the vehicles that were present at my address. The agent also recorded that my husband and I "were viewed to be moving about inside the kitchen." According to WorkCover, this 'spot check' is not surveillance. Vehicles are noted, you are watched moving about in your home, but this is not classified as surveillance...!

WorkCover went on to state that the agent's view of me and my husband was from his vehicle. He had the same view of the rear of the premises as any other driver or pedestrian would have had. Are they saying that surveillance from a vehicle is not surveillance? I don't believe it's possible that someone sitting in their vehicle some distance from my home can view activity in my second-storey kitchen. My home is situated on a hill, and the rear of my home looks down upon the road below, more than 100m from the fence line. Houses and many parkland trees that obscure a view into my kitchen border this road. Also, from the road you could not distinguish if this room was a kitchen or some other living area, but the word 'kitchen' was recorded, so the agent must have been very close and not in his vehicle all the way down the hill. It's possible the agent viewed my home from an elevated vacant block up the road using a telescopic device, as he had on previous occasions, when a video was taken from this vantage point with me arriving home with my 'new' car.

I don't know if all identifying information collected through surveillance was collected in a lawful, reasonable and appropriate manner. That was the purpose of my privacy complaint: to have an independent body assess my concerns. Another point I would like to make, is that as Herbert, Geer & Rundle were the legal panel firm co-ordinating the surveillance activity, why was Minter Ellison conducting the FOI case before VCAT? At this time, Minter Ellison were not listed as approved panel solicitors. Coincidently, they happened to be my ex-employer's legal representatives and were their representatives in my discrimination claim. There may well be an explanation why two different law firms were used for the same issue, but I believe it must have been my former employer who requested the surveillance take place.

The response from WorkCover has never satisfied me that this degree of extensive surveillance was justified; they stated it was because my claim had significant potential, but if this was to be truly believed then why then was my claim rejected and why did it remain rejected? Accepting the claim would have saved much grief, time and money for all involved, and would have had a far more positive outcome.

WorkCover attempted to justify surveillance on the basis that, in their view, my claim and the Magistrates' Court proceedings had significant potential on the basis that I was seeking weekly payments of compensation to date and continuing. Yet at no time was I seeking weekly payments of compensation, as I had already been paid for this period and my employer knew this, as they approved such payment.

My former employer was attempting to use section 82(2A) of the Accident Compensation Act as their defence to my claim. This Section states: "Compensation is not payable in respect of an injury consisting of an illness or disorder of the mind caused by stress unless the stress did not arise wholly or predominantly from reasonable action taken in a reasonable manner by the employer to transfer, demote, discipline, redeploy, retrench or dismiss the worker; or a decision of the employer, on reasonable grounds, not to award or to provide promotion, reclassification or transfer of, or leave of absence or benefit in connection with the employment, to the worker; or an expectation of the taking of such action or making of such a decision." Many claims have been lost under this section, because in my opinion it was written purely as an escape route for employers. Staff who bully can use the above actions as tactics to bully without accountability.

WorkCover argued that given the nature of my claim and of my allegations, and the elements of the section 82 (2A) defences, they were entitled to obtain and rely upon surveillance in order to test my credibility and to adduce evidence of my level of incapacity or impairment. My allegations were proven correct and section 82(2A) was not successful as a defence. My employer was fully aware of the treatment I was subjected to and should have reasonably known that this treatment could potentially cause anyone incapacity or impairment.

I understand why in some circumstances surveillance is undertaken, but in my case why did it continue over a long period of time when earlier surveillance did not provide any evidence? Why did my credibility need to be tested over and over again? There had never been any occasion during my period of employment where my credibility or integrity had been called into question. And what was the surveillance they relied on? After driving my husband's and daughter's cars for a few months, I bought a pre-loved car with my termination pay. I don't know or understand why this was so important to them. What did it prove?

The WorkCover system is the only legal arena where you are guilty until proven innocent. From my experience, it appears to be a system that has no desire to prove injury and innocence, but will go to extraordinary lengths to find evidence that can be spun into guilt.

To use surveillance to adduce levels of incapacity or impairment will be highly effective when a WorkCover claim is one of physical injury, but how surveillance assists in adducing whether someone is anxious or has a psychological impairment would be incredibly difficult. Many people with these conditions go about their daily business like 'healthy' people. No one can make a diagnosis of an injured worker's level of incapacity or impairment simply by looking at them or observing them in public places – some injuries aren't visible.

Further in their defence, WorkCover responded that during the period of surveillance, the claim and the proceedings were both on foot, and I was seeking substantial arrears and ongoing weekly payments of compensation. I was not seeking weekly payments at this time – I wasn't aware that I *could* claim weekly payments after I had resigned. And I was not seeking substantial arrears, as I had already been paid my full salary up to the date of resignation; my employer knew this and surely would have informed WorkCover that I had already received full payment for 82 weeks. Given this, my legal advisors at this time believed my claim was of little financial value, and yet WorkCover were stating that my claim had 'significant potential', so obviously WorkCover knew something my lawyer did not.

If WorkCover had information that led them to believe my claim had significant potential then they must have been of the belief that my claim had merit. They could have used this information to objectively reassess my claim and possibly avoid expensive legal costs down the road. Another justification put forward by WorkCover was that there were significant discrepancies between medical reports, a view in which I must disagree: there was but one unsupportive medical report (from Dr Shan), compared to nine supportive medical reports from a variety of medical practitioners. An undeniable and clear majority.

WorkCover cannot substantiate the need for surveillance on this point; surveillance was an exercise in clutching at straws. But just in case Privacy Victoria could be coerced, WorkCover provided all my medical reports to them, which I believe was unnecessary for the complaint at hand, and another breach of my privacy. I am guessing it was hoped that in some way Privacy Victoria, upon reading my medical reports, would be convinced that surveillance was indeed necessary. WorkCover was wrong again.

WorkCover state they are required to investigate claims lodged under the Accident Compensation Act and it would be an abrogation of their statutory responsibilities to simply accept without question information submitted by injured workers. But remember what was stated by WorkCover when my claim was initially denied: as I did not have a claim, I had no right to the supports offered by WorkCover. But I apparently had a claim for the purposes of surveillance? When is an 'investigation' not an investigation? I feel sure most in our community would agree that a claim should not be accepted without question, but how far should this go – at what point in time does WorkCover cross the line?

In my situation, WorkCover did not accept without question the information submitted by the injured worker, or information submitted by a number of medical professionals, who all diagnosed the same condition, with the same causation. Not to accept information simply submitted by an injured worker is understandable, but not to accept the consensus diagnosis of a number of medical professionals, their own Independent Medical Examiners included, is at the very least questionable. Yet at this point in my story, WorkCover had enough evidence in their possession to support the claim to be genuine.

I had resigned in April 2002 from my employment effective from June 2002, and no further WorkCover Certificates were presented after April 2002. I was of the belief that as I had resigned from work, certificates of incapacity were no longer required, as there was no employment to be incapacitated from. It was only a day or so before the hearing in February 2003, that my lawyer added weekly payments to my claim to cover the period from July to November. Why this was done, I do not know. Surveillance took place from June 2002 until January 2003, and commenced well before the claim for weekly payments was made in February 2003. I had been told on two occasions that I was not required to attend work, and yet in defence of my privacy complaint, WorkCover or my former employer stated that surveillance was necessary to ensure that I was not working.

WorkCover went on to say in their view that it was "necessary for the surveillance footage to have been collected for the purposes of defending the Magistrates' Court complaint. Surveillance footage was not collected for the purposes of investigating your WorkCover claim or determining whether it should be accepted or rejected." My response to this is that I find this statement contradictory; surely the motive for surveillance is investigatory.

The purpose of the Magistrates' Court proceedings was to have my claim accepted. The only information gathered in surveillance, which was used in court, was that I bought a car. I don't see how this assisted WorkCover's defence. Their barrister did say in his closing address to the court that my undisclosed discrimination settlement—and by inference to my luxury car—showed that I was not financially embarrassed. Perhaps he was insinuating that I should pay for all my own work-related medical expenses, as I had the means to do so. The magistrate made no response to the barrister's comment, and nor should he have – surely an injured worker's rights under law do not depend on the make of car they drive or how 'well off' they appear.

At the end of November, I received a letter from the Privacy Commissioner which stated: "I have reviewed the file including relevant aspects of Cambridge's response and your recent letter and I have decided that it is not appropriate to decline to entertain the complaint under section 29 of the Information Privacy Act 2000." At last, a government regulator that acted with integrity! I had experienced so little of this and felt the Privacy Commissioner to be a person of great integrity, conducting his position without 'fear or favour'. Unfortunately, he left his position not long after this.

Next in the dispute process was conciliation of the complaint, which was unsuccessful, and early in the new-year the complaint was referred to VCAT for determination.

In May, WorkCover's legal representative requested my participation in mediation of the complaint, and I agreed, as I knew this was part of the legal process and I had no real choice – not to do so would have been looked upon unkindly by the Tribunal. I feel that mediation is a tool used by those in power to hide bad behaviour and stop it from becoming public; I have not had good experiences around mediation, as there is always an imbalance of power, and the less powerful are rarely satisfied with the outcome. But I had no desire to take it to hearing – I had made my point and had it investigated by Privacy Victoria, who had found in my favour, and that was enough for me.

I entered the mediation room with an experienced barrister, Paul, someone who in a previous career had been a psychiatrist, so I felt in very good hands. I felt any tricks played would be expertly handled on my behalf by Paul, a handsome man, tall and lanky with a voice that was both authoritative and kind. I was glad I had briefed a barrister, as WorkCover had five agency and legal representatives in attendance. This is an example of the 'indirect costs' incurred by publicly funded institutions that I often refer to.

I vividly remember Paul leaning back in his chair, hands behind his head, his long legs stretched out in front of him, and stating very matter-of-factly: "We need to settle this matter, as we don't want the media involved, and this is what will happen if it goes to hearing." I could literally see the other side quiver in their chairs, and the degree of satisfaction this gave me was immense. The mediator entered, and after a short discussion we had time out in another room. The mediator joined us for a few minutes and then left to chat to the other side. This is where I experienced another shock (as mediators are supposed to be impartial): I must have stood as she was leaving, maybe to open the door, as I was seated the closest to the door, and when she was outside the room and outside the earshot of my barrister she hissed at me, "If this goes to hearing you'll lose." My faith in the independence of mediators was again shattered – up to this point I was feeling quite satisfied with the process; she needn't have worried as I had no intention of taking it to a hearing, as I'd already held WorkCover accountable.

Fortunately, I had every intention of settling this matter, so all that was left was the conditions of settlement, and Paul and I arrived at a settlement figure that was agreeable. I told him if he negotiated a higher figure then those additional funds were his. He did, and the matter was settled and all were happy, or so I thought – this was to come back to bite me five years later.

At this time, Privacy Victoria had a link on their website that took you to submitted privacy complaints and the outcome, and given mine was recognised as a breach you would think mine would be there, but no. This is when I first came to understand the word 'transparency'. Mine was not there I believe for two reasons: one, Paul C was no longer the Privacy Commissioner, and two, I had been successful against a government department and this was going to be hidden, and it was.

Surprisingly, when I finally received my legal file from my former lawyer, I found in this file memos from my former lawyer to MPOL dated May of 2010 and after my Supreme Court action had concluded in April of 2010. I was quite perplexed as to why my former lawyer was providing information regarding my phone contact details, my home number and my mobile number to a private investigation company, especially given MPOL was the company having me under surveillance in 2002 and 2003.

As I was taking steps to have the April settlement set aside, I can only imagine why my former lawyer thought this necessary, but there are at least two occasions over the coming year that I believed I was indeed being followed. In April of 2011, I spoke to an inspector of police (who I had previously met in regards to an assault in 2010), asking whether he knew if I was under any kind of surveillance (because of the perpetrator of the assault) and he assured me that VICPOL had no reason to do so – he felt it was more likely my former lawyer, and given the found memo to MPOL, I believed him to be correct.

SIX

Unions Not So Unifying

After I finished my employment, I had plenty of time on my hands and began to read and conduct research into what exactly had happened to me. I had an insatiable need to understand. In May 2002, I was perusing the Australian Services Union (ASU) website where I found an article that stated, "If you're not an ASU member – Why join? People join the ASU to have a voice in their workplace and industry and use this voice to protect and improve their rights . . . ASU members have access to vast resources such as legal and industrial expertise; specialist advice, industrial advocacy at the workplace level and before tribunals . . ."

In my experience, the above statement is nothing more than an exercise in beguilement. It didn't match my treatment as a union member, and I didn't experience the benefits the above article articulates. This is misleading to people deciding the benefits of union membership and could be considered false advertising, or even deception. The Anti-Discrimination Tribunal is a Tribunal, and the article stated that the ASU provides advocacy at Tribunals. Industrial Officer John H stated in October 2001 that this was outside the union's jurisdiction. Or is the Anti-Discrimination Tribunal not given legal status by the ASU?

The article went on to say:

Unions Not So Unifying

"What are my rights regarding harassment and bullying in the workplace? The ASU believes all workers are entitled to a safe and inclusive workplace. Workplace bullying is inappropriate, unacceptable behaviour that should not be tolerated. There may be a number of remedies available to you including actions under Occupational Health and Safety or anti-discrimination legislation. Talk to your local ASU representative or industrial officer. Demand the bullying behaviour stop."

I did not experience an inclusive workplace; I was offered no support and was left to fend for myself. I respectfully asked on many occasions for the bullying to stop, but it did not. I now feel I understand the reason for this; by this time, everyone believed either their own lies or the lies spread by management. There's nothing more dangerous than an individual—or even more concerning, a group—who truly believes their own lies; we only have to look at Nazi Germany for a tragic example of this.

I cannot remember when or where I read this (though I made a note of it at the time, so I must have thought it was important) that during a debate with Tony Abbott, Bill Shorten stated the following, regarding unions:

"Then they gain a real voice in their workplace. Then they are empowered. Then they no longer have to rely on the goodwill of the employer alone. The Howard Government simply misunderstands or misrepresents why unions and the Commission exist. Unions exist to rectify power imbalances in the workplace. Of course, we want the workers to get an extra dollar. We want them to get a fair go. We don't believe all bosses are bad, there's a couple I can think of. The unions exist because the market, if left to itself, will produce a very unequal result on many occasions. It isn't because we believe we need to tell workers how to think. Unions exist because the market does not always deliver a fair go."

I agree with this, as the market or system rarely delivers a fair go to the powerless.

I believe parts of Bill Shorten's comments to be generally true: unions play a vital role in keeping the rights of workers on the political agenda, but sadly, in some cases they fail. Remember at the end of November 2001 when ASU

Industrial Officer John H wrote me a letter stating that "they are aware of the unfair and discriminatory treatment I have experienced and state that I have not been afforded natural justice in the process." It appears there's little else they can do, they failed me and other union members. I am still coming to terms with the failure of organisations to do what they say they will do.

I was definitely involved in an industrial dispute. Was the Commission so notified? No. And the union industrial officer told me that representation at VCAT was outside their jurisdiction. I believe that if the union can represent at the Commission then surely they can represent at VCAT. It is accepted they are different jurisdictions, but I feel that representation at either would be part of the union's role.

I read somewhere that a Union may sue and be sued, and, importantly, is able to sue its members to recover fees, levies or dues payable under its rules. In addition, it can protect against employers' attempts to weaken the union's position by discriminating against its members. My discrimination determination at VCAT that my employer had a *prima facie* case to answer for direct and indirect discrimination obviously fell on the deaf ears of the union.

Trade unions do have a common law liability, and are recognised as legal persons by the law. They are subject to the law of tort in the same way as other legal persons in Australia today. There are three torts particularly applicable to today's modern trade union conduct. They are: inducing breach of contract, intimidation and conspiracy.

I often wonder if the union industrial officer was guilty of inducing breach of contract. Did I have a contract with the union? I would have thought so – I paid a fee for certain union services, and these services were denied to me. Basically, my understanding is this: inducing a breach of contract occurs where one party (my former employer) induces another (the union) to breach their contract with me.

The other tenet of the above list that I feel is relevant to my situation is the 'Conspiracy to Injure'. I have no doubt that the Union Industrial Officer had meetings with Craig, Director of Organisational Change, as he had told me one day after we had met that he had a meeting with Craig that afternoon. They would have discussed me and my situation, and I feel they would have come to a decision as to my position. I have no idea if the Industrial Officer spoke on my behalf to settle this dispute, but I feel he would have negotiated with Craig a resolution the union would accept, but not necessarily one that I would accept.

Unions Not So Unifying

I just wanted assistance to return to work, a Return to Work Plan, and for my employer to follow the Accident Compensation Act 1985, the Occupational Health and Safety Act, the Workplace Relations Act, the Equal Opportunity Act 1995 as well as their own policies and procedures. They followed none and it didn't matter, as both the union and WorkCover did nothing to enforce the law. I have now come to understand that many of these laws are 'window dressings' to make it appear there are laws to protect us, when in reality there are not. On occasion, an exception to the rule is made to give the impression that the laws do work, but not in my or many others' experiences.

And further to the above article:

"Although trade unions have been granted legislative immunity from criminal conspiracy, they are still liable in certain circumstances for civil conspiracy. A civil conspiracy occurs where two or more persons combine together to injure a Plaintiff and act in pursuance of that combination in such a way as to cause him loss. The act or means of injuring the Plaintiff may be either lawful or unlawful.
The High Court has limited the liability of trade union members for conspiracy by lawful means to cases where the combination is motivated by the sole true dominating or main purpose of harming the Plaintiff. [Was losing my employment harming me? I believe so.] In most cases trade union officials are able to establish that their combination is motivated by the purpose of improving the terms and conditions of employment of their members, and therefore, providing they do not engage in unlawful means, it is difficult to succeed in an action for conspiracy against them.
If union officials or trade union members combine together with an intention of harming the Plaintiff and act in pursuance of that combination by unlawful means the scope for the Plaintiff to recover damages against them is far wider."

The statement 'their combination is motivated by the purpose of improving the terms and conditions of employment of their members' certainly was not true for me.

So I pondered as I read that "many strikes are unlawful (the action taken by the resource officers was unequivocally unlawful strike action) and therefore a combination or agreement to strike engaged in with the intention of harming a plaintiff (this certainly appears to be the case – the resource officers were acting with the intention of harming me and harming my return to work) will amount to an actionable conspiracy at common law." They were union members and the union supported their action by inaction on my behalf. I do not know legally if this fits the definition of 'Conspiracy to Injure', but they planned it together and it caused me harm, so in layperson's terms I believe it does fit the definition.

The unions lack of support can only be attributed to one of the following, or both. I was just one union membership against many, so was it an economic decision, or they were swayed by what management wanted. Was the union involved with the commission of a tortious act?

In 2006, I attended an open forum in Geelong to discuss workplace bullying. Many in attendance were from the City of Greater Geelong, one or two from other regional councils, plus a few teachers and a variety of professionals. I was gobsmacked at the extent this insidious behaviour was occurring within Geelong workplaces. A workplace bullying support group was founded and I enjoyed meeting with others who understood – I had found a new tribe which gave me much support and validation. From my understanding, many bullied workers have been let down by their union.

The union's Constitution and Objects, which states in part:

"To watch over, improve, foster and protect the interests of its members; to obtain and maintain for its members reasonable hours of work and fair wages and industrial conditions; to obtain preferential treatment for members in all aspects of their employment; to improve the social and economic position of its members; to assist members or their families in distress; to assist members in enforcing their rights under any law relating to industrial conciliation or arbitration or compensation for illness or injuries or any other enactment; and to secure redress for any grievance to which members or any of them may become subject."

I felt I did not have the benefit of these lovely 'motherhood statements'.

In September 2000 the union magazine ran an article with the headline 'Always Defending You', with the same article on their website titled 'How can the ASU assist me with individual problems and grievances?' It stated:

Unions Not So Unifying

"The ASU can provide expertise and advocacy in matters relating to WorkCover, Superannuation, Disciplinary Procedures, Unfair Dismissals, Appeals and Grievances and of course representation in industrial tribunals and courts, such as the Australian Industrial Relations Commission (AIRC) and Equal Opportunity Board. Furthermore, the union can provide members with free legal and financial advice. Your relevant industrial officer can assist you with any of the above."

The article further states that "the union advertises that they have situated in their branch an Industrial and Legal Coordinator who will provide expert support to members in legal matters. Workers pay union fees to be eligible to access this legal support."

Section 4 of the Workplace Relations Act 1996, highlighting the definition of what a 'trade union' means. The Act states it is an "association of employees a principal purpose of which is the protection and promotion of the employees' interests in matters concerning their employment." This appears very straightforward, yet in my experience this once again did not happen.

The union advertises that it provides legal services to their members and services provided by a qualified solicitor and therefore is in a position of 'trust and confidence', but when I attempted to access these services very little was provided. Supposedly the union must act in their members' best interests; not my experience.

Under English law an individual union member can bring an action due to a breach by the union of its Rules, even where there are arguably multiple causes of the damage. The employer's conduct does not release the union from vicarious liability or culpability, especially when there has been protracted failure to deal properly with a complaint, the union will be liable for damages, but there is no case law regarding this in Australia.

During this time, I became familiar with Tim Field, a recognised British researcher in the area of workplace bullying and the author of the book *Bully in Sight*. I had emailed him in the early years of my situation asking for help to understand what had befallen me in my workplace, and he told me that without doubt I was the target of a bully. People from all over the world were contacting Tim with similar stories of woe. From what he was being told by targets concerning unions, he wrote the following:

"Sometimes the local (unpaid) trade union officer is helpful and supportive, but once the case moves up to a paid union official, the member finds their case frustrated. Many people report that their paid trade union official appears indistinguishable from the management and that their trade union, despite the rhetoric, appears to be more interested in maintaining its good relationship with the employer than meeting the legally-binding contractual obligations to its members. Some trade unions encourage personnel officers to join the union in the full knowledge that their members are or will be in conflict with the same personnel officers. The notion that trade unions exist to support, protect and fight for the rights of their members seems to have fallen by the wayside – especially if bullying and stress are the core issues."

This again is a familiar story, but it should be noted that these comments are from around 15 years ago, and it can only be hoped that the story with unions is a different story today.

In *Wisconsin State Employees' Union, Council*: "In determining whether a union violated its duty of fair representation, the Examiner must determine whether: a grievance existed; the union failed to pursue the grievance through the grievance procedure; the union's failure to process the grievance prejudiced the employee's rights; and there is some reason to believe that the union's failure to pursue the grievance was arbitrary or discriminatory or resulted from bad faith,"

Remember that when my suspension happened, I contacted six union delegates; all were absent on this day, and the Industrial Officer was uncontactable. Given this, they must have known that the interview was going to result in an unfair disciplinary action.

It is accepted practice that an employer has a duty to schedule meetings with employees "at a reasonable place and time to allow a union representative to be present."

In my case, they actually scheduled a meeting knowing there would be no union representatives, because they had coordinated their unavailability.

I experienced increasing hostility from my employer, irrespective of industrial, health and safety legislation and their internal policies and procedures. The union by their lack of action and concern for the wellbeing of their members allowed this behaviour to continue until my health deteriorated to work incapacity. The employer acted in breach of their employment contract, but the union ignored this fact and allowed the employer industrial immunity.

Had the union not failed in its agreements with its member and supported their member, the employer would have developed solutions to the issues. But the easier solution was that an innocent employee would be the scapegoat for poor management performance from both the employer and their union.

Since trade unions are recognised as legal persons by the law, they are subject to the law of tort in the same way as other legal persons in Australia today.

In discussion with an industrial lawyer, I asked: should the union be seeking to severely limit the extent of its contractual obligations to me? Did the union unfairly limit their contractual obligations? Can the union change the rules of the contract as it suits, and if so, what's the point of a contract in the first place? This lawyer responded "that there would again be a good deal of argument as to whether these contractual obligations have been breached, but given the information you have supplied, it does appear you have an arguable case." The union knew I were experiencing harassment, and that I was unfairly suspended, so did they not have more than a bystander responsibility?

I was on suspension for four months, even when the allegations made against me were found to be unsubstantiated. I cannot believe that any other union or worker in Australia would tolerate this behaviour as being acceptable – is this not a near perfect example as to why workers join unions in the first place? I feel I was owed a duty of care and were denied 'natural justice' – a duty recognised by law. Prior to my 'suspension' the union knew I was unwell, so they must have been aware that this action could put me at risk – was I not owed any duty of care due to our contract? Was I not owed some level of support at the suspension meeting? Did they not have a legal duty to see that I was safe, in reference to any Good Samaritan law?

If the reasonable hypothetical 'person' was asked the question 'Why do workers join unions?' then the response would be 'To protect rights at work, individual rights, collective rights.' I suggest that this would be the understanding of the vast majority of workers. If workers understood that their individual rights were not protected, that protection was only afforded to the collective rights of union members, then union numbers may dramatically diminish.

A point advanced by the union was that as a trade union, while it is incorporated pursuant to the Workplace Relations Act 1996, its activities were not properly characterised as being in trade or commerce.

For a breach of contract claim to succeed, it would have to be found that joining a union, gave rise to an enforceable contract between members and the union itself. There appears not to be any authority directly on this point.

I understand that for a contractual claim to be successful, a Court would have to find that joining a union gave rise to an enforceable contract between a member and the union. Mere membership of a union does not give rise to an enforceable set of contractual obligations on the part of the union to observe each and every one of its objects as a contractual condition in favour of each of the members.

Furthermore, the union can provide members with free legal and financial advice. Your relevant industrial officer can assist you with any of the above. The article further states that "the union advertises that they have situated in their branch an Industrial and Legal Coordinator who will provide expert support to members in legal matters. Workers pay union fees to be eligible to access this legal support."

I came to understand that union support was not forthcoming when on a bad day I rang Neil, the union legal officer, for advice, and his response was "What do you expect me to do about it"

SEVEN

Legal Lessons

I have undertaken extensive reading to improve my understanding and knowledge of our legal system and the rule of law. While still a novice, I believe that my understanding would match that of an educated layperson, and I quote a comment from a Federal Court 2015 symposium 'Is Access to Justice a Right or a Service,' which states, "the pursuit of justice is a normative concept in the mind of every person who feels that he or she has been done wrong."

It goes on to say: "A system of justice is an institution for the redress of grievances. It can only command the respect of society's members if the trust that it is impartial, equal, transparent and a principled system that gives effect to the rule of law." I recently read a comment by a leading judge: "You cannot always do justice according to law."

As stated in the Magna Carta, "to no one will we sell, to no one will we deny or defer right or justice," and this value is supported by our Constitution and Article 10 of the 1948 Universal Declaration of Human Rights. We may well have our human rights, but who is to prosecute when they are violated? No one that I am aware of – occasionally a judge of a court attempts to redress, but they often fail. A question put forward recently by a leading barrister asks "Are our judges honest?" and "Why are lawyers unpopular?" Hopefully after reading of my experiences, you will be able to answer these questions for yourself.

I recently heard a prominent Melbourne barrister state that "those who cheat must be found out." This fortified my courage to tell my story without fear or favour.

It was with these principles in mind that I pursued my rights in an impartial, equal, transparent justice system, but sadly I came to understand that justice and the law are two different things; some litigants get a shield while others get a sword. I often got the sword, but on occasion I experienced the shield.

Anyone whose responsibilities revolve around making decisions in the interest of the public must be of unimpeachable qualities. They must be of the highest integrity because they are trusted to act for the greater good of the community and not in the furtherance of narrow or vested interests.

In *Hamilton v. Oades* a NSW Court of Appeal Judge McHugh J.A. observed: "The speedy trial right is a common law right. It does not depend on statute. It needs no Constitution to enshrine it."

Delay is the preferred strategy by WorkCover – they purposely delay over years and years, and then use this delay against you in court by saying that your circumstance was 10 years ago so you should have improved. Gullible juries fall for it nearly every time.

The judges of the civil courts, imbued with the western and common law notions of the rule of law, are obliged by their commissions to dispense justice without fear or favour. According to their tradition they treat all litigants in their courts equally and apply the law and legal sanctions to them regardless of their power, influence and political muscle. If the jurisdiction of these judges was excluded at the expense of the jurisdiction of the industrial experts, one can well imagine what will happen.

I do not have to imagine what would happen – I lived it for nearly 20 years.

Prior to 2010, I had complete trust in what I thought was our justice system, but now through experience I have come to understand that most of the time we do not have a justice system but a legal system – a system that exists to ensure that those privileged to work within it are protected for the wrongs they commit and make a handsome living off both those who can afford their wares and those who cannot.

My first venture into this mysterious world was in 2002, when I hired a law firm to represent me at the Anti-Discrimination hearings at the Victorian Civil and Administrative Tribunal (VCAT). This action settled at mediation, and I remember quite vividly the moment Helen the supervisor and John the manager entered the room with their legal team. I felt my legal team sitting next to me shiver, and afterwards I asked them why. "We know what you mean," they responded. The presence of John and Helen created a negative physical response in these hardened and experienced professionals.

Sometime later, I read a document written by my then-lawyer and found it incorrect. I asked him why this was so, and he suggested that since I had read it earlier and said nothing, I must have agreed to it. I asked him when I was supposed to have read it and he said, "I gave it to you last time you were here and you sat in the lounge area with a cup of tea and read it."

I was shocked by his statement as it was completely untrue. He had lied to me, and with this, I knew I couldn't continue to be represented by him. I was still very naive at this time, and believed changing lawyers was necessary. Thus, I made the fateful decision towards the end of 2002 of changing to Clark Toop Compensation Lawyers.

I had read about my new lawyer Patsy in a book titled *Bullying in the Workplace*, and I met with the author over a coffee and she told me that Patsy had been bullied out of her previous employment at a large Melbourne law firm – she had personal experience. I was to later find out that this may not have been true, and the issues Patsy may have had were not related to any bullying, but of course I cannot be totally sure. After my eight years of experience with Patsy, I came to the conclusion that she had not been bullied, because if she had she would have treated her bullied clients in a more compassionate fashion than she did.

In the WorkCover system, injured workers are required to jump through many hoops (whilst sick and injured); as we have no choice but to rely on the 'no win, no fee' law firms. I cannot speak of other law firms, but I can for the two I had represent me. When I refer to a lawyer or barrister, it is a lawyer or barrister who operates in the personal injury field, and I make no comparisons with lawyers who work in other fields of law.

For many WorkCover claims, there are three major legal hoops the injured worker is required to jump through. An initial major hoop is having your claim accepted as work-related; if your employer or WorkCover does not accept the injury as work-related then it has to be taken for adjudication in the Magistrates' Court.

Another major hoop is having your injury accepted as a 'serious injury'; if WorkCover does not believe it is 'serious' it has to be taken for determination in the County Court. If the injured worker has successfully jumped the previous two major hoops, then it is off to either the County Court or the Supreme Court for a hearing for compensation, but only if you can prove your employer was negligent and there was no 'foreseeability'.

Through this part, I will relate my experiences with this process and how it fails vulnerable injured workers (not just me, but many others) and how we are set up to fail by those we think are looking after our best interests. They are looking after nobody's interests but their own; we are just 'lambs to the slaughter', a means to their ends.

My discrimination claim settled at mediation in mid-2002, and my Work-Cover claim was heard in the Magistrates' Court in early 2003. Why the Magistrates' hearing went ahead when nearly all the evidence supported the claim is just how the WorkCover system works. They don't care how much evidence you have in support of your claim, they will fight on regardless and in breach of the Model Litigant Guidelines.

My injury was accepted as work-related, but with no order for weekly payments as it was determined I had a work capacity. But did I really? I tried very hard to give the impression I could return to work, as this was all I had ever wanted. As I have said earlier there was an occasion when I had an appointment for assessment by a medical practitioner, and wanting to be found to have capacity, I stayed in a motel around the corner from his office. I arrived at his office early in the morning, not stressed or overly anxious as I could be after the peak-hour trip from my home in Geelong to Melbourne. I knew I couldn't do this trip in peak-hour traffic and arrive on time without being highly stressed. It is often claimed that injured workers exaggerate their injuries, yet I was downplaying mine.

Proceedings in the Magistrates' Court finished with my claim being accepted. If I were still at work, this would have been a beneficial determination, as my employer would have to make concessions to get me back to work. But this determination was too little, too late. We were told to go away and sort out 'The Terms of Settlement'. I didn't understand what this meant at the time.

I was satisfied with Magistrate McGauran. I felt he gave me a fair go and a fair hearing. However, I was not happy about six months later after reading a document I found in my lawyer's file titled 'Terms of Settlement' (and supposedly sent to me six months earlier after the Magistrates' hearing) and signed on my behalf by barrister S, an agreement I had not seen and one I would not have agreed with had I seen it. This barrister had signed away my legal rights to pursue an injury that would have met the 10% minimum requirements for automatic compensation.

This behaviour started to sow a seed of doubt as to who my own legal team was working with other than me, but I squashed this doubt. I asked Patsy (my lawyer) what the next step was, and she told me that if WorkCover didn't accept my injuries as 'serious' a hearing in the County Court would need to take place. I was very conscious of time, as my injury occurred in 2000 and it was now 2003, and I needed resolution so I could move on. I directly asked Patsy how long it took to finalise a resolution, and she responded, "Two years." I couldn't believe it: another two years of this nightmare. Had she been honest with me at this time and told me it would actually be another seven years, the outcome may have been very different.

The only other thing I found concerning around the Magistrates' Court was sometime in mid-2003 (after my February hearing) I attended the registry and requested a copy of the audio transcript of my hearing. The registry officer left the front desk and I could see out of the corner of my eye she was on the phone and trying to hide this fact. She returned to me and stated they didn't have the recording as they recycle the tapes, and mine had been erased. I was disappointed, but I understood and left the building. A week or so later, while reading the Magistrates' Court website, I came across information that said if a recording has been requested by either party they must hold the audio for three months. I was within the three-month period and I felt damn sure my former employer would have requested a copy. So with this knowledge, I went back to the court registry and told them that as my employer had requested a copy and it was within the three month period they must still have a copy of the tapes.

I was duly supplied with some of the tapes, while some others had been 'recycled'. Surprisingly, the missing tapes only consisted of my testimony; this was just too big a coincidence. I felt I was not allowed to have a copy of what I had said in court, lest I use it to refresh my memory, and of course it would be to the defendant's advantage if I later said in another court something that contradicted what I had said in the Magistrates' Court. I had always told the truth and never varied from the truth, so there was no need to refresh my memory, so fortunately these 'missing' tapes did not cause me any problem, but the fact they were missing was of concern.

Later in 2003, I had my second experience with the legal fraternity. I met Julie at a Whistleblowers Australia meeting in Victoria and immediately felt drawn to her. I joined Whistleblowers Australia in early 2003 as I had done quite a bit of reading about this topic and felt I may have belonged, as once I submitted my WorkCover claim I was effectively 'blowing the whistle' on my former workplace. I exchanged emails with Dr Brian Martin from Whistleblowers Australia, who explained to me the concept of 'whistleblowing', and he believed I met the definition.

He arranged for me to meet and have coffee with a Victorian representative, and so I was introduced to Associate Professor Kim Sawyer. He was a marvellous person who gave his time generously and assisted me to understand what had happened to me. During coffee one day I asked Kim why the law isn't followed, as this is usually what leads a person to become a 'whistleblower', and his response really put it into perspective for me. He said, "The laws are currently devised as signals, rather than the real thing. The laws are there as a deterrent, but only usually to the ethical employee or employer. Miscreants are rarely deterred. The only thing that deters them is the real thing, i.e. prosecution."

I was still struggling at this time to find a place where I felt I belonged – my search for my new tribe. Kim has continued to give me his support over the years and we have become friends.

I found Julie to be a vivacious and funny lady who told me of her experiences in the Family Court during a property settlement dispute. She told me stories which I found incredible. One story she told me was about an issue she had with court recordings, as she believed they weren't an accurate account of what had occurred and had been tampered with. I had a great sense of sympathy for her as I thought she was clearly unwell.

I now have my doubts, as some time later she asked me to come with her to a hearing being held in the Family Court regarding the property settlement. I won't go into the background to her property dispute as it's not relevant to my experience, but an experience I had there is. Julie had made her thoughts and feelings known to the court, as she believed she wasn't getting a fair go. Whether she was or not I don't know, but on this day, I was surprised by what I had witnessed in court.

I cannot remember much of the hearing, but I do remember the court adjourning for the morning break and Julie being told to read a 'settlement agreement' provided by the defendant. She was hastily trying to take in and understand what this document was saying in the short amount of time allowed. I remembered seeing the first page and seeing a settlement figure.

Legal Lessons

We returned to court and Julie was returned to the witness box. My memory is that she was being encouraged to sign the settlement, but she refused. Then came out the 'big guns' – if she didn't sign, the judge was going to order that her affairs be placed in the hands of the state trustees. Julie was horrified by this prospect, and didn't want to be found incompetent in handling her own affairs. Without her knowledge, either the court or the defendant had arranged for Julie's psychiatrist to attend court, give evidence and undertake an assessment as to her mental capacity. This was a catch-22, because if Julie was found to have incapacity the state trustees would be appointed, and if no incapacity then the court hearing could continue without Julie later making any claims that she was incapacitated so therefore the ruling was unfair.

Julie was found to have capacity, and returned to the court and continued to refuse the property settlement agreement. Over the next couple of minutes, I'm not sure what happened as I was distracted by a person entering the court, going to the defendant's bar table and placing some papers on the bottom of a pile of papers that were on the desk. I thought this strange, as you would expect that new papers would go on top, but this person gently and quietly placed these new papers on the bottom.

I looked back to Julie and she was clearly upset, but I had missed why. She said, "Give them to me then and I will sign," or words thereabouts. What caused me concern was what happened next: the defendant barrister deftly pulled the papers from the bottom of the pile of papers on the bar table and they were given to Julie. I felt my inner voice shouting *Do not sign without reading again!* but she did. I felt sick and horrified by what I had seen, but was hoping all would be okay. Well, it wasn't: I later saw her copy of the settlement and the front page was different to the one I had seen earlier in the morning, but I did not say this to Julie – she was exhausted mentally and physically and all I could hope for was that she was happy with the settlement she had signed and all her legal disputes were over. Rightly or wrongly, I felt the court would be glad they had dispensed with an obviously difficult litigant.

I stayed with Julie that night to keep her company, secretly hoping she didn't realise the document she'd signed was different to the one she read during the morning recess. But at around 3am I heard her on her computer, and it was then I knew that she knew.

Julie moved on not much later and I lost contact with her, but wherever she is I can only hope she is happy and has put this experience behind her. Despite this experience, I naively continued to have faith in and totally trusted my barristers.

Over the next five years I muddled through my life, attending to medical appointments and counselling to keep me healthy and sane. Keeping in mind by this time I knew my health issues and mental state were not the result of my physical illness or my imagination. This was confirmed to me by Dr Benjamin who said "what you think is happening is happening."

By the year 2003 I finally accepted that I was the target of the domestic violence of the workplace, now known as workplace bullying.

Finally in 2005, the insurer accepted liability for all my injuries and diseases. They basically had to, as my medical specialists and their own independent medical assessors attested in their reports that in their opinion these injuries were caused by my former employment. By this time, I even had the dreaded Dr Shan onside, as well as the amazing and highly regarded doctors Nigel Strauss and Lester Walton. I felt sure I was sent to the last two because WorkCover believed they would find me at fault and write a report that would suit their purpose – but Dr Strauss and Dr Lester were no 'hired guns', with Dr Strauss clearly stating in his report, "I have no doubt this lady was harassed and victimised in the workplace."

So here we were in 2005, and the two years to resolution, as told to me by my lawyer, had passed with resolution nowhere in sight. I felt very concerned, but what could I do – I was powerless, I had to believe that Patsy was doing everything she could to expedite an outcome. I only learned much later this wasn't the case.

The first role of government is to protect its people, but I now know given my experiences, that it is not to protect an individual person but the collective of people.

Basically, you are on your own when you need protection from the system, as you are an individual and no one is mandated by law to help you; there are no lobby groups and no community outrage about how vulnerable injured workers are mistreated.

During this 10-year period of feeling very alone in my quiet quest for justice and fairness, I learnt much about the systems of WorkCover and the legal profession. It's information I wish I didn't learn, but I have an enquiring mind that demanded I search for answers. In a country such as ours, this quest should never have started, and yet it had taken longer than the combined duration of two world wars to get to a horrific conclusion.

Legal Lessons

When Labor had come to power in 1999 and Rob Hulls was ordained Attorney-General, I really warmed to his maiden speech to Parliament, as it gave me a sense of hope and security. He coined the phrase that an "accessible, equitable and fair justice system" was his goal. My claim ran over the same period as his term of government, and sadly throughout the 10 years in his role as Attorney-General this stated goal was not attained – nowhere near it. I felt foolish in believing that government truly cared for the wellbeing of litigants accessing the legal system.

Accessible? It took more than two years to have my claim accepted, more than a further five years until my serious injury was accepted, then more than two years to have my negligence claim heard. Nearly a decade in total, hardly fitting the definition of 'accessible'.

On Saturday 16 November 2019, the *Age* newspaper reported on events concerning the case of the Inflation Nightclub, where two patrons were shot by police from the Critical Response Team. A reported comment: "The conduct of Victoria Police's lawyers, taking more than two years to settle the proceedings on the eve of the trial, was 'absolutely atrocious'." What is also 'absolutely atrocious' is WorkCover taking nearly 10 years in settling claims of injured workers. Why there is no one in our justice system outraged by this, beggar's belief.

Equitable? The insurer is an agent of the Victorian government department of WorkCover, and as such both must abide by the Model Litigant Guidelines, but they didn't. The Model Litigant Guidelines attempts to level the playing field, but WorkCover, insurers and defendant lawyers ignore these guidelines and demonstrate a 'win at all costs' attitude, because lawyers do so to line their own pockets at the expense of compensation for injured workers.

The approach of 'delay and deny' equates to money for the legal profession. There is a whole network of businesses that ensure they get a piece of the legal money pie, but it is acceptable that an injured worker gets nothing, not even one crumb of this deliciously profitable pie.

This is taxpayers' money, and with my newfound enlightenment I believe one function of the WorkCover system is to be a vehicle that syphons public money into the legal profession and associated entities, which may well be owned by the legal fraternity.

Fair? Coupled with all of the above and the rest of my story, is the system fair? I do not believe so. In December 2013, I read an article in the *Sydney*

Morning Herald which reported that WorkSafe pays law firms bonuses to minimise victim's payouts. An excerpt of the article states:

> "Victoria's work authority is paying lawyers millions of dollars in confidential bonuses to payouts in compensation cases brought by alleged victims of workplace accidents. In at least one case, a firm representing the authority received more than $1 million in bonuses over 12 months on top of legal fees. Leaked files from law firm Landers & Rogers reveal that it has made about $5 million in WorkSafe bonuses over five years by minimising payouts to alleged Victorian victims of workplace accidents."

From my experience, for many injured workers—especially for those who have been bullied or mobbed—financial compensation is merely the 'icing on the cake'. We want to be believed, vindicated, validated or even hopefully have some accountability paid for by those who caused the injury, and in some cases, such as mine, those who purposely caused injury.

The defendant in these cases has access to unlimited taxpayers' and employers' resources, while injured workers without 'no win, no fee' would have to risk any assets they have, primarily the family home. It doesn't seem fair, given the employers under law had to pay a premium to protect their workers – this money should be used to help them, not the legal profession. WorkCover is the bagman of the protection racket that is going on in this state. But don't expect the state to do anything about it, as WorkCover is a lucrative business that gives them hundreds of millions of dollars, some of which go into the state coffers and, once again, not to injured workers.

Finally, in April 2008, five years later than the two-year timeframe my lawyer told me it would take, I had my County Court hearing in front of Judge Misso. I feel the question here should be: why did WorkCover not settle at this time and spare the expense of a trial? Up to this point my direct claim costs were approximately $161,440 (this figure doesn't include any direct or indirect costs of claims management) and this doesn't include any costs my former employer may have incurred.

At this time, WorkCover had in their possession around 39 medical reports, a report from a human resource expert Jim Bailey, two reports from Donnally Ayres (consultants), and extensive surveillance reports, all of which supported my claim and honesty. In 2005, the insurer accepted liability for my workplace injuries, and yet with all this evidence WorkCover would not issue a 'serious injury' certificate, and I subsequently had to issue proceedings. A 'serious injury' certificate gives permission for compensation for both pain and suffering and loss of income. A negotiated settlement at this time would have saved taxpayers' money and allowed me to get on with my life. Once again in breach of the Model Litigant Guidelines, WorkCover soldiered on accumulating costs, believing they would win at the County Court and I would fail in my 'serious injury' claim.

I was successful in my claim in the County Court, no doubt to the horror of WorkCover. In his decision, Judge Misso stated:

> "It is clear when a comparison is made between what the plaintiff says occurred and what the various deponents and makers of statements say occurred that there is quite a dramatic conflict in evidence."
>
> "In the circumstances, I accept the plaintiff's evidence that the events she describes did occur and that her work was a significant contributing factor to the onset of injury."

This accords with Dr Benjamin's assessment when he stated to me, "What you think is happening, is happening."

So there we have it: a judge of the County Court, after hearing all the evidence, agrees that I was bullied and harassed at work and that this caused me a serious injury.

I found Judge Misso to be kind, understanding and fair. During the trial I could barely see his face, and his head was covered by the usual wig, but what soothed me throughout the hearing was his voice. His tone of voice was soft and calming during this period of chaos – I could have listened to him speak for hours. I felt a person gifted with such a lovely voice would have to be kind-hearted and full of integrity. Would I have felt different had I not been successful? I don't know, but I don't think my opinion of him based on his voice would have changed.

In getting back to costs, which are in the value of the dollar of 11 years ago, and, as previously stated, prior to the County Court hearing, they were around $161,440, and with the addition of the hearing costs of $135,423, the total was approximately $296,863. These figures are based on the receipts I have access to, but do not include indirect costs, and indirect costs are important to keep in mind because hidden costs are rarely open to scrutiny.

As I was successful in gaining a court determination of 'serious injury', WorkCover was required by law to make an offer of settlement, which they did in May 2008. Their offer was $0 – obviously they still weren't accepting the evidence, or even more surprisingly the judgement of Judge Misso.

By law I was required to put in a counter offer of settlement, which I did in June 2008. I did so for the amount of $350,000, keeping in mind that I would be lucky to get a small portion of this as legal fees eat up a large amount of injured workers' compensation. This offer wasn't accepted by WorkCover, and therefore the next hoop required was to issue proceedings for compensation in a court of law. Had WorkCover made a counter-offer of say $250,000-$300,000, I would have accepted the offer.

The direct legal costs for this period were approximately $360,905. Now, keep in mind there was an offer of settlement in June 2008 for $350,000. WorkCover actually spent nearly $11,000 more than my offer fighting the claim rather than accept the offer of settlement. This was again in breach of the Model Litigant Guidelines, and I wonder who, if anyone was monitoring this stuff? It appears that WorkCover preferred to spend employer's premiums on income for the common law legal profession than assisting injured workers.

Therefore, up until the last account was paid in 2011, the combined direct legal costs of my claim were a staggering $663,173. Now add to this my former employer's conservative costs and we have a total of $963,173. The system made a lot of money for the pigs with their snouts in the trough, but the injured worker received no compensation for her injuries. As mentioned, it's also been reported that WorkCover pay a bonus to their representative firms that successfully ensure an injured worker receives no compensation. Occasionally a pyrrhic victory is allowed, but this usually gives the injured worker very little after legal costs, and that's how they like it.

A bonus added to the above figure makes it all so much more obscene, especially when in September of 2001 I made an offer of settlement to my employer. Remember, this offer included returning to work, the payment of medical expenses of $3,000, and $1,000 in recognition of the pain and suffering I had endured in the false complaints against me. Paying $4,000 would have been a far better outcome than paying more than $1 million, and saved all the additional human suffering. People lost jobs and careers, and for what? Because someone somewhere was adamant they were not wrong, and there was no way any of the guilty were going eat a crumb of humble pie. This turned out to be one very expensive crumb.

Nick Starling, ABI director of general insurance and health, said: "A compensation system that can deliver £2,000 of compensation at a cost of as much as £5,000 is dysfunctional. Excessive legal costs are a symptom of a civil litigation system that is broken and in urgent need of fixing."

This may be in reference to the UK system, but I know it happens here too, and I certainly agree. Our system isn't just broken, it's crushed.

I remember reading a quote somewhere which may be relevant to many injured workers, especially those who develop psychological injury due to bullying: "Sometimes people pretend you're a bad person so they don't feel guilty about the things they did to you."

I found this quote to be accurate for those in my former workplace, and for those who formally represented me and were tasked with protecting my human and legal rights. I am not a bad person and I did not do anything that justified the level of abuse I endured.

When I first read this quote from *The Confessions of Artemus Quibble* (written by a lawyer) I thought it was a joke: "There are three golden rules in the profession . . . the first . . thoroughly terrify your client. Second, find out how much money he has and where it is. Third, get it." Given my experiences, I now believe it's not a joke.

Around 2006, I felt I needed to do something meaningful with my spare time and once again took to volunteering. My mother was a great believer in helping others – most likely a carryover from her nursing days, a career she loved but one she had to leave to become a wife and mother. I now look back with admiration at how difficult her life was: being a stay-at-home mum in the 1950s, with all her family living in another state.

It was likely this sense of loneliness that led her to volunteering. I learnt this from my mother and started to help her when I was about twelve. In my adult life, spanning a period of 30 years, I volunteered in many different capacities. They were all enjoyable, but my favourite was the Red Cross. Whilst I was still not recovered from my workplace bullying trauma, I embarked on my first volunteer experience with this highly respected organisation.

A year later, I became a staff member (while still continuing as a volunteer) and could not believe my good fortune, hoping this would assist in my recovery back into the workforce.

The position I attained at the Red Cross ticked all my boxes and made extensive use of my skill set. I really enjoyed the company of and the interactions with the members and volunteers. They were exceptional people, full of love, caring and compassion for others and I adored my new tribe.

It was difficult leaving that job, as I truly loved the work and the positive relationships I had with the volunteers, but I knew my time was up when three events unfolded which told me that it was time to go. The first was early 2009 during the terrible bushfires that ravaged the state. My supervisor had been seconded to Melbourne, which left two staff in the Geelong office. It was an emotionally torrid time dealing with a distressed public. One morning the other staff member motioned to me with a crocked finger to come into her office, which I did. She looked at me and said, "You may feel that I am cold, but could you stop being so caring and just flick the calls." My eyes were glistening when I left this interaction feeling very disheartened.

The second was just a few weeks later when my Supervisor asked me not to be so social. It appears I was too caring and friendly for this workplace.

The third was a few months later, when Melbourne management called and asked me to delegate work to my supervisor. If they believed the Supervisor wasn't performing I feel it was their job to address this not mine.

After 18 months in the position, I started to feel uncertain, insecure and unsupported; it was only the caring of the members and volunteers that kept me going.

I was offered another extension to my contract. Around this time, I came to the realisation that my time at the organisation had come to an end, as my past experiences were screaming at me to get out. So I did. I knew I'd miss the wonderful caring members in the craft shop, but the shop was being closed anyway as the office was moving to another location.

I continued as a Red Cross volunteer for another four years, even after my son Dan went missing. It was a distraction, and I certainly needed that, but sadly a wonderful Irish gentleman I visited through the Red Cross Community Visitors Scheme passed away, and with that came my decision to leave.

Between 2008-2010, I waited patiently for a hearing date in the Supreme Court. There were a number of legal steps needing to be taken, one being court-ordered mediation, with the hope this mediation would lead to resolution.

EIGHT

Maybe Mediation

Mediation was supposed to lead to resolving the issues in good faith. Through my experiences, I came to believe that the term 'in good faith' was rarely used or even understood by some officers of the court involved in ensuring justice was not just delayed, but denied.

As I'd been successful in the County Court for a Serious Injury Certificate, the next steps were to prepare for the compensation hearing. A County Court order of October 2008 and later a Supreme Court order stated the proceeding was to be referred to a mediator for mediation, which was to be finished no later than 20 May 2009. Despite making numerous requests through February, March and April for this to occur prior to 9 May (as I was to be away from this date until 26 May to attend my best friend's son's wedding overseas), I received no response to my requests to have the mediation heard prior. I left for my trip wondering when it would occur, as my return date was after the deadline of 20 May 2009.

I was concerned that the order date of 20 May would be missed, but to my surprise while I was overseas a letter arrived at my home stating mediation would be held on 14 May. It appeared my emails sent regarding the mediation date weren't read, and my absence until 26 May not noted. This kind of behaviour from my lawyer caused no end of frustration. The order wasn't met and mediation was rescheduled to 27 May – the day after I returned from my trip.

Overall, I felt that this wasn't a big problem, for it was apparent to me that court orders are missed all the time, and extensions are given to tardy lawyers, and it just adds to the strategy of delay and makes the waiting harder for the plaintiff. You need to have things happening, having things moving along, especially after so many years of sitting on the sidelines.

The change of date of the mediation cost more than $400, and the venue was also changed from the glass conference room at Clark Toop offices to the chambers of Andrew Ingram, and my account was charged $300 for this venue change. I wondered why this was done, and later wondered if it may have been because there were no representatives from the defendant in attendance and I would see this in the glass room. Mediation procedures as set down by the court state that all parties must ensure that persons with the proper authority for deciding whether to settle the dispute, and terms of any settlement, and the lawyers who have the ultimate responsibility to advise the parties in relation to the dispute and its settlement, attend the mediation. I didn't see anyone from WorkCover, nor the insurer, nor my former employer, nor the defendant's legal representatives in attendance at the mediation. They may well have been there, but I didn't see anyone, and so a doubt was raised in my mind.

Irrespective of my jet lag, I found mediation a peculiar experience. Due to prior mediations, I had expectations that this session would take maybe half a day to a full day, but it took less than 30 minutes. In the past, I (and any support person) had been required to sign a document titled 'Attendance Record' prior to the mediation commencing, but this didn't occur on this occasion.

The mediator arrived, I was briefly introduced, and then I never saw him again. Usually in mediation all participants meet, and then quite often one group retreats to another room with the to-ing and fro-ing commencing. I'm not sure how many times my legal representatives left the room to speak to the 'other side'; it could only have been once or twice, given the notably short duration. I was quite surprised when my senior counsel returned to the room and said to me, "The defendant has informed me that they have spent $1,000,000 so far and will not settle. The defendant's legal team is happy to go to trial as it will be good income for them." Model Litigant Guidelines ignored again.

A good income for them, but a bad loss of income for any barrister who represents me, as WorkCover appeared adamant I would never be successful. WorkCover's offer of settlement was $50,000 – one my lawyers and I could not accept as it would only pay a fraction of the legal fees incurred. The legal fees for the two barristers who were in attendance on my behalf for the half-hour conference prior to mediation and the less-than-one-half-hour mediation alone were around $8,690. Other costs included the mediator at $900 for a half hour and of course the printing costs of the file for the mediator of $800, and $700 for mediation changes of date and venue. Roughly around $11,000 charged to my account for virtually nothing. And if the 'other side' was in attendance then no doubt their costs would be similar, therefore we had a cost of around $20,000, which in my opinion is money wasted but in the legal opinion money well-deserved.

Back to the court order of October 2008, which stated that prior to mediation a copy of all pleadings, particulars and a copy of the order were to be delivered to the mediator. Interestingly, in 2014 when I finally received my file from Clark Toop (after instigating an action in the Supreme Court to get my file as I had been refused access) there was a copy of these documents (around 500 pages) prepared for the mediator in a file. This file was pristine – it hadn't been 'worked through' as one would expect. Not one dog-ear, not one pencil mark, not one smudge, fresh off the printer. Maybe it was handled with kid gloves, or maybe the mediator already knew he didn't have to read the extensive file. Or maybe he simply didn't have time, as the records show that this file wasn't delivered to the mediator until 26 May 2009, the day before mediation.

Lastly, the court order stated after mediation that the mediator is to report to the court. The Supreme Court has a document titled 'General Form of Order' which outlines the procedure required in regards to mediation, and it states, at point 4: "The mediator not later than [date] reports back to the Court whether the mediation is finished."

In the Minutes of Consent dated October 2008 it says, "By 2 June 2009, the mediator reports to the Court, by the Associate to the Master, whether the mediation is finished," and further, "By [date left blank] the plaintiff reports to the Court, by Associate to the Master, whether mediation was finished by the date fixed on behalf of this order."

The County Court 'Mediation Procedures' state, "Within 7 days from the date of mediation the mediator will complete the 'Notice of Mediation Result' and file it with the Court.' I feel the Supreme Court would have a similar system to the County Court, being a superior court and all. I believed this notification to the Supreme Court would be a physical form (like the County

Court form) and not just a phone call, but no record of this completed form or any phone record exists in my Supreme Court file or my legal file held by my lawyer.

I began to doubt if I had experienced a real mediation, as the court order date was missed with no apparent concern, there was no request to sign an 'Agreement to Mediate,' no 'Statement of Agreed Facts' was supplied to me (and likely not supplied to the other side), the mediation took less than 30 minutes, the venue was changed from a glass conference room to counsel chambers, I never met the 'other side', the mediator's file was pristine (I doubt it was read), there were no reports to the court when mediation was finished, no record of offers made and rejected, no records of instructions or advice of myself, my support person or legal representatives, no documents recording date, who was present, duration of attendance by barristers, no record of substance of advice given or confirmation of the barrister's advice in writing to me and no record of my response and/or instructions. No records at all regarding mediation or any outcome documented in any of my files.

These realisations were the moments I began to wonder if mediation happened at all or if it was just another act procured by those who supposedly had my best interests at heart.

I can admit I may be wrong – I am not legally trained, and this may well be how mediation in preparation for the Supreme Court works, but the experienced me, the common sense me, and the fact no records of any kind exist all leads me to believe I'm not wrong. It's one thing to fake mediation with an unsuspecting plaintiff and a compliant 'other side', but it's another thing altogether to fraudulently sign your name to official records for the court that you know are false. Is this what occurred? I don't know.

What I did find on the Supreme Court website under mediation is the following, "The mediator brings the parties together face-to-face in a private and confidential setting. The parties inform the mediator of their objectives and the mediator tries to explore options with the parties and search out areas of agreement." *Face to face!*

The games are beginning, with players taking their positions and no referee in sight.

NINE

The Compensation Con

This is the part where I get stumped. Where I tell you of my experiences concerning the complex and nefarious behaviour of my legal team to get the outcome wanted by them and WorkCover, but not the outcome wanted by me. Their planned outcome trumped mine, and that was to continue to work in the system that benefitted them, WorkCover and the government, at the expense of injured workers.

Prominent Australian lawyer John-Paul Cashen once said, "Anyone who's needed a lawyer in their life will know how much they need them to be on your side. To have a lawyer turn on you and act against you really does strike at the heart of the justice system."

Delay

My compensation hearing was set down for April 2010. The two years to resolution had become seven years, and a full decade since my injury date of 2000. I'd like to think most people would consider this outrageous, but I now know the legal profession and WorkCover use delay as a tactic to wear an injured worker down, which is highly beneficial for them.

Firstly, an injured worker may give up and walk away. However, I was already too invested to do so. Secondly, an injured worker may die, and I was told by a barrister that this is viewed as a reasonable option. Lastly, it is hoped that you will not perform successfully in front of a jury, as the delay causes a number of issues that can be used to discredit you with the jury (legal proceedings are considered one of life's most stressful experiences, impacting litigants in a number of ways).

After two long years since my County Court hearing, my 'negligence' hearing was set to be heard in the Supreme Court on Tuesday 13 April 2010. I asked my lawyer why the Supreme Court (rather than the County Court, where I'd had previously had success) and she responded, "Better judges and bigger payouts." For an experienced personal injury lawyer, she couldn't have been more wrong.

Difficulty in getting representation

On the Friday prior to my hearing date, I was informed by Travis (a lawyer working for my lawyer and a man who had lied to me on a number of occasions regarding details of my claim) that they were going to adjourn my matter because they were unable to retain senior counsel.

During the later years of my case, I instructed my lawyer to brief particular barristers on my behalf. In December 2008, I requested she brief a barrister named Ian who I had conferred with previously about getting a costs agreement. I found him to be a lovely man and very experienced in the subject matter of my case. She told me, "He doesn't have enough jury experience."

When it was apparent that there was difficulty briefing a barrister to represent me, I later asked Travis to contact Ian. Travis responded that Ian was unavailable because he had been made a judge of the Supreme Court. I later looked on the Supreme Court website and couldn't find notice of any such appointment. When I next saw Travis I mentioned this to him and he said he must have been wrong, that it was the County Court. I then looked at their website – no notice of such an appointment. I sent an email to Ian congratulating him on his appointment to the court and his response was, "I have neither sought nor been offered a position on any court. I am content for now representing people. You have been strangely misinformed."

Coincidentally, my lawyer was representing another injured worker by the name of Karen who had her matter listed for 21 April 2010 (starting a week after mine), but it had to be adjourned because the lawyers had failed to brief a

The Compensation Con

barrister to represent Karen. The transcript of Karen's case dated 21 April 2010 states that Patsy Toop (under oath) said to Judge Forrest during evidence supporting her request for an adjournment that she had contacted a number of barristers including Ian to represent Karen. I spoke to Ian concerning Karen's brief and he responded that Ms Toop had not contacted him regarding a brief for Karen or any other matter.

An important question must be asked here: why are workers injured by psychological bullying not able to get representation? I suspect many would wish they had instead been physically assaulted or physically bullied, as it would likely evoke sympathy and eager legal representation.

My naivety at that time led me to believe they had either left it too late or were not ready, and were hoping for an adjournment (which of course I wouldn't have accepted after such a long period).

One excuse I was given was the difficulty in retaining senior counsel for a trial with an anticipated duration of five weeks. The defendant had requested the time of five weeks; I knew my case very well and even I couldn't see how it could take five weeks, unless every little point of evidence is going to be minutely examined. As much as I would have liked this, it wouldn't be good use of court time and resources.

I believed a possible reason was the defendant knew I wouldn't get counsel for five weeks on a 'no win, no fee' basis for a claim such as mine – bullying claims were more difficult to prove than physical injury. I can look back now and see there was no intention of running a trial for five weeks; this was a scare tactic, to force my legal representatives into a corner, a corner the defendant controlled. My compulsory offer of settlement in 2008 was $350,000, and to have gone to a five-week trial at a cost of around $500,000 would be negligent in itself. This is the conundrum suffered by the legal system – it is often said there should be no price to justice, but there *is* a price. A price that most litigants can't afford because legal representatives have priced their services so high people can't access the very system that exists for their benefit. This often leads to plaintiffs becoming self-represented litigants. To me, this is control.

I'm not confident I can fully explain to you what happened next. I refused to accept an adjournment – after 10 years I'd had enough. I was disappointed that my previous barristers wouldn't take on the case, as my case had been lucrative for them in the past. But I didn't know then what I know now. I was prepared to represent myself rather than have the case adjourned, as I felt no one really understood my case as well as I did, and I believed I could achieve the same outcome or even better. I certainly didn't think I'd achieve any less. Had I represented myself the judge would be required to give me assistance in presenting my claim, guidance as to the court procedures and processes, and most importantly to ensure my legal rights were not violated. In actuality, by being represented my rights were violated and I could do nothing about it, because the ones mandated to protect my rights were the ones violating them.

I remember reading a few years ago about a Greens candidate for Melbourne, a Mr Brian Walters, who was forced to defend his work as a barrister for an alleged Nazi war criminal. He accused the Labor Party of running a smear campaign and said the legal requirement was for him to accept briefs regardless of a person's views. Mr Walters said the legal system required him to accept briefs on cases involving a wide range of people because of the 'cab-rank rule'.

He stated that the suggestion by Labor that he should pick and choose is a suggestion that he should behave unethically and that the rule of law does not matter. Prominent human rights activist Julian Burnside KC slammed Labor's tactics as a "disgrace" and said, "The cab-rank rule is fundamental to the independent bar. It exists to protect the community by ensuring that even unpopular clients can get representation in court."

In support, Jack Rush KC also defended Mr Walters: "There are plenty of cases where people have been required to accept the unpopular, the distasteful brief, but they're still required to do it."

I agree with the ethos of Walters, Burnside and Rush, but why wasn't I able to gain representation, a senior counsel to run my case in the Supreme Court? Even the unpopular, the distasteful, have a philosophical right to representation. But not an innocent injured worker. Or does this ethos only exists for fee-paying clients, not those of us in the nightmare of the 'no win, no fee' arrangement? If anyone can answer this question for me, please make contact.

I had Richard McGarvie and Andrew Ingram represent me in the County Court and they were successful. I had Senior Counsel John Richards and Andrew Ingram complete the necessary legal tasks for years prior to the Supreme Court hearing, and yet they were supposedly unavailable represent me. In a status report dated June 2009, written and signed by Ingram, he stated "Mr Andrew Ingram of Counsel is intended to be retained on behalf of the Plaintiff." I was told that Richards was not available, and later I found a note in my legal file dated December 2009 that said John Richards could not do my case as he was appearing in *Allbutt v. State of Victoria* on 20 April 2010.

Court records state that on 10 March 2010, the hearing date of 20 April 2010 for Allbut was vacated and the proceeding was listed for hearing on 20 May 2010. Therefore, Mr Richards was available to run my case, especially as he had conducted many of the interlocutory steps including mediation. I wondered why he would not take my brief even though my lawyer was desperate for senior counsel. I kept asking myself what did all these barristers know that I did not; obviously there was some issue, but something not disclosed to me.

Trust

In December 2009, I was informed by the lawyer Travis that Phillip Jewell SC had agreed to conduct my case, and that the briefing would take place in late January. I was so relieved to think things were finally happening. But it was short-lived, for as of mid-March I hadn't met Mr Jewell, and contacted Travis to find out when I would be meeting him. He responded that one or two days before trial would be enough time. Sometime in late March or early April, I was informed that Phillip Jewell was not taking my case, and when I later contacted him he stated he knew nothing about my case and hadn't ever been briefed.

Another time during this period, Travis told me that Tim Tobin had been briefed and then Dyson Hore Lacy SC would be conducting my case, and yet when I spoke to this barrister a few months later he responded that he told Travis he would not take the brief. I was told on 9 April that Ron Meldrum had been briefed, but a short time later that afternoon he stated he was not available. Two years since the successful County Court hearing and days before hearing the hearing in the Supreme Court and still no counsel. All this happening just days before the hearing – I trust you can understand my frustration.

In June (after I made a submission to have the April Settlement set aside), the court requested I attend and cross-examine my former legal team. The junior counsel in my case, Matt Walsh, stated under oath that he was retained with Mr Tim Tobin SC, then briefly with Mr Meldrum KC. I had a barrister and then I did not – this scenario played out many times prior to my April hearing. The worst of alleged criminals get competent legal representation. I again wondered what was going on.

When I accessed my legal file a few years later it contained a Memorandum of Advice dated May 2009 that stated, "For the Plaintiff to anticipate that Counsel will run her trial on a no win no fee basis is unrealistic." If I was being unrealistic, I should've been informed of such many years prior. I honestly held the belief that because I was genuine and with the evidence I had, a barrister would be happy to take my case. But that's before I knew how the defendant would play its game.

I met with Travis on the Friday afternoon prior to the trial starting the following Tuesday, during which he took a call from Matt Walsh (who had been briefed as junior barrister) and I heard Travis make the comment "$150,000 all-in." I was to later hear this same comment many times. I had a junior barrister but no senior barrister, and Walsh would not take the brief without senior counsel. It was at this time I had decided to represent myself and terminate the services of my lawyers. I informed the court of this and was then on my way to my lawyer's office to inform her, but just as I arrived, I was told senior counsel had accepted the brief. I can't prove it, but I feel the court contacted my lawyer to let her know my plans; plans the court would rather not have to deal with. Self-representation is accepted by the court, but I believe judges do not like conducting these kinds of cases for a variety of reasons.

Surprisingly, later that Friday afternoon, Lennon's Clerk for Senior Counsels called at around 5pm to accept the brief on behalf of Craig Harrison.

On the Monday and Tuesday of the following week, I met with my barristers Craig Harrison and Matt Walsh and felt pleased that something was finally happening. I was just so relieved, and it was amazing how quickly I trusted both Walsh and Harrison. I would have trusted them with my life at this time; I thought they were going to fight for me and I was just so grateful.

I felt the trust developed because on a number of occasions over those two days, while I was in Harrison's office, I heard him on the phone. He mentioned how his daughter in Mildura had MS and he had the care of her two children, a six-year-old and a three-year-old who had a disability, and I heard him talking to his wife on their wedding anniversary. At this time, he came across to me as a man of great compassion and I felt compassion for him. I thought I had the right person and expressed to my husband that evening how fortunate I was to have him represent me.

I wonder now if anything he said on the phone was true, given he knew I could hear him; I had become overly trusting as I didn't know what may have been occurring behind the scenes. If I had, I would have run from them both.

This is where my story really gets especially complicated; I hope I can succinctly tell it to you. I was so hopeful at the time that my story—the truth—was finally going to be told.

My hearing started a day late. I was surprised that no judge was available on this date, as my case had been set down in the court calendar about a year earlier. I believe my lawyer wasn't ready to proceed and had discussions with the court regarding an adjournment. When it became apparent I wouldn't agree to an adjournment and would conduct the case myself after terminating the services of my lawyers, a judge was hastily found, but not one experienced in personal injury.

Judge or Jury

On the Monday or Tuesday when my lawyers were informed which judge would hear my case, I remember Travis stating that "we got the bad judge." I must admit I felt a little concerned, but this was a judge, a judge of the Supreme Court, so it had to be alright. If it had meant waiting another week or two to get a judge experienced in this jurisdiction then I would have waited, but Travis was insisting I adjourn to November, which I now know meant the following year, and another year was a distance too far. My lawyer had another case which originally was to start on 13 April, the same day as my case, but this was adjourned to 28 April, whereas I was told that I would have to adjourn to November.

On the Wednesday (the first day of trial), the morning was consumed by jury selection. I didn't want a jury and I had previously told my lawyer to go with a judge alone. I had always felt a little conflicted about juries, and given this I sought expert opinion from a medical expert and a legal expert as to their assessment as what choice would be best for me. I cannot remember which one said it, but the advice given was, "A jury won't like you – you're too middle-class. Go judge alone."

So you can imagine my disappointment when I found out that the defendant has the choice of a judge or a jury, not the plaintiff. This was seriously to my detriment, as now WorkCover had control and they're known to employ 'bastard barristers' to do their dirty work. They're masterful manipulators and juries are putty in their hands. This is my opinion of the personal injury field, not the criminal field where barristers fight to get the guilty off. In my field, they fight the injured worker to be guilty, guilty of something, anything, and if nothing can be found they just make it up.

Victim-blaming

Knowing that I was a good person with a genuine workplace injury and lots of evidence to back this up, I felt confident my barristers would be able to deal with it and convince the jury my former employer was negligent. That was supposedly what this trial was all about: was my former employer negligent? For an employer to be held negligent, the injured worker's illness or injury must have been reasonably foreseeable. In other words, if a member of staff's psychological collapse comes with no warning signs, then the courts will not hold the employer to account for it. But in my case my former employer had many medical reports attesting to my injury and illness, and yet set about taking unreasonable actions that would further harm me. Negligence.

My claim was accepted, I gained a 'serious injury' determination, the insurer had accepted liability for my injuries, many medical specialists reported my injury to be genuine and caused by bullying in the workplace, but under law the jury was not allowed to know any of this. How convenient; the government enact laws that protect their sources of income and cause seriously injured workers to have to work harder proving their case to a jury, a jury selected and manipulated by the defendant. Mother Teresa would fail before a jury after a barrister victim blamed her for all the wrongs in the world.

Not so many years ago, women were blamed for being raped: for wearing a short skirt, for being drunk, for walking alone, for generally 'asking for it'. They were victim-blamed on the stand by defendant barristers, blamed for being raped, blamed for past sexual behaviour, their private lives open to the most hurtful scrutiny. It took a while, but with newfound enlightenment society now realises this is wrong and unfair.

Now we have the scenario where injured workers, especially those with psychological injury and especially those who are bullied, are the new rape victim: blamed for being injured. Theirs is no workplace 'accident'; their injury was intentional, which makes the injury even more profound. Where is the outrage of this behaviour? I see none, because our community has been brainwashed to believe injured workers are 'rorting', as often depicted on shows like *A Current Affair (ACA)*. I would hope that WorkCover doesn't promote such stories, but can't help but wonder about their origins. It's not the injured worker dobbing themselves in.

Overall, I believe plaintiffs with 'serious injury' claims are disadvantaged in the common law court system because the defendants are in the position of power, due to the usual defendant or co-defendant being the Victorian WorkCover Authority who fulfils two roles; one as regulator and one as defendant, which creates a conflict of interest. Defendant counsel are paid whether they win or lose, and the defendant calls the shots (e.g. jury/no jury). I feel confident that defendants prefer juries, as they can easily be manipulated by skilful barristers, and plaintiffs have little chance surviving days of character assassination, gaslighting and victim-blaming. Experienced personal injury judges must see through this strategy, but some seemingly don't care enough about the rights of an injured worker in comparison to keeping the system working in a manner that suits the major players and major beneficiaries.

Defendants often give timelines for trial they know may not be accurate, and call dozens of 'potential' witnesses to increase the time the case will run, knowing it's advantageous when negotiating settlements, as plaintiffs cannot get counsel for cases running for many weeks, irrespective of the 'cab-rank rule'. Hopefully, as you read, you're understanding why.

The defendants can and do manipulate the amount of time the trial needs by time-wasting and going down lines of questioning which may be—or are —irrelevant.

For example: in *Li v. Toyota* the case ran for eight days and there were nine witnesses; my case ran for seven days and there was one witness: me. I had witnesses who were prepared to give evidence in my support, but over all the years of my case no witnesses were interviewed, no statements taken. I had spoken to some witnesses who report they were not contacted by my lawyer in regards to their evidence or testimony. On the first or second day of trial, two family members met with Walsh in his office where they talked about the weather, his impressive office and view over the city. Walsh later claimed that this was an interview with two witnesses and fulfilled the witness criteria. I disagree – detailed witness statements are critical in any trial, and the earlier they are taken the better, as taking them years later may compromise the evidence.

FLYING MONKEYS

The powerless against the powerful

Plaintiffs are in a position of powerlessness due to all the above, and being unwell and waiting years for the case to come before the court they are worn down; both sides take advantage of this. Plaintiffs have no choice but to go 'no win, no fee' and legal counsel appear reticent to being involved in a supposedly three-to-five-week trial where they risk not getting paid if the plaintiff is unsuccessful. They are fully aware of the strategies defendant counsel will use against their client. Recently I was told by an injured worker that she was encouraged to accept a settlement rather than risk being "slaughtered" by the other side. I believe this is why I was asked to attend with Harrison at 8am on Friday 23 April 2010, when court was not in session until 10:30am, and also why I was told to give my family a "break" on this day and not have them attend.

My legal team should—or at least attempted to—have my case heard in front of a judge alone, given the defendant was insisting the case would take five weeks. In *Trevor Roller Shutter Service Pty Ltd v. Crowe* the judge states:

> "Court and judicial resources are scarce. We no longer have the luxury of allowing parties to run their cases for twice the length of time they would otherwise take simply because one party or the other prefers a particular mode of trial. In my view, where a court identifies substantial time and cost savings that can be made by changing the mode of a civil trial, then, in the absence of some compelling reason not to do so, the court is bound to change the mode of trial to the more efficient, timely and cost-effective mode.
> The present case is such a case. I am satisfied that as a cause, this case will take less than half the time it would take to hear as a jury trial. In circumstances where there are other litigants waiting to have their matters determined in this Court, I am persuaded to dispense with the jury and to order that this proceeding be heard as a cause."

I believe some lawyers in the personal injury field aren't being forthright with their clients, not disclosing the truth, by not telling them they will wait for years and may get little satisfaction, let alone any compensation; this is how the system works. The government is part of the system, so no good will come of telling them of your plight.

The Compensation Con

The Victorian Government introduced legislation that required employers by law to pay a levy to protect their workers in case of injury. This levy is a huge income earner for the government, just behind stamp duty and TAC registrations in terms of revenue. As mentioned earlier, I liken this levy to the old-style mafia protection racket, where bagmen forcibly collected money and were offered protection in return. But the difference today is that the government doesn't like paying out too much of the protection money, and will fight to pay the seriously injured workers as little as possible – they actually prefer to give the compensation to the legal fraternity. It figures; most members of government are lawyers, so they'd prefer to look after their mates.

On occasion the odd case wins a large payout – this is to give the impression to the community that the system works. WorkCover enjoys informing the media of a 'rorting' injured worker who can be shamed on *ACA*. This gives a false perception to the community that injured workers are 'rorters', when in fact WorkCover knows that the percentage of 'rorters' is very low – I believe around 1%. The WorkCover procedure an injured worker is subjected to is extremely difficult, and only the most honest make it to a 'serious injury' application or a common law damages claim.

Plaintiff lawyers may well end up with a conflict of interest, as defendants make offers of settlement far below the worth of the claim but will cover a good chunk of the lawyer's costs. A settlement is in the best interests of plaintiff lawyers, as it is a 'bird in the hand' and the settlement isn't eaten up by further court hearing days. The fact their client may get very little or nothing usually doesn't concern them.

My lawyer's other cases of Allbutt, Hudspeth, and Newton all concluded at trial because there were no settlement offers on the table – or if there were, they weren't enough to cover even some of their legal fees. Those cases also display the negligence of my former lawyer, with Judge Dixon stating in Hudspeth that a judicial review would be held into the legal representative's behaviour. Whether this occurred or not I don't know. Fortunately, the court intervened and protected the rights of those plaintiffs. I feel there was no intervention on my behalf, because just days later I claimed negligence by my legal team, whereas the others had not gotten to that point as yet.

The case of Turner went to jury judgement, as no offers, and Carr and O'Keeffe settled as offers were made. I can only guess that Allbutt, Hudspeth and Newton settled prior to judgement as no judicial decision appears on the official record and because of errors made by counsel a jury trial was dispensed with and they proceeded as a 'cause' in front of a judge alone.

I believe that the defendants in common law trials for injured workers make a valued judgement on how effective they assess a plaintiff will be in front of a jury and how many angles can be twisted to make the victim into the perpetrator of their own injuries.

Therefore, we can ascertain that:

Not Good = Low or no offers
Good = $100,000
Very Good = $150,000
Excellent = $350,000.

In my case, all in all, it was only about my lawyer's income. Lawyers take a gamble that defendants in common law personal injury cases will make an offer that covers their true and basic expenses. So the injured worker receives nothing, but they should be satisfied, nay, happy that WorkCover had to pay out. Receiving no compensation is one thing, but to be belittled, humiliated and derided in a court of law only adds insult to injury. You are innocent and genuine but the system works against you to protect itself at your expense. You are guilty of being innocent and they cannot have that.

Currently the total direct costs in my case amount to $724,651, with legal costs alone being $536,474. All this because an injured worker forgave the bullies and just wanted to return to work. WorkCover works when the claim is small or catastrophic, but a barrister did say to me if a worker becomes a quadriplegic, it's better to have full brain function, as the 'pain and suffering' payout is greater than if the injured worker is in a 'vegetative state' and does not know they are suffering. I also asked this barrister why the process takes so long, as I may be dead by the time it's resolved, and his response was that death would be viewed as a good outcome, as death payouts are smaller because the injured worker does not require full-time care or lifelong payments.

Injured workers are one of the most vulnerable and marginalised groups in our community, fearful of being stigmatised and fearful for their future. There is no one in any position of power on their side. They may think their kind and caring common law personal injury lawyer is on side, but they are sadly mistaken.

After all the problems with retaining counsel, I was later surprised to see in the 'Civil Callover Form for the Defendant' document dated two weeks before trial in April 2010 that the plaintiff lawyers were ready to proceed on 13 April 2010. But of course, this wasn't true – no senior counsel had been briefed at this time. A month before this 'Callover' was sent, which confirmed date of hearing and if a party were *not* ready to proceed, they were to provide a summons and affidavit in support as soon as possible. I found no evidence of these documents in my file. Given all the court deadlines or orders that weren't met, I began to wonder if they had any relevance or meaning, as the courts rarely enforce them – things are just changed to suit the legal representatives, which is either a known or unknown strategy in the game of delay, or a reward for tardiness, incompetence and negligence.

I believe there was an apparent attempt to minimise the seriousness of the manner in which my case was heard in front of Judge Robson, if not a straight cover-up. I will attempt to explain this to you by using court documents, transcripts and documents found in my lawyer file, and my knowledge at the time.

The Supreme Court Hearing

Firstly, let me tell you a little more about my actual Supreme Court hearing. I met with my barristers on the first morning of trial, with rather odd comments being made by counsel, one being that the defendant barrister, a Mr Paul Jens, had offered his own funds to assist with a settlement, and that my former employer and the insurer wanted to settle, but WorkCover was insistent they wouldn't settle because of previous action by me. This could only be the privacy complaint, so someone somewhere had an axe to grind—most likely whoever ordered the illegal surveillance—and I was going to be victimised again for pursuing my legal and human rights.

At the first day of trial, before a jury was empanelled, my senior counsel Harrison told the judge that there was one matter in his submission that ought to be ventilated. He asked if the judge had received a copy of the court books the day before, or the plaintiff's court book at least. According to the Supreme Court Rules on Civil Procedure, court books must be provided seven days before commencement of trial. This not being done adds weight to my belief that the decision to adjourn my hearing was made and the court book was hastily completed once it was known I was not agreeable to the adjournment.

Judge Robson wasn't asked for leave to serve the court book late, nor did he make any comment regarding this omission – it appears he ignored the breach of this rule. The judge responded that he had received the court book yesterday and Harrison asked if the judge had an opportunity to look at it. The judge responded, "No, I haven't. I have had the opportunity but I didn't avail myself of it."

I felt this comment from the bench showed a lack of interest, and this would have been clearly evident to both parties. I became concerned about this reinforcing the "we've drawn the bad judge" comment.

Harrison went on about the other matter and informed the judge that he had prepared some further particulars of breach of duty, which his learned friend Mr Jens had only just seen and had not had an opportunity to peruse. It was much later when I got the opportunity to see this unsigned document 'Further Particulars of Breach of Duty of Care Owed by the Defendant to the Plaintiff,' dated 14 April 2010. There are 14 particulars, and included among them are four new particulars that would impact on my ability to prove 'foreseeability' – it was changing my case from a workplace bullying case to a physical injury case. Graves' disease was now included, and there was previous argument that my employer didn't know I was ill with Graves' disease and, as I had not formally advised them of such, there was no foreseeability and therefore no negligence. I was dumbfounded as to why my legal team thought this adjustment was in my best interests, and had I seen this document prior I wouldn't have agreed with it being tendered.

My Graves' disease was already declared by Judge Misso in my Serious Injury Application as a red herring, and he was indeed correct, so why raise it again now? Mr Jens responded that he didn't anticipate this was going to cause the defendant any difficulty. Of course it wouldn't cause the defendant any difficulty – this was highly beneficial to the defendant, and they must have known this. Mr Jens stated he anticipated that he'd get instructions to concede that this amendment is made by consent. But he also anticipated that his instruction would be to ask his learned friend Harrison to make application to the judge to formally amend the pleading in front of the jury.

Amendment by consent – certainly not by *my* consent, and I feel that this addition at this stage of trial should have been questioned by the judge as to why this pleading was not relied on earlier with the other pleadings. Now comes the funny part: Mr Jens indicated that the judge may be a long way in front of the barristers insofar as any relevant law is concerned in relation to the ultimate proceeding. But in due course Jens would be making some submissions, based on a particular High Court authority, and he wondered if he could just mention that to the judge now.

In my opinion, the judge was not a long way in front of the barristers regarding the relevant law, as evidenced by the kind of questions the judge was asking. I think Mr Jens should have raised that the defendant was going to rely on *Koehler* in their earlier pleadings and they did not. The defendant didn't because it was their belief my claim did not come under *Koehler* – that is until Harrison added to the 'Further Particulars of Breach of Duty of Care Owed by the Defendant to the Plaintiff.' In hindsight, I believe that my pleadings were changed so the defendant could use the High Court authority of *Koehler v. Cerebus*, as I believe this case was not cited in any verbal or written submissions of the defendant because if it had my lawyers should have mentioned it to me.

Now I wonder why Mr Jens was so keen to have this authority tendered before the hearing had even commenced – I believe it was because he wanted the judge to be aware of this case and have it influence him. I feel Mr Jens knew at this time that *Koehler* would not be raised during his final submissions because he was not going to deliver any final submissions; my case was never going to get that far. But he had to get it to the 'black letter' judge, and he was successful.

The judge asked if he should read the authority, and I wonder: should a judge read a prejudicial authority before they have heard any evidence? I believe it would be in conflict with the 'open mind' principle, but he did not read it then and probably never has.

The judge's next question really floored me: "Isn't the hearing to determine whether the injuries she claimed she's suffered are serious? That's the issue, isn't it? No, but that's what it's about isn't it? Whether they're serious. If it's serious."

I thought to myself *no, serious injury had already been decided by the County Court, and this court case was not about that,* but the judge appeared not to understand this and appeared confused about what exactly was at issue in this case. The defendant barrister attempted to explain the law to the judge, who once again responded, "Do you want me to tell the jury about that at the beginning, and say that before she got to here, she went through a hearing in the County Court and got leave, or is this it?"

The defendant barrister responded to the judge that that was not required. I was concerned because the judge was unclear on procedure and appeared not to understand the Accident Compensation Act 1985 which states that a jury is not allowed to know that the injured worker has already been successful in gaining a 'serious injury' certificate from the County Court. A little time later the judge said, "My role as the judge is to ensure a fair trial and the parties are entitled to your verdict uninfluenced by others." I agreed with this sentiment, without knowing that my judge and jury were to fail. You will read more on this later.

The first day of trial came to an end, and only with the passage of time did I realise how concerning some of the judge's comments were. We started the next day with the judge asking me what a P-file was, the one referred to in the top of a memorandum handed to him in questioning, and I responded that a P-file is an individual's personnel file where all one's personnel records are kept. Maybe I'm wrong, but I felt an experienced personal injury judge should have known this. Not my judge. How much else did he not know?

During the first three days of trial, various offers of settlement were supposedly made by Mr Jens and rejected. On Wednesday 14 April, the settlement offer after costs was $50,000. In hindsight, this was the best offer. On the Thursday, the offer was (after costs) $30,000. In hindsight, this was a good offer. On the Friday the offer after costs was $20,000.

In a later proceeding in June, Mr Jens gave evidence that he only ever made one offer and that was on the Wednesday 21 April. I don't understand who was making these offers, as I believe Mr Jens' testimony on this matter that the defendant's first offer was on that Wednesday.

My evidence was given over two and a half days, and from memory, nothing was remarkable – I was just answering typical, expected questions. What I found shocking was that on the last day of my evidence, Harrison handed to me and the jury a copy of a document titled 'FDC Staff Complaint'.

An unsigned document of baseless allegations! The jury didn't know that, though. It was a Friday afternoon and they had all weekend to digest the document before cross-examination commenced the following Monday. No barrister wanting to win his client's case would tender such a prejudicial document. A primary rule within the law of evidence is that hearsay statements are inadmissible. The defendant couldn't tender this so-called hearsay evidence because it would be incumbent on my barrister to object to this being a breach of the Evidence Act under the 'hearsay rule', but luckily for the defendant my own barrister did this for him.

Later in the day, the defendant barrister objected to a question put by Harrison and said, "Someone said to me that someone had said to her – in my submission that is clearly hearsay and inadmissible. These witnesses can be called if anyone wants to call them, if it's a relevant issue." And to me, the staff complaint document was not a relevant issue because it was clearly hearsay and therefore inadmissible, but Harrison tendered this document without any objection of hearsay or inadmissibility by Mr Jens.

I wasn't yet aware of the famous quote by Cicero the Roman lawyer: "When you have no basis for an argument, abuse the plaintiff." But that's exactly what happened to me. I naively entered court believing I would be treated fairly and with respect. How wrong I was. I think I would have been better able to survive this experience if I had prior knowledge of the dirty tactics seemingly common across all courtrooms.

Examination in chief concluded on the Friday, with cross-examination by the Defendant to commence on the Monday. I'll try to not go into too much detail, but will attempt an overview so as to convey why I feel I didn't get a 'fair go'. Sometimes questions weren't questions at all, but statements of fact put forward by the defendant barrister. For example, from the transcript:

> MR JENS: You even attempted to contact the Director of Public Prosecutions about it, did you not?---**No, not – no. (Applicant)**
> I suggest to you that you attempted to contact the then Mr Paul Coghlan. I suggest it's quite the contrary, you contacted him and you were referred to Worksafe?---**No.**
> MR JENS: I suggest to you that you contacted the Director of Public Prosecutions, indeed written him a letter.

The defendant's own affidavit of documents clearly shows that it was WorkSafe who wrote to the DPP. Mr Jens would have known this, and so I feel he was misleading the jury. Given the judge's earlier statement at the beginning of the trial, about not availing himself of the time to read the court books, he may have not as yet read this part of the court book. Mr Jens knows this to be untrue, and then asked the same question three times and I denied it three times. The judge could have asked Mr Jens to tender the letter in evidence or my legal team could have objected or requested the letter supposedly written by me to be tendered into evidence. It could not be, because it did not exist.

Throughout the entirety of cross-examination, what I believed to be irrelevant questions abounded. Mr Jens kept repeating erroneous matters, such as explaining issues like: Work Car, Olympics, Gull Bus, Holidays, RDO's, TIL, On-Call Allowance, and finally, yes, asking "What kind of car do you drive?"

Interesting how the make of car I drove after I left employment was so important – surely this was no one's business but mine. There could be only one reason for asking this question, but no objection was to be heard anywhere from my counsel.

Remember in Chapter Two I explained in detail how the on-call allowance came into being, and yet here I was accused by Mr Jens of negotiating, initiating and agitating the on-call allowance for the purpose of more pay for myself. He went on to say that I was seeking to negotiate extra pay from my employer. This was not the intention; the on-call allowance was for my staff to be paid when they took the work phone whilst I was on leave towards the end of 1999. I had carried the phone for three years without making an on-call claim, but my staff refused to carry the phone without an on-call allowance, which was their right. But I was going on leave and would be interstate, uncontactable, so I needed to ensure the out-of-hours phone was managed. It was this dilemma that initiated my contact with the Manager of Organisational Change.

It was this manager who suggested that as there were funds in the Family Day Care budget, and given it was an award condition, that the allowance be back-paid to the start of the financial year – that is 1 July 1999. Contrary to what Mr Jens stated to the court, it wasn't me who wanted it back-dated. Mr Jens pushed the point that I would have been the major beneficiary of this back pay, and suggested it was my self-interest that pushed for the on-call allowance. Mr Jens concluded this line of questioning by saying, "I suggest to you that it was your initiative and you were seeking to have your pay increased by virtue of having the on-call allowance paid," and "So that the major beneficiary of this agitation by far and away was to be you." This line of questioning could only have one purpose, and that was to promote to the jury that I was not an injured worker, just a greedy and selfish employee.

I give the above as an example of how a dedicated employee who was doing something for nothing, out of commitment to her job, was cast in a bad light by defendant barristers, barristers who twist the yin into yang and yang into yin. It must be remembered that injured workers on the stand under cross-examination are especially vulnerable, and questioning is purposely convoluted to cause confusion, adding to creditability issues. I was asked to give evidence of events in 1999, then to events in 2001, and then to events of 2000, and then back to 1999, and then back to 2001, and then back to 2000. I must say I found this confusing, but I feel given the circumstance I handled it rather well, as I had lived this evidence for ten years. What I really found to be impressive was the barrister could do all this jumping around with ease, without losing his own train of thought.

There were times during questioning where Mr Jens made comment of things that were untrue and then apologised for his mistake. I believe these 'mistakes' were purposeful, as once they are said it is impossible to take them back, and the jury is legally unduly influenced.

Mr Jens stated that both parties were very conscious of the time this matter was taking. Yet the time taken could have been less if relevant questions were asked rather than time-wasting ones. Most members of a jury would understand these basic life and employment terms. I won't further explain, but will just say that the words "bullying" or "harassment" were not used at all during cross-examination, as this case wasn't about that, but about me and how awful a person I was.

Dishonesty

I'm going to make three references to the transcript which I believe are vitally important to my claim of dishonesty by the defendant, and maybe even my own legal team. During cross-examination Mr Jens stated, "I will give an undertaking to the court that Mr Circosta will be called and will give evidence," and "Mr Circosta will give evidence that it was not part of evidence to put a letter on the file," and "I don't want to go over this again, but as you know Mr Circosta, I suggest you already know this but he will give evidence."

It appeared that Mr Circosta went overseas just a day or two after the case 'unexpectedly' finished on Friday 23 April, so exactly when did he book his holiday and where was he going to give this evidence? Did Mr Jens give an undertaking to the court which he knew was false?

On the last day of hearing—it being unknown to me that this was the last day of hearing—and in response to a question I answered that I would never submit another WorkCover claim, a juror supposedly made the remark, "Yeah, sure." I didn't hear this remark, but supposedly both Matt Walsh and the judge's associate (AC) heard it. I later made contact with the judge's associate and asked if he had heard the comment, and he stated that he was not a lawyer and to ring the Supreme Court Registry for this information. I rang and spoke to a man who answered that this was not a matter for them. I was never able to confirm whether the associate had heard the comment or not.

Mr Jens informed the court that he had completed his cross-examination at the end of Thursday 22 April 2010. My senior counsel Craig Harrison confirmed that cross-examination was finished, so he could confer with me. The court then adjourned to 10.30am on Friday 23 April 2010. On leaving the court, Harrison suggested that as the next day would be an easy day for me, just re-examination that I give my support persons the day off from being at court, waiting outside for seven days, idly waiting to give supposed evidence. It was tiring for me so it must have been tiring for them, so naively I agreed. My eldest daughter who had little legal understanding of what was going on and little involvement (as she had her own family and worked full-time) was coming on that Friday to spend the lunchtime break with me. Harrison asked me to attend his chambers at 8am. I didn't question why so early—2.5 hours prior court, when it was supposedly going to be an easy day for me—but I soon found out when we crossed the road to the court and entered a small conference room.

I was promptly informed by Harrison that Mr Jens had sought leave of the court to continue cross-examination and leave had been granted, but I later discovered this to be untrue – there are no records or transcript of Mr Jens seeking leave of the court to continue his cross-examination and the court granting leave, either on the Thursday or Friday morning or overnight. Unbeknown to me at this time, counsel sought a brief sitting in the absence of the jury to have the matter adjourned to noon.

I was told by Walsh, "Your case cannot continue, as at least one juror is against you, and in our experience that's all it takes." Walsh told me that on the previous afternoon during cross-examination he'd heard a juror comment "Yeah, right" or "Yeah, sure" in response to my evidence that I was never going to make another claim.

After ten years of hell in the WorkCover system I would be vehemently reluctant to ever make another claim. Later, when I did suffer an injury at other employment, I paid the costs of medical treatment myself. Mr Jens knew this, but of course this was not told to the jury.

Walsh often referred to the juror in question as "the unemployed Greek truck driver juror." This was not my comment, but in Judge Robson's decision it reads as if I made this reference. Under the Evidence Act 2008 it is stated that "A person who is a judge or juror in a proceeding is not competent to give evidence in that proceeding. However, a juror is competent to give evidence in the proceeding about matters affecting the conduct of the proceeding."

The Compensation Con

Why wasn't this juror interviewed to ascertain if he indeed made this comment? A comment such as this would be very prejudicial to a plaintiff, and may well cause a dismissal of a jury and for the hearing to continue as a 'cause'. Why did my legal team not raise the issue of prejudice? I protested at the time, as I felt sure that my witnesses, who were yet to be heard, may change the juror's mind. My counsel said, "No, once a juror decides they do not like you, that's it."

In the June hearing, I was attempting to get the settlement agreement set aside. My lawyer said in her evidence that if she knew how a jury's mind worked, she would be a multi-millionaire. Well, obviously she did know, and her response was in conflict with the statements made by Walsh and Harrison on the morning of the eighth day, where they were conclusive that the jury did not like me. So *they* knew how a jury's mind worked, but my lawyer did not.

On the last day of hearing (which I wasn't aware was the last day of hearing), I was in the conference room for nearly four hours. I was subjected to oppressive behaviour from Walsh, Harrison and Travis when at the third hour my lawyer joined the mob. I feel this was because they only had until midday to force a settlement out of me and I wasn't budging. My lawyer suggested my daughter be with me, but by this time my trust was in decline. I knew what they were doing, but strangely I had no power to overcome it. What they were doing was wrong, and I didn't want them to use my daughter in their quest. I felt they would use her to get me to settle, which would be unfair as she had little knowledge of the details of my case. I just knew they would convince her that I must settle, and if I settled on her advice or recommendation, I didn't want her or me to regret this later. And I knew I would. I was reluctant to involve my children in my sorry tale of woe – only one knew the details, and she wasn't there.

For those four hours in that little room, I suffered a combination of Stockholm syndrome, the Stanford Prison Experiment, battered wife syndrome and battered plaintiff syndrome. These guys were experts – it took them only four hours to achieve what others take days and weeks to achieve. The day prior, I would have trusted these highly ranked legal professionals with my life. They gained my trust so easily and so quickly it was astounding. I felt that they relished in the power they had and took pleasure in the harassment.

I was told that if I settled, the defendant would vacate a formal order in the defendant's favour from the County Court. This related to my Serious Injury Hearing that was scheduled in the County Court in October 2007, but my legal representatives didn't want the judge we had drawn, so made up an excuse to have the matter adjourned. This took no more than an hour of legal time, yet the costs were around $10,000, therefore because my legal representatives requested the adjournment, I was ordered to pay the costs of the defendant. I find it difficult to understand why these costs weren't paid at the time, rather than waiting nearly three years, but I now believe these kind of costs orders are later used as carrots by both sides to help sweeten settlement negations or to add to the financial threats your legal team throw at you.

Undue influence was exerted that finally broke me, and under duress I signed what they demanded. Harrison and Walsh hurriedly left the room, leaving me feeling bewildered and emotionally numb, and through tears I apologised to my lawyer, though for what I do not know. She was busy playing on her Blackberry, and looked at me with the coldest eyes I've ever seen and said, "Don't be so selfish."

I can particularly relate to the following part of Justice Hayne's talk, title 'The Vanishing Trial', at the Supreme and Federal Courts Judges' Conference held in Sydney in 2008:

> "Third, resolution of disputes according to law is usually best achieved with skilled and experienced representation for the parties. It is a deliberate process that takes time. It is therefore expensive. It is expensive because of the need to use skilled representatives and because the process takes time and effort. If cases are settling because the prospect of trial is too horrid for parties to contemplate, settlement may mark the failure of the system, not its success. If cases are settling because they are managed to the point of the parties' exhaustion, the system has failed them. If cases are settling because one party is able so to prolong and complicate the litigation as to outlast a financially weaker party, the system fails. Settlement in those circumstances is a mark of failure not success."

My trial definitely vanished because of the above, and the 'no win, no fee' fear of my lawyers. *A bird in the hand is worth two in the bush*. Well, $150,000 in their hand was better than the risk of nothing, even if it meant ignoring my instructions, which they did on numerous occasions, and ignoring their legal ethics, which they also did on numerous occasions – too many to mention, but this book shares some examples.

The Compensation Con

I later read a statement by Robert McClelland, Commonwealth Attorney-General in 2009:

> "Today welcomed the passage through the Senate of the Access to Justice (Civil Litigation Reforms) Amendment Bill 2009. More than ever before, it is imperative we have a well-functioning justice system better equipped to assist people when they most need assistance, advice and guidance. Australia cannot afford a legal system where the cure of litigation is worse than the affliction of the dispute."

My cure was equal to my painful affliction suffered so many years ago. This period of time was actually far more complex and surreal than I have written, but to give you more would make it so unwieldly and complicated you may have left after the first page (that is, if you're still here!).

I mentioned Karen earlier. We shared the same lawyer and had many of the same experiences with them, so we had a bond. I eventually came to meet her; I'm not sure now as to how it came about, but I found her to be a smart and eloquent person and was saddened by her experiences of workplace bullying. She sent me a copy of a letter she had sent to some members of parliament; I won't name them, but I doubt any of them took the time to write a heartfelt or meaningful response.

Karen's letter (to various addressees)

Dear _____,

Injured Workers (Victims) are not Criminals – why are they treated as such?

For the past six years I have been living in a nightmare of trying to achieve justice for a workplace bullying situation that has (come close to) destroyed (ing) me emotionally, financially and professionally.

I feel criminals of the worst persuasion get their day in court with easily accessible legal representation, and within a reasonable time frame, but not so for Targets of psychological workplace bullying. During 2003/04 I was subjected to workplace bullying that resulted in an emotional breakdown, suicide attempt, and second emotional breakdown a few weeks after returning to work. My employer took a hostile stance and did not lift one finger to try to mediate, re-employ or assist me with my complaint, which only exacerbated my fragile state of mind, and has continued to do so during the ensuing years while I have been trying to pursue compensation for being unable to continue working.

In brief:

- A WorkCover claim was lodged and accepted in November 2004.
- In 2009 a Serious Injury application was successful in the County Court Melbourne for both Pain and Suffering and Economic Loss.
- Compulsory Mediation following this outcome resulted in WorkCover offering total compensation of $50,000 with the assertion that if this amount was not accepted, the next offer would be $0. This unrealistic offer was rejected and the $0 offer currently stands.

My Common Law compensation action in the Supreme Court was scheduled for 21 April 2010. Due to circumstances not of my making, the case was adjourned until November 2010. I have now been informed that my case has again been delayed and relisted for March 2011 – again through circumstances not of my making.
Bullied injured workers and in particular psychological injury cases are treated with suspicion, contempt and derision by all parties involved including lawyers, barristers, the judiciary, jurors, some medical professionals, but most of all by WorkCover. Which is in direct conflict with Minister Hulls' many media statements highlighting his distaste for this abhorrent behaviour.
The WorkCover legal process appears to be a game plan among key players (whether structured, planned or entirely innocent) and seems to exist to wear down the litigant emotionally, financially and in any way that will help to defeat the claim. But are premiums not paid by employers to ensure their injured workers receive fair compensation? These premiums should not be a "cash cow" for the state government at the expense of the injured worker.
Those without a supportive and nurturing network of family and medical professionals have no hope of enduring the process – it is a

mind, body and soul-destroying process to endure, designed (in my opinion) to wear down the individual to the point where they:

- unwillingly withdraw from their case;
- accept a paltry compensation payment that in no way depicts a true reflection of either their pain and suffering or economic loss;
- or emotionally break down and suicide rather than continuing in a no-win situation where everyone seems pitted against them – despite many claimants having very legitimate claims.

On the other hand, the alleged bully(ies) and negligent employer(s) suffer no loss whatsoever. They continue to enjoy their career, ongoing income, no censure or visible punishment, no loss of social interaction/standing, no criminal charges etc. In fact, some project a demeanour of contempt and annoyance that they must have their lives inconvenienced by being involved in litigation, knowing full well that they only have to sit back and wait for the "system" to destroy the plaintiff during the process.

I do not expect any of the addressees of this letter to even acknowledge it let alone take any serious steps to remedy an unconscionable situation, but I did want you to hear from at least one seriously injured worker so that you know what it is like for a person who was an intelligent, hardworking, well respected, gainfully employed, self-supporting, long term taxpaying citizen of this country to find themselves caught in a heinous and grossly unfair compensation system that offers them no respite or fair restitution for their workplace injury.

Please explain why there is no justice for so many injured at work and why the "no win, no fee" really is an oxymoron?

Yours Sincerely,

Karen

I totally agree with all Karen has said, and I doubt the current situation for targets of workplace bullying has changed in any significant way, but I'd be very pleased to be wrong.

Around the same years, there were other cases of workplace bulling before the courts – namely Turner, Carr, Willet, Finlay and Brown. And also, Doulis,

Loiterton and Di Petro – surprisingly the latter three were all successful, while the former were not. The main differences I can see are that the former were all female and the secondary ones all male. Males were successful while the females were not. I ask myself: is there sexual bias or misogyny playing out here with either WorkCover, the courts or legal representatives allowing this, or at the very least, encouraging it? If a man says he was bullied it's believed, with compensation paid. If a woman says it, she's just hormonal, being emotional, or it's a personality clash, and no compensation is paid.

WorkCover is broken. We need to fix it.

TEN

"I Think" to Justify

Under WorkCover legislation, it is stated that any compensation gained by the injured worker must be paid directly to him/her. While this may sound fair, there is another section in the Accident Compensation Act 1985, Section 134 AB (30) which allows lawyers on application to the court to have the sums paid directly to them. As stated in Judge Robson's decision:

> "I then fixed Friday 30 April 2010 for the hearing of the application of the plaintiff's solicitors. On 28 April 2010, I signed a general form of order as follows: Subject to any claim that the plaintiff's solicitors may make under sub section 134 AB (30) of the Accident Compensation Act 1985."

Judge Robson signed the general form of order on the 28 April, maybe *just* after he had been informed by court registry staff on 27 April that I was seeking to have the settlement of 23 April set aside.

So, in effect, the previous piece of legislation is voided by this second piece, and—as always—it's in the lawyers' favour. In my case, my former legal team requested the settlement monies be paid directly to them straight after the court adjourned on Friday 23 April 2010. The judge set down 30 April to hear their application, and given my application I feel the judge was unsure of what to do. By this time, I had terminated the services of my legal representatives. I had a large number of family and friends with me in court on this day, and rather than risk giving the impression of unfairness the judge adjourned the court to take my application into account.

While waiting to hear from the court, I received another invoice from my former lawyer for $232,958.

Unknown to me at the time, the solicitors for WorkCover had written to my former lawyer informing her they had become aware that I had terminated her services, and given this they intended to request their client (WorkCover) to pay the settlement sum directly to the injured worker. That same day, my lawyer wrote back to them requesting they do not do so until she had applied for an injunction that the settlement monies be paid into court, pending the resolution of my "mooted appeal" or further order. They asserted a professional lien in respect of the settlement sum of $150,000, and this led to an *ex parte* application the next day. If only my lawyer had acted with such haste when she was representing me.

During this May 2010 *ex parte* application (according to the transcript), Mr Harrison states—relying upon what's called a "fruits of litigation lien" in order to restrain the payment out of a settlement sum to the plaintiff directly—that "disregarding her former solicitor's claim upon that settlement sum, impartial satisfaction of costs and disbursements incurred."

I was not given adequate notice of this proceeding so that I may attend; I was phoned and given notice 10 minutes prior to the hearing. I live in Geelong, and even if my broomstick was operational at this time, I wouldn't have made it by 3pm. Therefore, I was denied the opportunity to give oral evidence regarding matters in dispute, and to be considered fair, this hearing could have been held the next day to give me time to attend.

I believed my former legal team purposely orchestrated this *ex parte* application to deny me the opportunity to be heard in my own defence. Sadly, after reading the transcript of this hearing, I contend Mr Harrison was not truthful with the court. Had I been in attendance, I would have given sworn evidence of the following: that the affidavit filed by me in the Supreme Court on 17 May 2010, and mailed to my lawyer on 19 May 2010, was true and accurate, and my lawyer's affidavit (unsworn) in response to my affidavit contained errors of fact.

Part of their application related to the County Court costs of 2008, and these costs should have been claimed by my lawyer long before May 2010.

"I Think" to Justify

Why a lawyer waits so long to receive costs due to them mystifies me, but I'm sure there is a reason, and that it's advantageous to them. My lawyer eventually received the County Court costs in January of 2011.

According to the transcript, Mr Harrison states, "I think she had requested and the firm intended to request their client to pay the settlement sum directly to her." Further into the transcript he states, "As well as the specific advice to the defendant's solicitors Thomson Playford Cutlers that she wishes to have the settlement sums paid directly to her,"

Both of these statements made by Mr Harrison were untrue, as I had never expressed any specific advice or request to the defendant solicitors that their representatives pay the settlement sum directly to me. Mr Harrison had no evidence that I had made such requests, because I did not, and yet he told the court that I did.

Mr Harrison often used "I think." He never seemed sure enough to say yes or no.

I have read that using a justifier like "I think" introduces uncertainty. When "I think" is said, the person is inserting doubt, a lack of confidence and knowledge – and most importantly for me, ownership. If Harrison stated "I know" then he would not be telling the truth, but "I think" introduces "I am not lying, I am just unsure." Even when the speaker is not unsure and knows exactly what they are saying, there is no perjury because they prefixed it with "I think."

Mr Harrison's direct quote from same transcript: "outside the reach of those who've striven long and hard." Long and hard for almost ten years is what I endured; my lawyer could have prevented much of this delay by working in her client's best interests. Long delays are only in the best interests of defendants, and in some cases even your own lawyer. Given what I read in the transcript, I suggest Mr Harrison could've joined the local drama group if he wanted to act as poor Hamlet in a Shakespearean stage play.

The transcript records a lawyer from Thomson Playford Cutlers as being present in court; he remained silent when he knew Mr Harrison was not telling the truth, even though this lawyer knew I hadn't given any advice to him or his firm regarding having the settlement funds paid to me – they did this themselves of their own volition.

I believe Thomson Playford Cutlers wrote to my lawyer to give them a 'heads up' of what would be occurring, according to law, and to give her an opportunity to take the appropriate action. This wasn't about professional courtesy or a legal requirement – it was to make sure I did not get the funds; a case of lawyers looking out for lawyers. I'm still flabbergasted that Work-Cover was intent that I would not get any compensation, and preferred lawyers receive the funds rather than an injured worker.

I'm not sure I've ever fully understood the ruling at the end of the transcript, but it states that the judge adjourned the hearing to give me sufficient opportunity to respond to my lawyer's summons, to receive copy of the transcript, and to be served these documents immediately that afternoon. So the further hearing of their summons was adjourned to the following week, with the settlement monies paid into the Supreme Court's Senior Master to be held until final determination of the matter.

This judge appeared to be fair and reasonable – she no doubt understood *ex parte* applications often take place without the knowledge of the other party, but I'm unsure if this is the reason, as I don't know enough about these legal processes.

The adjourned hearing took place on the following Wednesday in the Practice Court. I attended on my own, unsure of what was expected of me. The lawyer Travis was in attendance on behalf of my lawyer, and I quietly said to him, "You threw my case" and "So if I do not agree to your summons then you plan to charge me another $232,958?" and he replied with a snarl "Every cent of it." Mr Jens was directly behind me when this comment was made; I have no doubt he heard it.

The case was announced, the lawyers made oral applications, and the judge requested I respond. I simply said, "Your Honour, it appears that if I do not agree to have the settlement funds paid out to them then I am to be charged a further $232,958." The judge adjourned the court to consider my response, returning around 15 minutes later to say that I was to return to the court the next day in front of Robson and cross-examine my former legal team.

With little opportunity to prepare a case, I did the best I could over that evening to prepare to present my claims against my former legal team. This was incredibly stressful – I was up against two lawyers and three barristers who, in my opinion, appeared happy to attend to be cross-examined without being subpoenaed or ordered to by the court. Now, given the outcome of the June hearing, I am unsure if this opportunity was legitimate, or simply provided the scene for my demise.

The next day, in front of Robson, I duly explained my position that Work-Cover treated bullied workers unfairly even when the truth was known that the claim was legitimate, and that given the funds expended in my name, my case was a matter of public interest. I believed my case to be a strong one, and I believed it was a case that needed to run to full trial for the real issues in dispute to be examined. There wasn't the opportunity for that; I think, hopefully, through the evidence presented, that I was asking the judge to either continue with the hearing himself or to adjourn it to be heard without a jury and hear it as a matter – hear the matter as a cause. I would have been greatly assisted at this June hearing if I had a copy of the April transcript, but this was denied to me. Therefore, I was denied procedural fairness; later after a number of requests WorkCover reluctantly gave me a copy on 22 July 2010 – too late to be of assistance. It should be noted that even though the case cited my former employer as the defendant, the real defendants were my former legal team.

I was unsure then—and am not completely sure now—as to the purpose of this 'opportunity' to cross-examine my former legal team. One reason I have considered is the 'doctrine of advocates immunity', whereby immunity does not extend to advice given in relation to settlement offers because the advice did not affect the judicial determination of the case. I estimate that it was known at this time that I was not the kind of plaintiff who would go quietly after such an experience, and that advocate's immunity would not afford the required protection for my former legal representatives against any action I may bring – what was needed was a judicial determination, a determination bad enough that I would forever be discredited and silenced. Dissidents no longer have to disappear in the dead of night or be sent to Siberia to become powerful martyrs – now with the advent of the internet age, they could be silenced by the written word. The word of a judge is rarely questioned – even less so by those fortunate enough to have never suffered an injustice. On occasion, their words carry far more weight than they deserve.

I have gone into some detail in this chapter compared to other hearings because the June hearing was the one and only opportunity to get to some truth of the matter – which I did, but unfortunately the judge did not agree with me. I believed my former legal team had scandalised the court with their concept of truth, all while under oath. Lawyers are artful when questioning those on the stand, but when these roles are reversed, it was surprising to see how poorly they responded – they were flustered, contradictory, confused and at times untruthful.

My first witness was the defendant's barrister, who only the day before had made a nice comment to me, stating, "You're an intelligent lady and the ASU case and the way you did it basically showed that." I also remember a comment made in open court from the barrister who represented the defendant at the County Court: "Your Honour, Mrs O'Keeffe obviously has superior managerial skills." And yet all through the defendant's sworn witness statements, my former management team made allegations that I was an underperformer. We had two very different accounts, one made by intelligent barristers the other by workplace bullies.

I put to the witness I wasn't convinced that many of his questions in cross-examination were relevant – questions like "What kind of car do you drive?" I couldn't comprehend how that could be relevant to a workplace bullying injury damages negligence trial. I asked the witness if he felt that it was a relevant question, and he responded, "Yes.' (I guess he really could not respond in any other way, because to do so would be confirming the question was irrelevant.)

I put to the witness that there seemed to be quite a lot of questioning on things such as rostered days off, time in lieu and on-call allowances, and those questions were put in two or three different ways and I was asked over and over again what they meant. I questioned if he thought that a jury of reasonable people would understand what a rostered day off was, or what time in lieu or on-call allowance was, and his response: "May or may not."

These questions from him, especially the 'on-call allowance' one, were designed to inflict the notion that I was selfish and paid myself more of these allowances than my staff. In Chapter Two and Chapter Eight I explained in detail why my on-call allowances were greater than my staff's, and yet there appeared to be a lot of court time spent on clarifying those very simple work practices to the jury. His response: "Was there?"

I was asked questions by him such as, "Have you been overseas?" I had travelled twice in the 10 years awaiting my compensation hearing, and I didn't believe that to be unreasonable. The trips were both for family reasons which were important to me. I'm guessing once again that they were used to discredit me with the jury, as this was the best the defendant could muster—to denigrate my character—as no evidence existed that supported any wrongdoing by me. Also, there were a lot of questions expended on my volunteer work, especially at the 2000 Olympics, which once again delayed valuable court time. We weren't actually getting to the issues that were in dispute, expending time on issues that weren't really issues at all. We weren't actually getting down to

"I Think" to Justify

what happened in my workplace, about how I was injured, and showing foreseeability, which we never even got to. When I asked him about this, he said: "Right."

I stated to the court that I felt I was being prejudiced with the jury by being asked questions that really had no bearing on the case, questions designed to denigrate me in the eyes of the jury. Of course, I now know this is called 'victim blaming'. During cross-examination there was a particular comment made by the defendant's barrister that I found to be quite offensive. "Your claim of serious injury was an assault on the City of Wyndham." Now, obviously that was quite inflammatory, and in my turn at cross-examination I asked the witness if he agreed that this comment was inflammatory, and he responded, "I can't remember that aspect of it, but no."

In Victoria, there is a section of the Evidence Act that lists the type of questions deemed to be improper to ask a witness and which are not allowed. These include questions that harass or intimidate a witness, as well as questions that are misleading, confusing or "have no basis other than a stereotype."

The Act states that the court may disallow an improper question or improper questioning put to a witness in cross-examination, or inform the witness that it need not be answered. Not only did my legal team fail to do this, the court did too. Judge Robson in his judgement stated that the cross-examination was tough but fair; I respectfully disagree.

Given the evidence, I felt that I was the one under assault; my claim was upheld by the Magistrates' Court, my discrimination claim successful, my privacy complaint was upheld by the Victorian Privacy Commissioner, and the County Court issued a serious injury certificate. Combine this with the fact that the insurer accepted liability for all my injuries and illnesses, and various medical practitioners had all been supportive of my claim, and yet I was apparently the one making an assault on my former employer. Walsh later under re-examination stated in his evidence that my pursuit of these actions displayed a personality which was unreasonable; if it's deemed unreasonable to pursue your legal rights when they are violated then I believe we as a society would have little use for lawyers. The legal profession relies on people who act reasonably and unreasonably when it suits their agenda and their pocket.

It was Walsh's evidence that some of my more bizarre conduct included a complaint to the DPP. In a democracy, we have a right to write to any government official about any matter that concerns us. Yet, now added to the 'unreasonable personality' we had 'bizarre conduct' added to the list of my faults.

Had Walsh been aware of the facts he would have known that it was Work-Cover who wrote to the DPP, and as I have stated earlier this letter from Work-Cover to the DPP was discovered in the defendant's affidavit of documents. Had Walsh been properly prepared he may have known this. Or maybe he did.

The jury wasn't allowed to know my claimed injury had already been found to be serious and genuine, but they were allowed to know what kind of car I drove. This was of great advantage for WorkCover; to pit the injured worker against any prejudices or bias the jury may feel. In my opinion, it may well be said that a jury should leave these attributes at the jury door, but in reality, it is extremely difficult to divorce oneself of preconceived bias and judgements gained over many years. I believe the asking of what kind of car I drove falls into the section of the Evidence Act which says, "have no basis other than a stereotype."

Those claims or questions weren't designed to get to the truth – they were to prejudice me in the eyes of the jury as being a difficult person. I don't believe I am a difficult person, nor was I then, when all I was doing was enacting my legal rights. I like to obey the laws and have others with an obligation to the law do so as well. Most organisations have a complaint process – the VWA (Victorian WorkCover Authority) has a complaints process, even the Supreme Court has a complaints process. As such, I asked the witness if he felt it was necessary to continue to discredit me with the jury by insinuating I was a constant complainer, when all these organisations have complaint processes and I was justified (successful) in my complaints. Why have complaint processes if you're not supposed to use them? Why, if you do, are you labelled as difficult? His response: "I like to . . . extract relevant facts which I think advance my client's case."

If I did become a 'chronic complainer' (which I refute) maybe I became a chronic complainer because I experienced and suffered from such chronic misbehaviour.

I would argue these kinds of questions are not seeking relevant facts, and are only relevant if you want to assassinate a person's character, because this is what has to be done when no evidence exists that the injured worker committed any crime. If a crime could be found—even if the crime is of no relevance to the injury—you are doomed in front of a jury.

All the evidence at hand to the defendant made it quite clear I was the one assaulted, not my employer. This kind of comment strikes at the heart of an injured worker, minimising their pain and maximising their blame. Lo and

"I Think" to Justify

behold, any injured worker having a holiday, attempting a return to work, volunteering or travelling must be rorting the system... I believe this is why these kinds of questions are asked. Yet under law an injured worker must attempt to mitigate their loss and attempt to repair their good health through rehabilitation and attempt again to be a functioning member of society. If you do not participate in life, then you are personally doomed, and if you do participate, WorkCover dooms you.

The judge interjected with sympathy for my view, but stated the defendant barrister was just putting his client's case. Mr Jens obviously thought the questions were relevant, but at the end of the day the judge stated that it was up to my legal team to object if they were irrelevant questions and then he could've ruled on it. The judge went on to say that they didn't object, but they still had evidence-in-chief and they could've picked it up in re-examination, but in my opinion evidence-in-chief (which was to occur on the 23 April) was pre-planned never to take place for all the reasons previously and currently canvassed.

I put to the witness that we never actually got to the part of the hearing where the aspects of the bullying, the harassment, the intimidation, discrimination and victimisation that I was subjected to were covered, because I felt that Mr Jens was delaying the process by asking irrelevant questions that were taking up a lot of court time so that we actually didn't get to the relevant parts of my case. His response: "Well, I'm not sure whether I should say thank you or not." I'm not sure what to make of his comment – I'm not sure what it means.

It is obvious the defendant gained access to my application for a position with the Red Cross, and once again insinuated I was lying in this application. I stated to him that as an experienced personal injury barrister, he would understand that when applicants or potential employees fill out the section on their health information, they do still have a right to privacy under the Equal Opportunity Act and are not required to declare every injury or disease if they chose not to. It simply means that if you don't include this information, you are not covered if you have a subsequent aggravation – you cannot make a claim under the WorkCover Act. "Yes, I heard you give that answer," he said. This answer is the legally accepted answer under law, but a jury may not know this, and the defendant further brands you as dishonest. It is at these times that the inexperience and naivety of the jury plays into the defendant's hands.

The judge interjected here, saying my explanation for not including this information could have been got out by my team in re-examination, but as I stated earlier, re-examination scheduled for 23 April was never going to happen.

Towards the end of my questioning, I asked another question of the defendant's barrister, an important one: I put to him that on the morning of 23 April, at approximately 8:30am, I was told by my former legal representatives that he had requested leave of the court to continue with his cross-examination, and such leave was given. My former legal team told me Mr Jens wanted to continue his cross-examination regarding my voluntary involvement in the organisation of a conference in 2004 (once again, how is this relevant?), and his reply was, "We didn't ever get to this" – and that is because the trial terminated on 23 April, as it was supposed to.

As the transcript shows, I continued to press: "But you asked for leave to continue cross-examination on that Friday morning?"

"M'mm, and leave was granted."

I queried: "And leave was granted?" He responded that the case ended shortly after.

I probed further, asking why he wanted cross-examination on that organisation, but the judge interjected, "Well, is that really relevant? I mean, he didn't."

I respond that Jens sought leave of the court to do so, so he must have thought it important, and the judge's response was, "Yes, he ended up not doing it, so."

It was not until a few weeks later that I finally received a copy of the April hearing transcript, and there was no mention in that transcript of the defendant's barrister seeking leave of the court to continue cross-examination and no mention that the judge gave such leave. I then realised my former barrister had told me this at 8:30am, even though court was not in session until 10:30am, so I wonder when exactly Mr Jens had sought this leave and when the judge had granted it.

There is no evidence that proves the seeking of leave and the granting of leave, and yet the defendant barrister under oath states, "M'mm, and leave was granted and the case ended shortly after." By reading this, I get the impression that leave was granted sometime in the morning, as the case ended shortly after at around 12:30pm. If this is correct then it should be in the transcript, but it is not. Coupled with the fact the judge would have known this was untrue just further illustrates to me how the judiciary supports the legal fraternity. Earlier

"I Think" to Justify

in the hearing, the judge in response to a question from me said, "But, it's Mr Jens' duty and he doesn't have any personal discretion about the matter at all. It's his duty to put his client's case." I know barristers have a duty as an officer of the court not to mislead the court, but if the transcript is correct, he used his personal discretion and the duty he may have felt to his client's case to support the untruth fed to me by my former barristers, and in doing so swore under oath to something he knew to be untrue.

My opinion is that he did not seek this leave at all – that it was a designed tactic by my former barristers to force me to settle. I feel they may have been of the opinion that further cross-examination on this topic in some way would scare me, even though there was nothing untoward about my voluntary involvement in this conference and I had no reason to be scared. This tactic failed, and my barristers scrambled to find other ways to scare me into settlement. More on this later.

This barrister had earlier said in response to my question about my case being settled on 23 April and not running for the five weeks, as instigated by the defendant: "It had nothing to do with me whether you got that far or not." Once he had misled the court, it had everything to do with him – he was putting his duty to his client's case above his duty to the court. Had he attested he did not seek leave of the court to continue cross-examination, I would then have proof my legal team had lied, and I may have had a chance to have my case reopened and heard as a 'cause'. His client WorkCover and my former legal representatives would not have wanted this; their wants trumped fairness and integrity in legal proceedings.

Another tactic employed by my legal team was to tell me on the first day of trial that the defendant barrister didn't want to do this case, inferring my case was in some way awful or ugly, and the barrister had offered his own funds to help in the settlement of it – that's how ugly my case was. As this barrister was under oath, I asked him the question, "Did you make that statement that you did not want to conduct the case?"

"No," is all he said.

"You didn't make that statement?" I probed.

"No, I said I didn't want to be stuck in a case of this nature for five or six weeks."

The worst offenders of the worse crimes get legal representation for the length of their trial, and yet it appears that a workplace bullying trial is not worthy.

I remember clearly that in the first days of trial, my lawyers informed me of daily offers of settlement made by the defendant. I asked Mr Jens if he could remember the offers, and he stated he could remember the exact amounts of every offer made to my side and the dates when the offers were made. I was glad to hear this, as the timing and the amounts of offers was rampant during the first week of the trial and quite confusing for me.

"Okay, Mr Jens, your first offer was on Wednesday 14th of April?"

He responded, "The first offer amount that I exactly know about was Wednesday 21st April, which was $120,000 inclusive of costs."

Mr Jens was confident of his evidence that the first offer was on 21st April, which does not accord with what I had been told by my legal team. On the first day of hearing on 14 April, I was told prior to court there was an offer of settlement from the defendant. Upon me stating this, Mr Jens suddenly recalled that there was an earlier offer in the first week of the trial after he had already testified, "I exactly know . . . Wednesday 21st April."

I went on to say that on Thursday 15 April, the advice I received was that the defendant had made another offer, and after legal fees I would have received $30,000, and Mr Jens responded, "No idea."

I pressed; did he not make an offer on Thursday 15 April?

"The only offer that was made prior to Wednesday 21st, that is the $120,000, was an offer that was considerably less, and I think it was $80,000 or thereabouts."

What about an offer on Friday 16 April?

His response: "It may have been 50, I've just— I just don't have that note." And yet earlier he testified he knew exactly the dates and amounts.

Mr Jens went on to give evidence that after making an offer on Thursday 22 April, he received a phone call from Walsh that evening asking him whether the $150,000 was still available. But there wasn't any offer of $150,000 being made to me on that Thursday, so how could he ask if the offer of $150,000 was still available?

Then on Friday 23 April we get to the final offer, which is $150,000, and legal fees set at $150,000. Coincidently this is the amount I heard my lawyer say to junior counsel on the phone on 9 April before the hearing commenced: "the amount of $150,000 all-in." So it was known from this date the offer was $150,000 and would never be any more, and I believed my 'Claytons' trial was just an attempt to expend this offer on legal fees and to give me the trial for which I had waited ten years. In my now-educated opinion I believe that 'settlement offers' are in actuality a 'bribe' to your legal team.

Mr Jens testified that he knew the exact amounts and on what day they were offered, but he later stated "No idea" about the offer made on 15 April and 16 April. "I just don't have that note" – I understand the above may be quite complex to understand, but I was trying to point out that it appeared my legal team was making bogus settlement offers to me, and Mr Jens was changing his evidence as we went along to support the position of my former legal team.

I'm yet to be convinced otherwise that although my case was set for a five-week hearing, there were plans that it wouldn't run for five weeks. Nobody really had the time or was prepared for a five-week trial when one side was operating on a 'no win, no fee' schedule. I now believe this to be the reason why it was difficult for my lawyer to get counsel to run my trial. I'm coming to the opinion that plaintiff law firms are certainly at a disadvantage to the 'cashed up' WorkCover defendant. Just the threat of a five-week trial by this kind of defendant recreates a conflict of interest for plaintiff law firms, and just as Mr Jens said: "Well, I can assure you there were no plans, and my instructions were to conduct this case and take it to verdict, however long it took."

However long it took? If as Mr Jens contends through his evidence that he would have run the case to its conclusion, why did his main witness go overseas the weekend after my case terminated on the Friday? When did John the manager book his flights, and how did he know he would be free to travel on those dates? I wish I knew this at the time and could have put that question to Mr Jens, but unfortunately, I didn't understand the relevance of this until about three years later.

"However long it took" – he would still be paid no matter the outcome, and my lawyers only paid if we had won, which is very concerning in what is supposed to be a fair, accessible and equitable justice system. I conservatively estimate the costs of just legal representation alone for a five-week trial would be around $500,000, with associated legal costs of $140,000, and for the defendant barristers around $160,000 and for my barristers around $200,000, as my barristers were charging $10,000 per week more than the defendant barristers. So if I had been successful after a five-week trial the defendant would be required to pay my reasonable costs and their own. I suggest my barrister costs wouldn't have been allowed at the figure agreed to by my lawyer, and would have been discounted to the defendant barristers rate. We are back at that magical figure of $320,000.

WorkCover could have settled this claim after a 'serious injury certificate' was granted in the County Court for $300,000 two years prior. And I believe the above proves my point that they'd rather give the compensation due to the injured worker to the legal profession, utterly disregarding the 'Model Litigant Guidelines' and the Judiciary Act of 1903 (which include the standards for how the state, its departments and agencies behave as a model litigant in the conduct of litigation and how it should behave as a party to a legal proceeding).

Briefly, the state is required to: act fairly in handling claims; act consistently in the handling of claims and litigation; deal with claims promptly and not cause unnecessary delay; pay legitimate claims without litigation; to resolve the dispute by agreement, including participating in appropriate dispute resolution processes or settlement negotiations. Where it is not possible to avoid litigation, to keep the costs of litigation to a minimum, including by: not requiring the other party to prove a matter which the state knows to be true; not contesting liability if the state believes that the main dispute is about quantum; monitoring the progress of the litigation, and, where appropriate, attempting to resolve the litigation, including by settlement offers, offers of compromise and ADR; and to participate fully and effectively in alternate dispute resolution. In the chapter on mediation, you will have read about how the defendant participated fully and effectively in my alternate dispute resolution.

And further: "Do not take advantage of a claimant who lacks the resources to litigate a legitimate claim." I feel this is where injured workers relying on 'no win, no fee' are greatly disadvantaged. My favourite: "For the state to consider apologising where the state or the agency is aware that it or its representatives have acted wrongfully or improperly."

In essence, being a model litigant requires that the state and its agencies, as parties to litigation, act with complete propriety, fairly and in accordance with the highest professional standards. The expectation that the state and its agencies will act as a model litigant has been recognised by the courts. The obligation to act as a model litigant may require more than merely acting honestly and in accordance with the law and court rules. It also goes beyond the requirement for lawyers to act in accordance with their ethical obligations.

To my knowledge of the Model Litigant Guidelines, WorkCover shouldn't pursue cases at all costs no matter what, and that the duty of counsel acting on behalf of the VWA or the State of Victoria is obligated to act fairly.

Finally, I asked Mr Jens one more question: "After the conclusion of my case on 23 April, were you— did you appear in another case within the next week or two?"

His response: "I'm sure I would have. ---I'm sure I would have. Once I was – when I say with due humility once it was realised I was available I would have been snapped up."

This answer gives me the impression that he possibly knew this case would be completed in time for him to accept a brief for the next week.

There are a number of requirements to have a judgement set aside, one being that it must be shown by admissible evidence that the successful party was responsible for the fraud which taints the judgement under challenge. It must be shown that a party in so acting was in concert with the party who derived the benefit of the judgement. Given the evidence already outlined, most of which is contained in the transcript, I might suggest Mr Jens may have been complicit with my former legal team to get the judgement desired by them, while at the same time assisting his client, WorkCover, to get the judgement they wanted.

I felt Mr Jens exhibited no personal malice towards me – he was just doing his job as he saw it and how the legal brotherhood and the state (in total disregard to the Model Litigant Guidelines) demanded it.

My second witness was my former barrister Matt Walsh, who I had met the day before trial, a trial scheduled to run for five weeks. What was of concern to me was the fact I would need witnesses to prove my case and there was little contact with my witnesses and certainly no witness statements were taken or discovered by the defendant. Mr Walsh gives evidence that he prepared a list of witnesses which was provided to His Honour, and he identified the order and the likelihood of those witnesses giving evidence. I didn't see this list on the day, nor was there evidence of this list either in my lawyer file or the Supreme Court file. Maybe it was lost or never existed in the first place. I contend there was little witness preparation because no witness was ever going to be called, and this was proven to be correct.

To support his contention that he had taken appropriate steps in regards to witnesses, Walsh testified that he did discuss the matter with Mr Richard McGarvie before the case commenced, and that he had read the judgment of Judge Misso and discussed with Mr McGarvie the issues pertaining to liability in my case, and that he believes this was relevant. Maybe it was relevant, but not more important than having witnesses prepared before hearing.

My case terminated on Friday 23 April, and so I asked Walsh if he had organised conduct of any trial the next week or the following week, and his response was "Yes, there were – I may have been involved, and I am very sure that I have been involved in other cases in the next two weeks, yes."

During this June hearing, Walsh under oath stated that he did conduct a trial the following week – the week commencing 26 April 2010.

I asked Walsh if he was one of the counsel that Mr Jens made an offer of settlement to on Wednesday 14 April (keeping in mind Mr Jens initially swore in his evidence that his first offer was on 21 April, but then after further questioning by me remembered an earlier offer). Walsh confirmed it was indeed him, and I asked if he remembered what that offer was, and his response was that he did and he stated the offer was $150,000 all-in. This was not the offer made to me on this day; the first time this offer was made to me was on Friday 23 April.

I pressed further, and asked Walsh if there was another offer on Thursday 15 April, and he responded that he believed there was an earlier offer made, and he believed the first offer was about $80,000 all-in, or thereabouts, but that he could be wrong about that. Walsh was becoming confused, as he stated here the earlier offer was $80,000, but he had previously responded the first offer was $150,000.

I stated to Walsh that in reality, during this whole process, there was never going to be any compensation for me, that there was only ever going to be costs for them. I felt Walsh became quite flustered; his response was somewhat bizarre and not relevant to the question asked. He said, "Well, Your Honour, this is very, any lawyers? Can I just say this, Your Honour. If Your Honour is minded to accede to this application, ah, Your Honour, there's a matter that Your Honour probably needs to know about the statutory offer process. And if that were the case, ah, Your Honour would have to disqualify himself from hearing the case."

There had been no evidence lead during this hearing or the April hearing in regards to the statutory offer process – why Walsh raised it here is unclear. Later he stated that he wasn't in a position to disclose what the offers were, but this was not the question being asked, and there was never a question asked about the statutory offer process or any offers made. His above testimony is nonsensical – what was he really trying to say?

"I Think" to Justify

I put to the witness that on the morning of 23 April he made a statement to me that he had heard a comment by a juror, and he responded, "Ah, yes, I did indicate to you, ah, that I had heard a comment by the unemployed Greek juror." This was the first I knew that an unemployed Greek juror was on the jury. In response to a question from the defendant regarding my application to the Red Cross I said, "I was never going to make another claim." And this is when the Greek juror muttered audibly, "Yeah, sure."

It appeared the defendant had a copy of my file from the Red Cross, and in that file would be an incident report about an injury I had suffered, but that no WorkCover claim was made for and that I paid the medical expenses. I feel Mr Jens would have known my answer was true and correct, but the saviour for them all was the unemployed Greek juror's comment.

I questioned further, and Walsh stated it was audibly heard by him, Travis and the judge's associate. He testified, "I understand that, um, for— Your Honour, for the record, what I heard was that, ah, the Greek juror, um, and perhaps in context, and I've put this in a memo which I prepared after the event and before Ms O'Keeffe decided to take this action."

Before I had decided to take this action? I didn't decide to take this action, the Practice Court the previous day ordered this action be taken, but I did swear and serve an affidavit on 27 April to have the settlement set aside – maybe this is the action he is referring to. The April hearing terminated on Friday 23 April; the following Monday was a public holiday, and I filed my affidavit on Tuesday 27 April, but Walsh's evidence is that he put this in a memo which he prepared after the event and before I filed my affidavit.

I understand barristers no doubt work weekends and maybe even public holidays, but I would suggest that my case wasn't important enough for Walsh to do so. In later evidence he stated he wrote this memo setting out the basis of the resolution of the claim on 27 April and provided it to my lawyer on 28 April, and the first time he became aware of my application to have the settlement set aside was when he was back in court on the Thursday (29 April) for their costs application, and it was then that he was provided with a copy of my affidavit.

The court return date was Friday (30 April), not 29 April as said by Walsh. My affidavit was served on my lawyer on Tuesday 27 April, so I find it hard to believe my lawyer didn't inform Walsh of this action prior to him finding out in court three days later. In my opinion, if Walsh wrote this memo at all, it was after he had knowledge that I was taking action to have the settlement set aside and not before. In a later taxation of costs hearing, I attempted discovery of this document—the Costs Court order the document be discovered—but it was not provided.

Walsh's evidence continued: "In response to this, His Honour's associate also heard something mentioned, and it wasn't that word." This is interesting: "and it wasn't that word" – how did Walsh know it was not that word? He must have had discussions with the associate to know this, and yet later when I asked the associate to confirm what he had heard, he refused and stated he was not a lawyer and to ring the Supreme Court Registry for this information. I rang and spoke to a male person and his response was it was not a matter for them but a matter for the court.

Was there really a comment and was it ever confirmed by the judge? Did his associate really hear the comment? I would imagine that a 'black letter' judge would want to know the answer to these questions.

Walsh also stated, "Mr Jens I understand may have heard something, but he wasn't quite sure what it was." Now on the morning of 23 April, when the seriousness of the juror's comment was relayed to me, there was no mention of Mr Jens hearing this comment, because if he had they would have included him in the list of persons who had heard the comment. I believe it was sometime later Mr Jens was informed of this comment by Walsh or Harrison.

I said to the witness, "So everyone's hearing negative comments from jurors?" Walsh responds, "It's very, it's very— Can I just say this, it's very weird to hear anything from a juror."

I respond, "Well, I would have thought so too – yes, it wasn't my understanding of how a jury would work." This was the point at which I believe the jury should have been discharged, and if my lawyers were keen to run my case, as Walsh said in evidence ("But I can say this, that there was no greater priority on my legal calendar on 23 April, when this matter resolved, other than your case") they had a golden opportunity to have the jury discharged and to go judge alone. My lawyer knew that had always been my preference (judge alone), but they refused my instructions to seek leave of the court to have the jury discharged. Yet in his evidence, Walsh swore I did not instruct him to discharge the jury. He confirmed we discussed it, but I didn't instruct them. It is inconceivable that I would let such an opportunity pass, given that if I accepted the settlement offer, I would receive nothing, let alone any vindication I was seeking to restore my damaged reputation and the affront to my integrity.

"I Think" to Justify

I was deeply concerned about the behaviour of this jury member, as it was this statement that was used against me to force the settlement, used by my barristers as proof the jury did not like me. This confirms that juries must personally like you to be successful, and evidence and facts play only a small part in their deliberations – and experienced barristers must know this to be true.

The Juries Act 2000 states that a judge may, during a trial, discharge a juror without discharging the whole jury if it appears to the judge that the juror is not impartial, or if it appears to the judge that, for any other reason, the juror should not continue to act as a juror. In my opinion, if the whole jury had heard this comment—which would have had to have been probable—a request from my legal team to seek an order the jury be discharged would not have been unreasonable.

To be fair, the judge could have asked the other jurors if they had heard the comment (undoubtedly likely, since both Walsh and the judge's associate said they'd heard it). The judge could have compelled the juror who made the comment to admit to it and to ask other jurors if this would have influence over their deliberations. I feel confident that in a criminal trial a defence barrister would fight to the end to ensure their client's right to a fair trial, and make a charge that the jury be dismissed. But in my experience of personal injury trials, this isn't the case – your lawyers don't fight for you in the same way. Their fight is based on economics due to the 'no win, no fee' structure injured workers have to submit to if they want legal representation.

Lawyers and barristers suffer a conflict of interest – their financial interests versus the injured worker's right to a fair trial. These lawyers are conflicted because of the costs of running the trial versus the risk of them not getting paid. I don't know who decided my case would run for five weeks at an approximate cost of $500,000, but I'm guessing it was a strategy of the defendant law firm, knowing full well that my legal representation wouldn't be prepared to do so. Even if successful, any possible compensation mightn't even cover the legal costs, therefore my case was destined to run for one week, and one week only. It was an economic decision. Justice *does* have a price!

It's understandable – we can't have legal counsel in the field of personal injury constantly working for nothing. But it's a fault of the system. It's the system's plan to pay the big bucks to defendant law firms, bonuses to boot, and big dividends to government. Not to care about injured workers, or those who had their cases compromised. WorkCover is a money-making venture for government to get more in their coffers, so they can spend more making it look like they are doing a marvellous job when it comes to re-election. Injured workers are just a means to their end.

Throughout my trial I was continuously confused by the relevance of the questions asked by the defendant barrister (e.g. the car one). I couldn't understand why such questions were necessary when the case was about determining whether my former employer was negligent or not, and if this negligence caused injury. Surely, the car I drove wasn't relevant to this matter. To me, it simply demonstrated that the defendant barrister knew the jury would judge me on this irrelevant fact.

I often looked towards my barristers during this kind of questioning, expecting an "Objection, Your Honour," but it never came. The Evidence Act states that a party may object to a question put to a witness on the ground that it is an improper question, but I'm not sure if Harrison was even aware of what was going on as he was always busy writing in his blue notebook.

The Evidence Act states, "However, the duty imposed on the court by this section applies whether or not an objection is raised to a particular question." So Judge Robson's imposed duty led him to believe this was a perfectly relevant question? He didn't ask himself the pertinent questions, like what would be the purpose of such a question, would it be prejudicial, and is asking such a question against the law? According to the Act it is, and Walsh's comments come flooding back to me: "This is his first personal injury trial," "He does not like doing these kinds of trials," and "This is his first jury trial."

As I stated earlier, the Evidence Act says that during examination in chief and re-examination the court may disallow an improper question or improper questioning put to a witness in cross-examination, or inform the witness that it need not be answered. I could see why Harrison wasn't doing anything about this as he was too busy elsewhere, but why did the judge allow this kind of irrelevant questioning? The Act also states that the court must disallow an improper question or improper questioning put to a vulnerable witness in cross-examination, or inform the witness that it need not be answered, unless the court is satisfied that, in all the relevant circumstances of the case, it is necessary for the question to be put. I was a vulnerable witness, but nobody informed me that I need not answer irrelevant questions. Also, how necessary was it that the court—and more importantly the jury—know what kind of car I drove? The court in no way could be satisfied that there existed a need for this question to be put.

"I Think" to Justify

My understanding is that a question or a sequence of questions put to a witness that are: misleading or confusing; or are unduly annoying, harassing, intimidating, offensive, oppressive, humiliating or repetitive; or are put to the witness in a manner or tone that is belittling, insulting or otherwise inappropriate (I experienced many of these and I feel quite confident that many plaintiffs in the personal injury field experience this as well); or have no basis other than a stereotype, for example, a stereotype based on the witness's sex, race, culture, ethnicity age or mental, intellectual or physical disability.

The stereotype used against me may have included a little of each, but the main stereotype the defence barrister was pushing to the jury was 'greedy bitch' – and therefore if you drive a luxury car your rights under law to compensation from a workplace injury are void. The only reason I could have been asked this question was to get the jury of my 'peers' offside, and it worked wonderfully. This question was clearly prejudicial – I may have had so called legal representation, but no one in the court stood up to protect my legal rights. I felt my head was on the chopping block, with Madame Defarge knitting another stitch to cheers from both sides.

My instructions were ignored because that wasn't the plan – the plan was that my case finished on 23 April, as they had money in the bag. If they continued, the money in the bag may disappear, and such a risk wasn't to be taken purely for the sake of their client's rights and instructions.

I put to Walsh that on the morning of 23 April he said to me, "This judge is bad and very harsh. It is his first civil personal injury trial and he does not like these kinds of cases. Trust me, I know him personally." I asked him to confirm he made this comment. His response was that he did not say this and he rejected the comment.

I replied that I did not agree with his rejection of this statement because that is exactly what he had said to me. It was his statement that caused me to suffer anxiety, panic and a psychological reaction to what was happening in that room. I became upset and was crying, and I didn't know what happened to my request to have the jury discharged.

In regards to the $150,000 offer, I asked Walsh if he made the comment, "That won't even cover our costs, so we'll have to take a reduction and we'll just have to accept the full $150,000 as payment." He responded that he recalled that, and that Mr Harrison indicated that they were certainly taking a reduction in what they would normally charge. That 'bird in the hand' flies again. Further, Walsh stated, "You will owe us nothing," and at that point, of course, the realisation would be that after 10 years of illness, unemployment, working my way/battling my way through the WorkCover process, that I was actually going to get zero compensation. His response: "That was, ah, unfortunately, the—." The end of his testimony was not transcribed, but I believe the word would be "case," and I responded, "I think that would make anyone cry – did I cry?"

Walsh testified that I wasn't crying through this process, but later submitted there may have been tears, but not crying.

I was getting towards the end of Walsh's testimony, but I had one more detail to present to the court, and that was the physical behaviour of my lawyers during the morning of 23 April in the small conference room – behaviour I felt was threatening. I stated to the court that both Harrison and Walsh were standing over me and pushing and pushing and pushing me to settle. I asked Walsh if he was hovering over me, standing over me while I was seated. His response: "Ah, no, I was sitting. You were sitting, I was sitting and I was sitting to your left and almost behind you and, ah, I believe that um all members of the legal team were sitting."

I put again to the witness that he was standing. His response, "No." I reiterated to him that he was standing to my left and Mr Harrison was standing in front of me slightly to my right with his arms crossed. His response, "I believe that we were all sitting." The use of the term, "I believe" is very similar to the term "I think," and used for the same reason.

It was much later, around September, that I became aware that there were two people in the court environs on that day who witnessed (through the window of the room) the behaviour of my legal team, and both confirmed in affidavits that both Walsh and Harrison were indeed standing over me while I was upset.

On the last day during the distressing settlement negotiations, I instructed my legal team to the run the case for one more day, and I said I'd pay the costs right then, as I had my chequebook in my handbag and I had an excellent witness waiting to give testimony, but Walsh denied I said this. Interestingly, he stated that I *did* indicate I wanted another day, but I had said this on a number of previous occasions and not on *this* day, according to him. Simply wrong: 23 April was the first time I had requested just one more day, because on the previous days I was of the opinion that my case was still to run for at least another three weeks.

The judge interjected here and asked Walsh, "And did Mrs O'Keeffe refer

"I Think" to Justify

to her chequebook?" His response: "Ah, Your Honour, she did not refer to her chequebook. And whatever she had in her handbag, Your Honour, if she— Certainly I was never— At no stage advised she had a chequebook, and when I first read this affidavit which is about the— Probably about 28th or 29th April, it was, ah, it was, um, news to my ears." Walsh testified earlier that the first he knew of my affidavit to have the settlement set aside was at the costs hearing on 30 April, and yet now he testifies it was 28 or 29 April.

I confirmed I had finished with the witness, and Mr Ingram of counsel, who had previously acted for me but was now acting for my former legal team, stood to re-examine Walsh. It was at this moment Walsh stated that he wished to clarify costings. But without mentioning a word about costings he went on to make what I consider to be a bizarre statement. His statement as recorded in the transcript and at page 87 is below:

MR WALSH: Your Honour, could I just clarify one issue regarding the costing? I know that Your Honour was interested in that comment? Can I ask you some questions, Your Honour, about this?

HIS HONOUR: Yes. You clarify the costings first?

MR WALSH: Your Honour, one of the— When you're acting for a plaintiff who suffers in particular psychological injury as a consequence of a workplace issue, it's always been in my view very important for counsel to look after a plaintiff and advise them along the way, and particularly if they're facing a very adverse finding at the end of it. This was heightened to me just recently when I acted in the case of *Febriano v. State of Victoria* in 1999. The plaintiff ran— It was very long trial, it took 24 days before a jury, and the plaintiff was unsuccessful. I recently saw Judge Harbison about two years ago, in fact I believe it was the opening of Clark Toop's offices in West Melbourne, and she advised that Mrs Febriano shortly after that case committed suicide. So Your Honour, sometimes the outcome of these cases can have detrimental effects, and particularly if the desired result is not met.

HIS HONOUR: Thank you Mr Walsh. Mr Ingram, do you want to ask Mr Walsh a question?

MR INGRAM: If I could please, sir.

MS O'KEEFE: Can I just make a response to that first—

HIS HONOUR: No, no we're just [indistinct] here, you've had your go.

How the above statement relates to costings is a mystery to me, but I certainly felt great sympathy for Mrs Febriano. In my opinion, Walsh wasn't looking out for my welfare but looking after his own. I don't know why he felt it necessary to testify to the judge that "facing a very adverse finding at the end of it" and "detrimental effects, and particularly if the desired result is not met." At no time during my experience could I say that my lawyer or barristers gave a *hoot* about my psychological injury – it was just about the money, nothing more, nothing less.

I became interested in the abovementioned case, and in March 2011 I attended the County Court Registry and made an application to access the file of *Febriano v. State of Victoria* from 1999. There were no records pertaining to this case or variations of that name. Fabriano, Fibriano, Fubriano, Fobriano. Registry staff suggested I attend the Supreme Court Library, as the case may be stored there. I did so and spoke to the librarian. She could find no record of a case cited as *Febriano v. State of Victoria* or any variations of that name. I mentioned to her that unfortunately Mrs Febriano took her own life just after judgement was handed down. The Librarian suggested that I contact the Coroner's Court, as if it was a suicide, they would have records. I used the phone in the library and called the Coroner's Court and made enquiries regarding a Mrs Febriano and variations of that name. The Coroner's Court staff stated that there were no records pertaining to that name of any variations of that name for a death in 1999 or 2000.

Later in March, I emailed a request to the judge of the County Court who supposedly heard this case for the file number for *Febriano v. State of Victoria* that Walsh said Judge Harbison presided over in 1999. The judge's associate refused to provide the file number and said "Her Honour makes no comment on this matter." Maybe there was nothing sinister here; it may have been simply a case of confidentiality that required all court records to be wiped because of the defendant in this case and the poor outcome for the plaintiff.

During this time, I undertook an internet search to find any reference to a

"I Think" to Justify

Mrs Febriano. There were no listings in the White Pages, Ancestry.com or any article recorded online. I wondered if this person ever existed. Was Walsh giving the judge a message? Was he implying that if I was unsuccessful in my case then I may well go the way of Mrs Febriano, solving my former legal team and the court's problem of me raising further issues of possible corruption?

The days of using technology to message a judge are over if the message is not for a proper purpose, as there is always a 'footprint' of this contact. Given this, I now believe any contact of this nature is hidden in plain sight in the court room, as there were a couple of occasions during my trial where comments made by barristers appeared odd, to say the least. I wondered if hidden messages or codes were relayed in this manner. I am sorry that I can't quite put my finger on it, but words such as 'theory' and 'conspiracy' and 'James Bond' and 'Walter Mitty' were flown around at intermittent times, times when they had no relevance to the current line of questioning.

On the first day of my cross-examination, the defendant barrister Mr Jens strangely made this comment to the court: "It doesn't need to be transcribed but I have got a burst eardrum so I am having difficulty hearing. It is not causing me any inconvenience, save that sometimes I am having difficulty hearing the witness and I don't want to bring that to the jury's attention or anything but sometimes—." The rest of his comment is not transcribed. The judge responded: "Is there anything we can do? Do you want to stand closer to the . . ." Mr Jens said, "No, I can hear Your Honour perfectly."

I feel this is very odd – a highly paid professional raising in the court he had a burst eardrum, and then stating it isn't causing any inconvenience, that he can hear the judge perfectly who is sitting further away from him than the witness. Was there a message here, and if there was, what was it? Fortunately for me, a number of medical specialists have confirmed that I don't suffer from paranoia, and that what I thought was happening was happening, with this being confirmed by the judge in the County Court who found "In the circumstances, I accept the plaintiff's evidence that the events she describes did occur."

I was still curious about the name Febriano, and wondered if the name may have been transcribed incorrectly in the transcript – could it have been 'Fabriano'? As Latin is the language of the legal profession, my enquiring mind told me to get a Latin dictionary and look up the term *'fabriano.'* I found the word *'fabri'* from which our English word of fabrication is derived.

Further, in Mr Ingram's re-examination of Walsh, the judge stated he was confused about the evidence given regarding my instruction to seek leave of the court to have the jury discharged – and if my application had been successful, would it not have changed the advice by my counsel to settle? The response from Walsh was they had taken the view that His Honour, on the evidence before him, would not find in the plaintiff's favour, therefore it wouldn't matter which way the judge decided the application, so there was little point in seeking to have the jury discharged.

Judge: "No?"

Mr Ingram: "In our view, the evidence before Your Honour was sufficient, we believe, for Your Honour, if—

His Honour: "Having the jury discharged isn't going to solve the problem?"

Mr Ingram: "It wasn't going to solve the problem."

His Honour: "Sorry Mr Ingram, I just wanted to clarify that."

Mr Ingram: "No, thank you, and I think the reason that you felt that was the case with respect to His Honour was that you felt *Koehler* applied to the facts that have been unfolding in this case? Correct?"

Upon my reading of this paragraph, it appeared that Walsh and Ingram were telling the judge that the evidence before the judge was sufficient to tell him that discharging the jury would not solve the problem, and the reason that the judge would feel this way was because he felt *Koehler* applied to the facts that have been unfolding in this case. In my opinion, we have a clear case of the barristers telling the judge how he should rule and how he should feel. There is no evidence that the judge had read and understood *Koehler*, keeping in mind that up until this time the judge was not the trier of facts, this was the jury's role, not his Honour's.

Judge: "All right. The next matter was that you—?"

Ingram: "No, can I also say that we were also very concerned about an application by the defendant and it wasn't raised at the time, but it was on the back of our mind, about an application to discharge the jury on the basis of no reasonable jury could have found negligence in the circumstances and that was a live issue. We didn't discuss it with the plaintiff, but certainly it was something that I was alive to, and the defendant, mind you Your Honour, did not indicate at that point that that was something within their contemplation, however it was something that could have happened."

Ingram's statement regarding an "application by the defendant and it wasn't raised at the time, but was on the back of our minds" appears to me again to make no sense. How did Mr Ingram know about an application by the defendant that was not raised at the time and yet it was in the back of their minds? I feel again that the judge is being told what to think that "no reasonable jury could have found negligence in the circumstances and that was a live issue." Mr Ingram did not represent me at the April hearing and played no part, and yet he refers to the collective of "our minds." Given this, I believe this was a later invention which may have come about in meetings or discussions with my former legal team after the hearing terminated and when it was known I was seeking to have the settlement set aside. I am guessing that such a meeting could well have occurred in May.

If "no reasonable jury could have found negligence in the circumstances," my expert witnesses certainly did and would have attested there were indeed negligent circumstances, but the jury were destined to never hear this evidence. If there was no negligence, why were we even in the Supreme Court? If my lawyer believed this, why did she continue with her representation for eight years? Why wasn't I informed of this "live issue?" This is a re-creation after the event to bolster the barrister's positions; in my opinion, the above transcript makes no sense.

The next witness I called was my former lawyer, and I asked her if she had a full understanding of my case and what was going on with my case. She responded in the affirmative. If she had this full understanding, I question why I was never informed of the difficulty of proving negligence – I suggest because it was never a "live issue." Before my case commenced, the lawyer Travis stated to me that my case was strong because throughout the ten years my story had not changed, and he suggested the value of my case to be around $600,000. I asked her if she agreed with this estimate, and she responded "No," even though her own actuaries report stated it to be more than $700,000.

She confirmed why there was so much difficulty securing senior counsel – this was because the trial was scheduled to run for five to six weeks on a 'no win, no fee' arrangement and so no counsel were interested.

I asked if she had filled out a 'Civil List Callover Form' in my case, a listing in which she stated she was ready for trial when she clearly was not.

I then asked the witness if I said to her on the morning of 23 April, "Can we please proceed with requesting leave of the court to have the jury discharged and go judge alone?"

Toop: "No. Um, the, um, the background was that, um . . ."

Not a convincing reply. She could have simply said yes or no, and even more surprising was her following testimony: "Ah, and then, um, we, ah— Mr Jens was about to make an application to have the plaintiff re-examined."

What? "Mr Jens was about . . ." *Was about.* This does not accord with previous testimony from Mr Jens, who in response to my question, "But you asked for leave to continue cross-examination on that Friday morning?" said, "M'mm, and leave was granted."

This witness's testimony is certainly in conflict with what I was told on the morning of Friday 23 April by Harrison and Walsh, who stated that Mr Jens had sought and had been given leave to continue re-examination. In this regard, I believe her evidence over the barristers'. There is no doubt in my mind here that the judge knew the truth and chose to ignore it.

I asked the witness if she felt that a juror making the comment "Yeah, sure" would be a pre warning and the defendant would be advantaged.

The witness's response: "I don't— I'm sorry, I don't really quite know what . . . I'm just trying to clarify that your . . .? I don't think that that could be — I don't— I usually . . ."

Another version of the "I believe and "I think"!

I asked the witness if she had heard junior counsel state, "This judge is bad and very harsh. It's his first civil personal injury trial and he does not like these kinds of cases, trust me, I know him personally."

Witness: "No, I didn't. No, I didn't."

The witness was correct – she was not present in the interview room when this statement was made; she attended at around 10:30am when I believed she was contacted by counsel to come and assist their endeavours in the settlement process because I was not budging from my position. But interestingly, the judge wanted to know.

His Honour: "I think it would be of assistance if Ms Toop did— Was there some sort of conversation about me?"

Witness: "Yes, yes, there was, Your Honour."

She may not have been in attendance, but she told the court, "My note just says" about Walsh's statement to me, though her version was very different to mine: "Matt advised Lori that he knew the judge and that he was a good man, but that this was his first jury trial. Further, that he would probably be conservative, but moreover he had a reputation for being an excellent black letter lawyer." This is in direct conflict with her earlier evidence that she had not heard the negative comment about the judge when had she made her note.

"I Think" to Justify

The issue of undue pressure or undue influence to get a party to settle quite often results in a court judgement being put aside. Is being visibly distressed and crying not proof enough of undue pressure? We already have Walsh giving evidence of my tears but not crying, plus Ms Toop's evidence: "No, I do, but look you certainly became tearful." Later in her evidence she stated I was teary, but that I composed myself, and later again she confirmed that she did offer me some tissues to clean my face because I had been crying so much that my makeup had run. I asked the witness if she gave me a mirror out of her handbag to clean my face, and she responded, "I may well have, I'm not sure, because the mirror I was carrying around that time was a piece of broken glass so I don't believe I would necessarily offer that to you, but I may well have."

More versions of the "I believe and "I think" are "I'm not sure" and "I may have." What happened to a simple yes or no?

No definitive answer, and I believe these words or phrases are used when skirting the truth is required – avoiding perjury with indecisive wording. The mirror I was given was a lipstick case red in colour with gold embossing and it wasn't until I described the mirror to the witness that she conceded that yes she had given that to me and she gave it to me that on that morning to clean my face.

Toop gave further evidence that on the morning of 23 April, when counsel wasn't in the room, she had a discussion with me—a long discussion—regarding the pros and cons of settling. I guess by stating this, it appeared I was given every opportunity to discuss with her my concerns and she was performing her fiduciary duties. She confirmed that I certainly did become tearful, but that I composed myself. The only problem with this is that there were no discussions between Toop and myself at this time – she was busy on her Blackberry and totally ignored me. She stated further she had notes about the discussions, but how can this be – notes about a discussion that did not take place? I wondered again just when and where she made her notes, but she later stated in evidence, "I sometimes take notes on my phone." But notes of a discussion that didn't take place? She was doing something on her Blackberry, but I believe it certainly was not about me or my case.

Toop goes on to say that I accepted the advice to settle, and that I signed an authority and that was the end of the matter. I asked her if I made the comment at any time that I didn't want to sign, that I didn't want to sign these forms, and her response was, "No, not at all, absolutely not, no." This was precisely the reason she was called from her office to attend at the court: because I was refusing to sign. I would suggest that if I was happy to sign the settlement offer then why was I crying or tearful, and why did it take nearly four hours and an adjournment of the court to achieve this happy settlement?

The day before, my support persons were told not to worry about coming back to court until Tuesday of the next week. I was told by counsel on the Thursday night to give them a day off, as the next day (Friday 23 April) was going to be an easy day of re-examination by my counsel.

Walsh had stated in his testimony that it was early Thursday evening when he realised the significance of the juror comment and contacted Mr Jens around 5:30pm, asking if the $150,000 was still on the table. At 8:30am the next morning (Friday) I was bombarded with all the difficulties with my case. If the settlement process was going to be conducted in a fair manner, I believe that Walsh or Harrison should have contacted me either the night before or early in the morning concerning the need to have my family with me, as there were going to be big decisions made. They made no such contact because they did not want any witnesses to what was coming. They needed total control to break me down in record time; having others in attendance would have slowed the process.

I asked the witness if I had instructed her to run the case for one more day, and that I would pay costs. Her response: "We did have that discussion when counsel was out of the room."

From my memory, we also had that discussion when counsel was in the room, and I put that to her. Her response: "I can't recall that, but I do— I do have notes about the discussion that I had with you about that matter."

All these notes being taken without my knowledge or awareness, and no copy of any of these supposed notes in my file.

An addition to the "I believe" and "I think" and "I'm not sure" and "I may have" is: "I have notes."

We returned again to the juror's comment – I asked the witness about her knowledge of this, and she responded that it would be unsettling—and it was —but notwithstanding that comment, she stated that they had already provided extensive advice to me, and that Harrison had provided extensive advice that the case was not travelling well. This is not true – Harrison did not provide any such advice or any extensive advice. The first time this was raised was on the morning of 23 April, and if the advice is in writing, none exists in my file.

Further in evidence, I felt Toop attempted to support her and the barrister's position by stating to the court that the 'foreseeability' as required in negli-

"I Think" to Justify

gence cases was weak. But once again, no evidence of this existed in my file. My response to that was, if she believed that—and given she knew my case very well—why did she continue to bring proceedings? Would it not be perverting the course of justice?

I called my next witness, the lawyer Travis. I asked him if he was also in the room on the morning of 23 April, and if so, whether it appeared to him that I was happily signing the settlement agreement. He responded, "Happily." *"M'mm?"* "I don't think you were happy about it." He went on to testify that I had senior and junior counsel, and two solicitors, and my husband advising me the day before, on the Thursday, that the case was not travelling well. My husband refuted this occurred the day before, as do I, because that was the afternoon my barristers told me to give my support persons a rest from coming to court. We did meet on that Thursday, in the morning for around 30 minutes, but that was not part of the conversation. The conversation was around an offer the defendant had made – I do not remember the offer, but it certainly was not $150,000. This meeting took place prior to the juror's comment, and yet it was this comment that was used by my former legal team that caused them to reconsider running my case.

The witness further stated that he had written instructions from me to try and settle the case the day before, on the Thursday; he also stated he dictated notes of that. That could only have been during the morning meeting mentioned earlier in regards to an offer; there were no instructions by me— written or otherwise—to settle. No such documents were in my file, and if I had given written instructions to settle, why was the case not settled that day?

The judge asked the witness, "Did you observe Mrs O'Keeffe crying?" Travis: "Um, I— I saw her teary," and, "The only time I saw her quite teary is once."

I stated to Travis that the outcome that was actually achieved that morning was really no different to the outcome that we may have achieved had we run the case, but there was obviously a decision made sometime between himself and counsel that they were no longer prepared to continue with the case. His response: "Oh, no, that's not true. I would have followed it all the way to four to five weeks, that's no win, no fee on a case is exactly that. Um, it was— The facts were that counsel, um, aren't, don't work on the same basis." Once again, the 'cab rank' rule is not applicable to personal injury claims.

Finally, we get to the point I was alleging: that counsel was not and never was prepared to run a five-week case, and I felt by his testimony Travis confirmed this to be true.

My next witness was barrister Craig Harrison. I asked him when he was briefed to take my matter, as sometime after this June hearing I found evidence to support the date as being Friday 9 April, with the hearing starting the following Tuesday.

His response, "I don't remember to be honest. I— I really couldn't— It— It certainly wasn't months beforehand. It was . . . it was possibly a week beforehand or two." (I would like added to our little list: "It was possibly…")

As my evidence clearly showed, it was late in the day of Friday 9 April, with the hearing scheduled to start on Tuesday 13 April – this is two business days, not a week or two. I put this to Mr Harrison, and his response: "In fact, I think that probably is right."

I put to the witness that it was late on the Friday when his clerk contacted him regarding the taking of this case and the briefing of this case, and he responded, "I think he just told me that I'd been briefed," and later he stated, "I was available."

His response was interesting, as it gave the appearance that he had no say in whether he took the brief or not, and that he was available.

Strangely, Harrison was listed on 2 February 2010 to represent Loiterton in *Loiterton v. McKillop Family Services* in the County Court, but the hearing didn't go ahead on 2 February as the plaintiff barrister (Harrison) requested an adjournment, and yet the defendant lawyers agreed to pay the costs of this adjournment. This is not the usual practice; whoever asks for the adjournment usually pays for it. This may have been an occasion to provide the carrot, just in case one was required for Mr Loiterton.

The case was adjourned to the new date of 13 April 2010 – coincidently the same day as my hearing was scheduled to be heard in the Supreme Court. I do not believe this was just a coincidence – I believe it was purposely orchestrated so that this case started the same day as mine. Two workplace bullying cases being heard on the same day, one in the County Court and one in the Supreme Court, one destined to be successful and one not. I can understand how relieved Mr Loiterton must have felt to have it all over, and to feel validated and to prove that the system 'worked'. Mr Loiterton was an ex-police officer who was bullied by a teenager in his care, a situation I feel any defendant barrister would've had a field day with, but it appeared not. I don't want to be unkind to Mr Loiterton, as I understand

"I Think" to Justify

how complex bullying can be and the profound impact it can have on a person.

Even more strange, was that Mr Phillip Jewell SC, who at one time was to be my counsel, later returned the brief stating he was unavailable in April. Surprisingly, he became available on 9 April to represent Mr Loiterton. So, in effect, the two plaintiffs swapped barristers, me from Jewell to Harrison and Loiterton from Harrison to Jewell. Harrison wasn't available to take my brief, but obviously some wheeling and dealing took place, and by Friday 9 April Harrison was replaced in Loiterton by Phillip Jewell. Why situations such as this occurred takes some contemplation. The only reason I can conjure is after the possibility of no pay (due to the 'no win, no fee' scenario), it was known my case was to be 'thrown', the 'bribe' accepted, and that the barristers—initially briefed, once aware of this—refused to participate.

I surmise that Harrison took the brief on the promise that my case would be finished by 23 April, around the same time that Loiterton concluded, and that his costs were guaranteed, as they would've been if he acted in Loiterton.

I spoke to Mr Loiterton and asked why he changed barristers so late in the day on 9 April. He responded that he didn't know – he just followed what his lawyers told him.

Now, if you remember my chapter on my workplace bullying experience, you'd be aware that I was attacked by not one bully, but by two, with a mob in support and with a very compliant management team. Given this, why was Loiterton successful and I was not? I can only think of two reasons, but there may well be more. One: I had been outspoken over the years, an advocate for myself in the WorkCover system, much to the ire of WorkCover. Two: I was a 'woman at the well' sharing my story and advocating for other women to tell their stories. I was a threat to the system, a system that didn't want bullied injured workers supporting one another; I had to be shut down, and the hope stripped from those waiting behind me.

I asked the witness if he had any other matters in which he was briefed to appear in the following week. His response was interesting: "To the best of my recollection I had a mediation on the afternoon of the Friday, the 23rd, when I was supposed to be the mediator. I— I recall that, but that's the only thing I recall. I may've had other matters but I— I don't recall".

I put to the witness that 23 April was one of my hearing days of a five-week trial, so what plans had he made for doing the mediation? His response: "Well, I wasn't going to be able to do it."

I asked if he had made arrangements for someone else to do that mediation for him. "No, as it turned out I hadn't."

I exclaimed, "You hadn't?" His response was, "I had been very heavily embroiled in your matter, and I had completely forgotten about it I'm embarrassed to say, and in fact after your matter settled, I went and did it, and it lasted about 40 minutes."

I asked what time the mediation was scheduled to commence. "I think it was set for 2:15pm."

I put to the witness that as it was set for 2:15pm, what would have occurred had my case not settled at 12:30pm? "I would have rung the solicitors, both of whom I know, and said I'm terribly sorry, I've made a blue, I'm not going to be able to be there. We can do it at 4:30pm if you want, or you'll have to accept my apologies and you'll have to refix it for another date, or I can do it at the weekend if that's suitable."

I asked Harrison if he ran his own diary or was it something his clerk did for him. His response: "I have my own diary which I'm still struggling with – in my word processing thing there's a little box that you— And I'm getting better at it, but I'm better at it now than I was in April."

I probed a little further and affirmed he was booked for the full day on 23 April in my case, and he agreed he was, but that he had a mediation at 2:15pm. I asked if there was some kind of alert on his diary, or did he check his diary of a morning before he left to go to court. He answered, "No, I don't, but I know now there's a thing that comes up and says you've got to do this, but I don't think there was that then, or if there was, I don't think I knew how to work it, because otherwise I wouldn't have forgotten about this mediation."

I asked if his clerk assisted in the running of his diary, and he said his clerk did not remind him of his day-to-day commitments, but they did record his court commitments. Further, I asked if they had a record of the mediation, and he responded, "That's a good point, but probably they should have, and he would have— It would mean that the system probably slipped up there as well, because they should have rung me and said you're not going to be able to do this mediation, we'd better ring the solicitors and get someone else. They didn't do that, so that either means they slipped up, or I hadn't told them about it."

Feeling incredulous, it was about this time that the judge put his elbows on the bench, arms upright, and placed his head in his hands. By his actions I understood how the judge felt – this testimony was unbelievable.

"I Think" to Justify

I probed further with the witness and stated that it was quite fortuitous that my case actually settled at 12:30pm, and he responded, "It meant that I didn't have to inconvenience the litigants in the other matter, which I had mediated on one previous occasion, and it was sort of an adjourned mediation. That's true, it was fortuitous."

As Harrison had mediated on one previous occasion with the parties in this mediation, I felt that gave more reason to remember it rather than forget it. Given all the evidence heard by this stage, there could be little doubt my case was planned to finish on 23 April, around lunchtime. And if there was any doubt to that, Harrison had just eliminated that doubt.

I felt emboldened and pleased with my legal performance while under immense pressure. The witnesses, under much scrutiny were contradicting themselves and were only changing their testimony as I pleaded the facts. A person sitting in the court claimed my cross-examination was something she'll never forget, that it was truly marvellous. She said I was so impressive, and she enjoyed watching these legal experts squirming in their seats.

Back to Harrison. I asked him to confirm that I had instructed him to request leave of the court to discharge the jury. His response: "Well, I'm sorry but I disagree with that. The issue was canvassed and we gave you advice that we did not believe that it would be successful— Such an application, and you accepted that advice."

At first, he testified that he disagreed I had instructed him to request leave to have the jury discharged, but later stated that the issue was canvassed. Why would the issue be canvassed if I hadn't made such an instruction and I accepted advice for something not raised? Remember Travis's testimony, where he stated I had provided written instructions the day before to settle.

The witness affirmed that if there was success in getting the jury discharged the *Koehler* case would be my downfall if we went judge alone. He stated, "Your Honour was given a copy of the *Koehler* case in the opening on day one by my learned friend Mr Jens."

This supported my contention that the defendant was using WorkCover's 'go to' case of *Koehler*, even though once evidence was explored it wouldn't have been a relevant authority. But evidence explored was not planned, as my own legal team by this time were also pushing *Koehler*. As you read, I hope you're coming to understand why my own legal team would do this.

Harrison went on further to state, "We believe that the *Koehler* principle was a— We always were— I mean we discussed it in conference before the case started. We were always very apprehensive about it . . ."

I asked if he had discussed that in conference with me. "Absolutely, we discussed it with you before the case began. Well, my recollection is very clear that we discussed it in conference prior to the case starting. You were aware of it, you knew about it." Yes, I knew about this case from 2005, but was never concerned about it as it was a very different case to mine. It was certainly never discussed with me by any member of my former legal team.

If the witness had discussed the *Koehler* case with me, I felt confident I would have remembered this, as I knew of this case, but once again no evidence of these so-called discussions were anywhere to be found. I knew this case hadn't been discussed, because had it been, I would've found a computer and read the case again to get my head around what he was referring to. My lawyers had never mentioned *Koehler* to me – they would have made a file note of said discussions. No such file note exists.

I asked the witness about the juror's comment, and he responded that he didn't hear it. Yet on the morning of 23 April, Walsh had stated to me that Harrison *had* heard the comment. Harrison thought there might have been something said, but he had no idea what exactly was said. He said Walsh heard it and was immediately concerned, and as soon as Walsh could he told Harrison. This comment by the juror occurred around 3pm, before the afternoon tea break. Since Walsh was immediately concerned, he told Harrison as soon as he could (at the said afternoon tea break). As such, I query why was I told at 4:30pm that same day (22 April) that the next day would be an easy day and to give my support base the day off.

I put to the witness, "So even though I instructed you to at least approach the judge to have the jury discharged..." Witness response: "Well, I reject that, my clear recollection is we discussed the issue, and you accepted our advice that an application to discharge the jury was likely to be unsuccessful, and you don't make applications you're going to lose."

I agree you don't make applications you know you're going to lose, but if instructed by your client to do so, and without knowledge of how a judge may rule, an attempt is not unreasonable – and at that point I had nothing to lose. But the lawyers sure did.

Harrison testified that the first offer of settlement was on the first day of trial, on 14 April, and was for $50,000 all-in – there was no mention of the offer made on the previous Friday before trial of $150,000 all-in that I had heard Travis discussing on the phone with Walsh. He further stated, after referring to his notes, that he was certain the offer made on 21 April was $150,000 all-in and that I rejected this offer. Not true: the first time the offer reached $150,000 was on Friday 23 April – or was it on Friday 9 April? The arrogance of Travis to discuss this settlement offer on the phone in my presence is breathtaking, and convincingly proved to me how powerless he believed me to be.

Harrison further testified, "Wednesday the 21st, and that the distressing thing about that was we had discussions, and at that time on the Wednesday I think Mr Walsh and I had already agreed to reduce our fees, and as at the Wednesday my recollection is there would have been something for you out of the $150,000, in the order of about $20,000, whereas by the Friday that benefit to you had disappeared." My response to this: I was under cross-examination on this day, the Wednesday, and no such discussion took place. A discussion took place on the Thursday morning, but there was no offer for $150,000, as previously attested to by my husband.

I confirmed with the witness that Walsh had testified that this occurred on the Thursday, not the Wednesday. Unfortunately, Harrison was not in court when the others gave testimony, but I am surprised there was little conversing overnight to get their stories straight. The offer of reduced fees was made on the Friday morning, not Wednesday and not Thursday. This offer was another carrot dangled to induce settlement.

Given the conflict in this evidence, I now believe the first offer made by Mr Jens to be on 21 April for $120,000, and the other offers were made by my legal team. I would suggest that in this situation, where there appears to be some controversy, there should be a form which highlights the date, time, offer made, rejection or acceptance and signed by both lawyers and clients. I tend to think that offers recorded on scraps of paper, on the bottom of transcript pages, simply are not good enough.

I asked the witness if he was present when Walsh stated "this judge is bad and very harsh, and it's his first civil personal injury trial" and he replied, "No, no, just a second, I don't recall— I disagree with that." On the Tuesday, the day before trial, I was with Harrison in his office when Travis attended and said we had drawn "the bad judge."

Then Harrison testified, "There were discussions embarrassingly about His Honour's attitude – my recollection is they were on the Wednesday." It appears he must be referring to Wednesday 21 April, when testimony has already proved that we did not meet or have any discussion on this day. He stated, "No, no" and then admitted there were discussions "embarrassingly about His Honour's attitude." On this evidence, I would suggest that a discussion concerning the judge did indeed take place in his office on Tuesday 13 April before the hearing had commenced, and again on the morning of Friday 23 April.

Harrison was asked if on the morning of 23 April I stated, "Can we please just run the case for one more day?" He responded that "Yes, you did say, 'I would like to go on for just one more day.'"

I asked him: "Did I make the comment that, 'Can we please run for one more day? I've got my chequebook in my handbag'?" His response: "I think you— Yeah. I think you did say something about your chequebook in your handbag."

Keep in mind that now both Harrison and Toop testified I made this comment, while Walsh testified that I did not make this comment. The only time I made this comment regarding my chequebook in my handbag was on the morning of Friday 23 April, and yet Harrison testified that this conversation was on either the Wednesday or the Thursday—and possibly both—and again on the Friday. He had already testified that we didn't meet on the Wednesday; I believe he was attempting to give the impression that discussion around settlement started as early as the Wednesday, a day we did not meet at all, and the Thursday, when we met for half an hour with no discussions involving my chequebook. My husband was at this meeting and he said there were no comments about or references to any chequebook.

I asked the witness if he was present when I signed that authority on the blue note sheet, and he responded he was. I asked him if he noticed that my eyes were full of tears and I couldn't actually even read what I was signing as I was crying, and he stated in response that if he had seen me crying, he would've said, "Everybody out of the pool. We'll take a break and we'll, you know, come back in half an hour if you feel you're up to it." But Harrison didn't have a half hour – the pressure was on; he had to be back in court in a few minutes or the judge was going to adjourn to the afternoon and then he'd miss the mediation he was planning to attend at 2:15pm. My case then would have been adjourned to the following Tuesday (as the Monday was a public holiday) and the manager John, the defendant's main witness, would most likely already be in the air for his overseas trip.

I told the witness I was crying prior to the signing and I couldn't even read

"I Think" to Justify

the words on the blue paper as my eyes were so full of tears, and the witness responded, "I don't believe that's right because I think my— I— I— I think you went through it and turned it over and— Before you signed it. I don't recall— I— I might not be right about that but I think you did." That word "think" again. I did not go through it or turn it over, as it was a page attached to a pad, one cannot just turn over a single sheet unless it's removed from the pad, and it was not. I told Harrison I never read that document and I therefore would have to disagree with his testimony.

He went on to say, "Well, I think Mr Fewster might've— I think he read it — He read it to you. 'I, Lori O'Keeffe, hereby instruct' after he'd written it out." No, that's not correct either, it wasn't read out to me and I didn't read it. I just signed it as I felt under a lot of pressure and duress.

During the settlement discussions I was beginning to feel guilty because counsel was talking about how they were all taking a loss. I did state verbally a number of times, "I don't want to sign this." And then Mr Harrison, while he was standing in front of me with his arms crossed, said quite sternly to me, "Mrs O'Keeffe, will you please instruct me to tell the— To tell them the offer is accepted."

I asked the witness if on the morning of 23 April he made the statement, "You've had a win. This is the best we can do – at least you've got the comfort that even though you're not going to see any money from it they have had to pay $150,000, and if you go on, they don't even have to do that, so you've extracted something." I found no comfort in his statement and felt I extracted nothing but a pyrrhic victory, which didn't resolve any of the issues. The only people who would extract something were the lawyers.

My next witness was my husband, and I asked him if he was in attendance on Thursday 22 April in a morning conference with Harrison and Walsh, who both stated in testimony that the offer on the Thursday was $150,000. I asked, "Do you have any recollection of an offer of $150,000 being made?" His response: "None whatsoever." This accorded with my memory that the first time this offer was mentioned to me was on the morning of Friday 23 April. Toop in cross-examination of my husband asked if I had given instructions at that conference on the Thursday to settle for $180,000 all-inclusive of costs and disbursements, and his response was, "No."

A further question by Toop: "Did she give any instructions to put any offer?" His response: "The only instruction I recall was that she wanted to proceed."

My question to the witness: "You were aware that I was very keen to have my matter, my full matter, the full merits of my case heard." His response: "Yes."

In my opinion, the evidence certainly leaned to the fact that at no time was I seeking a settlement. I wanted my case to be heard – money was not my motivator. No amount of money justifies you giving up ten years of your life – ask anyone severely bullied in the workplace.

There must be a reason for counsel attempting to convince the judge that these discussions took place when they did not, but I don't know what that reason could be.

After my husband was a witness, there was a flurry of authorities put before the judge by the defendant with the comment, "That there has been on our submission no fraud, certainly" and Toop further submitted that there has been "no duress" with the judge commenting "or improper conduct." His Honour stated, "Secondly, that any that did take place was not known to the defendant, so the contract stands."

Is the judge stating here, "that any that did place" appear to be a suggestion that some indeed did take place? The challenge I faced here was that the defendant's position was that it was dealing with the practitioners who were representing me, and they had either actual or ostensible authority to bind me. This is a conundrum faced by many in the 'no win, no fee' arena, a condition being you have to abide by the legal advice provided even if you do not agree. If you disagree, then your representation is ceased, and this often leads to many litigants seeking legal representation over and over again, and finally turning to self-representation because in the end you can only trust yourself. The legal system cannot abide by those who seek self-determination; the system is basically one where you can only have as much justice as you can afford to pay lawyers.

In final submissions, the judge commented that Toop in her evidence had conceded that she knew I had always wanted to go judge alone, and that he did have the power, were he so minded, to discharge the jury. But unfortunately for me, this request was not sought. Toop in closing said some of the matters raised by me are matters for the Taxing Master, if in fact there was a dispute relating to costs of course – which there was. I wasn't aware that this was a possibility, but then I knew there was another avenue open to me if I was unsuccessful in the current matter.

The judge refused to make a decision as to whether my original claim was doomed to fail, stating that we hadn't really heard argument on that. He said that it wasn't the issue – the issue, as far as he could see, was whether, in some way, as I alleged, the agreement was improperly obtained and that I was intimidated and signed the document under duress. He refused to express any views about the strength or weakness of my case.

He went on to say there's the legal argument that even if I was subjected to duress, that wouldn't upset the settlement that had been submitted to him because the defendant shouldn't be deprived by having the settlement set aside. I believe this to mean that when a defendant agrees to a settlement they agree in good faith, and the belief that the other party's representative has actual or ostensible authority to do so, and so the court has no jurisdiction to set aside the judgment.

In most circumstances I'd agree with this, but the defendant must have known their major witness would not be available to give testimony. Even more importantly, had the defendant barrister been complicit by giving evidence he knew to be untrue? If the answer to either of these questions is yes then, in my opinion, the defendant loses the chance of having the settlement stand on its merits.

The final question: Did the evidence elicited at this hearing provide proof was I overborne or oppressed in giving my consent in the settlement of my matter?

Judgement was handed down Thursday 2 September 2010. Since the hearing only lasted about seven hours, I was surprised it took three months for the judge to come to his decision. During that period, with every passing day I came to accept that I would be unsuccessful.

Unlike previous occasions, I attended court alone to receive the decision; I didn't want my grief and sadness witnessed by loved ones. When I read the judgement, I went from grief and sadness to anger. I've only been angry a few times in my life, and for me, anger is a motivator. I believe the judgement was planned to be 'the straw that broke the camel's back' given it was unnecessarily cruel and made judgement of facts that were not facts at all.

I previously felt the judge tried to get to get to the truth and displayed some doubt about the testimony of these witnesses, but in the end it seemed he had to find in favour of the legal representatives. Otherwise, the administration of justice may have been brought into disrepute, and it's critical that the public interest rests with confidence in our judicial system.

Of course, judges and barristers socialise together, and maybe went through law school together. Can they completely separate themselves from these relationships in the courtroom? On most occasions they probably can, but in cases where their legal brothers and sisters are called to account, perhaps not. Keeping in mind that my former barrister Matt Walsh stated he knew the judge well – they were family friends, as Matt's father was also once a judge. It appeared that before becoming a judge, Robson and Walsh worked together in the area of estate planning. It may well have been another Matt Walsh, but I doubt it.

At the time of writing, Walsh and the judge are friends on Facebook. It is stated on the Supreme Court website that when a judge goes on circuit there is an expectation that the local legal fraternity show the judge some hospitality. Judge Robson and Mr Jens have both attended circuit in Warrnambool, where no doubt they were shown some hospitality, so to me there's no doubt that a degree of mateship exists. Would these relationships pass the pub test? Surely impartiality, independence and the absence of bias would be almost impossible.

It's a well-established principle that a judge is entitled to immunity in respect of any act done by him in the exercise of his jurisdiction, and I agree that any honest mistake can be rectified on appeal. But what about the occasions when it's not a mistake – what then? We may well argue that the public interest is best served by an honest judiciary in a sincere search for the truth and one not hiding behind immunity, but that's just my dream (not my reality).

I felt the judge had failed his oath of office to adjudicate without fear or favour; his premediated decision to do me harm was concerning. I am fortified in this belief because almost immediately after giving his decision the judge closed his chambers for three and a half weeks. It appeared to me he may have been "heading out of Dodge," as the court had only reconvened in August after the winter break and Judge Robson had had two weeks off over this period, meaning that as of 2 September he'd only been back at work for six weeks. This supports my contention that he was showing favour to my former legal representatives by silencing me, damaging my credibility/reputation so I would never be believed, and diminishing the possibility of any future successful action against my former legal representatives. My thoughts turned to Mrs Febriano.

If the judge suffered some emergency, or his absence was due to sudden illness and he can provide evidence of this, then I offer my sincere apologies.

It was about a year later, that I had an epiphany and finally understood the

"I Think" to Justify

significance of being allowed to cross-examine my former legal team. Advocate's immunity would not protect them, but a witness is protected from defamation when giving evidence under oath, even if this evidence is false, and this hearing gave my former legal team the opportunity to defame without consequence. I now understood the concepts of 'witness immunity' and 'proceedings immunity'.

A few days later, I again read my judgement, and noticed there was a judgement by Robson handed down the day before mine cited as *Shirreff v. Elazac Pty Ltd*, which ran for 10 hearing days (from 26 July until 9 August 2010). My last hearing day was 4 June with a combined seven hours of hearing – nowhere near 10 days. And mine was completed nearly eight weeks prior to Shirreff. I wondered why the Shirreff judgement was handed down the day before mine, and—more importantly—why his case was heard initially with a jury, but then by a judge alone. There may be a number of reasons for that, but one that strikes me is the fact that a judge alone hearing creates a written decision—a jury trial does not—and this written decision is publicly displayed on the internet, thereby supporting optics that the WorkCover system works and judges are 'good'.

This injured worker was hugely successful, with a million-dollar compensation award. Admittedly, physical injuries are easier to litigate than physiological injury, and especially so when said injury was caused by bullying, and more so again when WorkCover seemingly disallows workplace bullying claims to be successful to ensure those waiting in the wings will give up. By this time, I knew many of those waiting in the wings, as I had been one of them. I attended a number of workplace bullying support groups over the years, and it was common knowledge in those groups that there was a big case 'in the wings', and that all other cases were delayed because of this. I now feel it was mine that was 'the big case waiting in the wings'.

The hearing of my claim against my former legal team terminated on 4 June and the last hearing day of Shirreff was 9 August. Given the two-month difference, I believe my judgement should have been handed down before Sheriff; mine on the Wednesday, his on the Thursday. My logic says if you're going to do something bad, do something good first, so your badness is not questioned because of your goodness.

I wanted to understand the judge's decision, so I looked at 20 random cases he had presided in over the previous couple of years to compare details of those cases to my own. My hearing ran for around seven hours (roughly 1.5

hearing days) spread over three days. Of the sample of 20, I had the least number of hearing days but the second largest judgement (46 pages). Two other cases had hearing durations of 10 and 11 days but only 52 pages of judgement, while the longest running case at 12 days only had four pages of judgement. Out of the random sample, I had the second most transcript referrals at 70, while Shirreff exceeded this with 110 references to the transcript (but Shirreff had 10 hearing days). It appears on the face of it that my written judgement by comparison commanded much more attention to detail than the other 19 judgements.

There are a number of categories of possible misconduct by the judge, including the following: case prejudged; failed judicial oath; outside of jurisdiction; denial of procedural fairness; bias; reasonable apprehension of bias; lack of impartiality; and lack of independence. There may be more, but I'm not legally trained so cannot comment further.

Though, Independent Broad-based Anti-Corruption Commission's (IBAC) Acting Commissioner Bonighten's December 2012 speech—where he spoke about perceptions of corruption in Victoria—did resonate:

"History has shown that if integrity in government breaks down, it will break down in business also, and have a knock-on effect elsewhere in society. Corruption in the public sector and the police, for example, will result in unjust processes and outcomes leaving citizens feeling angry, vulnerable and distrustful."

ELEVEN

Judgement of the Judgement

In July 2010, while awaiting judgement of my June case, I read Joel Gibson's article in the *Sydney Morning Herald*, which I've set out below in full due to its relevance to the predicament I found myself in with my own lawyers.

Fees policy no winner for clients, says Judge

Lawyers acting on a 'no win, no charge' basis are compromised in their ability to provide the best objective advice to their clients, a senior NSW judge has warned. Justice Patricia Bergin, the Chief Justice of the Supreme Court's equity division, said that controversial but widespread practice of charging contingency fees was "fraught with difficulties" and liable to produce "unsatisfactory by-products" for clients.

Justice Bergin made the statements in a case where a firm threatened to stop acting for a client if he did not accept a settlement offer, causing him to become "emotionally distressed."

A week before Alan Spence's hearing and after 2 1/2 years of work on his case, Gerard Malouf and Partners discharged itself from acting for Mr Spence, refused to release his file and claimed he owed $240,000.

Justice Bergin criticised the firm—whose principal was found guilty two years ago of professional misconduct for illegal advertising—ordering it to release the file and pay Mr Spence's costs.

"It is clear to me that the solicitors were very concerned that if they did not secure a settlement they would not be paid any fees or costs. I am satisfied that this concern caused the highly inappropriate threat to be made," Justice Bergin said.

"In a 'no win, no charge' retainer, when solicitors' livelihoods and incomes are bound up with, and dependent upon, the client taking a particular step in litigation, it seems to me that the capacity to provide the client with objective advice about taking that step is compromised. The greater amount of fees to be lost, the greater the prospect of compromise."

The president of the Law Society, Mary Macken, said the concerns were valid and clients needed to consider carefully what constituted a "win" for firms that claim almost 100 per cent success rate.

"A technical win may see the client walk away with very little . . . A lawyer taking on a spectrum of cases which includes extremely difficult cases would find it hard to maintain a 98 per cent success," Ms Macken said.

Lawyers should make it clear to clients that "if the case is lost, they may have to pay the costs of the other party," she said. Or, indeed, if the case is technically 'won' but costs are significant the win may be pyrrhic."

Mr Spence's solicitor, Shaye Chapman from the firm Lawjet, said the case "puts it back on firms to make it clear in their agreements with clients the basis of when they are entitled to their legal fees."

But Jnana Gumbert, the NSW branch president of the Australian Lawyers Alliance, which represents many personal-injury firms, said: "By and large, lawyers don't allow those considerations to affect the advice they provide to clients."

Contingency fees provided a community service for thousands of victims of accidents who would otherwise be fighting large insurance companies by themselves, Ms Gumbert said.

Gerald Malouf and Partners, which markets itself as having the "triple-C attitude – compassion, commitment and competence towards our clients," did not respond to requests for comment.

I was hopeful my judge read this article, but if he did, he seemed to pay no mind to it. This article confirmed what I'd experienced was not so rare, and was no doubt the experience of many injured workers. I wasn't concerned about paying the costs to the other side if I was unsuccessful, as I was aware that WorkCover rarely pursues their costs if successful, because to do so would render injured workers unable to pursue their rights under legislation.

I had a 'technical' win, but only a pyrrhic victory, and my lawyers likely knew this from the beginning. My heart skipped a beat at the comment by the Australian Lawyers Alliance representative: "By and large, lawyers don't allow those considerations to affect the advice they provide to clients." I couldn't disagree more.

It wasn't until writing this book that I again visited the judgement of September 2010 and for the first time read the judgement in correlation to the transcript. The transcript gives evidence that isn't included in the judgment. I feel this evidence was purposely withheld to give an impression (one that isn't supported by testimony).

There are a number of references to notes, written instructions, file notes and memorandums supposedly made by legal counsel, and yet none were tendered to the court, nor have I seen them, nor were they in my file. As I've stated earlier, it's one thing to write a 'note' you know to be untrue, but another altogether to put your name to it and have it tendered in court.

In the daily listings for the Supreme Court my case of cross-examination of my former legal team is listed as an application, not a trial.

Was this a fair trial, given I had less than one day's notice and thus had little time to prepare? Was it a legal hearing, as none of the usual legal steps were undertaken? No applications in reply, no affidavits of documents, no discovery, no interrogatories, no mediation. I couldn't possibly do justice to my case with one day's notice whilst also being unwell. Maybe the judge could have considered contacting the Victorian Bar to enquire if a duty barrister was available to assist me. I didn't know at this time that the bar offered this service, though I'm not convinced this would have made any difference.

There are comments through the judgement that I never put allegations directly, and maybe this is because of my inexperience in cross-examination and my fear of saying "you are not telling the truth." I was too scared to challenge a barrister, even when I felt he wasn't being truthful.

The transcript clearly shows on a number of occasions how flustered the witnesses were in answering my questions, and especially so for Harrison, who as an experienced barrister admitted he did not check his diary each day – this simply isn't believable.

All through the judgement there are references to the High Court decision in *Koehler v. Cerebus 2005*. I can state categorically *Koehler* was never mentioned to me at any time by any legal representatives, and there are no records pertaining to any such advice. If all legal counsel believed that I would lose my case because of *Koehler*, why wasn't I ever informed of this? Why were we in the Supreme Court wasting everybody's time and money? I had read *Koehler* in 2005 and I knew it was a very different case to mine and gave it no further thought.

I did instruct my legal team to seek to have the jury discharged and go judge alone. Why would I not do this? I state without any doubt that there was only one offer of settlement put by me and that was the required statutory offer of $350,000 in 2008, and reoffered during the April 2010 trial. I didn't make any other offers because money wasn't the motivator. The offers referred to in this judgement supposedly made by me were not made by me, but made by my legal team, and some without my knowledge.

My legal team saw that I was crying and that I didn't want to settle. Why would I—or anyone for that matter—'happily' settle for nothing? It makes no sense whatsoever. At no time prior to Friday 23 April was I informed my case was not going well. I had been in cross-examination since the Monday, so could not speak to my legal team. There was one half-hour meeting on the Thursday morning to discuss an offer from the defendant (before the juror comment of the afternoon) but no opportunity to be informed that my case was not going well.

Early in his judgement the judge stated he was informed that Mr Jens would be seeking leave to continue his cross-examination; strangely it was *my* barristers who told the judge that Mr Jens would be seeking this leave, not Mr Jens. Mr Jens testified he had sought leave and leave was given. This does not accord with "would be seeking" – it appears the judge was ignoring the contradictions in this evidence.

The judge stated that the solicitors would receive nothing in net terms, and yet they had received up to this date around $250,000.

The judge goes on to say that I had not appeared at the summons hearing of 26 May regarding having the settlement monies paid to the lawyers, giving the appearance of tardiness or not bothering. I was notified 10 minutes prior of the hearing time – impossible even if I had a helicopter.

I was accused of denying my lawyers natural justice – because I was unsure of court procedure, I hadn't served copies of all documents prior to hearing. However, I too was only served with their documents just prior to hearing, yet this was deemed appropriate. And the documents prepared for the above summons hearing in the Practice Court were provided *after* the hearing was finished.

It is recorded that Walsh stated that my case could not continue as at least one juror was against me, and in his experience that was 'all it takes'. It says that I protested as my witnesses who were yet to be heard may change the juror's mind. Walsh said, "No, once a juror decides they do not like you, that's it."

Walsh said he didn't believe that the comment itself would have justified the court's discharge of the jury, but I believe this was a decision for the judge. If in a criminal case a juror made a prejudicial comment to the defendant's case, I'm confident that representing counsel would request the jury be discharged. I have great respect for criminal lawyers who appear to work hard to ensure their clients rights are protected, but they are not practising in the 'no win, no fee' arena with their costs often being paid for by the taxpayer through the government-sponsored legal aid program. If only injured workers had similar access to legal funds afforded to alleged criminals.

The judgement states that Walsh read from a memorandum he had written of the incident the following week. Walsh had recorded in his memorandum that the Greek juror muttered audibly, "Yeah, sure."

This may be insignificant, but what was stated to me on the morning of 23 April wasn't "Yeah, sure" but "Yeah, right." If Walsh wrote this memorandum the following week he may have had a better chance of remembering what was said, but I believe he wrote this memorandum a lot later than he stated and that's why he got the wording wrong.

If Walsh had read from the memorandum, then I believe it should have been tendered into evidence, and it was remiss of the judge not to do so. I have no memory of Walsh reading from a document, but I cannot say conclusively that he did not.

In the judgement the judge states he asked Walsh whether it was his evidence that he did not leave my presence until he had my agreement to accept the $150,000, and Walsh replied, "That's correct."

I was in that room for nearly four hours during which he left my presence on a number of occasions. The court surveillance cameras would support my evidence, as they are situated just outside the door to the ante room. I wonder if the judge knew at this time that Walsh's testimony was wrong, or if he just missed the discrepancy.

The judgement records that I then said, "I was crying but both counsel had left the room at that time." I was crying whilst counsel was in the room and made no such statement from the bar table. My affidavit of April 2010 supports I stated that counsel was in the room when I was crying, but there was no weight given to my testimony, as it must be shown that the barristers didn't know I was crying, because if they knew, that would prove I was under duress. But hold on, the transcript records Toop, Travis, Harrison and Walsh confirming there were tears.

The judge recorded that I questioned Harrison about his engagements, which suggested that he had recommended settlement of the case so that he was free to do other matters. The judge says I never put this to Mr Harrison directly, and this was because I didn't know how to address this in court. It's very concerning to allege an officer of the court may be lying under oath. Harrison's evidence is that he overlooked the mediation booked for 2:15pm on the afternoon of Friday 23 April, but could have rescheduled it if my case had continued.

The transcript clearly shows Harrison was flustered, and it was at this time the judge buried his head in his hands. For an experienced barrister not to check his diary each day is not credible, as a judge would likely agree. In the transcript, Harrison stated that he was anxious to have my matter settled, and I believe this was why I was put under immense pressure: because of *his* anxiety to get to mediation and not to have it cancelled.

It is recorded in the judgement that Harrison checked the authorities to see whether it provided grounds for an application that the jury be discharged. I only instructed Mr Harrison to do this on the morning of 23 April, and from what is recorded he must have checked the authorities before he knew my instructions.

Harrison agreed that the discharge of the jury was discussed on the Friday morning, but that he and Walsh were the first people to raise that issue. I was the first person to raise the issue as it's what I'd wanted all along – to go judge alone.

He said he formed the view that given the circumstances it was unlikely that such an application would be successful. I instructed Harrison to seek leave of the court to have the jury discharged; it was the judge's view that was important, not Harrison's. I had nothing to lose by this application. Again, I can't help but imagine it would be very different in a criminal hearing context.

The judgement states that I put to Harrison that he was aware that I had always wanted the matter dealt with by judge alone. He denied that, and said it was the first he had heard of it.

My lawyers knew I wanted trial by judge alone – this was admitted in cross-examination and recorded in transcript and I tendered an email into evidence. Harrison, an experienced barrister, would have known that it was going to be difficult to persuade a jury after days of victim-blaming by the defendant, given I didn't look unwell and that I was too 'middle class'. He should have jumped at the opportunity to go judge alone, but again supported his position that if the matter proceeded with a judge alone the case would not improve because of the problems faced by the High Court's decision in *Koehler*.

The judge found that Harrison had advised me that the evidence was pretty clear that there was no basis upon which my former employer would've had knowledge of my particular psychological susceptibility, but I ask how this can be true when dozens of experts support that they *did* have knowledge, that they *did* know that bullying causes psychological susceptibility. It was Dr Strauss that said: "I have no doubt this lady was harassed and victimised in the workplace." This was the legal conundrum for WorkCover as their own Independent Medical Examiners supported my Claim as did a County Court judge. They did not fight my claim because they felt it was bogus, but because they knew it was genuine.

In paragraph 113 of the judgement, it is recorded that I asked Harrison on the Wednesday to run my case for one more day, as my position had worsened (I believe he was referring to the juror comment that would worsen my case), but we had no discussions on the Wednesday because I was under cross-examination, and Harrison testified that we didn't have any discussions on the Wednesday. But later it was recorded that Harrison expressed the view to me that it was over and I was not going to be able to turn the matter around. I wonder why Harrison would say this on Wednesday given the juror hadn't made the comment until Thursday, and that he'd earlier testified we had no meeting on the Wednesday. The judge got this fact wrong – whether it was intentional I don't know. I understand that this paragraph is complex – it's indicative of the complexities when analysing a transcript with a judgement.

The judgement recorded that Harrison testified that Mr Jens was going to be given leave to continue his cross-examination about the conference and the whistleblowers organisation. *Be given leave.* The judge knew at this time that Mr Jens had already testified that he had already been given leave but he is silent on this fact. Once cross-examination is over no barrister wants their client recalled. Harrison informing the court that the defendant would be seeking leave was odd, to say the least – acting on behalf of the defendant wasn't their role. This was their case, not mine, and it was a game of manipulation for their benefit only. Never mine. This was a case of planned system failure for me and planned system success for my former legal team and WorkCover.

His Honour further records that Harrison did agree that there was discussion about putting the equity in the family home at risk, and Harrison also said that my husband was not supportive of the matter continuing. This is not true – there were no such discussions regarding putting the family home at risk, and the evidence my husband gave was discarded in favour of the evidence of the lawyers. This discarding of contrary evidence occurs all through the judgement. I do understand a judge has the discretion as to who he believes and who he does not—that is inherent in the role of judge—but he chose not to believe a word I said.

Further, he records that my ownership of the house that I jointly own with my husband could be jeopardised if the case continued. Walsh said that was one of the factors they considered in the totality of the situation; though Walsh may have considered the ownership of my home, he never mentioned it to me and we never discussed it.

The judgement states that Walsh said I didn't say I had my chequebook in my handbag, but I did indicate that I wanted another day and I said on a number of occasions that I wanted one more day. Where's the indicated evidence of me asking for one more day and when did these "number of occasions" take place? It certainly wasn't in the first week of trial, nor the second as I was under cross-examination with the only (and very brief) meeting being on the Thursday morning. The only occasion was on the Friday morning. According to the transcript, both Harrison and Toop testified I did say I had my chequebook in my handbag and yet the judge makes no mention of the alternative testimony of Walsh in his judgement.

Walsh said that he had discussions with my husband on the Thursday at lunchtime during which he recommended I accept the $150,000. However, there were no discussions with Walsh on the Thursday lunchtime. We were asked to return early from lunch to meet, but neither Walsh nor Harrison turned up. My husband testified to this and that the offer of $150,000 was not mentioned on the Thursday.

Judgement of the Judgement

The judge recorded my history of complaints against a number of organisations, including complaints against my former employers. The complaints against my former employers were the submission of a WorkCover claim, an employee right under law. The complaints concerning those working within those organisations were my responses to their complaints and false allegations they had made against me. The judge stated this to be unusual to say the least. The complaints were susceptible to an interpretation that I was particularly aggressive and unreasonable – was the judge suggesting that I had no right of reply, or right to natural justice or procedural fairness? I don't understand how my right of reply is considered aggressive and unreasonable. My behaviour was consistently exemplary, in spite of how difficult a time it was for me.

My responses to these complaints were made on the advice from my union against those who had bullied, mobbed, harassed me and who had lied to the WorkCover investigator.

I do not believe it is aggressive and unreasonable to use the law to fight for your legal and human rights. Should I have gone outside the law? I'm not a violent person so it wasn't an option for me, but if I had taken physical action I would have been out of jail years ago. My belief is that the judge had to support the myth my former legal team were selling, and he did so unequivocally. There is absolutely no evidence in existence that proves I am or was an aggressive and unreasonable person, not one incident, because had there been it would have been used to terminate my employment.

The judge stated further in his decision that some of my bizarre conduct included a complaint to the Director of Public Prosecutions (DPP). As stated previously, I did not write to the DPP, nor has he ever written to me – the evidence shows it was WorkCover who wrote to the DPP. If the judge had availed himself to read the defendant's affidavit of documents, he would have seen that it was WorkSafe that had written to the DPP, and the defendant barrister would have known this as being true. It's not the job of a defendant barrister to point out something detrimental to its case; the trier of the facts is the judge, and because he didn't avail himself the task of reading court books he made an erroneous decision of fact.

The judge made reference to my application to the Red Cross and how I had not included all my illnesses. He formed the impression that the jury wasn't impressed with me. Of course they wouldn't be impressed – they'd just sat through four days of denigration, defamation and victim-blaming. My application to the Red Cross was true and honest according to law, and a black letter judge would understand this, but not necessarily a jury. A black letter judge would also understand that all the evidence has to be presented before a determination can be achieved, yet he was simply silent on this.

The judgement records a note my lawyer supposedly made regarding a conversation about the judge, but the judge remained silent on the rest of the testimony. I had asked her if she had heard junior counsel state, "This judge is bad and very harsh, it's his first civil personal injury trial and he does not like these kinds of cases, trust me, I know him personally." My lawyer states she didn't hear that statement being made. So how did she write a note about a conversation she didn't hear? The transcript states that Harrison testified that there were "discussions embarrassingly, about His Honour's attitude," and I believe this supported the evidence I gave concerning what Walsh had said to me about the judge as being true.

At paragraph 90, the judgement stated that my lawyer referred to the evidence that I had not reported to my superiors that I was suffering from Graves' disease until the mediation on 25 October 2000. I take issue with this statement, as my lawyer didn't give any testimony regarding this matter and there's no record of this in the transcript. So what is the evidence referring to? I am concerned that the judge was making judgement on issues not raised in court. My lawyer knew this was incorrect. I told my supervisor in early July 2000, I told the PA to the director of my department that I had Graves' disease in early August, and there was a comment from a co-worker on 1 September 2000 regarding my supervisor's knowledge of my illness – plus the fact I told everyone who asked. As my former lawyer, Toop understood my case "very well". She would know this.

Toop didn't make this statement to the court, but the impression was given that she did. I believe this was done to support the no 'foreseeability' concept – that supports my former legal team's position of doing what they did in my best interests.

The judgement stated that I said I didn't want to settle, but again my lawyer read from her notes—notes I believe were reconstructed after the event —and once it was known I had made an application to the court to have the settlement set aside, I don't believe that my lawyer read from any notes. The contents of this note are untrue – this wasn't said to me, and the judge should have had this note tendered into evidence. I didn't see this note and didn't understand the tendering process at this time. This was an opportunity for the

Judgement of the Judgement

judge to ensure my legal rights as an unrepresented litigant were protected, but he failed.

The judgement refers to my lawyer offering me a mirror to fix my mascara as I had been crying, but makes no reference to the fact she initially denied giving me a mirror. That was until I explained the distinctive characteristics of the mirror she gave me – then she changed her mind and agreed that this was correct.

At paragraph 98, the judge records that Travis (the lawyer looking after my case) said he had written instructions from me to try and settle the case the day before. But that day would be Thursday 22 April, so when and where did I give those written instructions, and why wasn't a copy put into evidence or tendered? I was still under cross-examination on 22 April, and the only time we met was for 30 minutes mid-morning, and this was certainly not discussed. My husband was at this meeting and he concurred that no such discussion took place.

The judge stated that I indicated I wanted to call a social worker who helped me understand what had happened on Friday 23 April, but he refused to allow me to lead that evidence on the basis that it would be hearsay and inadmissible. I don't understand how it would constitute as hearsay – she was giving evidence of what I said to her, not evidence of someone else saying what I had said to them. All throughout the hearing lawyers deferred to conversations with others and referred to notes written but not produced, so how this would be inadmissible or hearsay I do not know.

I wrote my notes on Saturday 24 April, the day after the event. My witness was going to confirm that this took place. All through their evidence that legal counsel referred to—memos, memorandums, notes, file notes—none were tendered and none were proven to have been written at the time they were stated to have been written. The judge allowed this, but wouldn't allow my witness to testify that my notes were written on 24 April. The transcript does not state that I used the word "reconstruct" – the judge used this word in his decision. The word "reconstruct" has an air of being fabricated after the event.

Again, in paragraph 127, the judge states the court was informed that Mr Jens would seek leave to continue his cross-examination, but I was told first thing on Friday 23 April at 8:30am in the ante room of the court that Mr Jens had leave of the court to continue cross-examination, and Mr Jens himself states he sought and was given leave. This is clearly wrong – the transcript does not support the judge's statement. "Would seek leave" does not equate to did seek leave, and to me it seems an attempt at covering up this important detail.

Under the judgement heading 'Finding of Facts' there are a number of findings that were not facts – for example, he stated that my daughter accompanied me to court but that she did not sit in on the conference. My daughter did not accompany me to court, as both barristers would know, as I met them at 8am on my own. I didn't know my daughter was present until around 11am, three hours after the commencement of the conference, and this was only after my lawyer attempted to get her to join me. By this time, it was too late – I had an understanding of what they were doing and I wasn't going to allow them to use her to meet their ends. I believe this was stated to give the impression I had support available from the beginning of the conference to give the appearance of fairness.

Further, the 'chronic complainer' title rose again – the judge didn't appear to appreciate that my case had been running 10 years, and that all these 'complaints' in effect related to the original WorkCover claim and the frustration and unfairness caused by delay. He would be familiar with the saying 'justice delayed is justice denied'.

The judge states that Mr Jens may have presumably used these complaints to challenge my credibility as well. A judge shouldn't take guesses, and cross-examination had finished without Mr Jens attacking my creditability in the way suggested. It's disheartening seriously injured worker's so often have their integrity constantly attacked. Medical support and expert reports are therefore crucial. However, despite my medical treaters and independent medical examiners all accepting that I was seriously injured by my former employer, they were never going to be heard in my case.

These experienced professionals knew me, admittedly some more than others, but they believed me. No concerns as to my credibility were ever raised by them. The judge didn't take his mind to this and in a short period he knew better than those professionals who had been involved in my case for many years. The judge made a presumptuous and erroneous decision based on his inexperience in the WorkCover legal processes. As a judge, he must have known that any issues of credibility elicited during cross-examination could be addressed in re-examination and witness testimony. He didn't put his mind to this – it is a basic court procedure, whether civil or criminal, but he simply accepted Walsh's evidence at face value.

The judge did not understand that, colloquially speaking, "an injured worker has many hoops to jump through" before he/she gets to a damages hearing. Walsh and Harrison knew me for 9 days and that is all they needed to know how to manipulate and intimidate me.

The judge reported that counsel expressed the view that my case was doomed, but in the trial transcript it was recorded that the judge responded "it was not necessarily so."

It was recorded that when back in court, there was no indication to any observer that I disagreed to counsel's submissions to the court that a settlement had been reached. That was because I was traumatised, numb and in a state of shock – I hadn't expected such behaviour from my own barristers. If the judge understood the nature of my claim, he would've known that this is exactly the kind of behaviour a traumatised person would display. An experienced personal injury judge would face this in most trials where a plaintiff suffered post-traumatic stress disorder.

He further stated that I appeared to be a strong, independent and competent woman more than capable of handling my own affairs, and this is the only time he refers to me in a positive light – because it suited their agenda. I had to portray myself as an independent and competent woman because that was all I had left; I was powerless in the system. Those in the system charged with my care abandoned me; I had to fight for myself, and this couldn't have been achieved if I lacked credibility. I fought very hard to remain credible.

The judge decided that in the witness box I was subjected to very tough but fair and proper cross-examination by Mr Jens, and I displayed a strong character in dealing with this cross-examination. My reply to that is yes – because I had to. This was to be my only chance at validation and vindication. I had to convince the jury that I wasn't the person portrayed by my former employer. The judge wouldn't have understood this; it's something only those who have experienced workplace bullying can relate to. Travis gave evidence at trial that I "was really a silly woman, who would not cry in front of others." All parties at this relevant time knew I suffered a chronic anxiety condition triggered by intimidation, and yet the judge made the assumption that I was in a fit condition to make a decision to cancel the trial for which I had been waiting a decade.

If I continually cried in front of others I would've been labelled as histrionic. I couldn't win no matter how I behaved. On most occasions I remained composed, as maintaining credibility was all I had left, but my stoicism was used against me.

According to Yale Professor John Langein, "cross-examination is often an engine of oppression and obfuscation, deliberately employed to defeat truth." Justice Fox says, "Cross-examination may help the elucidation of the truth, but it can also obscure the truth, and quite often is designed to that end – a clever cross-examiner can make even the most reliable testimony look questionable." Did my judge put his mind to any of this? Doubtful, as the cartel protection racket swung into action.

My lawyers had achieved so little in the resolution of my claim over the course of eight years, I had attempted to take charge of my own affairs. In December 2009, Travis demanded I agree to my case being adjourned to another date, a date no one would give me, so I stood my ground and said I wouldn't agree to an adjournment. I had to start looking after my own affairs because it seemed abundantly clear that my lawyers weren't.

The judge found that he wasn't satisfied that my lawyers had any reason to believe that I felt under pressure, at a disadvantage, threatened or intimidated. I had previously requested my lawyer not attend the hearing as our relationship had broken down, but just after two hours she was summoned to come to the settlement session because I was not budging on my position and she was required to add to the pressure.

The judge further stated after hearing the evidence that had been elicited to date, that he wasn't surprised that the case ended as it did – and he of course had a *completely* open mind at that stage. The pathway of the judge's reasoning to this decision is inadequate; having an open mind means you will give fair consideration to all possibilities. His decision failed to consider that any one of those five lawyers could have given an untrue answer; even when it was elicited in evidence the judge explained it away, made excuses for it or totally ignored the discrepancy. He stated that it wasn't necessary for him to comment on any other matters I raised, yet he made comment on matters not raised. My matters were significant, but he wouldn't allow me to raise issues of creditability, which in the situation we found ourselves were particularly relevant. I have evidence that Travis lied to me regarding a very senior counsel, and that my lawyer under oath to a Supreme Court judge gave evidence she knew not to be true.

The judge denied me the opportunity to put all my evidence forward, and then made no decision regarding the evidence I did tender. He also didn't refer to any authorities, especially *Dwyer v. Calco Timber, High Court of Australia*

2000, a decision regarding that a plaintiff's stoicism should not be used against them.

He stated that he carefully observed Mr Jens' cross-examination, and in his view, his questioning was proper. The judge gave no pathway to his decision that the cross-examination was proper, but I'm still at a loss as to how the make of car I drove was in any way relevant to a personal injury claim relating to workplace bullying and harassment. Not to mention the asking of the same question four times after it had been answered, or the supposed seeking of leave to ask me about where I met a friend from Whistleblowers Australia. In my opinion, it equated to annoying or harassing questioning under the Evidence Act, an Act the judge appears not to understand.

He stated Mr Jens was seeking to show that there was no basis for my former employer to know I had any psychological susceptibilities; the susceptibilities were not due to my Graves' disease. Blood tests showed normal thyroid function from around September 2000. It was the intimidation, harassment, discrimination, victimisation and bullying that caused my psychological susceptibilities from 2000 to 2002. It had been stated in evidence that my supervisor Helen started a rumour at work that I was unwell around August 2000, and she did not mean Graves' disease. Helen being a former nurse, senior management gave too much credit to her opinion, and it's ultimately what led to where we are today. Even if I did, initially, have some kind of emotional response to the Graves' disease (though friends and family state they didn't observe any such emotional behaviour), this was rectified by September 2000 with effective medication to control the symptoms of the disease.

The next decision made by the judge would instil anger and pain to any victim of workplace bullying, and was the dagger-through-the-heart moment: he stated that my "complaints of bullying were baseless." This comment flies in the face of all the evidence, which he obviously chose to ignore. Evidence from about 20 professionals, who all agreed that workplace bullying *did* occur – and even the decision from another judge, who stated in his decision that he accepted I was seriously injured by my former employer due to bullying and harassment. Judge Misso stated in his decision that "I believe what Mrs O'Keeffe said happened did happen," but no consideration was forthcoming from the judge, the 20-odd professionals were all wrong, and he was right – completely unbiased.

When I finally got my legal file from my former lawyers I found some pages of transcript from the April hearing of my cross-examination, and on these pages are notations by one of my barristers – which one, I'm unsure, as I don't know their handwriting. The notation on page 44 states "deliberate bullying," page 51 "bullying," and page 63 "more bullying by John." Coupled with the above, this proves to me that my barristers knew that my complaints of bullying were not baseless.

The judge again mentioned my history of complaining, in that I had made a similar complaint against a previous employer around 10 years earlier. Once again, this was a WorkCover claim, and the only complaint in my 10 years of employment – now that it is established that a WorkCover claim is a complaint, I was successful in this complaint. I was proven correct that a local law was directly and indirectly discriminatory and it was rescinded. This is not a bad history.

The judge seemed to take pleasure in making decisions on issues not raised in this trial, so that I had no right of reply, or ability to give evidence in my own defence. During the trial he stated—and it is in transcript—that the hearing was only about one issue, and one issue only: was I overborne in giving my consent to the settlement. There was no mention in this hearing transcript of any discussions or evidence around my staff not wanting to work with me, yet he stated that my complaints arose primarily because my own staff had indicated that they didn't wish to work with me.

This is incorrect. My WorkCover claim was dated November 2000 and didn't involve any issues with my staff – it arose before the staff complaint of April 2001. The judge appeared to be stating that my response to the staff complaint was a complaint, when it really was a response to their complaint – my right of reply. The judge didn't seem to understand 'natural justice' but was on the trail to prove my 'chronic complainer' label. The judge was making assumptions not based on fact, but had no intention of addressing his errors because he didn't think it appropriate to make observations about whether these points were well founded. If he believed this, then in all fairness, he shouldn't have included it in his decision. Make an accusation, without a balanced view, because he had to give Mr Jens reasonable grounds for taking the line of cross-examination that he did, a line in conflict with the Evidence Act.

The judge goes on to cite a High Court authority that includes the following: "would suffice to render a simple contract void, or voidable or to entitle the party to equitable relief against it, grounds for example such as illegality, misrepresentation, non-disclosure of a material fact where disclosure is required, duress, mistake, undue influence, abuse of confidence or the like." If by now I haven't created at least some doubt in your mind, then perhaps the following will. The misrepresentation that my legal team was available for five weeks of trial, despite court records showing this to be untrue, and their own evidence stating that they did have cases the following week (and let us not forget Harrison's 2:15pm mediation). I've accessed some records which support the view my case was finishing on Friday 23 April; the barrister's account for services rendered dated 22 April with the discount or 'haircut' included, a transcript account for services rendered to 22 April, and the court hearing setting down fees for each day of trial to 22 April, not 23 April. The evidence I have supports my contention that my case was running for seven days and seven days only.

The judge goes on to talk about when a settlement is binding between the defendant and the plaintiff, but in my opinion any evidence given that a defendant was complicit should null and void that principle. I believe Mr Jens knew what was happening in the court conference room, and he testified that he spent this time waiting in the courtroom, and yet it's my understanding that the court is locked when court isn't in session. My friends sitting outside the courtroom door state they didn't see Mr Jens when they occasionally looked in the court to see if anything was happening.

Obviously, there were times when court was in session according to the transcript of 23 April 2010, but nobody told me or my friends that court was in session. I feel it may well be prudent of a judge to directly ask a plaintiff to ensure, and see for himself, that the plaintiff wants to settle. All judges should do this when faced with vulnerable clients to ensure the legal rights aren't being trampled on by their own legal team, but I doubt that would suit the system.

The authority of counsel briefed in the cause to bind his client to a compromise of the litigation is governed by the certain principles, but for me the only principle made clear was that my rights now belonged to my legal team.

The judge referred to Travis's testimony, and once again ambiguity reigned. Travis exhibited a disclosure statement dated 23 June 2009, provided by his firm to me, and he said that although it wasn't signed by me, he was informed by my lawyer and believed that the letter was sent to me and that I acknowledged receipt. He stated further that I discussed its contents and agreed with the same in a conference with my lawyer at their offices shortly after it was received by me. This statement was untrue – I never met with my lawyer to discuss this document, a document for which I had been asking for eight years. It wasn't supplied until June 2009, after I met with another partner of the firm to request the document. I provided evidence to the court regarding this failure by my lawyer, but again the judge made no comment. In an affidavit, Travis attested to my being sent five disclosure statements, but he could only be referring to the one letter of 23 June 2009, as there were no further letters. If these other letters existed, they should have been tendered, but you can't tender something that doesn't exist. I provided an affidavit in response to Travis's attesting to this, but the judge appeared to ignore my evidence and didn't undertake any form of analysis to get to the truth. This paragraph of his decision seems an attempt at giving my former lawyer a façade of competence.

The judge was again giving my lawyer a 'leave pass' when he stated that she deposed in court and in an affidavit of 30 April that at all material times I had been aware of the existing costs agreement and that I would be charged solicitor/client costs. I believe that all material times related to the commencement of briefing your lawyer, not some eight years later after a number of court cases and legal steps had already been taken.

He went on to say that I was aware of the costs and disbursements incurred in running my statutory benefits application, serious injury application and common law proceedings. Incorrect – I did not know. Upon what evidence did he base his assumption – the evidence of my former lawyer, which I had attested by affidavit that I had sent her a number of letters requesting this information but my letters were ignored? This was why I had to meet with another partner of the firm in mid-2009, which was after the serious injury application of 2008. The judge remained silent on my evidence.

Towards the end of his judgement, he stated that matters I raised went to questions that may well be dealt with at taxation or other proceedings that deal with the terms of my retainer, and I wonder why he would make such a statement when all through his judgement he supported the position of the lawyers. If he believed other proceedings could deal with some matters then he must have felt these matters were legitimate.

In my opinion, the judge didn't pick up on any contradictions in sworn evidence and never believed I was telling the truth. The judge made statements of fact that were not recorded in the transcript; maybe this is an accepted practice, but it doesn't feel right to me. For example, paragraph 19 stated: "In March 2009, she informed Clark Toop Taylor (CTT) of her desire to attend the directions hearing scheduled for 3 June at the Supreme Court as she had instructed CTT that she wanted her hearing listed in 2009."

The email response from Patsy Toop was: "I am concerned that you will attend a directions hearing. If you wish to take over the conduct of your litigation and represent yourself personally, please advise and I will file the necessary papers to withdraw as your practitioner."

To me, this confirms that my lawyer roughly one year before trial had decided she no longer wished to continue. She hung in there just to cover her costs.

On 2 September 2010, late in the day, Judge Robson delivered his decision, and as expected, I was unsuccessful. In not so many words he simply stated that he didn't believe me or my evidence, and that all five legal representatives were beyond reproach. Yet no other professional involved in my ten-year battle doubted my word. The judge made finding of fact that I was strong, independent, competent and capable, and that I possessed a strong character when it suited the desired agenda, but when it did not, I was aggressive, unreasonable, a chronic complainer and exhibited bizarre conduct.

If the judge saw my positive attributes, a jury may have felt the same way. But that wasn't the desired narrative – me being an aggressive, unreasonable, chronic complainer exhibiting bizarre conduct exonerated his legal brothers and sisters. I had no doubt that these experienced legal folk would worry about a disenchanted client who was strong, independent, competent, capable and possessing a strong character being a potential threat down the track, so the track had to be unforgiving. I am fortified in this belief, because they came willingly to be to cross-examined, they were not subpoenaed, and made no excuses about having other cases, as it was their big opportunity to make that track as unforgiving as needed. I must say here that I don't believe the judge in the Practice Court was part of this plan, when he referred the case back to Judge Robson. At least, I hope not.

After reading the judgement I knew I would have to appeal because he was just so wrong – he made many erroneous decisions of fact and his judgement was plainly unfair. I believe the judgement was to elicit the 'Febriano effect,' and I feel fortified in this belief because of the personal 'dagger in the heart' comments which were unnecessary to the matter at hand, which was simply: was I put under duress to settle. Had he just stayed with the matter in dispute without all the erroneous decisions he made, I may have not have experienced the positive anger that spurred me on for many years. It appeared to be an accepted practice that particular care should be taken to avoid causing unnecessary hurt in the exercise of judicial function, including observations made in reasons for judgement. As C.J. Gleeson stated in his monograph of 2004, "A judge should never cause unnecessary hurt."

It was the day after his judgement was handed down that I emailed the judge's associate to inform of my decision to appeal, and it was the next day (a Saturday) I received an out of office reply which stated that Justice Robson's chambers were on leave from Friday 3 September until 27 September 2010. He closed his chambers after delivering my judgement – I thought I would just have to wait until Judge Robson's return. Until I have evidence that Mrs Febriano existed, I believe the judge closed his chambers so he wouldn't be around if there were any 'Febriano effects'. If Febriano had a different defendant other than the State of Victoria, like *Febriano v. ABC Plumbing*, I would have been able to follow up myself, but having the State of Victoria as the defendant made this impossible.

The following Monday, I rang the Supreme Court Registry to enquire as to the appeal process, and was informed that I could only appeal on the orders; I said I had the decision. I was told I couldn't appeal on the decision, that I could only appeal on the orders. The orders were mailed to me a few days later. Had I not contacted the court I wouldn't have known that the orders were already written on the 2 September. Why I wasn't given a copy when I was in the court is unknown to me. Had I waited until Judge Robson's return from leave I would have been out of time to lodge an appeal.

I felt the judge failed in his duty to a self-represented litigant, and if he is, as he has claimed to be, a black letter judge, he would have ensured I received a copy of the orders before taking off on leave.

I don't believe I experienced judicial independence, or the observance of the principles of natural justice, or the right to an unbiased adjudicator. Everyone who comes before the court should be treated in a manner that respects their dignity. If the judge's abuse of power was designed to silence me, then he has failed – I will speak my truth without fear or favour.

I particularly appreciate the ethics of Mr John Jess, a federal member of parliament in the 1960s, who was a seeker of justice in the fight to have the 1964 collision between the HMAS Melbourne and HMAS Voyager properly investigated. He stated that he:

Judgement of the Judgement

"believed that the truth was what it was, not a prefabricated idea put forward by a powerful governing body that had something to gain at the expense of the ordinary person.
I think the individual has got to be prepared to stand and be counted and that's what we are short of in this country.
It is a question of justice in this country and whether justice is based on fact and whether fair and open inquiries are worth fighting for . . . I do not think it is any good talking about communism, corruption or collusion in others if we are not prepared to watch that it does not happen in our own area . . . We need to be vigilant. We need to see at all times that the little man is not victimised."

When an individual is seen as a threat to those in positions of power, tactics to discredit the individual are strategically deployed. In regards to the 1964 collision between the HMAS Melbourne and HMAS Voyager, Gough Whitlam said, "the board saw Cabban as a threat and he had to be discredited." Voyager executive officer Peter Cabban fought for years to have the truth known that Captain Stevens, the captain of the Voyager, was unfit for command, but the Navy didn't want the truth to be known. Cabban suffered immense discrediting so the truth could be hidden, but with John Jess on his side, fighting for justice and truth, after two Royal Commissions, eventually won out.

One of many addresses Jess made to the House of Parliament included: "I say to all honourable members of this house that unless we are prepared as individuals to stand up occasionally on behalf of a particular person, unless we are prepared to take an interest in what happens to an individual when the big machine appears to be against him, we have no right to be here."

I personally know of many occasions where an aggrieved person has made contact with a Member of Parliament and they are either ignored or got a letter thanking them for bring it to their attention and then nothing. There are very few, if any, John Jesses around today.

Another statement of Jess's I completely agree with is: "The judicial system of this country must be one hundred per cent right or it is one hundred per cent wrong."

I believe that on most occasions the judicial system works well, but every now and then someone comes along to challenge the system for its real integrity. That someone has no doubt discovered wrongdoing or a failure within the structure of the overall system; be it police, government or the judiciary itself. Usually, this person has a strong moral compass and a deep sense of justice, and is naive about the parallel system in which we sometimes live, until they speak out. They have an expectation that they matter, and the wrong committed against them therefore matters too. But they're just an individual—worthless, expendable—and the system works for the 'greater good'. Society must have confidence that things *work*, which is why the failings by those named are best usually hidden.

Maybe in hindsight I should have re-joined the 'greater good' sooner rather than later, but I was compelled to learn if our legal system did indeed work, and if our judicial officers were beyond reproach.

Below are excerpt from two pieces that I believe are supportive of my position and that prove that many in the legal fraternity and the judiciary are aware of trends relating to their practice.

'Evidence law and the mess we are in' by Geoffrey Gibson

> A primary rule is that the evidence must be relevant to the proof or disproof of the matter in issue. Arguments here turn on the degree to which that issue has been crystallised in the pleadings filed by the parties.
> The failure properly to control the trial process is most evident in how judges handle the examination of witnesses. Some cross-examination goes on for hours, days even. This is a real flaw in our process and a denial of fairness both to the parties and the taxpayers who fund this gravy train. There is, in my view, no reason why time limits should not be imposed on cross-examination, and judges need to come down harder on cross-examination that is inept, oppressive or slippery. The court has the power to disallow questions that are misleading, confusing, unduly annoying or repetitive, insulting or otherwise inappropriate. And the court must take action against such bad cross-examination even if counsel for the witness takes no objection.

> Lord Mansfield was Lord Chief Justice for 32 years. He decided about 700 causes a year. He insisted on clearing his list about once each term. He knew that delay and increased costs come from the lawyers, and that no litigant with a fair case ever wants delay. He outlawed adjourn-

ments even by consent. He knew instinctively what all judges should know and act on: delay and expense favour the rich and powerful. The point is simple. If the trial process takes too long, it isn't fair. Since Magna Carta entered our forensic fabric in 1215, it has been axiomatic that justice delayed is justice denied. And if the judges at Nuremberg and at the ultimate courts of Australia, the US, and the UK imposed strict time limits, why on earth can't our trial judges do that at the trial?

I'll end this chapter with words from *J'Accuse*, written by French writer Emile Zola in 1898 in support of the falsely accused Alfred Dreyfus, which still has some degree of relevance today:

"When judges begin verbally bullying the people they accuse of wrongdoing, when there is no wrongdoing, they are themselves guilty of wrongdoing by trying to enforce a law which does not exist, therefore they are breaking an existing law which they swore to uphold."

TWELVE

The Supreme not so Supreme

After I finally received the court orders of the judgement, I proceeded to prepare my case for the Court of Appeal. I'm afraid there'll be further repetition in this chapter, but I feel it's necessary for your understanding of what I was alleging in my appeal.

For an appeal, it's required you make submissions regarding your grounds of appeal, and so with this I included the necessary documents, which comprised an analysis of transcripts for 14 April 2010, 26 May 2010 and 3 and 4 June 2010. To me, this showed two things: one, how the judgement being appealed wasn't supported by the transcript evidence, and two, the poor quality of the transcript. I also included my written response to Judge Robson's judgement.

Unfortunately, the defendant was still listed as my former employer, when in reality my appeal raised issues mainly to do with my legal representation at trial and in the June hearing, and to my knowledge at this time the defendant hadn't played a significant role in this. I didn't know until many years later that the defendant had actually played a major role.

The orders I was seeking were that the orders of the Robson decision, dated 2 September 2010, be quashed, and that the matter be remitted expeditiously to re-trial by an experienced judge of the Common Law Division Major Torts List as a cause.

My submissions regarding the grounds of appeal were that Robson was inexperienced in this jurisdiction of law and that he was a specialist in the Commercial List not the Common Law Major Torts List. According to my former barrister Matt Walsh, Judge Robson had never presided over a jury trial in this jurisdiction prior my case, and this inexperience was obvious when I read the transcript of the April hearing.

The transcript shows he relied on advice and explanations from counsel as to the Accident Compensation Act 1985, and he accepted a document titled 'Further Particulars of Breach of Duty of Care Owed by the Defendant to the Plaintiff' dated 14 April 2010. Minutes into the proceedings, this document was tendered despite it being unsigned. These further particulars included new claims that would bring my claim under physical injury, an injury my employer was supposedly unaware of, so no 'foreseeability'. I felt it was an error of the judge to allow a document purporting to be something of significance when the signatory line was blank.

I didn't realise at this time that Mr Jens handed up *Koehler v. Cerebus High Court of Australia 2005*. Colloquially speaking, I suggest that Mr Jens, knowing of Judge Robson's inexperience, was leading him down the garden path. I don't know if the judge was in error to have accepted the authority, or whether it is usual for a judge to allow a party to raise authorities at the beginning of proceedings.

It appeared to me that Judge Robson did not undertake any detailed analysis of my evidence compared to what my lawyers said in their evidence – he just accepted at face value what they stated, and what they stated could have easily been supported by sworn exhibited documents or by being tendered at court. Was Judge Robson remiss not to request that these tasks be completed? As I am not legally trained, I don't know.

Any reasonable person on reading the analyses of the transcripts, affidavits and applications could not conclude that I received a fair trial. The public confidence in a fair, accessible and equitable justice system was cited by the then-Attorney-General Rob Hulls as a goal that must be maintained. Judge Robson made numerous erroneous decisions based on assumptions. For example, the bullying and why my staff wouldn't work with me were never fully canvassed at trial, because the April trial ended before we could. Robson gave a judgement without hearing all the evidence of the case, and made findings of fact that were not fact.

The issue regarding my inability to see what was written on the blue settlement paper due to problems with my eyes was never fully considered, and as can be seen by the April transcript, it is stated on 10 occasions I was having difficulty with my eyes. Counsel was anxious to have the matter resolved by midday and certainly didn't take the time to read it to me. Once it was signed counsel was out of there like 'bats of out hell'. Judge Robson never turned his mind to other possible scenarios, and missed or misunderstood evidence that may have been more fairly considered.

I submitted that I was disadvantaged because I couldn't access the transcript of my trial until 22 July 2010 – too late for the June hearing. Up until this date, no one would give me a copy; as Judge Robson knew, from 28 April 2010 I was a self-represented litigant, in justice and fairness he could have organised that I received a copy. As it was on email it would not have cost the court anything but a few clicks of the mouse; mere seconds could have made all the difference to evidence I led at the June hearing.

With respect, Judge Robson was a specialist in the field of Commercial Law, not Personal Injury – he didn't have the knowledge and experience to be the judge in a claim so complex. He didn't have knowledge of world trends on the subject matter before him. It was unfortunate for him that he drew my case, and unfortunate for me as well, and in my opinion his decisions lacked the proper pathways to his reasoning.

Australian law is supposedly based on English law, yet Australian law is far behind English law. Decades, I would suggest. With the wonders of the internet, this shouldn't be so. In England, cases such as mine are routinely settled in two to three years. I gave as an authority the case *Green v. Deutsche Bank 2006*. I highlighted an English guide which was written and conceived by John Hamilton, Head of Safety, Health and Wellbeing at Leeds Metropolitan University and a visiting lecturer in health and safety law at Salford Law School, University of Salford.

This guide is for employers and is titled 'Work Related Stress: What the Law Says'. It contains the practice an employer is required to take: identifying a problem; monitoring working conditions to spot signs of stress; being aware of working conditions that could cause ill-health; consulting with employees to get their views on the workplace; and giving consideration to employees with specific health needs or disabilities. It goes on to state the importance of preventing harm, assessing the potential impact of workplace stressors, and identifying measures that could prevent ill-health and ensure employees are aware of preventative measures.

It states that protecting individuals and taking action where harm to indi-

The Supreme not so Supreme

viduals is foreseeable is key, and to consider the needs of individuals and make reasonable adjustments to meet specific health needs or disabilities. To manage the workplace by monitoring the ongoing impact of work on vulnerable individuals, avoiding discriminating against individuals because of their health needs or disability and preventing workplace bullying and harassment. Evidence exists that shows my former employer failed in all these areas and this would prove 'foreseeability' and 'negligence.'

My employer did nothing relating to the above behaviours that I was subjected to even despite Victorian Laws relevant at that time. Judge Robson's decision was made blindly, because he was blinded by mateship.

I argued that the community's belief in the trustworthiness of lawyers is that they are consistently rated low, while nurses, teachers, doctors and community workers are rated in the top 30%. My career choice would have placed me in the top 30% – thousands of parents trusted me with the care of their children.

Judge Robson in his profession would have been aware of this community attitude, no doubt formed by those who had experienced the legal system, and he reinforced it. Not a skerrick of a benefit of one doubt was given to me.

On the morning of 23 April, Mr Harrison did make other comments to me regarding other barristers. He said other senior counsel told him that I was very "lucky" to win my claim at the County Court. That nobody expected me to. Harrison said that they all rang his firm that morning: Richard McGarvie, John Richards and Andrew Ingram. I cannot remember what he said they said, but I remember how I felt: intimidated, threatened and confused as to why these barristers would call Harrison, especially John Richards SC, who hadn't played a part other than to sit in on mediation and undertake some of the interlocutory tasks.

I gathered up the courage and went to visit Mr Richards on a Monday in May and asked him why he had called Harrison. He said that he couldn't remember. He stated that he believed *Koehler* would be a problem for my case. I responded that I had read *Koehler* and that it was a very different case to mine – *Koehler* wasn't a workplace bullying case. This was the only occasion I mentioned *Koehler* or discussed *Koehler* with anyone, and yet in evidence one of my legal team referred to me knowing/mentioning the *Koehler* case to them. This was untrue as only John Richards and myself had had a short conversation regarding this case in May, after the April hearing and before the June hearing.

That evening, Mr Richards called me at home around 10pm, which took me by surprise. He said he didn't call Harrison on that morning, but that he *had* spoken to Walsh. I was curious as to why Richards, who had little to do with my case, would call me at 10pm at night when the matter didn't seem urgent. And my question still is: Who rang who on 23 April, and why?

I sent an email the next morning to Mr Richards asking that very question, but got no response – he refused to answer whether he called Walsh or Walsh called him. I find it peculiar that a barrister unconnected to your legal proceedings would ring so late at night. Perhaps there was some kind of meeting that afternoon or evening around what the barristers should do about me, and that's when the decision was taken to use *Koehler* as the red herring (since I'd discussed it with Richards the day before – they knew I knew about this case). The die was cast for this case to be used as a strategy against me and to support their positions in any future action I may take.

I then spoke to Richard McGarvie, the barrister who represented me at the County Court serious injury trial. He confirmed that he did speak to Harrison on the morning of 23 April prior to the recommencement of my case. He didn't remember who rang who. I asked him if I was "just lucky" in my success in the County Court, and he responded "no" – that Judge Misso is sympathetic to injured workers, but he would have based his judgement on the evidence.

Judge Robson makes no mention of the Model Litigant Guidelines and the failings of WorkCover to abide by such. If he had, he could have introduced a possible point of appeal. I also included some authorities citing when a contract is not binding because of duress. The point may well have been that the defendant's position wasn't a safe binding contract in the support of the settlement. Judge Robson didn't ask of himself if I was competent at this time to enter into a contract. I was an unwell person; I had been on the stand for seven days and staying away from home, and I was sleep deprived, all of which added to my levels of anxiety and distress. On the settlement date, my support persons weren't there with me (as instructed by my representatives). He made the judgement that if I looked well, I must be well. That if I appeared confident, I must be confident. That if I appeared competent, I must be competent. As a judge he would understand that just because it *looks* right does not mean it *is* right, but maybe this is how a black letter judge operates. It'd be a different story with an experienced personal injury judge, facing injured workers every day in their court.

The Supreme not so Supreme

I raised that Australia has agreed to uphold the human rights set out in a number of international treaties and declarations; the ones I believe are relevant to my present situation are the following: International Covenant on Civil and Political Rights; the Universal Declaration of Human Rights; and the Convention on the Rights of Persons with Disabilities.

I believe Judge Robson was in error and missed his obligations under these Acts, primarily because he was a specialist judge in the Commercial List.

It was mentioned to me a couple of times that Judge Robson was a black letter judge and for a time I felt that perhaps I was a black letter litigant. I've since come to realise that I wasn't – what makes me a good decision-maker is that I use *both* my head *and* my heart (you have to in a career working with vulnerable young children).

The Common Law has evolved over centuries – law made by judges, because judges have used their heads and hearts in their decision-making processes. It isn't government law, as this is usually head-based. I imagine in Commercial Law, it's appropriate to be a black letter judge.

But I feel I was failed due to Judge Robson's lack of experience in using heart for decision-making.

The five weeks of trial time was the excuse given as to why I had to wait so long for the court calendar to fit my case into the court's busy schedule. There were other personal injury cases whose date of injury was after mine, but had their case heard years before me. I submitted that I held the belief that it *was* in the Public Interest that I be given a retrial; I only used 1.5 weeks of my allocated court time of five weeks.

I stated that if the court so ordered I was prepared to go judge alone, to offer most of the evidence on the papers and to only call 10 witnesses, which should've expedited the process. And if the court so ordered, there was a good chance I would be able to get legal representation.

The 'open court' principle includes making judgements accessible to the public. To protect my privacy, I requested the judgement be listed as unreported, as I was aware that many cases go unreported. I don't agree that injured workers' rights to privacy should be rescinded because they have invoked a legal right. I found Robson's response concerning. He said that as I had raised serious allegations against my legal team, they had the right to be vindicated. I had waited 10 years for my vindication but it never came because those entrusted with its care failed, and now *they* needed to be vindicated for their failure!

There are situations where the court will suppress names or apply a pseudonym, but only in sexual abuse cases; I hope one day psychological abuse is afforded the same sensitivity. In my opinion, abuse is abuse, and the abuser shouldn't have the pleasure of seeing their victim embarrassed and ashamed.

I found a number of references to unreported cases that were not displayed on the internet, such as *Grey v. State of Victoria 1999 VCAT, Dawson v. State of Victoria CC 2004, Filippou v. Dimitroso and TAC 2001, Hatswell v. State of Victoria February 2010*, just to name a few, and these unreported cases are not of a sexual abuse type. So it can happen, but seemingly only if the defendant is the State of Victoria. Is something being hidden from view? I couldn't find one reference anywhere for *Febriano v. State of Victoria.*

I then submitted to the court my arguments against the decision of Robson. I won't go into too much detail, as by now you have an understanding of my arguments, but I will highlight a few of note.

The judgement was riddled with factual errors – many dates were wrong, a statement saying my husband had discussions with counsel was wrong; as at no time did my husband meet with counsel where I was not present. Walsh stated some of my bizarre conduct included a complaint to the DPP, yet I've never written to the DPP nor has he ever written to me and the simple production of the letter could have proven or disproven this fact.

In his decision, Robson stated that Walsh was asked whether he conducted any trial in the week following the settlement. Walsh said that on the Tuesday following he was in chambers, but he probably did appear the next week. It was put to him that he had cases ready to go and he explained that that was not an unusual situation. Robson suggested that if I wanted to put to Walsh that he had urged me to settle because he had some other commitment that I should do so expressly and that I did not do so. I did not do so because I was simply too scared to challenge a barrister, despite knowing he wasn't truthful. Maybe Robson could have considered the power imbalance, my inexperience and my ill-health and just accepted that Walsh had another case starting the next week as he had testified. Why did the fact of the matter depend on me asking this question 'expressly'?

Robson stated that he asked Walsh whether it was his evidence that he did not leave my presence until he had my agreement to accept the $150,000. He replied, "That's correct." Now that answer is incorrect – as I have stated before, I was in that room for nearly four hours and he did leave my presence on a number of occasions. The court surveillance cameras would support my

The Supreme not so Supreme

evidence, as they are situated just outside the door to the ante room. Judge Robson was at times in court when Walsh was in court, so Judge Robson missed this discrepancy – that Walsh did not leave my side until the settlement was signed. Walsh's testimony was plainly wrong.

Robson confirmed Walsh's testimony that I did not say I had a chequebook in my handbag, but Robson made no mention of the fact that both Harrison and Toop both swore that I did say this. Robson again stated only half the truth and supported the evidence of Walsh that he had discussions with me and my husband on the Thursday lunchtime, and that Walsh recommended that I accept the $150,000. Both my husband and I testified that there were no discussions with Walsh on the Thursday lunchtime, but Robson ignored our testimony and didn't even say that he preferred Walsh's testimony over ours (which I believe to be the usual practice). Robson appeared reluctant to make comment about any of our evidence in case it raised a doubt in someone's mind.

Robson decided that Walsh's testimony about the juror's comment merely confirmed Walsh's belief that he was of the view that discharging the jury wouldn't solve the creditability problem. After days of cross-examination and victim blaming, I'm sure all plaintiffs suffer a 'creditability issue', but it's through re-examination and witness testimony that the truth can be recovered and/or uncovered.

Robson recorded that Walsh confirmed he thought the High Court case of *Koehler* applied to the facts of the case. If this is indeed true, why didn't Walsh mention this on the settlement morning as part of his strategy to get me to settle? Because he didn't (at this time) consider the case relevant to my case. As I said earlier, I feel this may have been a later invention, just maybe after the May meeting with Richards. Counsel was using this case to justify their behaviour in the June hearing. Had my whole case been aired it would have been seen as different to *Koehler*.

Robson decided to accept that Ms Toop said there was a conversation about the trial judge and that she had made a note of it, though no note was tendered in evidence because she was not present at the time this comment was made.

Robson confirmed Ms Toop said that despite the observation by the juror, Harrison had already provided extensive advice that the case was not travelling well, though once again there was no reference to my contrary evidence that Harrison did not provide me with any such advice.

Surprisingly, Robson reported that Ms Toop said there was no evidence of complaint by me that the stress caused by my work had any detrimental effect upon me. It was not my actual work that caused the stress and distress, but the bullying. Toop's testimony is quite bizarre. My WorkCover Claim is evidence of complaint and the fact she took my case. Why would any lawyer work on a case for eight years in the absence of evidence? He stated further that Ms Toop referred to the evidence that I had not reported to my superiors that I was suffering from Graves' disease until the mediation of October 2000. Ms Toop knew this was incorrect, as I had provided evidence to her when she took my case about when my employer knew about this, even though it was not Graves' disease that was impacting on my ability to work but the harassment I was subjected to from the beginning of 2000. As Judge Misso stated, he believed that the Graves' disease was a red herring and he was right – my WorkCover claim wasn't about Graves' disease making me too ill for work, but about workplace bullying, mobbing and harassment.

Robson recorded that I had put to Ms Toop that she had offered me a mirror to fix my mascara because I had been crying. However, Robson mentioned nothing regarding how Toop initially lied about this until I described the distinct mirror (then she agreed that this was correct). Again, the yin without yang.

Robson further stated in his judgement that Travis said that he had written instructions from me to try and settle the case the day before, but I say that day would be Thursday 22 April, so when and where did I give those written instructions and why wasn't a copy put into evidence or tendered? No such written instructions were found in my file because none existed.

Robson stated that Travis had a bit of a chat to me while counsel was out of the room, and yet counsel testified that they were present in the room the whole time – Robson makes no mention of this contradiction. He stated that Travis said that he would have run the case for as long as it needed to be run, but no mention yet again of my evidence that Travis had the case of Patterson booked for trial starting 28 April.

Robson goes on to say that I questioned Harrison about his engagements, which suggested that I may have been putting that he had recommended settlement of the case so that he was free to do other matters that he had been engaged to do, but those allegations were never put to Mr Harrison directly. I say when an allegation is made to a witness then that is "directly put." Robson says that nevertheless, he was asked questions about his engagement, and in

The Supreme not so Supreme

particular Harrison said that he did have a mediation booked for 2:15pm on the afternoon of Friday 23 April which he had overlooked. He said, however, that if the case had gone on, he would have sought to arrange the mediation for 4.30pm or otherwise accommodate the requirements of the parties. This sounds all so cordial, but it didn't actually transpire in the manner Robson stated it did, and the transcript clearly showed that Harrison was ruffled. Why did Robson put his head in his hands at the exact moment the experienced barrister suggested he didn't check his diary each day?

In my experience, rearranging a Supreme Court mediation is no mean feat. At my mediation in May 2009, there were four legal representatives, the mediator, the plaintiff and defendant counsel—at least eight people—and when the date of my mediation was changed it cost around $700. To coordinate a change for so many, and considering any court orders and commitments of those involved, Harrison's evidence shouldn't have convinced Judge Robson, and it clearly did not. In the transcript he stated that he was anxious to have my matter settled and that's why I was put under immense pressure.

In his judgement, Robson said that Harrison checked the authorities to see whether it provided grounds for an application that the jury be discharged. But —as I've already touched on—I can't fathom *when* exactly he checked the authorities, *what* authorities he checked and *why* he checked said authorities when there was supposedly no instructions from me to seek leave to have the jury discharged. Harrison agreed that the discharge of the jury was discussed on the Friday morning, but that he and Walsh were the first people to raise that issue. Incorrect: I was the first person to raise the issue – I had never wanted a jury in the first place.

Robson recorded that Harrison said that I said that would seem to be a good idea, but that he and Walsh advised that such an application would be unsuccessful and therefore there was no point in making it. I didn't say this would be a good idea – I actually instructed them to seek this leave. Harrison categorically rejected that I had instructed him to apply to the judge to have the jury discharged; again, Robson found for Harrison and rejected any evidence I gave.

Robson stated that Harrison advised me that the evidence was pretty clear that there was no basis upon which my former employer would have had knowledge of my particular psychological susceptibility which had been established by Mr Jens' cross-examination. My response is fourfold: one, once they had a WorkCover Certificate of Capacity they were on notice of the psychological susceptibility; two, many professionals supported the said diagnosis and cause; three, if this was truly believed then why did my lawyer and barristers attend my case over eight years; and four, what exactly had been established by Mr Jens' cross-examination? Robson did not need to make this finding – it was not necessary or anywhere near factual.

It was recorded that I cross-examined Harrison about the various offers of settlement that were made, and Harrison began by saying that he had made a note of the various offers. I suggest this was another reconstruction after the event – another note not tendered and not seen by me or the judge. However, Robson stated that as events transpired, Harrison was unable to identify with accuracy on which day the various offers were made. I have already discussed in detail the situation surrounding various offers, so won't repeat here.

There was a reference to the fact that the judge was reputed to be a black letter judge and therefore would apply the law, and he said that issue may have been revisited on Friday in the context of discussion about discharging the jury and the discussion about the risk faced because of *Koehler*. I say that this issue was not revisited because it had never been visited in the first place.

In his decision, Robson recorded that I put to Harrison that during the discussion on the morning of Friday 23 April, when the offer of $150,000 was being discussed, that there was a comment regarding the Victorian WorkCover Authority being annoyed or angry because of concerns I had raised. Harrison did not recall that, and I felt he did not recall because to do so would show that either I was placed under duress or the VWA was victimising me because of previous issues (such as the privacy complaint).

Although, Harrison did concede a statement may have been made that the VWA did not like what it colloquially called "psych claims." To me this comes across as possible discrimination – my claim included a number of physical illnesses for which the defendant had accepted liability.

The comment, "No, I do instruct you to accept the offer" was recorded. Untrue: I made no such statement, and that Harrison said he thought he may have said something to the effect of, "Look, I don't want you to sue me." If I was happy to settle then why did Harrison give evidence that he made said comment – why would such a comment be necessary?

Harrison went on to say that WorkCover would have to pay $150,000, and if I went on, they didn't even have to do that, so I will have extracted something. I felt that I had extracted nothing (as opposed to the legal system that had extracted an income of around $600,000). My concerns remain unresolved

The Supreme not so Supreme

and WorkCover got out of an expensive claim for $150,000, none of which went to the seriously injured worker. If the case had continued, WorkCover would have had to cover the costs of their legal team at around $300,000, plus my legal costs (if I was by some chance successful) as well, so Harrison's comment that they didn't even have to do that is non-sensical because they *did* have to do that or the case would have continued accruing even more costs.

Harrison said my claim was doomed and it was prudent to get out of it on the best terms possible. My claim was doomed because it was set up to be doomed, and it was prudent to get out on the best possible terms for the lawyers. There's that 'no win, no fee' oxymoron again.

Robson recorded that Harrison agreed that such conversations took place either on the Wednesday or the Thursday, or possibly both, and then again on the Friday. I say that there were no such discussions on the Wednesday or Thursday, only on the Friday. Both counsels had already testified that there were no discussions on the Wednesday and just a short 30-minute meeting on the Thursday morning to discuss an offer – my evidence and my husband's confirmed this. The explanation that my case was doomed was because of the juror comment, but this comment wasn't made until the Thursday afternoon. In my opinion, Robson appeared to be attempting to give the impression that there were a number of discussions regarding my doomed case before the Friday morning, so further discussion on the Friday morning shouldn't have been a surprise to me, but it was a surprise. Is this part of the judgement designed to say that any duress would have been lessoned due to my prior knowledge?

Robson went on to his 'Findings of Facts.' It's interesting to see how many findings of fact are actually fact; I hope I can relay the complexity of the true facts in an understandable manner.

At the end of Thursday 22 April, Mr Jens indicated that he had concluded his cross-examination. I agree with this, and that Mr Jens had not sought leave of the court to continue cross-examination. Robson went on to state that the court was informed that Mr Jens would seek to continue his cross-examination but Robson failed to say that it was Harrison who stated to the court that Mr Jens would be seeking such leave, and also ignored the fact that Mr Jens under cross-examination in the June hearing stated to the court that he had sought leave and leave was granted. Robson remained silent on this contradiction in evidence.

Robson found that on Thursday 22 April 2010 the defendant offered me

$150,000 all-in inclusive of costs to settle the matter, and that offer was rejected. He made no comment about who rejected the offer and when. He gave no reasoning to this finding of fact because it is not a fact. For it to have been rejected on 22 April means I must have rejected it that evening after Walsh supposedly called Mr Jens to see if the offer was still on the table. My testimony was that the first time this offer was made to me was on Friday 23 April, fact, and my husband's testimony that no such offer was made on 22nd April. Also a fact.

Another fact found by Robson was that during Mr Jens' cross-examination that afternoon, after I said that I would never submit another WorkCover claim, a juror supposedly made the comment "Yeah, sure." Was this a fact? I didn't hear it and no one swore to hearing it, and Robson had a responsibility to ensure fairness; he has taken Walsh's evidence at face value and he could have easily asked his associate if he had heard the comment; this would have once and for all given credibility to a supposed fact that a juror had actually made this comment.

Robson's fact that I made a complaint to the DPP is not a fact. If Robson had read the defendant's affidavit of documents he would have seen that it was WorkSafe that had written to the DPP; the defendant barrister would have known this to be true.

As Judge Robson did not complete the simple task of carefully reading court books he made an erroneous decision of fact, but I feel he was attempting to give fodder to the 'chronic complainer' label that was to be used to discredit and to denigrate.

Robson found that the possibility of making an application to discharge the jury was discussed, but he wasn't satisfied that I instructed my counsel to apply for the jury to be discharged. He wasn't satisfied? What an easy way out – given all his findings of 'fact', how could Robson state that I did not instruct my counsel do so? The evidence showed that I wanted to go judge alone from the beginning; my lawyers knew this and the juror's comment supported why I would want this. Judge Robson's decision was erroneous after he knew I had been fighting to have my case heard for many years; the statements he made further in his decision does not support that I would not instruct my counsel to apply to have the jury discharged. I had nothing to lose by so instructing, but my legal team did: if I continued and was unsuccessful they would get nothing.

Robson found that I was advised that the High Court decision in *Koehler* presented insurmountable difficulties for me – this is not a fact as I was never so advised. Where is the evidence of this advice? No note, no memo, no recorded of he said she said. I was not advised of this, and Robson again made an assumption in favour of my former legal team. He accepted all their verbal evidence without any documentary evidence to support, and yet accepted none of my evidence.

During the settlement discussions Robson found as fact that Harrison and Walsh weren't standing but were sitting at a table. I stated in my evidence that both Walsh and Harrison were to-ing and fro-ing from the ante room and certainly were not wasting time sitting down; they were standing over me while I was seated. This found fact is wrong, but I wasn't then aware that there were witnesses in the court precinct who saw Walsh and Harrison standing over me; at one time Harrison stood with his back to the wall in front of me with his arms folded across his chest. Of course, we all know that this form of body language gives the message, "I'm not interested in what you are saying" or "I'm fed up."

Robson found as fact that counsel discussed that they would be discounting their fees – "they would be;" they already had. I found in my file an 'Account for Services Rendered' to my lawyer dated 22 April, $40,000 to Harrison and $20,000 to Walsh. Given Mr Jens' fees were lower at $30,000 and junior counsel's at $15,000; this wasn't much of 'haircut'. This supports my belief that my case was always destined to conclude on the Thursday and was not ever going to continue on the Friday.

Robson found as fact that my lawyers didn't have any reason to believe that I felt under pressure, at a disadvantage, threatened or intimidated. I stated in evidence that the lead-up to my case would create pressure, and make any plaintiff feel threatened and intimidated. My former legal team gave evidence that I had a tear, but was not crying; I was crying, but composed myself, and the fact it took nearly four hours to convince me to sign the settlement agreement should have caused some doubt in the mind of Robson.

Had Robson availed himself of the facts in many medical reports, some doubt may have been raised, but I feel he wasn't looking for any doubt. He found that after hearing the evidence that had been elicited to date, he wasn't surprised that the case ended as it did. He, of course, had a *completely* open mind at that stage. The pathway of Judge Robson's reasoning to this decision is inadequate; having an open mind means you will give fair consideration to all the evidence. His decision failed to consider that any one of those five legal people could have even remotely given an untrue answer; even when it was elicited in evidence Robson explained it away, made excuses for it or totally ignored the discrepancy.

In his decision, Robson felt that it was not necessary for him to comment on any other matters I raised. These matters were significant; he would not allow me to raise issues of creditability, which in the situation we found ourselves were extremely relevant. My creditability was allowed to be attacked on all fronts, but not theirs.

Judge Robson denied me the opportunity to put all my evidence forward, and then made no decision regarding the evidence I did tender.

At the beginning and end of the trial, Judge Robson spoke glowingly of the worldliness and common sense of juries, and yet Mr Jens spent hours of cross-examination time on irrelevant personnel practices that most average people of today would be aware of, such as the use of work cars, RDOs, time in lieu, on-call allowances, personnel files, and professional development reviews. My case had been running 10 years, yet more time was spent on my holidays and my private life since I left the workplace than spending precious court time on events in the workplace that actually caused injury. I felt Robson didn't understand the Evidence Act, especially the section on irrelevant questions.

Robson stated that Mr Jens sought to show that there was no basis for my employer knowing that I had any psychological susceptibilities and my complaints of bullying were baseless. I have outlined earlier where Robson was simply wrong; there had been no evidence lead regarding this matter in June hearing and there are no references in the transcript. He made no comment concerning the evidence contained in the court book; he thought himself right and the 20 or so other professionals, and a County Court judge, wrong. Robson made an error of fact that no reasonable person based on the evidence could find, so his decision was without merit.

He recorded my history of complaining, in that I had made similar complaints against a previous employer. I say that one complaint in 10 years, where I was proven correct, is not a bad history. My written response to the staff complaint was not in itself a complaint, but simply my right of reply. Judge Robson was making an assumption not based on fact.

How could Robson state that in each case Mr Jens appeared to have reasonable grounds for taking the line of cross-examination that he did? I keep using the car question here because it is the one question that is truly irrelevant. Robson believed it to be reasonable and I find this very concerning. It

The Supreme not so Supreme

was Mr Jens' job to discredit me. Victim-blaming was a tactic often used to discredit rape victims, and is still used as a strategy to discredit injured workers.

Further in the judgement, Robson said that my suggestion that Mr Jens was deliberately delaying the hearing had no grounds. One only has to read the transcript to know this was untrue and to have an understanding of how personal injury cases are conducted. One witness in nearly seven days of hearing was proof in itself when compared to other negligence cases.

Robson states that he was referred to two cases, one being *Bailey v. Marinoff*, where the High Court of Australia held that there is no inherent power in a court to deal further with an appeal which has already been dismissed by formal order, in conformity with an order pronounced, where the order was entered before the application to vary it was made.

My application to vary was filed in the court on 27 April, and on 30 April. Because of my application, Robson didn't pronounce or hand down any final orders. He gave the impression to those in court he would fairly consider my application, but in hindsight, given what had transpired, he didn't do this, and his judgment proved this to be accurate. To this day, I've not signed the formal settlement document which my lawyer sent me days later under the guise of being something else: a 'Solicitor Ceasing to Act Form.'

The directions hearing held on Friday 30 April was adjourned to a date to be fixed, but I didn't hear anything with regard to my application until my lawyer applied to the Practice Court on 26 May to have the settlement monies paid out to them. I didn't attend this Practice Court hearing for reasons previously given, and it was adjourned to 2 June.

The misrepresentation that my legal team and Mr Jens were available for five weeks of trial, when I am sure court records would show this to be untrue: Robson could have explored this in his decision. But nothing was explored if it didn't fit with my former barrister's narrative.

Delays in hearings tire and deplete already ill and vulnerable injured workers, and the defendant knows this and takes advantage of the situation. The defendant WorkCover is complicit merely by allowing law firms on both sides to drag out expensive claims and forcing injured workers to compromise their claims for much less than they are worth. I looked at 10 cases from 1999 to 2010, with six taking eight years or more to come to hearing and the other four around three to five years to hearing. It appeared to me that some cases are purposely delayed by WorkCover; an experienced judge in the Common Law jurisdiction no doubt is aware of this, but not Robson.

Robson cites *Donellan v. Watson Handley*, where a judge's associate of the New South Wales Court of Appeal set out the well-recognised general principles applicable to settlements entered into by lawyers on their client's behalf. Any instruction from the client which restricts the solicitor's authority to compromise the proceedings will only affect the other party who is on notice of that restriction. I feel lawyers and barristers act in concert without transparency; clients should always be in attendance when discussions are taking place; why this does not occur leaves the door open to mistrust and misuse. Harrison would not abide by any of my instructions – that's why it took so long, I was arguing for my case and Mr Jens must have been on notice of that restriction given that it took over four hours.

Robson found that the authority of counsel briefed in the cause was to bind his client to a compromise of the litigation that is governed by the same principles, and all I can say to that is it sounds correct; your rights now belong to your legal team. He stated that Harrison and Walsh had express written authority and the compromise is binding as any ordinary contract, but I say ordinary contracts are not always binding – 'cooling-off periods' apply as well as the legal principles of Undue Influence and Legality.

Robson made the statement that there was no suggestion that the defendants procured the compromise agreement by fraud, duress, mistake, illegality, misrepresentation or non-disclosure of a material fact. I have no doubt Mr Jens knew his major witness, John the manager, would not be available to give evidence, and if so, is this not fraud, misrepresentation and the non-disclosure of a material fact? I would have raised this at the time of the appeal had I been aware of it at that stage. In the June hearing, Robson stated, "the only circumstances in which – or one of the few circumstances would be that he (Jens) obviously can't mislead the court." I don't have a law degree, but I felt Mr Jens did mislead the court by making reference to John's evidence, evidence he *knew* would not be forthcoming.

The last few pages of Robson's decision deal with costs, and will be covered in another chapter.

Robson stated that it appeared that the only means of setting aside the settlement agreement would be by fresh proceedings and then relying on the limited legal and equitable principles that permit a contract to be voided or

The Supreme not so Supreme

otherwise set aside. He stated—as previously mentioned—that I had not made out any of these limited grounds.

Since it really hit the nail on the head, I included Joel Gibson's article in my appeal submissions (refer back to the beginning of Chapter Eleven for a refresher).

I became a victim of the pyrrhic victory – a victory with devastating cost to the victor; a victory that is offset by staggering losses.

The following paragraphs weren't included in the appeal documentation but are my thoughts as I write this many years later. This judgement was exactly what the defendant wanted, and Judge Robson could not see it; justice is blind, but she has many sighted friends!

In my opinion, a purpose for this judgement was non-judicial; it was to create in me an emotionally charged response and to have those that may have supported me to distance themselves because of the unnecessary derogatory comments. Did Robson act outside the scope of his judicial duties, and if so, did judicial immunity still apply? The main obstacle litigants like me face is discovery of the connection, and then getting anyone to take a close look at the failings of a judge, but now with the Dyson Heydon affair I can only hope that more notice is taken of civil litigants who are failed by the court system.

Joe McIntyre, senior law lecturer at the University of South Australia, stated recently, "Power inequity in law is the 'true cancer' and the legal profession is still very much dependant on personal and hierarchical relationships."

It is well accepted that Robson is a black letter judge – as was Dyson Heydon, formally of the High Court, whose legacy cemented his standing as the strictest of black letter lawyers, meaning he adhered strictly to legal precedent and avoided reinterpreting legislation. After experiencing what I believe to be an avoidance of any interpretation that may have been to my advantage, it seems injured workers need a judge who has the capacity to use his head and a little bit of heart in the courtroom. This would on occasion take some bravery.

Dr McIntyre went on to say that "the law is still an exclusive male dominated enclave" and interprets that "Australia's taboo about criticising judges, they're treated almost as a priesthood that their decisions are always correct, that there is no possibility for error and I think that is dangerous because it hides the fact they're human making human decisions." We all now know about the 'good' of the priesthood.

My appeal was heard in the Court of Appeal before Chief Justice Warren and Justice Buchanan and I represented myself. I was asked to stand and address the court and to amplify or add to the matters set out in my documents.

I commenced my opening submission, stating that workplace bullying over the previous 10 years had taken on quite a large public interest. There were lot of people being affected by workplace bullying, and in as much their families had been affected as well, and I was there today to try and right the wrong that I had suffered.

I said that I was there as a lay person and I had provided extensive submissions to the court, and I knew in some circumstances they may well have been emotive, but workplace bullying is an emotive topic and it couldn't just be viewed as a petty civil crime – that it's quite serious wrongdoing.

A point raised by the Chief Justice was that I should look at the prospect of taking legal proceedings separately against my lawyers. As such, there's a preliminary point I needed to address as to why I came to seek to set aside His Honour's orders, when in fact it may have been my lawyers I should be focusing on.

The Chief Justice went on to say that my former counsel in the ordinary course can take objection to irrelevant questions, and the judge can decide whether they are relevant or not, but my response is that my lawyers failed to do this.

The most relevant section in the transcript refers to Mr Wheelahan's (the defendants barrister for this hearing of the appeal) statements to the court – he made them from the bar table, so they cannot be claimed to be evidence given under oath. The Chief Justice asked Mr Wheelahan about two matters on which she could be assisted. First, the assertion by me that Mr Jens, the defendant's counsel, was said to have been given leave to further cross-examine me after the overnight adjournment between 22 and 23 April. And as she understood it, I said that this wasn't in the transcript, and the Chief Justice enquired that she didn't know whether I was in the court all the time, but I seemed to be inferring that no such leave was given. Her Honour asked if Mr Wheelahan or his junior were able to give her assistance with that.

The second matter she needed assistance with was if Mr Wheelahan would be able to clarify the position as to the memorandum referred to in His Honour Judge Robson's reasons. The Chief Justice stated that I seemed to be saying that there was no memorandum before the court, but that I acknowledged that it was mentioned in the transcript. She asked that it may be that Mr Walsh read it out in the course of evidence and therefore it was read into the transcript, and

The Supreme not so Supreme

asked Mr Wheelahan's knowledge of these two matters and if he could provide some assistance that would be useful.

Mr Wheelahan stated in relation to the first matter, his own review of the transcript in preparation for this hearing didn't indicate that leave was given to cross-examine further, and the transcript at the end of the last hearing day indicated that Mr Jens had finished his cross-examination. That was his interpretation of the transcript. In relation to the second matter, the memorandum was read out by Mr Walsh in evidence, but again he was unable to find any reference in the transcript to the document being tendered, and added that his learned junior said it wasn't.

It was recorded in the transcript that while the Court of Appeal had left the bench I provided two affidavits, sworn by the two witnesses who saw the behaviour in the ante room of the Supreme Court on Friday 23 April that both barristers were standing over me while I was crying. I don't understand why the transcript recorded that the court had left the bench and also stated, "Both affidavits as we understand it were provided by Ms O'Keeffe." Why those choice of words, "we understand"? This appeared to give the impression that the affidavits were given at some other time. I handed both affidavits to the judge's associate while the Chief Justice was on the bench. The transcript further recorded that the court had read both affidavits and they would be placed on the court file, but it appeared by choice that the Chief Justice made no findings as to these two affidavits and was silent on their relevance and veracity.

Another section of transcript which was incorrect was the manner in which Mr Wheelahan answered the two questions put to him by the Chief Justice, my notes record that his response to both questions was a simple 'no', but now I feel unsure if I had just recorded this in simplicity. I guess this doesn't change the outcome of what Mr Wheelahan did say, but I can't understand why the transcript recorded something that didn't take place. I've had a number of concerns regarding transcripts during my hearings, and found that they didn't always record what was actually said, and vital questions and answers were incomplete which made it difficult to follow when going back to a transcript weeks after the event.

It was here that my interest was first piqued regarding the "transcript" – I came to learn that this is the documented record of what happens in a court proceeding. It's a faithful record of what is said and by whom. It forms part of the official record of proceedings, and is frequently referred to by the parties and the judge during those proceedings. It really is a vitally important court record – one judge refers to it as an 'aid memoir', another, that parties to a dispute rely on it to be a true account. Proceedings are recorded directly by skilled stenographers in the court (or so it is said; I felt my transcripts left a lot to be desired) or by in-situ audio recording and transmission by tape or network to a team of skilled audio typists located away from the court. The publication of the transcript can vary from real-time transmission to a laptop or computer monitor in front of the judge and counsel to the provision of hard copy typed sheets within hours of the words being spoken in court.

The provision of the transcript is a requirement of all proceedings in the Supreme Court; in criminal proceedings the Victorian Government Reporting Service (VGRS) is the designated recorder. The VGRS was created specifically to develop standards and provide transcript services for Victorian Courts and Tribunals, and in civil proceedings the transcript is provided by contract providers engaged by the litigants. The cost of transcribing in criminal proceedings is met by the state, and the cost in civil proceedings is the responsibility of the parties. I feel anomaly rises here again – alleged criminals get their transcript for free while injured workers have to pay for theirs. It would be interesting to know who actually owns theses private transcription services, who the stakeholders are and whether there are any conflicts of interest.

After the April hearing I needed a copy of the transcript to prepare my case to have the settlement set aside, but trying as hard as I could, I found it was a most confusing experience. I asked the court who transcribed the hearing and I was told a service located in Bourke Street. I visited their office, and after a complex discussion with the receptionist I was told that they didn't do this hearing, and that possibly the service in Queen Street had the transcript. I visited there and there was another complex discussion with a receptionist who stated that they knew nothing about this hearing and it must've been done by the service in Bourke Street. After a number of phone calls and visits to Bourke Street it was finally confirmed that they had the transcript. I sent an email requesting a copy of the transcript and any costs, and that if this was a problem for them to contact me, and if I heard nothing in three days, I would refer the matter back to the court. An email was received the next day stating, "With respect to your request for transcript I confirm that the total cost is $8,336.92 covering 8 days of hearing, your portion (being 1/3) of the cost for transcript is therefore $2,778.97. Upon making payment of this amount, transcript will be made available to you."

The Supreme not so Supreme

I wrote to WorkCover the next day regarding the cost, and as they already had the transcript could they provide me with a copy. Fortunately they did, and on 22 July I finally received the April transcript, but too late for providing assistance with the June hearing. With the transcript I could have challenged Mr Jens more than I did regarding his testimony that he had sought and was given leave to continue cross-examination and whether his witness was in fact absent overseas.

Of course, I needed the June transcript, and with the same degree of confusion I set off on the trail again. I sidestepped the added confusion of the transcripts services and headed straight to a known source. I contacted the WorkCover law firm, who responded instructing me to contact WorkCover directly, which I did, and they stated that WorkCover were not a party to these proceedings and to contact the insurer. I contacted the insurer, who responded that they didn't have the transcript, but WorkCover did. I wrote to WorkCover requesting a copy of the transcript for the 3-4 June hearing, and it was in my hot little hands a week later.

I only needed the transcript now for the 2 June hearing in the Practice Court, and hence contacted the court to ask which transcript service was used. I was informed that the Victorian Government Reporting Service was used to transcribe the hearings in the Practice Court, which again I found confusing, as the Practice Court dealt with civil matters which should be transcribed by the private services. Anyway, the customer service from this department was excellent, way less confusing than the others. A couple of weeks later and after a payment of nearly $400 I had the transcript. The only thing I found unusual was in an email sent to me during this time by the VGRS which stated:

The Victorian Government Reporting Service covers:

Supreme Court criminal and practice courts.
Important Note: Not everything is automatically transcribed. Access to some transcript may be restricted by revisions and appeal status or may be suppressed or prohibited by the presiding judge. Transcript Services staff will alert you to such restrictions and provide you with the best course of action to follow.

Not everything is automatically transcribed? Why not? Access to some transcript may be restricted by revisions – revisions by who and why? Does that mean a transcript can be rewritten? Appeal status? So the transcript can be revised if an appeal is mooted or made? Suppressed or prohibited, by the judge – why? I thought the accurate transcriptions of court proceedings were vital, as they are an official public record.

I have given my experiences here because I feel they lead into the next issue of the transcript saga and explain what happened and why.

The transcript we are now discussing is the Court of Appeal transcript which states "JUDGMENT FOLLOWS" but then the next six pages of the transcript are blank and then go to arguments concerning costs. I have no memory of what the ruling was other than I was unsuccessful. What the Chief Justice said in her ruling was not recorded; why this section was blank I do not know. I didn't receive the written judgment for many weeks and cannot say whether it matched Her Honour's verbal ruling which was given at the end of the hearing. On this occasion I received the orders but not the written judgement, and yet in my June hearing with Robson I received the written judgement but not the orders. I feel there may well be a reason for this, but I should not make any guesses.

From memory, I didn't feel threatened during the hearing. I felt that both the Chief Justice and Mr Wheelahan treated me in a respectful manner and did not make any attack on my dignity. But I have to ask: was the ruling fair, given Mr Wheelahan stated to the court that there was no record in the transcript of Mr Jens seeking or being given leave of the court to continue cross-examination either on 22 April or 23 April? Should this one piece of evidence of possible perjury and the complicit behaviour of my own legal team and Mr Jens be enough to be granted leave to appeal? I believed so.

Approximately four weeks later I received a copy of the judgement. There were the usual preliminary words, then the Chief Justice went on to rule that in her view there was a fundamental threshold issue that I was unable to overcome. If there was foundation to my complaint against my former solicitors and counsel, any cause of action would lie against them. She stated there had been the suggestion, although not made out for present purposes, that the respondent was complicit in the alleged duress and that I asserted that this led to the settlement of the proceedings, and as far as she was able to ascertain the respondent was not aware of the duress alleged.

She went on to say that she expressed no view as to the efficacy or validity of my allegations with respect to my former solicitors and counsel, and my cause of action, if any, lay against those parties and didn't involve the respondent.

The Supreme not so Supreme

Furthermore, in the course of my arguments I also made allegations that would impugn the ethical conduct of my lawyers. This wasn't a matter for this court, but a matter to be taken up elsewhere, and so the case was dismissed. If only I had known at this time of the complicity between my own legal team and that of the defendant WorkCover regarding their statements to the court, and that John the manager would give evidence on these matters, while at the same time knowing he could not give such evidence because he would be out of the country. Would this have been enough to be granted 'leave to appeal'? Somehow I doubt it; another excuse would've just been found to dispense with my case.

The main problem I faced was that the action taken in June and then here was against the wrong defendant – the real defendants were my former legal team, but I had to run the appeal case based on my substantive case. I didn't know what else to do.

A year or so after my appeal, I read a remark made by the Hon. Marilyn Warren at a public forum held at the University of Melbourne Centre for Public Policy, that couldn't have been further from my experience. She stated, "Courts and our democracy – just another government agency? The events in the court room—that is, what is said—are recorded, evidence is documented and the case is argued in an open court room before an impartial, unbiased individual who is beyond corruption."

I was denied an impartial and unbiased individual with my judge. I refer back to previous chapters that explain how my experience so dramatically failed to meet such standards.

To refer to any individual as beyond corruption, especially so when in powerful positions, I believe, is delusional – they are still human and have human frailties; they are not gods (even though some may act as if they are omnipotent).

I cannot put into words how I was feeling towards the end of the year 2010. I should have been feeling happy and settled with all the legalities of the past decade behind me, but I was feeling the exact opposite. I had lived through a traumatic event and my trauma was forever compounded by my experiences of our judicial system. I was so confused; I felt like Alice tumbling down the rabbit hole not knowing when I would hit rock bottom. But as if by magic, I felt a maternal strength pulling me back up to the surface, and a few weeks later I enjoyed a fabulous Christmas with my family – and my last ever Christmas with my beautiful son.

THIRTEEN

High Appeal not so Appealing
_____

I wanted to re-open my case, as can be seen in this chapter, following up previous actions and pursuing actions that were to come. Broadly speaking, there are four recognised classes of cases in which a court may grant leave to re-open, but they are not exhaustive and judicial discretion always plays a part. These main four classes are: fresh evidence; inadvertent error; mistaken apprehension of the facts; and mistaken apprehension of the law. I felt my case would nicely fit into at least one of these categories, but at this time I didn't know how much evidence I actually had that may have fitted with any of the requirements.

I anguished as to whether I should appeal to the High Court for special leave to appeal from the whole of the judgment of the Victorian Court of Appeal given in October 2010.

I read papers that outlined the criteria for granting special leave to appeal and felt my claims were within reason and well-founded. My belief was that the High Court may have regard to any matters that it considers relevant, but *shall* have regard to whether the proceedings in which the judgment to which the application relates was pronounced to involve a question of law. I often felt confused as to what a question of law actually was, but came to understand that the question of law was more important than what was fair and just. A question of law could be whatever the lawmaker wanted it to be, and if that didn't work, discretion was administered that was not appealable. Courts declare there is public interest in finality of litigation, but there is also a public interest to ensure justice is dispensed without fear or favour, and that the finality of litigation principle should never eclipse an individual's legal and human rights; these rights cannot be subservient to this principle.

Given the damning evidence I provided I felt leave would be given if nothing more than to have the opportunity of the court to question the integrity of the judicial system, which I thought would be of some importance to them. But again, I learned that the interests of the administration of justice were more important than the interest of those who came to their door. In my experience, the needs of the administration of justice tactic is initiated whenever a case comes before the court that may bring the administration of justice into disrepute, and the protection of key players and the court is the top priority.

Without legal training, I completed the complex legal documents myself and decided on a number of grounds for the appeal. My beliefs were that the appeal justices erred by: on the evidence not declaring a mistrial because of the omission or failing to consider that the jury was compromised; ignoring any prejudice such compromise may have caused; ignoring or were oblivious to transcript inconsistencies for the end of April 2010, June 2010 and October 2010 hearings of my matter; making assumptions regarding affidavits as matter of fact without exploring evidence to ascertain such facts; and not giving sufficient weight to the evidence of the appeal in October 2010 as recorded in the transcript. This all supports that legal counsel for both parties misled the court, and counsel for the defendant under oath said something he knew to be untrue.

The orders I sought were mainly the following: the setting aside of the orders of the Court of Appeal; remitting the matter for hearing by the High Court of Australia or alternatively the Supreme Court as a cause; and that the respondent pay the associated legal costs.

My written case briefly contained the following: the High Court of Australia supports the principle that democracy is reliant on a fair, equitable and accessible justice system for all and all are equal under law, and if the High Court decides I have been denied my democratic rights, then the Victorian system of justice is a dismal failure. It had taken incredible courage and determination for me to have my concerns addressed, as I was powerless and I felt ignored – was I not part of the "all"?

The Model Litigant Guidelines developed from the Judiciary Act 1903, recently reinforced by the Commonwealth Attorney-General, are an excellent method to access justice for the people, but it only works if the guidelines are respected and implemented. Sadly, the State of Victoria did neither, in my experience.

I believed it was in the public interest for litigation to be concluded as soon as possible, the respondent did not, and caused long delays between the events in issue and the trial. This created difficulties for a fair hearing of the trial. I was hopeful this goal of our judicial system was also Their Honours' goal. But I felt opponents of this goal were lawyers and respondents who would not comply and would benefit by delay. So the battle continued, the principle lost in warfare, the guilty gone and forgotten with the innocent paying the price.

I had been ignored and powerless for too long, and I needed the High Court's assistance to listen to what I had to say, to fairly assess the evidence and to come to a considered judgment, because in the words of Martin Luther King, "Our lives begin to end the day we become silent about things that matter."

My integrity mattered; I had lived my life by those principles and valued them dearly, and then they were taken away from me without just cause. I believed the court had the power—and hopefully a legal heart—to have what was stolen returned to me.

I went on here, explaining my experiences of workplace bullying and mobbing during the years 2000 and 2002 when I was subjected to harassment behaviours, as stated in various and many expert and medical reports. I explained the impact it had on my health and how in 2008 I was successful in gaining a serious injury declaration from the County Court of Victoria on both heads of Pecuniary Loss and Pain and Suffering.

I explained the management of my case by my legal team, and how on 23 April, after the case had been running for seven days, I was coerced, placed under undue influence and duress to settle the claim for $150,000 which would pay the lawyers and barristers. I explained that just days later I filed three documents to rescind the settlement agreement obtained under duress and terminated my legal representatives. When this was heard around a week later, Judge Robson gave the appearance of keeping an open mind and that I would be given a fair hearing. After not hearing anything for a few weeks I was told that the application for the settlement monies to be paid directly to the lawyers (bypassing me) was heard *ex parte* in the Practice Court. The judge didn't make any such order and adjourned the matter to the next week in front of another Practice Court judge. I was unrepresented and had no real idea what was occurring or what I was supposed to do. The judge appeared fair and reasonable and denied my lawyer's motion for the settlement monies to be paid to her, and adjourned the matter until the next day for adjudication by Justice Robson.

Over the following two days I was given the opportunity to cross-examine my former legal team and the barrister for the defendant. I raised the issues of transcript which were of poor quality and failed to catch many of the questions asked and evidence given in reply. Many witnesses referred to notes, memos and memorandums, but didn't have copies with them. I did not understand that I should have asked that these be tendered – or that Justice Robson should, in fairness, have asked that they be tendered.

I did not understand why each of these legal witnesses sat or stood side-on in the witness box, in effect having their backs to Justice Robson, but I feel I now know. Of particular relevance was the testimony of Harrison, which by any standards was unbelievable; I have mentioned previously that this was the time Justice Robson put his elbows on the bench and put his head in his hands. I took this body language as a positive sign that Justice Robson also thought that the evidence was unbelievable. I don't know if the proceedings were videotaped, but if they were, it would support what I stated to be true.

I explained to the High Court that after many requests I finally received a copy of the April and June hearing transcripts on 22 July 2010, too late to assist me in the June hearing against my legal team. They would have been beneficial to me in conducting the cross-examination.

Three months later, Justice Robson handed down his decision and I was unsuccessful. He believed the unbelievable, even when the transcript stated differently. Justice Robson stated at the beginning of my compensation hearing that he uses transcripts as an "aid memoir," so transcripts *were* important, and yet mine were poorly recorded.

I further evidenced to the High Court how in the appeal of my matter, after a short break, the Chief Justice entered the court and read out her orders. I became confused because I hadn't presented my oral case. Her Honour stated that she wanted me to confine my evidence to a couple of major points, which I did; I felt that the decision had already been made without my opportunity to present oral evidence.

Two important issues the appeals court raised were the following remarks recorded in transcript:

CHIEF JUSTICE: "Yes, yes. Thank you, Ms O'Keeffe. Mr Wheelahan, similarly the court has had the opportunity to read the written submissions that you have filed. There may be matters you wish to amplify from the written submission, but there are two matters on which I would be assisted. The assertion by Ms O'Keeffe that Mr Jens, the defendant's counsel, was said to have been given leave to further cross-examine her after the overnight adjournment between the 22nd and 23 April. And as I understand Ms O'Keeffe she says that that is not in the transcript, and I don't know whether she was in the court all the time but she seems to be inferring that no such leave was given. If you or your junior was able to give me assistance with that, that would be appreciated."

It was here that Mr Wheelahan simply answered, "No."

CHIEF JUSTICE: "The second thing is if you would be able to clarify the position as to the memorandum referred to in His Honour's reasons, about paragraph 60 onwards of the judgment. Ms O'Keeffe seems to say that there was no memorandum before the court. She acknowledges that it was in the transcript. Now, it may be that Mr Walsh read it out in the course of evidence and therefore it was read into the transcript. I don't know but of those two matters if you could provide some assistance that would be useful?"

It was here that Mr Wheelahan again simply answered "No," meaning there was no memorandum before the court. I stated Mr Walsh did not read from any memorandum, because if he had I felt I would have asked for a copy, or the judge may or should have requested it be tendered.

I provided a detailed affidavit in support of my appeal, but the Chief Justice's decision just rubber-stamped Justice Robson's decision without any detailed analysis of the evidence. I felt the simple fact that two barristers, one from each camp, lied under oath regarding their involvement in my trial, and the defendant's new barrister Mr Wheelahan, acting with integrity, admitted he

High Appeal not so Appealing

could find no reference in the transcript any leave being given. I believed this should be, of itself, enough for the Supreme Court of Appeal to have granted a new trial.

And further:

> CHIEF JUSTICE: "Whilst the court had left the bench we were provided with two affidavits. One by BF dated 5 October 2010 and one by DO of 14 October 2010. Both affidavits as we understand it were provided by Ms O'Keeffe. The court has read both affidavits. They will be placed on the court file."

These affidavits supported my evidence of duress on 23 April 2010, but unfortunately I wasn't aware that these two witnesses existed until after mid-June 2010, too late to put before Robson.

I requested and paid for a copy of the 15 October transcript in late October 2010. The transcript was received a week or so later, and upon reading I realised that the transcript was not an accurate account of the proceeding.

I informed the High Court of my concerns regarding the transcript and how I called Legal Transcripts, the provider of the court transcription service, and spoke to Bev, and I expressed my concern that the transcript was not a totally factual dialogue of the hearing. And what did "Unrevised" mean? This word was written on the first page of the judgement. Bev expressed surprise and asked me not to do anything until she called me back the next morning. But she didn't call, and the ramifications of this are outlined in the next chapter.

The deadline to appeal to the High Court is 28 days after judgement, yet weeks had gone by without me receiving a copy of the Chief Justice's judgement. I had to contact the Supreme Court of Appeal Registry and ask if the judgment was available. I was advised that it was, and I requested it be emailed to me. Had I not taken the initiative I would have been out of time to lodge an appeal to the High Court.

The 'cab rank rule' appeared not to apply in my case, and Senior Counsel Craig Harrison was only effectively briefed one business day before the trial was to commence. In December 2009, I was advised that senior counsel representing me was Mr Phillip Jewell. I was later informed that Mr Jewell was not available.

Interestingly, I later found out that Mr Harrison was briefed to represent the plaintiff in *Loiterton v. McKillop Family Services*, commencing in the County Court on 13 April 2010 (the same day as my case was supposed to commence) and that he had conducted much of the pre-trial preparation. Mr Loiterton's senior counsel up to 9 April 2010 was Mr Craig Harrison, but it appears that as of the preceding Friday, Mr Harrison was briefed to run my case and Phillip Jewell briefed to run Loiterton. I was told Mr Jewell wasn't available for my case, but then he was available at short notice to run Loiterton.

I strongly believe the defendant was aware of the planned approach to the case given Loiterton and the late additions to the 'Further Particulars of Breach of Duty of Care Owed by the Defendant to the Plaintiff' by my legal team.

The trial judge that I had drawn was from the Commercial List, and this was his first personal injury case under the Accident Compensation Act 1985 and his first case before a jury. This was told to me by Matt Walsh, my junior barrister, who also made a number of negative comments regarding Judge Robson.

The judge gave the appearance of insensitivity to my case by comments he made on the first day of my compensation hearing, and later in the June hearing. Some of these comments are recorded in the transcript. In June, when the Practice Court judge refused the orders requested by my lawyer and referred the case back to Robson, His Honour made a statement along the lines that he hadn't read the 2 June 2010 transcript of the hearing before Justice Hargrave so he was unsure of why we were there that day. This statement was not recorded in the transcript for 3 June 2010.

Justice Robson without comment allowed the late submission of my court books, most likely late because my legal team hadn't planned for my case to go ahead, and the unsigned document titled 'Further Particulars of Breach of Duty of Care Owed by the Defendant to the Plaintiff'. He allowed the respondent to submit prejudicial authority before the trial had begun that fitted with 'Further Particulars of Breach of Duty of Care Owed by the Defendant to the Plaintiff' – a document written and presented to the court that morning, a document I had not seen, and if I had I wouldn't have allowed these changes. These changes caused 'foreseeability' to become an issue; it's quite unbelievable that your own counsel would jeopardise their client's case in this manner.

Justice Robson allowed mistakes in law to go unchallenged, mistakes that were prejudicial to my trial. He may have at least asked himself if he should clarify where there were possible signs of a respondent's counsel exploitative conduct by wasting time asking irrelevant questions and sometimes the *same question* over and over again, in beach of the Evidence Act.

In my opinion, this form of cross-examination bordered on attempting to imply to the jury that the plaintiff was giving falsified evidence or tainted evidence when they were not. I believe it was misleading the court by suppressing evidence the defendant knew to be true while at the same time insisting the plaintiff's evidence was false. Remember my earlier example of the defendant insisting I wrote a letter to the DPP when the defendant knew this was not true.

Justice Robson should have been alert as to why my own legal team weren't objecting to this line of questioning, for example the question, "What kind of car do you drive?"

The day *your* legal rights depend on such a trivial matter will be a sad day indeed.

Affidavits by my lawyers were taken at face value and could have been easily proven wrong. My affidavits in response appeared to have been ignored, even where proof was provided. As previously mentioned, the example of Travis (a lawyer with Clark Toop) writing an affidavit swearing I had been sent five Conditional Costs Agreements, which was untrue as I had only been sent one; when I received my complete legal file a few years later there was only the one Costs Agreement on file, not five.

I feel I was obstructed in my June hearing against my former legal team because I couldn't get a copy of the court transcript for April until after my Common Law hearing held in June of 2010.

There were many occasions where I asked my legal team to go judge alone, but this choice sat with the defendant. And why wouldn't they want a jury who could be swayed into believing wrong was right? I now realise that in early court preparation my legal team could have requested trial by judge alone given the defendant's statement that the trial would run for up to six weeks. In cases such as mine (that were destined to take up much court time) it is in the interest of justice for a court to dispense with a jury and to hear the matter as a cause. But of course, this didn't happen – my legal team were playing to a particular tune, the defendant's tune; they were the pied piper.

Through no fault of your own, or even when purposely injured at work, once a WorkCover claim is made, your rights to privacy (a human right under international obligations) are rescinded. You are embarrassed and humiliated for pursuing a right you thought you had.

It is accepted that the law must be seen to be done, but I see no benefit in not respecting the privacy of innocent plaintiffs. The worst of criminals appear to have a greater right to privacy than law-abiding citizens who through no fault of their own find themselves having to exercise their legal and human rights by accessing the judicial system. Past practice of archiving court files meant interested parties had to apply and travel to the court to access, but now with the internet, access is only four clicks away from the comfort of your own home.

I now feel this may be a legal form of defamation, used by defendants to discredit the worker. Irrelevant and hurtful accusations are made without proof, and of course the judge still has to consider this in his or her decision; even though the allegation is false they are given air in which to live.

In the past, a period in the stocks was shortly over and confined to your local village, but now once you pursue your legal rights you are in the stocks forever, and not just in your local village but throughout the world. I contend that to publish an ill-gotten judgement on the internet is in violation of the human right to privacy. I believe innocent, injured workers should be protected like many other cases, such as sexual assault or sexual harassment victims, and be given the choice of remaining anonymous – this still serves the judicial process as the law is seen to be done, others learn from the rationalisations of judges, the common law evolves and the brave individual can heal.

I also asked the High Court how a regulator like the VWA can, under statute, investigate a breach of a law while at the same time be a potential defendant in legal proceedings concerning that same breach.

My legal team knew my state of health at this time; I was staying away from home, living in unfamiliar surroundings and suffering from sleep deprivation that was only added to after being on the stand for seven days. My legal team suggested that on the Thursday (the last day of trial for me) I should give my husband a day off, as he had been sitting outside the court for seven days waiting (supposedly) to give evidence, and as the next day was only re-examination. Re-examination it was not: this was the morning full of threats, intimidation and bullying, with my major support person strategically absent. I was understandably exhausted and vulnerable and this should have been understood by the court, with the balance of probabilities at least being considered in my favour.

As this was the judge's first personal injury trial and first jury trial, was he just inexperienced? Is this why this happened to me? It's something I'll never know, but in a way I hope it was because he was inexperienced rather than through neglect or bias or something worse. He only had to view the CCTV outside the interview room just outside the courtroom to see what I was saying was true.

On the very next day I knew something was wrong, I knew the treatment from my legal team was wrong and I knew I had been harassed into a settlement, so I immediately set about setting aside what I thought was the draft compromise I had signed the day before, before the final orders hearing being heard the next Friday. Later, on 30 April 2010, the judge threw back to my former barrister a costs agreement because it was unsigned by me.

I felt that both the Supreme Court and Court of Appeal failed to accord procedural fairness to a self-represented litigant because orders of the court dated 28 April 2010, 25 May 2010, 2 September 2010 and 15 October 2010 were not sent to me, nor was the procedure to obtain such orders explained to me. It was only by chance that I gained access to these orders, and had I not been proactive in gaining the orders I would have been out of time for any appeals process.

I had at all times been honest and genuine, and this is reflected in the required legal actions taken prior to the damages hearing where I was successful. I was not at fault due to the extended time my claim has taken. I did everything within my power and control to expedite matters, but this was beyond me; I was powerless in the legal system. I felt the principle or right of a fair trial had been denied to me; after patiently waiting many years and doing all that was asked of me to have this taken unfairly from me by both my legal team and the defendant's is an insult to the rule of law, and the profession generally.

According to the Model Litigant Guidelines, as serious injury had already been decided by the County Court of Victoria, I was not required by law to prove it again. Yet, that's exactly what was happening – the hearing was being derailed by the asking of questions that didn't need asking or answering, but the jury didn't know this. They are encouraged to believe you're a 'rorter' and not genuine.

Any hint of a compromised jury should be investigated as prejudicial and a decision made. The court made no enquiries of which I am aware, and to this day Mr AC, associate to Justice Robson, has neither confirmed nor denied the existence of the dialogue he heard from a juror on the last day of trial.

It appears that representative error is common in claims such as mine, and the only redress is by taking legal action against your former lawyers. This is unrealistic, as by this time most plaintiffs are totally depleted, unwell, unemployed and on their own, and few lawyers would take on such a case against another lawyer on a 'no win, no fee' basis. These plaintiffs no longer have any rights to justice or the law as they no longer have any funds to feed it. I stood my ground respectfully and within legal boundaries, yet Justice Robson in his decision labelled me a chronic complainer because I had followed the law and invoked my legal and human rights when necessary. I feel the Supreme Court had lost sight of its role to ensure fair justice, which is the cornerstone of human rights and democracy.

I had experienced victimisation in the workplace because I followed OH&S laws and had the expectation that my employer would do likewise. I was victimised again because of my legal complaint to WorkSafe in 2004, and legal counsel informed me on the morning of my last day of trial that this was the reason WorkCover (as the behind-the-scenes defendant) was playing hard ball. They weren't just playing hard ball – they ignored their responsibilities under law, especially the Model Litigant Guidelines. The New South Wales case of *Patrick Stevedores Holdings Pty Ltd v. Fogarty* 2014 says it well:

> Allianz's behaviour is all the more disgraceful given that it is obliged to act as a model litigant. That means more than acting honestly and in accordance with court rules, and more than lawyers acting in accordance with ethical obligations; it must be a "moral exemplar" (*State of Queensland v. Allen* 2011, and *LVR (WA) Pty Ltd v. Administrative Appeals Tribunal* 2012.) It is obliged to pay legitimate claims without litigation. Mr Fogarty's claim was, without doubt, a legitimate claim that should have been paid without the need for litigation. Why it was not paid should also be investigated.

The defendant had at all times been obstinate, even in the face of: strong evidence to the contrary; acceptance of claim; acceptance by the insurer for liability for all injuries and diseases; acceptance of serious injury by a court; numerous documents supporting my claim; and acceptance by many and varied medical practitioners. Other claim/s for similar injuries by the same employer were accepted. The defendant continually refused to sincerely negotiate, mediate or conciliate or attempt any alternate dispute resolution process. The defendant ignored the Model Litigant Guidelines and had allowed costs to

High Appeal not so Appealing

escalate beyond what I was prepared to settle; these costs went to pay legal fees rather than compensate an injured worker. The government attempted to display equity and fairness in the Model Litigant Guidelines and attempted to level the legal playing field, but WorkCover, insurers and defendant lawyers ignored these guidelines and displayed a 'win at all costs' attitude while they were playing the game of justice – or I should say, injustice.

The defendant had enough information to know my claim was genuine, as other/s WorkCover claims had been made by employees in the same organisation. These claim/s were accepted and the original bully appeared to have been asked to leave after WorkSafe undertook an 'inspection' (I won't say 'investigation' because I don't believe one was undertaken, as the truth didn't want to be found) supposedly took place. On the last day of the April trial, another bullied employee was sitting outside the court waiting to give supportive evidence on my behalf. The defendant knew this was going to be damaging to their character assignation of me; of course the trial never continued as I had 'settled'.

In the past, WorkCover has prosecuted perpetrators of workplace bullying. I believe the reason they didn't in my case, was because I *had* a WorkCover claim, and to prosecute would bolster the veracity of my claim; they wouldn't have wanted an injured worker to get fair and just compensation. This coupled with the fact that the defendant was the third arm of government meant, in effect, that you have the government suing the government, which of course happens, but I believe this would be a huge conflict of interest.

I travelled to the High Court in Canberra, not because I felt I would be successful, as I knew by then how the system worked, but to give a face to the court number. If the court was going to deny my human rights, I wanted them to look me in the eye when they did so.

As I had to give my name on arrival at the court, I knew it would be known that I was present.

When the full court filed in, there were three male judges and one female judge; I was later to find out that the female judge was Matthew Walsh's (my former barrister) aunt. It's unknown what part—if any—she played in the decision to dismiss my application for leave to appeal, but her sitting on the bench when the decision was handed down wasn't a good look. Another one I'm confident wouldn't pass the 'pub test'.

On entering the court, Chief Justice French had his eyes downcast, and this was how it remained for the entire time I was in court (around 45 minutes).

When it came to my case, a simple 'dismissed' was the only action, with Justice French never looking up, as I feel he knew he would be looking right at me, as was my position in the court. I felt he didn't want to make eye contact because he was embarrassed, and if he was then there was hope that his actions weighed heavily on his conscience. The fact he seemingly had a conscience and that he hadn't lost his sense of human dignity was heartening.

I then went to another court and listened in on a hearing about the costs associated with a broken clay pipe. I wish my human and legal rights were as important as that broken clay pipe.

I still wonder now if the High Court, the highest court in our land, failed to consider the important question: was this case beyond reasonable doubt?

Associate Professor Kim Sawyer stated in his 2021 paper 'Beyond Reasonable Doubt' that "It underscores the maxim that is so often expressed yet so often ignored. Innocent until proven guilty, a principle of natural justice. . . . The ultimate test is whether the argument that determines a verdict is free of inconsistencies."

I feel, if nothing else, that my case abounded with inconsistencies, and just maybe this was one of the reasons it was dismissed, as to examine inconsistencies takes court time. In my opinion, the value of the litigant was considered and the decision made that this litigant wasn't worth valuable court resources to find the truth (which was wanted hidden anyway). And to top it off, this litigant wasn't paying to play.

Sawyer goes on to say, "Judges and jurors must focus on the question that matters and the evidence that matters." I have no doubt that judges alone suffering no bias do this every day, but I have grave doubts that a jury is capable of this essential separation of the 'wood from the chaff' when a barrister's complex manipulation is at play, where wood becomes chaff and chaff becomes wood.

As Sawyer states, "Complexity is the enemy of justice. Complexity anchors minds to the irrelevant." And this is exactly what happens in a jury trial, or in my opinion in a civil jury trial.

Further, Sawyer states, "The principles of a fair trial are that: all relevant evidence is considered, all irrelevant evidence is discounted; and the logic of induction is applied to all the relevant evidence." ('Induction' being the inference of a general rule from particular instances – opposed to 'deduction', in that evidence and evidence alone is used to make decisions.)

High Appeal not so Appealing

And: "The right to prove innocence is a fundamental right. It is the underwriter of natural justice."

I feel that many in the legal profession believe this statement, but on occasions it doesn't suit, they forget it. Sawyer would make a great judge, as I believe he has the integrity to actually live up to his stated opinions.

"Litigation: a machine which you go into as a pig and come out as a sausage."
— Ambro Bierce 1842–1914.

FOURTEEN

To Protect and Serve

It took me nearly 10 years to struggle through the WorkCover process. Such an experience does not assist injured workers to regain their health and wellbeing to return to the workforce. The process, in effect, makes a claimant almost unemployable and their life almost unliveable.

My claim ran for the same period as Rob Hulls was in office, and he made many 'motherhood' statements over these years that fitted in with my belief system; it lulled me into a false sense of security. In his maiden speech to parliament in 1999, Hulls made the statement backing a "fair, accessible and understandable justice system" and I fell for it. Plus, he also said that the "Bracks Government understands that 'justice' is not an abstract concept, but something that affects all our lives in a very real sense. Justice is about openness, transparency and accountability," and "It is about creating courts that are modern and accessible, not only in terms of our court buildings but in the way they dispense justice."

This didn't anywhere near describe my experience. The old quote "Justice delayed is justice denied" certainly rang true for me.

My estimate of the direct costs of my claim at this stage were in excess of $1 million. All I wanted was to return to the job and career I enjoyed. My crime: guilty of being innocent.

From memory, the first time I met Rob Hulls was in May 2002 at a Community Cabinet Consultation held on the Surf Coast, and for a brief couple of minutes I talked to him regarding my experiences of workplace bullying. I found him to be engaging and sympathetic and a potential warrior for change.

The following year in February, my WorkCover claim was accepted and around this time there appeared to be a renewed interest in workplace bullying.

Coincidently, a few days after my claim was accepted, the Minister for WorkCover Rob Hulls put out a media release stating that there must be accountability in the use of public funds. He gave a figure of $57 million being spent annually on this scourge in the workplace. That was now over 20 years ago; I can only guess what that cost is today, as bullying still appears rampant in the workplace.

Hulls went on to say that "Not only does workplace bullying have an unacceptable social cost, it also carries a substantial economic impact," and "Workplace bullying claims made to VWA totalled $57 million in 2001–02, up from $51 million in 2000–01. The full cost of workplace bullying, in lost productivity and absenteeism, is difficult to quantify, but some Australia-wide estimates have placed it at a staggering $3 billion a year."

Hulls went on to state, "These are real problems which result in injuries to employees and costs to employers and the community; the community at large accepts that bullying needs to be dealt with and the best way to do this is through preventing it happening in the first place," and "Employers need to be able to recognise the warning signs that bullying may have occurred," and finally "Victims of crime can be further traumatised by court trials and retrials, and it is important we reduce court delays and appeals to reduce unnecessary hardship for victims."

I wondered if an injured worker can be classified as a victim of crime. I have come to the conclusion that when an employer, once informed, allows the bullying to continue, then this is a crime under Occupational Health and Safety Act – but don't ever expect a prosecution to take place, especially when two key factors are at play: one, a WorkCover claim form is submitted, and two, the employer is the third tier of government.

I believe traumatised injured workers (especially bullied workers) are victims of crime, and yet they are left to languish for many years experiencing delays, no legal aid for them, just the horror of 'no win, no fee'. I wonder if Hulls considered this to be an unnecessary hardship on them? I would hope so, but given my extensive experience, I now believe that an injured worker is more frightening to the system than a criminal. If some get a dollar for their pain and suffering and loss of income, then others may believe that the system works and either confidently submit a claim or rort by the submission of a false claim. It no doubt costs more to keep a convicted criminal in prison for a few years, than to pay an injured worker a fair dollar, but this is exactly what happens, I can't for the life of me understand it.

My employer's senior management team were aware of all that happened to me, but simply chose to ignore their duty of care and their obligations under the OH&S Act, choosing instead to spend many, many thousands of dollars of public money concealing their incompetence. Then someone decided that surveillance of me, my family and home was warranted, and many more thousands of dollars of public money was spent on fruitless surveillance activity, the outcome of which was discussed in a previous chapter.

I read another media release, dated October 2003, that in part stated that a recent survey had found 14% of employees had been bullied in the workplace in the past six months. The Minister for WorkCover called on more employers to develop workplace bullying policies following the release of the survey. Mr Hulls said, "Bullying is cowardly and must not be tolerated in the workplace; intimidation in the workplace is a real problem that results in injuries to employees and costs to employers and the community. Bullying needs to be dealt with. The best way to do so is to prevent it happening in the first place," and that "Bullying can never be 'part of the job' and is never acceptable."

This 'warrior for change' appeared to be growing some teeth, and this gave me great hope for the future. Over the coming years I corresponded with Hulls, and in one letter he stated what I felt was a genuine response. He said, "The VWA has assured me that you will be formally notified of the outcome of this investigation" and "Thank you for drawing this serious matter to my attention." In my understanding, not long later, my serial bully was asked to leave her employment. But as I've stated before, no genuine investigation took place – only an inspection; that is what I was told.

I met Hulls again in 2009, some seven years after our first meeting. He was in Geelong to open the new Red Cross Blood Bank, and after the official duties were over refreshments were served in an adjoining room. I was hopeful to talk to him for a minute or two, but doubted I'd get the chance due to a number of others also keen to talk to him. With my cup of tea, I retreated to the corner of the room, and after a few moments Hulls entered and—to my surprise—walked straight over to me. We chatted for a few minutes, but I soon realised he hadn't actually recognised me, but that was fine and I knew such a context didn't allow for any in-depth conversation. His staff motioned to him that it was time to go, so he said goodbye and turned to leave, taking a step or two before turning back to face me, and he said, "Keep fighting." I can only assume that, as I was wearing my name badge, it finally came to him as to who I was. This comment sustained me over a number of years, giving me much-needed strength.

The next stage of this story began after the October 2010 hearing of my appeal, which I have detailed in the previous chapter.

After a number of requests and again seeking out the transcription service, I finally received an electronic copy of the appeals court transcript on 3 November 2010. Later that afternoon, I called Legal Transcripts and spoke to staff member Bev, and discussed with her my concerns regarding the fact the transcript wasn't an actual, real-time recording of the proceeding. She asked me not to do anything until she called me back the next morning at 10:30am. Bev didn't call me the next morning, or respond to emails I sent that day and a week later.

As I was going to Melbourne the next day (4 November) to drive a friend home, I thought I would attend the Supreme Court Registry to inform them that the transcript was incorrect, as I understood that accurate transcripts are vitally important to a judge as an 'aid memoir' which assists a judge in his/her decision making and writing of reasons. I think of my friend Julie and her claims about her transcript in the Family Court, and I have since discovered there are many unsuccessful litigants who make similar claims. Are we all wrong? Doubtful.

I attended the registry around the middle of the afternoon and requested to see the Self-Representative Litigant Co-ordinator, but he wasn't available. So I asked for the Practice Court Co-ordinator, but he wasn't available. So I then asked to see the Prothonotary, but he too was unavailable.

Since I was in the city, I decided to visit 1 Treasury Place to enquire if it was possible to see Rob Hulls. In his position as Attorney-General, I believed he needed to know that transcripts in civil proceedings were incorrect, and possibly being altered, as this was the second transcript I had received that was inaccurate. Given my previous interactions with Hulls and the fact he knew of my case, I mistakenly thought he might see me for a few minutes.

I honestly believed that Hulls would want to know about possible judicial misconduct. As I reflect back on this, I am prepared to admit that this was an example of 'bizarre conduct'. Who was I to think that a senior politician would see *me*, a powerless nobody? I fear I am now living up to the label Robson had placed on me just months before.

Late in the afternoon I entered the foyer of 1 Treasury Place and spoke to a person on the reception desk and asked if it was at all possible to see Rob Hulls for a few minutes. I was asked to take a seat, which I did, and then I was asked to fill out a form detailing the purpose of my visit. I was informed that it was unlikely that I could see Hulls as he was not in the building. I rang his personal assistant on my mobile phone and was told he wasn't in the building and no one knew where he was. I responded that he was more than likely in the shower, as I had just seen him jog through the main front doors of Treasury Place.

I continued to sit quietly on a small lounge in the foyer while my friend went for a walk. Sometime later, I'm not sure how long, a Protective Services Officer (PSO) approached me stating that I would not be seeing Hulls that day. I responded that I was happy to sit here on the off chance and also to wait for my friend to return from her walk. He went away and I continued to sit quietly on the lounge. A few minutes later, I am not sure of the exact time, the same PSO plus another PSO came over to me and stated that as Hulls would not see me that day, I had no business being in the building, and that my legal right to be there had been revoked and I was now trespassing.

I was told to leave, and I responded that I was happy to sit here until my friend returned. One PSO stated that I could wait for my friend outside on the park bench, and also told me if I didn't leave immediately they would forcibly remove me. At this point my friend had returned. Before I had packed up items to go back into my handbag, both PSOs each grabbed an arm and I was pulled off the lounge forcibly. Though shocked, I said, "I haven't done anything wrong," I didn't display any physical or verbal resistance and was escorted outside. Once there, both PSOs went back inside, and there were no further verbal or physical exchanges.

I was sitting quietly in a public space and never expected to be treated as I was. Early the following year, when Labor were out of power and Baillieu was the Premier, a group of rowdy protesters chained themselves together in the foyer – they were not forcibly removed by PSOs.

After leaving Treasury Place, I went to an address in Southbank Boulevard where I stayed for approximately 30 minutes, and upon returning to my car I discovered that I had been issued a parking ticket at 6.20pm when restrictions finished at 6:30pm. At the time I thought I was just unlucky. But later on, reading information on the duties of Protective Services Officers, I was surprised to learn that while most of their work related to building security, they also performed another main function: the issuing of parking tickets. I wondered if I had been followed from Treasury Place to Southbank by either the PSOs or by other/s unknown. This could only be ascertained by examining the evidence, evidence I am not allowed to access.

It was around this time, while driving to Footscray, I noticed that my right arm was aching. My friend and I decided to have a meal in a restaurant located near Paisley Street, and I parked in Paisley Street. During dinner my right arm was incapable of lifting even a small bowl of soup. Upon returning to my parked car about two hours later, I discovered that my car window on the right rear passenger side had been smashed and entry had been gained. Damage consisted of the broken window, and items stolen were the car log book and maintenance records, the driver manual and the first aid kit. The car was in disarray, but to my surprise, a mobile phone, prescription drugs, new high-end glasses and a variety of other goods were not taken. I didn't know at the time that the street was covered by a rotating CCTV camera. It was a constable at the Footscray Police Station who told me and said, "This would be good as we can see who broke into your vehicle."

I had attended the Footscray Police station to file a report regarding my car break-in, and by this time my arm was extremely sore, so I requested to make a statement regarding what I believe was an assault on my person by the PSOs. I reported both of these incidents to the constable and he took a report of my car break-in, and said that as it was parked in Paisley Street, Footscray that the incident would be captured on the CCTV that operated outside the Westpac Bank. He stated that he was too busy to take the report of my assault, but said to come back the following Wednesday at 3pm.

As requested, I returned to the Footscray Police Station the next Wednesday, but the officer said he didn't have time to take my statement, and he also said that unfortunately my car was not in range of street CCTV. I attended the Geelong Police Station a few days later but they too would not take my statement.

Two weeks later I attended the Geelong Police Station again, where a senior sergeant took my statement regarding the alleged assault by the PSOs. The constable from the Footscray Police Station first told me my car was but then later telling me it wasn't within range of the street's security cameras had made me feel I was being misled.

In early 2011, my friend who witnessed the assault at Treasury Place gave a statement to an Inspector Michael. Inspector Michael was the officer appointed to investigate my claims. I was informed in February 2011 by Inspector Michael that the CCTV footage of the assault confirmed my statement as being accurate. He also said that I would be "happy" with his report. I asked if I could see the CCTV footage and he responded that he didn't think that would be a problem.

A few weeks later, I visited the area where I had parked my car to see for myself where the CCTV cameras were located. I couldn't see any, so I entered the Westpac Bank and asked the security guard if there were any cameras in the vicinity. He responded in the negative and I said that was a shame as my car had been broken into. He told me that the cameras used to be there but there were too many complaints from the traders, so the council took them down. I asked when this was and he said, "1 March 2011." I asked him where they were located and he said 'just there', pointing to a telegraph pole on the corner, just outside the bank. My car was parked in the second car park from the corner, in full view of this whole-street CCTV camera which was in operation at that time. Local newspaper *The Star* had reported on the removal of this camera in March of 2011 due to complaints from traders in Paisley Street.

I next rang Maribyrnong City Council and spoke to the staff in the Parking Office and asked if the footage of the CCTV cameras was still available, and was told it was. I asked if I could view the footage and was told "No" – only the police could access.

Inspector Michael called me in mid-February and said the CCTV footage showed I was not violent or offensive at any time while I was at 1 Treasury Place on 4 November 2010. He clarified some concerns regarding the PSOs stating that I raised my fist to them and was threatening; he states that the CCTV didn't capture this and that he was concerned that my statement wasn't taken when I attended the police stations – he told me the constables would be spoken to. This was a relief; even though I knew I hadn't acted in an anti-social manner, it was good to have this confirmed by him. I was informed in early March 2011 that the police investigation was complete and I would receive a copy of the report by the end of that week.

Interestingly, in early March of the same year I was watching the news on TV when there was a feature on Rob Hulls being evicted—without explanation—by the Speaker of the House, the Honourable Ken Smith, a veteran Liberal MP. Mr Smith ejected Mr Hulls after he tried to raise a point of order over recent comments the Speaker made questioning why Mr Hulls was still in Parliament. What I remember most clearly was the comment from Hulls, "I haven't done anything wrong," or words to that effect.

Not long after, Mr Hulls became seriously ill and a few months later resigned to spend more time with his family. In October 2012, Hulls was appointed Adjunct Professor at RMIT and was invited to establish the new Centre for Innovative Justice as its inaugural director. The Centre's objective was to develop, drive and expand the capacity of the justice system to meet and adapt to the needs of its diverse users. I wonder how that's going, as it is now more than 10 years later and I certainly haven't experienced any capacity of the justice system to meet and adapt to the needs of its diverse users.

A few weeks later, after meeting my son Dan in Southbank for a catch-up coffee, I was driving home when I received a call from Ken Smith, who introduced himself as the Speaker of the House of Parliament. He said he had heard about me and would be interested in meeting up, which we did the following week. My daughter and I met at his office in Parliament House and he was very interested in what I had to say about my visit to Treasury Place and my other experiences with the court. I didn't tell him about the Mrs Febriano issue, as I wasn't yet aware of its significance. Ken showed us around Parliament House and was thoroughly engaging and I liked him very much. He asked for me to send some documents he was interested in seeing and we left. I sent him an array of documents the following week.

I met Ken again a few years later for the purposes of my book, and he kindly treated me to lunch at the magnificent dining room in Parliament House. I told him about my book and wondered if he had any further information which would help with this chapter. As it was now a number of years later, he had only sparse recollection, and suggested I access the Hansard for this period of time. I had undertaken so much reading that tackling Hansard was not particularly appealing, so I stuck with what I already knew.

I hadn't received said police report and contacted Inspector Michael, who stated that he finished it in March and it was "upstairs." I eventually received the report at the end of May 2011 and it was vastly different to what I was led to expect. I had gone from being the victim to being the perpetrator, as Inspector Michael's report made a finding that once outside the foyer of 1 Treasury Place, I turned to one PSO and threatened her and the second PSO had to draw his capsicum spray to protect her and warn me to stay back. Robson's label of "angry and aggressive" was gaining traction. This report was a fabrication; no such thing occurred, and this was supported by my witness, earlier comments made by Inspector Michael and external CCTV cameras – recordings CCTV cameras that I've never been allowed to see.

On a visit to police headquarters to meet with Inspector Michael I was introduced to the Assistant Commissioner Stephen Fontana, who appeared interested in my story and requested further details. I sent him an email regarding follow-up action on the issue of perjury in my case at the Supreme Court. Inspector Bill, on behalf of Fontana, sent me an email that stated, "I wish to highlight Victoria Police are only looking at your complaint against the Protective Security Officers and your allegation of possible perjury." I have never had a response from Victoria Police regarding the perjury allegation, and the assault allegation went nowhere.

Over the following months I requested—on a number of occasions—to have a copy of the CCTV footage of the assault and my supposedly threatening behaviour towards the PSOs, but this was never forthcoming. In May 2011, I submitted a Freedom of Information request form to Victoria Police for copies of both CCTV footage from Treasury Place and the car break-in. The response I received said, "Due to the large number of FOI requests received at this office, a delay in completing your request is expected. This delay may be in excess of the 45 days referred to in Section 21 of the Act." I since made a number of phone calls regarding this FOI request, but have never received access.

Around this time, I requested a copy of the statements made by the PSOs, as I believed—under the principles of natural justice—I would be entitled to have a copy of these statements. In regards to my formal FOI request for a copy of the CTTV recording from Treasury Place, the response from the FOI coordinator was, "I am advised that the footage is being used as part of an Ethical Standards Department (ESD) investigation. I am satisfied that the disclosure of the footage at this point would be reasonably likely to prejudice that investigation."

I didn't know what investigation was being referred to because I had been informed that the investigation was complete. I never at any time requested that my assault be treated as an Ethical Standards complaint – it was not a complaint, I reported a criminal act of assault, and this should have been investigated by police as such. I believe this investigation occurred because Inspector Michael had been delegated control of the matter, and because it involved Hulls, there was a desire to investigate it as a civil matter rather than a criminal matter. Inspector Michael never explained why he was delegated control of a matter I feel belonged in either the Criminal Division or Ethical Standards, not in the Counter Terrorism Unit.

I was concerned for the safekeeping of these recordings, as they could be lost or distorted. With this in mind, in mid-June 2011, I applied to the County Court of Victoria for a freezing order for CCTV tapes—the one from Treasury Place and the one from Footscray—and this was granted by the court. I wasn't sure at this time who the real defendant was, but there had to be a defendant named, so I therefore named Rob Hulls. The County Court decided Hulls wasn't the correct defendant, despite the fact Inspector Michael told me in early July 2011 that it was Hulls who gave the order that I be physically removed from the foyer of Treasury Place. When I can view these two CCTV tapes, it should be clear if it was a PSO involved in causing damage to my car and if there was any cover-up.

Moving into July of 2011, I still hadn't received a copy of the PSOs' statements, so I sent an email to the Ethical Standards Division requesting the statements by the PSOs be provided to me by 15 July 2011, but neither FOI requests were fulfilled on this date, or ever.

A 2021 paper written by Geoffrey Watson SC, titled 'Buried at Sea: The Loss of our Freedom to Access Governmental Information' includes the following statement: "Those supplying answers to requests for information routinely falsely claim exemptions which cannot be justified by a proper interpretation of the legislation. ... When a person seeking access challenges an adverse result they are confronted with skilled, government-funded legal opposition with the potential for expense and delay." This is certainly what I faced.

On the evening of 15 July 2011, I contacted the Geelong Police station to report that my son Dan was missing. I was told by an officer that they would attend my home to take a statement. After waiting around an hour and a half, I was contacted again and told that officers would be there soon. After waiting around another hour and a half I was contacted again and told they could not attend, but officers would come by to get a photo of my son, which they did at around 11:30pm.

Police finally attended our home a few days later to take a statement, but only after they had been contacted by media for comment.

There was an occasion around three weeks later when I called the officer in charge of Dan's case and asked if he had interviewed a witness (who reported seeing Dan on the day of his disappearance) yet. We needed information as to where we should best direct our resources and energy. His response in a loud and angry voice was "That's none of your business." Maybe it wasn't, but I felt his anger was defensive because he *hadn't* interviewed this person three weeks after knowing of their existence. Because of this (and a number of other concerns I had), I restricted my contact with Geelong Police regarding the investigation into my son's disappearance. It's impossible to convey how distressing this was for me.

Prior to November 2010, I'd had no involvement with the police in any aspect of my life, and believed that if I ever did need them, they would be there to protect and serve me. I was wrong, again.

I had two strange experiences between November 2010 and May 2011. A few days after my car was broken into, I was travelling through Melbourne to a doctor's appointment when I noticed a car behind me with flashing lights and dutifully pulled over. A young man looking like he'd just stepped out of the pages of a fashion magazine—tall, immaculately well-groomed and very handsome—asked me about the plastic covering my back passenger window. I told him about the car break-in, and after momentarily looking at my licence he smiled and returned to his obviously-unmarked police car.

I didn't notice this car beside me at any time, and from behind, the broken window would have been out of his line of sight. I felt I was pulled over for no particular reason and it's possible he would have just used his police laptop to look up my registration details so it was known who I was before he approached my car. I told this story to a friend who was a sheriff and his best bet was that it was counter-terrorism or an undercover officer.

In May, I was having dinner with my friend Anne for her birthday. Anne and I have been friends since kindergarten and as she lived in Queensland, we didn't see each other as much as we would like. We went to the Sands Resort in Torquay to share a meal and celebrate our time together, and as it was early in the week the only other diners were a table of four. When Anne left to use the restroom, I had a look around the resort. It was very quiet with no one in the bar or surrounding lounge rooms. Anne returned and we left, not noticing anyone in the car park or surrounds. When you leave the Sands, the way out is straight ahead from the driveway, but we decided to take the scenic route and turned right.

After a couple of turns around the residential area, Anne said to me almost amusingly that we were being followed. I saw headlights behind me and took the next left and so did the headlights. I took another left and once again so did the headlights. The street I turned into was a dead-end street and so I quickly turned the car around facing out. The headlights came into view, and as there was nowhere for this dark-coloured four-wheel drive with tinted windows to go but beside me. Without fear, I wound down my window—as did he—and asked him what he was doing. He responded that he was lost and was just following us to see if we could lead him out. It could've been true, but remember the way out of the Sands carpark leads you directly to the street you need to take to get back to the highway, and I didn't see him around the resort; it appeared he may have been waiting in his car.

In early July 2011, I had sent an email to Inspector Bill requesting my FOI request be fulfilled by Friday 15 July. It wasn't, but my attention was elsewhere since my son went missing on that date.

I was concerned that Inspector Michael's report may have affected how the police dealt with me during Dan's disappearance. I was also concerned about any reputational damage that may have occurred that I may never have been aware of. With this is mind, a few years later I made an application to VCAT for a copy of the PSO statements and copies of the CCTV of Treasury Place and Paisley Street.

In April 2014, there was a directions hearing at VCAT where I requested that both PSOs be subpoenaed to give evidence, or at least that I be provided with their statements. The sitting member refused, and it was then that I believed that pursuing a hearing would be a wasted exercise and that I now believe the PSOs made no such reports in their statements of possible violent behaviour or the drawing of capsicum spray. I believe this was an invention by police command for reasons known only to them.

As of writing this, there has been much in the media in recent weeks concerning police leaking a photo of a former AFL coach who was in custody, with those officers involved being charged with misconduct in public office. I fail to understand how my allegation of a report being purposely fabricated was not considered as misconduct in public office. The only difference I see is that the first case involved uniformed officers while mine involved high command. Different treatment again: the individual in custody had her rights respected, but mine were ignored, because those higher up the chain of command were to be protected. The cycle continues.

You may be asking yourself if I had a belief that Dan disappearing on the same date as my FOI email request was in any way related, but thankfully I never went down that rabbit hole as I knew it was purely a coincidence. Unfortunately, my acquaintance Sue (not her real name) went down that rabbit hole.

I had met Sue around five years earlier at a workplace bullying conference in Queensland and we bonded straight away. When you have a shared experience, either negative or positive, you have an alliance with that person. On rare occasions, you connect with a person who will later have a negative impact on your life. That's what happened with Sue. I would never have met her except for our shared experience of workplace bullying. I have met others through this experience that have made a positive impact on me and my life, and I now call these people friends.

Sue was different. I later discovered she regularly smoked marijuana, and I feel this may have been what led her down the rabbit hole – believing that Dan's disappearance was somehow linked to my activities with the police and the courts. It was Sue who led me to Melbourne on that fateful day where I was assaulted at Treasury Place, and it was Sue who I spent the day with on 15 July while she waited for her car to be serviced. Sue lived in Melbourne, but she had bought the car in Geelong and was having it serviced at the usual mechanic who knew the car. I offered to pick her up and have brunch together while the car was serviced. After brunch we returned to my home where we had coffee and chatted until her car was ready. Had I never met Sue, I may well have been home that morning, and I often wonder if this would have changed the outcome for Dan. Somehow, I doubt it. Fate will be what it will be.

FIFTEEN

Costs Corruption

Over the year from when my case terminated, my former lawyer sent me approximately four accounts, all for varying amounts which added to my confusion; she didn't appear to know what her actual costs were and she kept changing them. Given the case settled for $150,000 inclusive of legal costs, affirmed by Judge Robson in his decision of September 2010, she was not legally entitled to more. I felt this was done to scare me into thinking if I pursued a Costs Court application, I could end up paying even more. In an account for services rendered was the statement, "General skill care and responsibility in respect to the assessing of and advising you throughout the conduct of your action." Under consumer law, goods and services must be fit for purpose – all these fees were charged for services which were of no value to me.

I was of the understanding that I had the right to have a taxation of my lawyer's bill. I was ready to proceed on three dates in early 2011; it was my lawyer's initial actions that caused the lengthy taxation process to span over a year.

During this early period of 2011, I was sent a letter from my lawyer (after I had filed my application with the Costs Court) in the pursuance further costs. This letter states:

Therefore, based on the solicitor client costs and disbursements and the recovered party/party amounts, the non-recoverable costs and disbursements are calculated in the sum of $384,558.74. This figure exceeds the sum of $150,000 which we had previously accounted to you. We refer you to section 3.4.43(2) of the Legal Profession Act 2004 which states that we are not bound by the previous amount and matters stated in the lump sum assessment, if the matter goes to review/taxation.

I'm not sure I understood this and how it fitted with a court order, but receiving such a letter after such a harrowing court experience was deeply troubling, as I had learnt from previous experience that lawyers could do whatever they liked and the courts often supported it. I felt intimidated – blackmailed even, because I was being told that if I pursued my legal right to a taxation of costs my lawyer would demand further payment of up to $384,558.74. In my understanding, the role of the Costs Court constituted by a Costs Judge is to reduce the costs if costs are not reasonably incurred or costs are considered excessive. It may, for the purposes of the reconsideration, receive further evidence in respect of any objection.

With this is mind in, in February 2011, I made an application to the Costs Court for the taxation of my bill, and included a list of objections. At this time, I was only questioning if the settlement amount of $150,000 was a fair and reasonable amount, given my lawyer had already been paid for the Magistrates' Court hearing, the County Court hearing, and the necessary interlocutory legal steps, which are paid by WorkCover to the tune of around $100,000. In this application I requested I be provided a number of documents which I believed would assist me in my case to show that "due care and attention" was absent and yet I was heavily charged for this "due care and attention."

In my Amended Notice of Objection dated February 2011, I requested that the orders of Associate Justice Wood given verbally the day before be enforced – that I be provided with all documents as stated in my Notice.

There were a number of observers in court during the period of my cross-examination who made mention of Harrison writing furiously in his blue notebook, which was reassuring as I had also observed this. I don't believe he was writing about my case – I believe he was working on other matters during the time he was being paid by me, so to prove this allegation it was vital to see his blue notebook. I requested the original notebook used by Mr Harrison during the trial from 14-23 April 2010 be made available to the court, but this was not forthcoming.

Under cross-examination by me in the June hearing of 2010, Harrison admitted he had a 2:15pm Supreme Court Mediation booked that same afternoon of 23 April 2010, the day I claimed my hearing was purposely terminated. Upon further questioning, he submitted that he didn't know how to use his diary and as such did not realise he was double-booked. This is the evidence he gave in court before Judge Robson while under oath.

I requested Mr Harrison' diaries, whether electronic, paper or held by his clerk, be produced to the court, in particular the cases of *Loiterton v. McKillop Family Services* from 2 February 2010 then adjourned to 13 April 2010, and *McDonald v. National Parts and Victorian WorkCover Authority* with a hearing date of 7 May 2010, a date on which he should have been unavailable as my case was scheduled to run, according to the defendant, for five weeks till the 26 May – but Harrison obviously knew my case would be completed in time for him to appear on the 7 May. The request for these documents was not forthcoming.

I requested mobile phone records for the period 14-30 April 2010 for Mr Travis Fewster, Mr Craig Harrison, Mr Matt Walsh and Ms Patsy Toop be provided to the court – these were not forthcoming.

Harrison and Walsh both stated under oath in the June hearing that the *Koehler v. Cerebos* case would not fare me well; this had never been stated to me by any of my legal team throughout the five years since the *Koehler* decision. Why did my legal team persist if they believed my case was doomed because of *Koehler*? Because the excuse of the *Koehler* decision was a later invention. *Koehler* was different to my case – hers was a case where the employer did not know her work was causing injury, in comparison where my employer did know; this is a vital perquisite for proving negligence.

I requested all written legal opinions, notes of discussions or any other matter or thing that support these barristers statements given under oath on 3 and 4 June 2010 – none were forthcoming.

Walsh on the Friday morning of 23 April 2010 informed me of an alleged comment made by a juror, and that it was audibly heard by him, my lawyer and the judge's associate. Until proven, this comment made by the juror stood as unsubstantiated and may be a fabrication on behalf of the legal team to force me in concert with other threats to settle.

I requested the judge's associate attest to this by way of affidavit or in court under oath, but this did not happen.

Walsh stated under oath in the June hearing that the judge's associate heard the comment from the juror, and he put this in a memo after the event. Copy of this memo was requested, but not provided.

Walsh said under oath that he called the defendant barrister Mr Jens on 22 April 2010, and if this call occurred I believe it was to discuss the mutual strategy of ensuring the hearing finished the next day. Harrison had a mediation he wanted to attend and Mr Jens' key witness needed to prepare for his trip overseas. Sometime later, Walsh changed his story to include that Mr Jens had also heard this comment by the juror, when he had said earlier that he was the only one to hear the comment. If the comment was genuine, then my opinion is that Walsh told Mr Jens about this comment on 22 April.

I requested the phone records for 22 and 23 April for both Mr Walsh and Mr Jens, but none were received.

I feel Walsh was lax in gaining witness statements, and I contend he did not, as I spoke to some who stated that they were not contacted, nor were there any discussions. My daughter and husband said they met with Walsh for approximately one and a half hours on the first morning of trial, with most of the time taken up with social chit-chat, admiring Walsh's office and view. Walsh stated under oath on 3 June 2010 that seeing two witnesses in one and a half hours "was a significant period of time in the scheme of these cases." I disagree with this evidence, as this supposedly was a five-week trial and Walsh (and my lawyer) were not prepared. Walsh stated, "I prepared a brief of evidence from both your husband and your daughter."

A copy of this brief of evidence was requested, but nothing was supplied.

Walsh again under oath stated on 3 June 2010:

Me: And what was that offer?
Walsh: Ah, the offer was the defendant agreed, or offered to pay to you the sum of $150,000 all-in, that is inclusive of your legal costs, together with the retention of the benefits you had received to that point.
Me: Okay, so . . . Benefits as in?
Walsh: Weekly payments of compensation or any other benefits.
Me: I've never received weekly payments of compensation.

Walsh clearly had no clue regarding my claim, as I have never been in the receipt of weekly benefits and with due care and attention, he should have known this. The offer of $150,000 may have been made at this time, but it was also made at an earlier time on 9 April (prior to my hearing commencing on 14 April). I wasn't informed of this offer prior to the hearing, so it appeared that even before the trial started it was known that $150,000 would be the only offer on the table, and so the 'game' had to be played until the funds were eaten up in costs.

I particularly like the comment made that "the defendant offered to pay to you the sum of $150,000 all-in." Pay me that sum? I doubt it – the offer was a compromise (bribe) to my legal team, as $150,000 would only cover their fees; this was never about paying me any financial compensation. Fortunately for me, financial compensation was not my motivation.

From transcription of evidence given by Walsh on 3 June 2010: "And if there's any issue about that, Your Honour, I can provide you with a handwritten note that I made during the running of the trial." Copy of this handwritten note was requested, but not supplied.

In other transcript evidence, Walsh supposedly wrote a memorandum on 27 April, and Harrison made amendments and sent it to their instructing solicitors on 28 April. It's five pages long and Walsh has a copy, but it is not signed. My 'Affidavit In Support Of Application' was dated 25 April and filed on 27 April in the Supreme Court Registry. It is my belief that this memorandum was written *after* my former lawyer and barristers knew that I was challenging the settlement. Time is of the essence here; it's unfortunate I don't know the exact time I filed my documents. I requested a copy of Walsh's memorandum, but this was not supplied. When I later received my file from my lawyer there was indeed a memorandum dated 28 April with a covering email transmission stapled to it. Email transmissions confirm date, time and recipients, and these details confirm Walsh's statement, but something nags at me. If the email and the attached memorandum were printed at the same time as you would expect, and given they were stapled together, why are they on different paper? Is the email confirming the same document or some other correspondence? And does attaching it to the memorandum give it validity? If indeed this memorandum existed as at 3 June and Walsh had it in his possession in court, he rightly should have tendered it, and that would have been the end of the matter. But what if this memorandum was written later to reflect the testimony he gave in court, written later when it was known I was seeking my file? Sadly, that is a mystery I cannot solve, or maybe no mystery at all – but given the manipulation I have experienced at the hands of experts I now question everything.

Upon an application, the Costs Court shall—not may or should—reconsider all the taxation objections stated in a Notice of Objection, and as stated in the Rules may receive further evidence in respect of any objection. Interestingly, in my case these court rules appeared to be ignored, and not one requested or court ordered document was provided.

The Rules require the party who filed the bill to file any documents in the possession, control or power of that party. Also under the Rules, the court may direct the party to lodge any documents in the party's possession, custody or power that will be required for the purpose of evidence on the taxation. Associate Judge Woods had verbally ordered the documents requested by me be provided to support my evidence on taxation that I was presenting to the court.

I issued a summons in April 2011 because my lawyer had not complied with the verbal orders of Associate Justice Wood given in February 2011 to provide all documents as outlined in my Notice of Objection. This Notice of Objection did not just relate to accounts but to documents that would reflect the level of skill, care and attention paid by my lawyers in the preparation of my action. Unfortunately, my taxation of costs was delegated to a Judicial Registrar who ensured my summons went nowhere and that I would never receive requested documents that would have assisted me in proving my case.

I am not legally trained, nor have I studied law, and there may well be legal argument why some of the documents were not provided to the court, say due to client privilege or professional privilege. But documents that pertained to me or my case would not attract any such privilege. I believed that most or many of such documents could not be provided because they were not in the possession, control or power of my lawyer; I felt they either did not exist or they proved what I said to be true.

What is of most concern to the 'no win, no fee' plaintiff is costs, costs which seem to take on a life of their own. I believed that during my case, 'gilding the lily' was a practice my lawyer—and most likely many in the personal injury field—garden very well. Delay is the manure for the lily to grow and prosper. Delay increases costs, as there are years of interaction with your lawyer, which all come at a price; five years becomes ten years. After the compensation hearing and the second hearing to have the settlement set aside was completed, and after my appeal to the Court of Appeal, I took another avenue open to me to highlight what I believed to be wrong: the Costs Court. For a Costs Court hearing you really need to have a 'Bill of Costs' so that the court and the applicant knows and understands the costs charged, and so you can effectively respond to each charge with any argument you may have. Keep in mind that in May 2009 I was told by the lawyer Travis that my costs at that time were around $50,000, as my lawyer's fees (relating to other proceedings in which I was the successful party) were paid by the defendant.

According to the Rules, a lawyer shall be taken to have failed or refused to serve a bill of costs if within 60 days after service, the lawyer does not serve a bill of costs. I requested this Bill of Costs in December 2010, and after my request appeared to be refused the court finally ordered the Bill of Costs to be provided. In mid-April of 2011, it was.

It arrived well outside of the 60-day requirement as set down in the Rules. The Rules state that if the Lawyer is at fault "where a party fails to apply to have costs taxed within a time fixed under Rule 63.53(1) and the failure is occasioned by the neglect or delay of the party's solicitor; or in any proceedings before the Costs Court the solicitor for any part, is guilty of neglect or delay." The only consequence if a lawyer does not abide by this Rule is the threat of not being paid costs for attendance or for the preparation of the Bill of Costs, but in my understanding the Costs Court is a jurisdiction of no costs being awarded. And the provision of a Bill of Costs is at the lawyer's expense anyway; this highlights to me that lawyers really don't have to abide by the Rules if they choose not to. It's up to the court to make such an order if an order is necessary, an order seemingly rarely given. If there's no consequence for ignoring the Rules then why have them in the first place?

A Bill of Costs is a confusing document for a layperson, and in the Rules it states that a bill of costs for taxation under this order shall have charges and disbursements set out in separate columns, and the amounts in each column shall be totalled at the foot of each page and the total carried forward to the top of the next page. The bill shall also contain items numbered in chronological order describing briefly the work done by the solicitor for the party entitled to costs, and stating beside each item the amount claimed for the work and the amount of any disbursement made; at the conclusion of the chronological description of the work done should lie a description with regard to the work done, justifying an allowance of the amount claimed beside that item.

Unsurprisingly, the 'lily' had been gilded with such finesse any horticulturist would be proud. An item number included in the Bill of Costs was an amount of more than $4,000 for the preparation of the Bill of Costs. It was my understanding that this cost is to be borne by the lawyer, not the plaintiff, but if this can be included to fatten the bottom line then so be it.

I will, as briefly as I can, go through the costs that were gilded so that the lily would be large and healthy. I will not go through all the costs, some incidental but inflated, because to do so would be too large for the purpose of this book. In compliance with the Supreme Court General Civil Procedure Rules, a defendant is in breach if unnecessary or careless work is carried out; all through the Bill of Costs I found numerous examples of such work, and yet once again my lawyer simply ignored the Rules and suffered no consequence for doing so.

Sometimes I felt my lawyer was in the photocopying business rather than the legal business, as approximately 16,000 pages of photocopying was charged to my account and at a cost of nearly $30,000 (nearly $2 per page). I could have done this task myself at Officeworks for $1,250, (8c a page) but to be fair staff time must come into this as they need to feed the bundle of papers and come back to retrieve when completed. From memory, administrative staff at this time were paid around $30 per hour (but charged out at a much higher figure). So, allowing for their time at $50 per hour, the photocopying costs would be around $13,000, still undeniably good manure for them. In effect, each plaintiff covers the costs of a copier machine, sometimes two.

Even though there were no copies of faxes in my file, the Bill of Costs state that 111 faxes were sent or received at a cost of $9.90 to $38 per fax; this is just for the machine receiving the fax, not the writing of the document. An email cost of 2c would be more economical for the plaintiff, but this doesn't provide much gilding for the lily; I am aware email costs are now allowed at a similar cost as a fax.

One aspect of legal costs is adjournments – they cost a lot and achieve the delay your lawyer and the defendant may well want. For the County Court hearing my counsel were not ready, as they were only briefed the evening before hearing, and when we arrived at court counsel didn't want to go before the judge allocated and gave excuses for an adjournment, one excuse being that I was then again working and it may be best to adjourn the case to see how my employment affected my case. I didn't want this adjournment but, as always, I had no choice. The costs for one hour of court time was nearly $18,000, inclusive of the defendant costs of $10,000 and senior counsel approximately $3,500; it's this kind of costs order that remained purposely unpaid, only to rear its head years later in the settlement negations. "If you settle now the defendant will forgo the County Court Costs Order" – this costs order was used as a carrot to further coerce me to settle.

In my Bill of Costs there were many charges relating to my County Court action (which were payable by the defendant due to me being successful in my claim there) and yet there was a total item cost of more than $15,000, and added to this is a loading of 80% which takes a cost of $15,000 to more than $27,000. Uplifts of more than 25% are not allowed under law (as far as I know), and in the Costs Agreement sent to me in June 2009 it is stated that uplift fees will be 25%. There should have been no costs associated with the County Court action in the Bill of Costs, but I believe they were included to once again fatten the bottom line.

Even more surprising in the Bill of Costs was the totals of sections A+B+C which related to the County Court action, and this total amounted to nearly $84,000. As I had been successful in this action, this amount was due to be paid by the defendant, or was it the difference between what my lawyer was paid and what I owed? I don't know if this figure is justified (though I doubt it), but what isn't justified is the loading fee of 120% which took this claimed amount to $184,632. I don't believe this loading fee is allowable under the Rules, but is a loading fee different to an uplift fee? As a novice in this jurisdiction, I cannot answer that question.

Of course, there were numerous errors in my bill – maybe human error, maybe not. For example, 463 pages of photocopied documents sent to a medical expert, and a year later (when nothing had changed) another 463 pages of documents were sent. I felt that these may well be the same documents. Were they sent in error? Who cares, just more manure for the lily. The cost of 'Interrogatories' was claimed twice, and more than $40,000 in counsel fees from the County Court were included in my Bill of Costs. These costs were payable by the defendant, but I believe they were included to increase the bottom line. If a plaintiff doesn't go through the process of detailed analysis of their Bill, they may never be aware of such 'errors'.

From my understanding, there was only one defendant in my case, my former employer, and yet a 'Service of Originating Motion', which only costs around $40, was served three times, and the costs of a letter and subpoena (more than $300) sent to a doctor after I had informed my lawyer that he was deceased. There was a cost for more than $4,000 for a so-called 'S12 Conference', but there were no records of this conference on file and I certainly didn't attend any such conference. A change of date for mediation cost more than $400, even though this happened because of an error made by my lawyer; 'tasks' relating to the change of mediation venue, as requested by the defendant, were billed to me at a cost of $300. Mediation went for less than 30 minutes, a prior confer went for 30 minutes, and inclusive of barrister fees the costs for this less than one hour was a whopping $11,000.

I found many costs that did not appear to be legitimate, for example an Originating Motion 'protocol conference' for November 2006. I have no idea what this means, who attended and what it was about and there are no records in my file relating to this. According to the Rules, a fee for a conference shall not be allowed in addition to the fee of a solicitor or counsel for drawing and settling, or perusing, or advising on any document, unless for special reason the conference was necessary or proper. If there is no evidence in my file relating to such conferences then how can it be known if it was necessary or proper?

There's a claim for an 'attendance' at Slater & Gordon in 2005; I don't know how this relates to my claim, or maybe it belongs to another plaintiff and is just another error.

I was charged stamp duty on a number of subpoenas. I was not aware that subpoenas attracted stamp duty; there is no mention of this on the Supreme Court website. Subpoenas are pro forma and each read is billed at $41. I generously estimate read time to be around one minute.

One item I found unnecessary was a $60 fee for telephone attendance at the County Court, seeking copy of its judgement in my case, when counsel was paid to attend to hear judgement and the judgement was on the County Court website that same day.

I was billed more than $40 for the defendant lawyer's change of address notification to my lawyer. I was billed for the reading of an email I sent to my lawyer that simply said "Thank you," and billed for an email sent to me by my lawyer simply asking me for my phone number. I am guessing it was easier emailing me to get the number and be able to charge for this than spend her time getting my file or asking a staff member to get my phone number; I shouldn't have been billed for her convenience.

Included in the Bill of Costs was a claim for a letter regarding a meeting with another partner of the firm. I requested this meeting because over seven years I hadn't been provided with a Conditional Costs Agreement or any agreement relating to costs, and this was of concern to me and should have been of concern to this partner – again I was being billed for their failures. I was billed for a letter to me cancelling a subsequent appointment to discuss the fee agreement. This led to the Conditional Costs Agreement never being signed.

There are charges for items that do not appear to exist as there are no copies of these documents in the file, like a "Status report" that cost $237, and a Supreme Court Notice of Callover Form or Civil List Callover form not in file but which cost $93. Witness statements are billed and yet there are no signed witness statements. Also, there is a claim for "Drawing and Engrossing" witness statements of Sandra, Helene and Brenda when no witness statements existed in my file. There are many claims for "Drawing and Engrossing" but I don't know what tasks were completed relating to this as there were no copies of these in my file.

I didn't understand at the time why many letters and documents appeared so wordy, and often two pages were used when the document could have fitted in one page; often a letter would have a second page with just a signature on it which would have fitted on the first page. When I read the Bill of Costs I came to understand what a 'folio' is – for the purpose of calculating an allowance for a document according to the length of the document, it is measured by folio. A folio contains 100 words, which is approximately three sentences, and every word or letter was charged out at a little more than 44 cents – for example, 'procedure' 'the' 'a' or '2' are all costed individually at 44 cents, so each folio or three sentences or a hundred words cost $44. Given these charges, this chapter of my book, which consists of approximately 7,500 words would cost $3,300 just to type. Maybe I'm wrong, but it does appear to be excessive.

For the period of January 2010 to April 2010 the bill claimed 16,171 folios at a cost of more than $71,000.

If the folio word costs included the lawyer's time and expertise in preparing a document then this would appear to be more reasonable, but from my understanding it is only the costs for typewriting, as the "skill, care and attention" is claimed separately.

I terminated the services of my lawyers in April 2010, and yet I was charged more than $1,000 for phone calls and "necessary tasks" for my former lawyers' own expenses that occurred in May after a 'Solicitor ceased to act' was completed and filed.

Some of the claims in the Bill of Costs were not large, but these small costs combined together grow bigger with each human failing or error. If I am billed for an action there should be some evidence of this action in my file, but for many there was no evidence to assist me in my understanding as to whether the costs were reasonable or not.

It must be remembered that all the costs included here are costs of more than 10 years ago, and I feel quite confident that they have near doubled in that time to now. The total claimed costs in my 'Bill of Costs' was more than $459,000, which given what I have said earlier leads me to believe costs were inflated by 50% and by the inclusion of the Magistrates' Court and County Court costs of more than $84,000 (and the loading fee of 120%, which took this claimed amount to $184,632). I believe these costs and the highly inflated costs were included to allow for a 15% reduction if the Costs Court so allowed, and more importantly to cause fear and confusion as to whether I would have to pay these costs.

I feel legal costs are like the ocean ebbing and flowing depending on the wind and the client's ability to pay is the current. Lawyers add much padding to their accounts so that if they receive lower fees they are still paid handsomely. Both my former barristers declared on the morning of Friday 23 April that they were "taking a haircut" which I understood to be that they were charging me lower fees for representing me; I believe this was another strategy to make me feel guilty and to encourage me to comply with their order to settle. My former senior barrister was paid $40,000, with the junior barrister being paid just $20,000, and yet according to the records the defendant's barrister was paid $30,000 with the junior paid $15,000. Not much of a 'haircut' for my barristers, and as it appears, no haircut at all.

For further examples of comparison, I refer to two other cases run by my lawyer over the same period, *Li v. Toyota Motor Corporation* before Justice Forrest, where it was stated that the bill of costs prepared by Mr Li's solicitors amounted to $119,441.70. It included a number of items relating to the preparation for the trial as well as all of the trial costs (including counsel's fees). I'm at a loss to understand why Mr Li's fees were so low. There may well be something I do not know.

Li's jury trial ran for seven days, and a further two days after the jury was discharged. In total nine days, and eight witnesses gave evidence, and there were five judicial decisions. My case ran for seven days with one witness, myself, so how could my costs be greater than Li's? There appears to be a rather large costs discrepancy between these two cases, and there is no mention that counsel had discounted their costs for Mr Li.

Costs Corruption

The jury in Li's case was discharged after seven days of hearing, and the case proceeded with a judge alone, heard as a cause. Li's lawyers were the same as mine and they made application for a discharge of the jury because of the defendant's barrister irrelevant references in his address to the jury concerning Mr Li's entitlement to workers' compensation payments. The inference here being was that he was greedy and just seeking more money. This sounds very similar to what I experienced, and yet my former legal team flatly refused to seek to have the jury in my case discharged. There was a very live issue during proceedings concerning Mr Li's contributory negligence, which was eventually settled by the judge at 25%, and because of this and other deductions his compensation award was reduced to $268,463. I am surprised that given the contributory negligence issue that my former lawyer went ahead with the case, yet given there was no contributory negligence in my case it was still 'dumped'.

Mr Li was indeed fortunate: he had two very experienced Common Law judges in Forrest and Beach who took great care in ensuring his legal rights were protected. I am disappointed for myself that my former legal team refused to make an application to discharge the jury, and I believe that the offer of $150,000 sealed the deal, whereas in Li's case I believe no such offer to seal the deal was made.

My 'current' flowed to the tune of $459,000, and Mr Li's only $119,441. My lawyer received nearly $240,000 in legal fees from my case, which for some inexplicable reason was not discounted in the 'Bill of Costs', demanding another $459,000.

The court on a taxation may disallow the costs of any work which is not necessary or is done without due care, or where costs are incurred improperly or without reasonable cause or are wasted by undue delay or negligence or by any other misconduct or default or where from any other cause the amount of costs is excessive. Only costs which are reasonable and proper shall be allowed, and the Costs Court may assess those costs at a gross sum. This is the reason I gave such detailed information in my Notice of Objection, with the request of relevant documents and my analysis of the Bill of Costs to show exactly where I believed my costs were not reasonably incurred. After a long and drawn-out taxation process caused by my lawyer not being ready to proceed (and a variety of other delay tactics), in February 2012 my matter was taxed as unopposed. It was not unopposed as my year of evidence would show, but I was absent from the state at this time, interstate on a family matter. I informed the Judicial Registrar of my absence and requested an adjournment, and a request to be informed if the adjournment was not granted because if not, I would return to appear. I was not so informed, and unknown to me the Judicial Registrar went ahead with my case in my absence.

Did any of the Costs Court's own Rules matter? It appeared not, as the Judicial Registrar placed little if any weight to my arguments and found that I actually owed more to my lawyer than the $150,000. An order was made in February 2012 that my costs were taxed in the amount of $384,558, an order made in my absence and without my knowledge. I had initiated this costs review to prove my lawyer was undeserving of being paid $150,000, and yet my application was hijacked by my former lawyer filing a counter claim. I believe it can be seen by this example how on occasion the courts protect the legal profession even when they are wrong.

The Law Institute of Victoria, comprising judges, persons nominated by the Governor General and Queen's Counsel, usually make up a panel of seven members whose task it is to set Legal Practitioners Remuneration Costs under the Legal Profession Act. I query the independence or impartiality of such a panel, given it is largely made up of members of the legal profession. This could be likened to the fox being in charge of the hen house. Given that ordinary, everyday Victorians cannot access the justice system due to costs, another system needs to be considered, one that sits between the VCAT and the higher courts and one that does not rely on the 'no win, no fee' arrangements forced on injured workers. If an alleged criminal has access to legal aid, why not an injured worker? Surely they are just as deserving. Currently all the power sits with the legal representatives and not the client. Lawyers should work in your best interests, but in my experience they do not.

Discretionary costs such as fees and allowances shall be allowed at the discretion of the Costs Court. In exercising discretion, the court shall have regard to: the complexity of the item or of the proceeding in which it arose; the difficulty or novelty of the questions involved; the nature and importance of the proceeding; the skill, specialised knowledge and responsibility involved; the number and importance of the documents prepared or perused; and the labour involved and the time spent by the solicitor or counsel. Any other fees and allowances payable to the solicitor or counsel in respect of other items in the same proceeding. Unfortunately, there was little discretion that came my way.

If it was to be accepted that the Bill of Costs was accurate (which of course it was not) then we must accept that the defendant accrued similar costs of around $459,000, and maybe even more if a 'bonus' was paid to the defending law firm. This is a total of $918,000, and couple this with Independent Medical Assessors costs of around $11,000, plus my medical and like expenses to date of around $110,000 and the estimation of my former employer costs both direct and indirect of around $300,000, then my claim in total has cost $1,339,000. I believe a slightly more accurate figure is gained by using the records provided to me by the insurer of legal costs being around $632,000; adding the other factors results in a new total of $932,000. It must be remembered that these are mostly the direct costs I know about; there are undoubtedly more, and these are sums from ten to 20 years ago and would be more in today's dollars. All this expense because an injured worker who wanted to return to work wasn't allowed.

If my statutory 'offer of settlement' made in 2009 for $350,000 had been accepted, or a counter offer of $300,000 made, then that would have been the end of it. But their offer was 'nil', which made another court action necessary. The Supreme Court action appeared to cost both sides around $150,000 – a combined $300,000. So the defendant's preference was go to court and expend the $300,000 on court costs rather than pay the same amount to the injured worker, in complete breach of the Model Litigant Guidelines. I don't know who monitors these 'guidelines' – I am guessing no one. Guidelines carry no legal force and are just a suggestion to be followed; these guidelines should be made law, with a monitor, then a fairer outcome for injured workers could be had. If there had been a counter offer of say $300,000 and it was accepted, how much would I have received after legal fees? Going by my lawyers' Bill of Costs of $459,000, less the $150,000 (which was incurred by the negligence action), amounts to $309,000. I would have received nothing, and in effect would still have owed them another $9,000. This is the conundrum of the 'no win, no fee' system – even if you win you still lose.

If that doesn't convince you that the WorkCover system is broken then I doubt anything will. I still believe that the system is purposely set up to funnel employers' contributions into the legal system, government coffers, to the administration of WorkCover and not to the injured worker. Some employers would be shocked if they understood this, as many are genuinely caring towards their injured workers; to know that none of their WorkCover premiums go towards compensation for their injured worker may well convince them to self-insure. Not that I believe that system would be any better under a self-insured employer fund, because at some point lawyers get involved, and then the focus changes from compensation for the injured worker to income for them.

Remember back in late 2001, I offered to settle my claim with my employer for $4,000, inclusive of medical costs, plus a $1,000 payment in recognition of my pain and suffering and a supportive return to work. By this time my former employer knew my claim was legitimate, external investigators had found none of the allegations against me were substantiated, and my employer could find no wrongdoing that could be used for dismissal. I feel any wrongdoing at that time, no matter how minor, would have been used against me. Prior claims by the bullies of my poor performance were not proved, the Human Resource Acting Manager left suddenly after her part in the suspension, and finally other staff had come forward with their concerns regarding bullying in the workplace.

After requesting six weeks to consider my offer, my employers counter-offer was to advertise my position without telling me, and the bullying continued unabated. I could not stop it and no one would help me, not Work-Cover, nor the union, who both suffered a conflict of interest. I was alone, powerless and a victim of the by-stander syndrome.

It was at this time a true leader needed to intervene, a leader who actually worked the talk, but sadly none existed at my workplace.

My lawyer achieved what she set out to do, and that was to not have her costs under court scrutiny, and not to provide the requested documents – this being supported by the Judicial Registrar who refused to make the order or any part thereof and an order by the Judicial Registrar for me to pay the further demanded costs.

In May 2012, Associate Justice Wood (on appeal) sensibly decided against my lawyer's request for further payment as outlined in her letter of demand in April 2012, and scolded her for making such a request because the Settlement Agreement still stood as signed on 23 April 2010. He stated that such a letter would be distressing for me, and asked if it was explained to me that no further payment was required. Associate Justice Wood displayed displeasure upon hearing that my lawyer did not explain this to me. Associate Justice Wood delivered his verbal reasons, and stated that 'things' should go back the way they were before taxation commenced, and that both parties walk away as if it had never happened (or words very similar to this). He said he would leave the Judicial Registrar's orders of February 2012 untouched, but they held no consequence, and in his written reasons under Costs of the Review he stated that an order that had the effect of each side bearing their own costs was appropriate in the circumstances. So, by May 2012, that was the end of it – or so I thought.

I may have misunderstood this statement given the verbal reasons given previously that 'things' go back to the way they were and both parties walk away as if taxation never occurred. I accepted Associate Justice Wood's reasons that each side bearing their own costs was appropriate in the circumstances, and believed that that was the end of the matter until I began being harassed by debt collectors out of the blue. I was served with a Magistrates' Court Complaint for the amount of $7,500, issued by my lawyer dated August 2012, and my response was a request asking how the sum of $7,500 was derived. I was informed that there was no itemised account for this sum and I was just required to pay it. Given my circumstances over the previous year, I was physically, emotionally and mentally exhausted and could no longer fight the good fight, so my lawyer and I settled for an amount agreeable to her. Of course, I now know that this had a profound effect on the case I later brought against her.

SIXTEEN

Happy Times

In April 1986, I was at a co-worker's wedding when half-way through the evening I began to feel unwell. By 7:30am the next morning I was in hospital with excruciating pain in my abdomen with no idea what was happening. The pain was so great I couldn't let the doctor touch me – when he did it caused pain like I had never felt before. My husband Des was basically begging him to give me something for the pain, but he refused, stating that he had to do an examination first. It became obvious that an examination wasn't going to happen *until* I had pain relief. Des was becoming quite upset, a side of him I hadn't seen before, as he was always calm and in control. Eventually with Des's increasing frustrations I think the doctor thought he might be in for an act of violence; unaware that Des was the most placid and non-violent person you could ever meet. The good doctor finally agreed to administer morphine. I was examined, and my blood was taken and sent to a ward. Later that afternoon the doctor told me the blood tests showed I was pregnant, but they couldn't find any evidence of a foetus. I was shocked – I had an IUD as a form of birth control; it was this IUD that had failed and caused an infection in my uterus.

I was disappointed that I didn't know I was pregnant, but it also meant I hadn't bonded with my baby, so the grief was lessened. The worst was yet to come; I was told that the infection had done so much damage that it was unlikely I would ever get pregnant again. I may already have had three girls, but I was grieving for the future children I would never have, and Des was mourning the loss of the potential opportunity for a son. I was ill for six weeks and decided to never have an IUD again.

Three months later, I was pregnant. I remember pulling up outside our house and Des running from the front door asking, "Well?!" – "Yes!" He was so excited he grabbed around the waist and twirled me around.

The next few months were wonderful – the pregnancy was going well and Des and I were so excited to welcome our little miracle. Of course, over this time one of the most fun tasks was to try to pick the right name for our little bub. I remember we were hosting a dinner party at our home and a guest asked what name had we picked. I said "Amanda Jade," as I was convinced it would be a girl as we had already proved we had girls. Simultaneously, Des said "Daniel James" – he already had a name picked out, unbeknownst to me. I liked the name, but felt sure it would be Amanda Jade.

Our beautiful big baby boy arrived right on time, and we were both euphoric. I thought of all the joy this boy would bring us – and he did, his whole life.

Dan was a 'good baby' – during the day he'd be up for two hours then down for two hours, throughout the whole day. I could plan my day easily as Dan had put himself into such a good routine.

The girls adored their baby brother. I remember a particular happy day when Dan was a few months old – we had been on a family picnic to the You Yangs Regional Park, and Dan was a little fractious. We all sang his favourite nursery rhyme (adapted from The Farmer in the Dell): "We love you Danny boy, we love you Danny boy, heigh ho the derry-o, we love you Danny boy." He stopped crying, hearing his song, but when the song finished he would cry again, so we sang it all the way home.

He was the baby of the family and lovingly cared for by his three sisters. Then he turned two and all of that changed. Dan was a boisterous boy and loved doing boy things, and his sister Loren stopped being a little mother and became an adversary. They were the closest in age and so spent a lot of time together when the older girls were off to ballet, dance and all matters of artistic endeavours. At two years of age the doting from the sisters became less as Dan hit the 'terrible twos', but really he was a very normal, happy kid and there was nothing in his behaviour that concerned me. What concerned me was the beginning of the sibling war that ran for ten years. Dan and Loren were at each other every waking moment, every single day. The arguments and fights at times became physical, and I must admit I found this a very trying time to be a parent. I remember a time when Dan was around three years old and the fight between them was on. I looked over to where they were and Dan just looked up at me and said in a very cute three-year-old voice, "I know, I go to my room," and I said, "And you may come back when you are going to be happy." Seconds later—he would not have even made to his room—he stood at the doorway and said to me, "I happy now."

Dan was very good at self-discipline; I rarely had to say anything, as he knew when he had done the wrong thing. There was only one occasion when he was about 10 years old that I smacked him. I regretted it immediately and I have felt guilty ever since. Des had come home from work, all was well, the kids were playing and I was cooking dinner after a hard day at work. Des went to collect Kate from ballet, and not long after he left the fight was on, both Loren and Dan bickering and screaming. I suddenly heard Loren cry. I went to her in the next room and saw that Dan had broken her Communion necklace. I 'saw red', grabbed his arm and dragged him to his room, spanking him as I did so. Loren also got a smack and sent to her room. Des returned home with Kate – Loren was crying in her bedroom, Dan crying in his bedroom, and I was crying in our bedroom while I was packing my suitcase. Des asked what had happened, and through tears I tried to explain that I was a bad parent, that I smacked the children and didn't deserve to be their mother. Loren came into the room and said, "Please Mum, don't go," and we hugged and I was forgiven, but I have never forgotten that night. This was the one and only occasion I feel I failed as a parent, and I know that Loren remembers this night, but Dan never mentioned it over the years, so I hope in my heart of hearts he'd forgotten about it.

Des and I very rarely raise our voices, and arguments were few and far between. We had a healthy respect for each other, and Des was a wonderful role model for our son – he was kind, gentle and very caring towards all his children. Our home was violence-free (except for that one night); our children experienced a calm, respectful environment where they were treated with the utmost care. Neither Des nor I are the type to yell, so the children didn't experience being verbally abused in any way. The good thing about not being a 'yeller' is that when you do, notice is taken. I remember a nice winter's day when Dan was aged around 10 and Loren around 12 when we packed up the car for a weekend at the Mount Buller Ski Resort. Our house had a short driveway, no more than roughly 10 metres long; we hadn't even travelled down the drive when the fighting began. I turned with a raised voice and yelled, "Be quiet!" They both looked shocked, sat back in their seats and not a peep was heard during the four-hour drive to Buller.

Dan was a happy and contented little boy who made friends easily; we would only be at the beach for a few moments when he would bring over his new friends to introduce us. The girls were always outgoing, but slightly hesitant in new surrounds, and would take a while to join in with others on the beach. Dan was always very social, making friends wherever he went; he just loved being and playing with others, be it boys or girls. Socially, he was advanced for his age and showed a high degree of confidence when interacting with others.

One of my favourite memories is Dan's fourth birthday party. We had all his kinder friends and teachers come and we had the most marvellous time. Kate put on a show of dancing and magic which held the children spellbound, and Loren displayed her gymnastic skills, much to their delight. The birthday cake had magic candles – each time Dan blew them out they would magically relight to the awe of the children. Dan was just so happy and the video of his party is one of my most treasured possessions, but sadly one I cannot watch as the pain is too great. Maybe one day. We were big on birthday parties in our family and all the children had one every year until they reached ten years of age.

We had pirate parties, jumping castle parties, ghost parties, pool parties, bowling parties and dance parties, just to name a few. Even though it was a lot of work, with all food usually homemade, I loved seeing the joy and happiness in my children's faces – it made it all worthwhile. Another memorable birthday was Dan's 13th birthday, where he had 30 friends to a disco party. I was a little concerned about supervising so many, and came up with an idea to ensure the kids stayed inside with no wandering off. Upon arrival, all shoes were placed in a large basket and were hidden away to be brought out at the end of the night for a game of 'who can find their shoes the fastest'. This strategy worked and the party went off without incident except—there is always an exception—two noise complaints were made to police who visited our home twice, much to the joy of the children who believed it was cool having the police called to your party. The party finished at 10pm, not late, but as we live on the side of a hill the noise may have travelled across the valley and amplified.

Dan loved kinder and school, but at around five years of age, he was diagnosed with a learning disability. Over the coming years, while socially he remained positive and his behaviour exemplary, he struggled academically. I now feel this was the base that slowly eroded his confidence; he found it difficult to achieve in a standard schooling environment. Knowing what I know now, I wonder if things would have been better for him if we had taken a different approach, though what that approach would have been I do not know. The alternative education models we have nowadays barely existed in the early nineties.

We did everything we could to assist him with his learning, including tutors and tutoring schools, but nothing seemed to work. Des would spend an hour or two every night helping with reading and homework; I marvelled at his degree of patience and the manner in which he interacted with Dan. My job was assignments, which Dan found really difficult, so together we would work on them and he always had a presentable assignment to hand in, though no doubt the teachers knew there had been a fair degree of helping. I wonder now if this helping was actually a hindrance – should we have allowed Dan to fail, be embarrassed, humiliated or even shamed in front of his friends and to learn resilience along the way? No parent wants their child to feel these emotions; it has only been in recent years that the connection between failure and resilience has been realised. Even given this, Dan loved school, and barely if ever had a day off. He never resisted going, never made any excuses for not going. When he came of an age when he knew he couldn't complete his schoolwork like his friends could, his interactions with his friends seemed to make up for any feelings of inadequacy he may have felt.

What Dan lacked academically he made up for in other ways: he was kind, thoughtful and wise, and these qualities followed him throughout his years. Dan was a great conversationalist, a trait fostered by the number of kids—mainly girls—who would call him, seeking his wisdom. I can remember one Saturday morning Dan and I were out; on returning home, Loren gave him the list of girls who had called: five in two hours. Loren was surprised, impressed with this gift her brother possessed that was so appealing to these girls. Dan was in grade six at the time and the girls were already at secondary school! Over the next couple of years Loren learnt what it was: Dan was special.

When Loren hit 14 and Dan was around 12, their fighting miraculously stopped and a beautiful and close relationship between them began to grow. It was a joy to see. His two other sisters, Vicki and Kate, also began to see Dan for the person he was—kind, caring, gentle and wise—and then another sibling rivalry began – all three wanted to be his favourite sister. The coming years were beautiful, the children happy in their relationships with each other. This is a joy to any parent.

Loren was Dan's big sister, but Kate was a bigger sister, and I fondly remember two occasions when Kate protected her little brother. Dan was about 11, and he had a friend David (not his real name) who lived nearby in another street. On this particular day, after having a sleepover at David's, his father came to our door and accused Dan of taking some sunglasses – sunglasses that belonged to David's sister's boyfriend. I wasn't at home so Kate was dealing with this herself. She defended Dan from this aggressive father, who was stalking up and down the street, stopping to look into Kate's car. She called me, concerned, and I said I would be home soon. Then the father called me accusing Dan of being a thief, and I asked him to leave my children alone; I would talk to him when I arrived home shortly. I knew Dan would never steal, especially from someone else's home, but this man and his wife were adamant it was Dan. Both professionals, I was surprised at their erratic behaviour, at their accusations toward a child without any verifiable proof. The angry father said he'd call the police – and he did! I remember feeling so proud of Kate and the manner with which she dealt with this aggressive man and the faith she had in her little brother.

By the time Des arrived home from work, we were all in such a state, concerned about this man's behaviour and what he might do next. Des went to see him at his home, and it came to pass that the boyfriend hadn't worn his sunglasses to David's house that evening before and they were safely home on his bedside table. The father gave Des a haphazard apology, offering to have us over for a barbecue. The barbecue never happened, and Dan never saw David again. I felt so sorry for Dan – he had lost a friend through no fault of his own. Kate later ran into David's sister's boyfriend in a shop where he worked and he was profusely apologetic and embarrassed by the father's behaviour.

The second time Kate flew to Dan's defence was when he was around 15 years of age. While still at school, Dan had gained a part-time job in a local cinema, the same cinema Kate had worked in for a few years before going off to university in Western Australia. I arrived at the cinema to take Dan home after his shift and I noticed a very slight shift in his demeanour and so I asked him what was wrong. He had tears in his eyes as he relayed to me what was happening at work. I felt numb and I asked Dan if he knew what this was, and he responded "bullying." I asked him how he knew it was bullying, and he told me he'd heard me talk to Dad about this behaviour. Of course kids hear 'private' conversations in your home. Dan and I talked about what he could do about this, and the options open to him.

As soon as Kate heard about this, she was on the phone to Dan, giving advice and support. The bully turned out to be someone Kate knew, and it was clear to her why Dan was experiencing this. Dan was tall, dark and handsome – everything the bully was not. Kate was planning to talk to the manager and get the matter sorted out, but Dan in his wisdom made the decision to resign from his very first job. I wish I'd had Dan's level of wisdom when I experienced the horror of workplace bullying.

One funny memory I have of around this time was when Dan was 16 and asked if he could visit a friend that evening, and off he went. Around 11:30pm we were woken up by a commotion outside our bedroom window which faced the street. We listened for a few minutes and became concerned when we thought we heard Dan's voice. Des was up in a flash and out the front door, with me not far behind. There was a pyramid of arms and legs in every direction, and Des joined the fray pulling kids off each other to get to his son who we thought was underneath it all. It was such a sight, Des in his purple polka-dot boxers, attempting to save his son from this band of ruffians, who we learned had been at a party a street away where a dispute between two groups had arisen. They continued the dispute along the street until reaching the proximity of our house, where the fight broke out. By the time Des had separated the warring parties it was obvious Dan wasn't actually part of it.

During the ruckus I found a large knife on the ground, which worried me; I picked it up and ran back to the house and locked the door. I called the police, and while on the phone there was a loud banging on the door. I explained this to the police, who suggested it may well be my husband and to let him in, which I did. A few minutes later a small group of kids knocked on the door and asked to be let in to shelter, and we let them in and they told us about the fight. After waiting a few minutes while the coast cleared, they left just before the police arrived. We told the police what had happened, and they asked me where my son was, and rather shamefully I said I didn't know. They checked the street, but by this time the kids had dispersed, probably back to their party. I went to Dan's room, and to my surprise he was sound asleep in his bed, oblivious of his dad's heroic attempt to save him. I hadn't heard him come home; I desperately wish I had, then I could have proudly told police my son was home in his bed, where all good children were at that time of night. Years

Happy Times

later we still retell this story and have a good laugh – I will never forget the sight of Des on the nature strip in those purple polka-dot boxers.

Other fond memories are of Dan as 'the spider man'. Whenever I was accosted by a spider and Des wasn't home, I called to Dan. Dan and his dad were the same in that they would never hurt any living thing, even a spider. Dan would coach the spider into a glass jar and gently carry it across the road to a large garden surrounding a tennis court and let it go into the foliage. He performed this act with such tenderness that my heart just melted – he was the best a boy could be.

Dan was never interested in the standard, popular sports like football, cricket or soccer, but his love of being physical led him to breakdancing, rollerblading, skateboarding and finally Brazilian Jiu Jitsu. He was extremely talented at all of them, and we were pleased when he took to martial arts. I was initially concerned about the fighting component, until I went to watch a class and witnessed the philosophy of martial arts. I was impressed with the self-discipline required and the values being learned.

When it came to good taste, Dan had it in bucket loads. He was always immaculately well-groomed and well-dressed; his sense of style was amazing in someone so young. When he was about sixteen, I suggested we redecorate his room (which hadn't been touched since we moved in seven years prior); the walls were still the cream colour the whole house was painted in at the time. I got the colour swatches and asked Dan what he liked, and to my (almost) horror he chose navy blue, with a navy blue and green striped roman blind for the large window. Naturally, the striped option was the most expensive fabric in the samples, but Dan loved it so we went with it. When the redecorating was finished, I was pleasantly surprised – it looked stylish and turned out to be the best bedroom in the house for sleeping, as light didn't reflect on the navy walls and the trees just outside the window kept the room cool and shaded.

At 18 years of age, Dan went to the US to be a camp counsellor for Camp America. He had been assigned as a soccer coach, which was surprising because Dan didn't know much about soccer, but apparently he 'winged' his way through, and had the most amazing time there.

Loren had been a counsellor at the same camp in Ohio the year before, and had encouraged Dan to go. It was with great trepidation we sent our gorgeous 18-year-old son to another country, but we were confident in Dan who had always demonstrated good decision-making and was mature beyond his years.

Dan was expecting to be picked up at the airport by Josie the camp manager, but Loren had a surprise in store for him: she gave friends she'd made the year before (her teenaged campers that were now Staff in Training) Dan's flight details. When he stepped into the terminal, expecting an older solo lady, he was instead met with a group of young cheerleaders holding placards and pom poms.

Dan had a marvellous time at camp; the children and their parents warmly welcomed him to their homes on weekend visits and provided him access to classic American pastimes. He made some lovely friends, some who still contact us to this day.

Dan was never one for being the centre of attention, even though he often was. In 2008, rather than having a big 21st birthday party, we gave him a trip overseas. He travelled to the UK, and spent some time in central London in a share house of Loren's friends. He then went on to Scotland, staying in Edinburgh for a number of months, excitedly telling me all about the kings and castles he learned about while walking the streets. It was around this time he met Susie, an Australian girl from Queensland. He was smitten. They enjoyed a wonderful time together and were in love. Susie came home while Dan still had a few countries to visit, which he quickly breezed through as he was eager to get home to her.

I think it was around mid-2009 when Susie came to live with us, and this was a time of great joy – it was lovely to see a young couple so in love and devoted to each other. Susie was a wonderful house guest and I enjoyed her company immensely. I remember one evening arriving home from work and seeing a sight any working mum only dreams of seeing: Dan and Susie were cooking dinner and Des was doing the ironing. Pure joy!

Over the following year, Dan was immersed in his Brazilian Jiu Jitsu. In September—on his dad's 60th birthday—he won the Pan Pacific Purple Belt in the Light to Heavyweight Division. We were having a party to celebrate Des's milestone with our friends and family; it was a fantastic evening, and made more so when Dan arrived home from Melbourne with his trophy. He was just so pleased and we were just so proud; this was one of the best times of my life after so many years of hardship.

SEVENTEEN

Hard Times

I don't know any details, but sometime later, Dan and Susie were experiencing problems in their relationship and broke up for a few months. Dan was devastated, and I was too; we loved having Susie in our life.

They soon got back together but—for reasons unknown to me—their relationship was different, and by early 2011 Dan was having difficulties with his mental health. I didn't know the depth of these issues; Dan still presented as a loving and happy son. It wasn't until Susie told me about Dan's troubles that I became concerned. Those following six months are rather a blur, as I was reeling from my treatment in the courts and struggling to keep my PTSD symptoms under control. I didn't know what to do. I convinced him to go to Headspace (a mental health service for people aged under 25) with me. They chatted with him and told me to keep an eye on him, which was easier said than done – Dan was an adult, and living with Susie in Melbourne. I took him to a local doctor who gave us a referral to the Geelong Clinic (a private mental health hospital), and we went there that day. We were asked to wait in the waiting room and the doctor would be with us shortly, but after half an hour Dan became restless and left. I tried to convince him to return with me, but he refused. I contacted a counsellor I'd had in the past, but his policies didn't allow him to see family members of a patient he had previously seen.

I was at a loss. Dan wasn't exhibiting any concerning behaviour—no aggression, no outbursts, no crying, no drinking or drugs—but I realise now that he had crippling anxiety that he hid very well. I've experienced crippling anxiety myself, and know how well it can be hidden.

Susie had moved to Melbourne, so Dan spent most of his time there and I was grateful to Susie who took charge and sought help for Dan. I'm unclear of exactly what that help was, but I know it included some medication and counselling with a psychologist. We were hopeful all would be well, but it wasn't.

During those years I was dealing with my own experiences of workplace mobbing and the medical aftermaths, the confusion of being a pawn in the WorkCover and legal systems, while trying with all my might to still be a good mother and wife. Luckily my hardy personality saw me through and our family life continued on as before. I don't believe my personal challenges contributed to Dan's difficulties that began to manifest in early 2011. One of the last things I remember Dan telling me around this time was how proud he was of me for standing up for myself.

The weekend before my birthday in 2011, Dan cooked dinner for the family and we had a wonderful time. The following Tuesday was my actual birthday, and a night out at Crown Casino with my best friend was planned. We met Dan and Loren in the lounge area and had a few drinks, then Loren left and Dan announced he would stay and have dinner with us. We had a fantastic time; Dan was happy, humorous and appeared to be in a good place. This is another occasion that lives on in my heart. On the Wednesday before he disappeared, he came home from Susie's and appeared a little down, but there was nothing that overly concerned me.

I had a friend from the country staying that night, and after preparing dinner for Dan and Des, Lill and I went out to dinner to catch up on both our lives. Lill was bullied at work; I met her through the bullied workers network, and she was a lovely lady – we warmed to each other as soon as we met. The house was quiet by the time we arrived home and we sat in front of the fire with our coffee and chatted into the early hours – we had so much in common.

I was sound asleep when Dan crawled into bed beside me (something he hadn't done since he was a child) and told me he wanted to go away where no one would ever see him. We talked about his lack of motivation to continue teaching in his martial arts academy, which we had set up only a few months earlier. He was disappointed that the owner of the gym was renting out his space when he wasn't teaching, which meant all the very heavy mats and equipment had to be packed up each time; he'd been planning to use the space fully once his school membership increased. Dan told me he felt he had lost his school and was just renting floor space every week, and this wasn't what he had planned. We discussed the best way to handle this and once again considered the options, with the decision being that he would attend the next class and inform the students he was having a break. In hindsight, I feel that Dan really couldn't cope with this option. This is the second occasion I feel I failed in my parenting, as I didn't understand just how vulnerable Dan was at this time; it was a case of the vulnerable leading the vulnerable.

For the rest of that morning, Dan and I hung out at home. In the afternoon he appeared to be okay, and visited some relatives that lived nearby. That evening I cooked one of his favourite meals, not knowing it would be the last meal I ever cooked for him. As I wasn't hungry, I left the boys to their dinner and headed to the study where I spent my time writing down my experiences. At the time, I didn't know I was writing what would form the basis of this book. Dan came up to the study, put his arms around me and said, "Thanks Ma, that was a lovely dinner." These are the last words I would ever hear him say, and I hold them close to my heart. Later that evening, Dan asked his dad if he could have a campfire (something we did a lot of when the kids were younger and a favourite activity of Dan's). Being on a hill, our yard looked out over the horizon, and if you had your back to the house, you felt like you were out in the bush. Des and Dan built the fire on this cold winter's night and Dan sat there until bedtime. Regrettably, I didn't join in as it was too cold for me. I simply called out, "Goodnight Dan" from the balcony, unaware it was his last night on earth. I write this with tears streaming down my face, as precious memories of my beautiful boy flood my mind.

The next morning was a bright and sunny July morning, a morning that started out as any other. Des was up early and pottering around the garden when Dan joined him, and they shared a mandarin from the tree that was bearing fruit for the first time. It was a bitter fruit, not yet quite ripe, but Dan ate his pieces without complaint. Des went to the laundry to wash his hands before coming inside, and while there he heard Dan on the phone (just outside the closed laundry door). Des could only hear a little of what was being said, but was surprised to hear Dan swear – we'd never heard Dan use bad language.

I'm not sure what time I got up, but I showered and dressed and was ready to drive Des to work at around 10am; as it was a Friday, Des was having lunch with friends and couldn't drive home as he planned on having a few drinks. I went to Dan's room and he wasn't there. Des said he thought Dan was going for a walk, so I called him to make sure he knew where the key was (so he could get back in). I hung up when Des said that Dan knew where the key was, and we left. After dropping Des off, I went to pick up Sue. I mentioned Sue earlier – she was the one having her car serviced in Geelong even though she lived in Melbourne, and we were spending the downtime together. We went for brunch at a local café and then back to my house. Dan still wasn't home, but I remember not feeling worried by this as he had friends in the area who he'd visit when back in Geelong. Later in the afternoon, I drove Sue to collect her car and then headed to the supermarket. I called Dan to ask what he would like for dinner before he got the train to Werribee to speak to his class. He didn't answer so I left a message for him to call, and thus began our nightmare.

Later, around 6:30pm, Susie called to say Dan hadn't yet arrived at the gym. There were numerous calls over the next couple of hours to check that he was not just running late (maybe he missed the train?). Dan had recently been caught speeding and had his license suspended; we later learnt this was likely a suicide attempt. The police had taken Dan to the Werribee hospital for observation, then he was discharged into Susie's care. We weren't told about this incident and other behaviour that would have put us on high alert, had we known.

The nights and days following 15 July 2011 are a bit of a blur for me; it was so surreal, like watching a movie of someone else's life, but the twist at the end is that it's your life.

The girls all came home. Kate was overseas so she terminated her trip and flew home. I can remember us all sitting in the living room stunned, worried about Dan – where *is* he? Something must be wrong – he would never miss a class. We sat there not knowing what to say, not knowing what to think and not knowing what to do. The police were called and would arrive soon to take a statement. We waited and waited, then called again; they said they would be there soon. We waited and waited, then we called again, and they said they would be there soon. The last call was them telling us that they would not be coming, but a police officer would drop by and collect a photo of Dan.

Around 11-11:30pm, two police officers arrived at our door. The night was bitterly cold and blustery and the officers were invited in. I remember feeling that something was a little odd as they stood at the door hesitantly and declined the invitation. They were given a photo and left with hardly a word. Sometimes wonder if their behaviour was related to me – were they told to be careful, told that I have an "angry and aggressive" nature? Is that why two officers were required to pick up one photo?

The day after Dan went missing, a neighbour informed us that around 3am he was woken by three people walking around the street talking. Another neighbour reported he had seen three males walk up the pathway from the park at around 9am and get into a dark-coloured four-wheel drive, and that he had never seen this car in our street before. He didn't know if Dan was one of the males as he didn't know Dan very well. Our next door neighbour was out in his driveway between 8:30am to 10:30am that Friday and said he didn't see Dan leave our home. These occurrences were added to our endless list of possibilities to ruminate over, but eventually lessened in importance; we figured he must have left through the back fence.

A police officer finally arrived on the Sunday, only after the police were asked for a statement by the media. He was pleasant enough and even offered to organise family counselling (though this never eventuated). We asked if a search could be conducted or Dan's phone to be triangulated, but both requests were denied. There was no request from the police officer to see Dan's room or computer, even after we suggested it. The next weeks were a flurry of media, possible sightings and searches. A woman in Highton reported she saw Dan at a bus stop, and after three weeks of no information from the police I called and asked if this woman had been interviewed and was told, "That is none of your business." Maybe it wasn't, but I found the tone of voice quite confronting and unnecessary, and so began our dysfunctional relationship with this police officer.

A few days after Dan went missing, we noticed the VicPol website had incorrectly stated Dan's name as Daniel John O'Keeffe. My daughter asked if this could be fixed, but was brought to tears by a phone call from this very agitated police officer yelling, "Don't you dare try to tell me how to run my investigation!" It was distressing for Loren and for all of us. What was equally distressing was in 2015 when the Coroner's Court sent us a Coronial Brief of Evidence for a Daniel John O'Keefe who had died by suicide in the Shepparton area. I read a few pages—in shock—as it described how Daniel had died; my mind twirled in confusion. I put the report down and just stared at the cover page until it sunk in that this was another Daniel O'Keefe, not our Dan.

We asked the State Emergency Services (SES) who agreed to conduct a search for Dan, but Victoria Police wouldn't approve it. We again pleaded for his phone to be triangulated, but this was again refused. We sent out a plea for help through the Facebook page Loren had created, and around 100 people (mostly strangers) arrived on a Saturday to assist in our search for Dan in a 2km radius around our local area, which included various parklands and paddocks of nearby farms. We are eternally grateful to those who showed so much care and concern; many had travelled some distance to be there with us. We later learned that the police believed Dan had taken his own life, and would no doubt turn up one day, saving the expense of search and phone triangulation.

Around the end of July, I contacted a private detective through their website P.I.NOW, requesting information about his services and possible costs. I was called the next day and a discussion took place about the PI's ability to find Dan. The PI called me back the next day and offered his services pro bono in our search for Dan, with the proviso we advertised this on our website.

We were just so grateful to have *any* investigative help. That is, until a few months later when he called to tell me that since I'd withheld vital and crucial information, hadn't been honest and upfront, and had misled his investigation, he would no longer be working with us. I found this incredibly strange, as we had given him the same information that we had given to the police. He made these allegations but never provided any information that supported his allegations – he said he didn't need to go into the details, as he was sure I knew exactly what he was talking about...

I certainly did not know, and couldn't believe I was seemingly being attacked yet again. I mentioned to our lovely Dale (another police officer assigned to our case) what the PI had said, and he expressed his belief that the PI was just annoyed that he hadn't solved our case before the police. Dale suggested the PI was a 'cowboy', and said, "We don't encourage families to use PIs – they promise a lot and deliver little." I told Dale how the PI had told me he would find Dan before the police, and Dale concluded, "He's just angry because he hasn't found Dan, and needs to lay blame to cover this." I later came to regret telling Dale about these dealings with the PI. (I can only assume the police thought he might actually know something of relevance, of which he did not.)

This PI brought a psychic in on the case, which caused us much distress and wasted a lot of time. I like to keep an open mind; I'm not saying *all* psychics are dubious – but most seem to be, and I came to experience this firsthand. Take it from me: no matter how desperate you are, leave it to the experts, not PIs and psychics. I feel confident there are many private investigators out there doing a wonderful job for WorkCover, uncovering cheating spouses and the like, but do your due diligence before even considering hiring one.

In an email from this PI, he stated, "This is a complex case with numerous facts, theories or even conspiracies." Oh no, he had been speaking to Sue, the acquaintance I mentioned earlier who went down the rabbit hole, and I felt he was following her down as he lacked the skills and/or experience to realise what was happening.

In 2016, in preparation for Dan's Coronial Inquest, it appeared that the police wanted a statement from this PI. I spoke to officer Dale regarding his location and he stated, "He doesn't have an office where he says he does. We know this because we have tried to contact him there." I was at a loss to understand why a statement from this rogue PI was necessary, given we hadn't had any contact since the end of 2011 and he hadn't found anything of significance. This PI 'clouded' the work of the Coroner's Court by following up leads that he should have known were based on rumour and innuendo (found by contacting people listed as friends on Dan's Facebook page – 'friends' Dan hadn't actually seen for a number of years). I spoke to one of these people who informed me she had been contacted by the PI, and after speaking to her it became apparent to me that whatever she had said to the PI was based on rumour and conjecture. I honestly believe she thought she was in some way helping; my mind went back to the advice given to me by a woman named Jo in the early days of Dan's missingness.

The PI provided a statement full of unfounded allegations against me. I was horrified. At what point did the brief to help find Dan change to a brief to vilify my character, and for what purpose? Over the space of four days, he went from a position of support to completely abandoning his mission. His statement to the coroner was written some four years after these events, and he repeated his verbal accusations that I had withheld vital and crucial information from him, that I had not been honest and upfront, and that I had misled his investigation. He repeated the same accusations in a dozen different ways but always said essentially the same thing. His accusations hadn't diminished, but his vitriol had, oddly, dramatically increased.

I can only think of a few possible reasons that could have compelled this PI (though there be others): he had to justify his unsuccessful attempts to find Dan to protect his reputation; there was an ulterior motive or motives currently unknown; at the request or insistence of a person or persons unknown; he was firmly stuck down that rabbit hole with Sue. The effect his statement had on me was dramatic. Even though I knew what he stated was untrue, it nearly pushed me over the edge. How anyone, especially someone considering themselves a professional, could behave in this manner and cause such torment to a grieving family is unconscionable.

There were many reported sightings of Dan, and we believed that he was out there somewhere. Early on, I spoke to Jo whose son was also missing. She warned me that people would want to help and that we'd get lots of false sightings. She told me about an experience she'd had where a friend of her son Gary contacted her to say he'd seen Gary at a bus station. As it came to pass, sadly Gary was already deceased at the time he was supposedly seen. I came to understand that people *wanted* to help because they care about your plight. The trick is to not get too hopeful (easier said than done since hope is all you have at these times).

On the morning Dan disappeared, a friend of my nephew believed he saw Dan walking down Ryrie Street (a main street in Geelong). He was adamant it was him. I have some distant recollection that Dan had a meeting in the city that morning which gave credibility to the sighting. We contacted the police and asked to see the CCTV, but our request was denied because it would be a breach of privacy. I asked whose privacy would be breached, and I was told "those captured on the CCTV." My response was that a right to privacy didn't extend to public places. We couldn't understand why our request elicited such a response, but the Privacy Act was quoted. We researched the Privacy Act and found that this Act was not applicable. Being able to decipher a 'Point B' and thus knowing which direction Daniel left in that day would have been incredibly helpful – if it was Dan, we would've had a location from which to search. The police said it wasn't Dan, but the friend was convinced otherwise.

We asked again to see the footage and were told that there was no one on the CCTV that could have been Dan, and that the only person of interest had his back to the camera. I persisted, as I would recognise Dan from behind and by the way he walked. Our request was again denied.

Two years later, during a meeting with senior police, we asked again if we could see the tape. The response was, "That's not going to happen." A few months later, I was told the tape had been destroyed. Regardless of whether or not it was Dan, any associated angst we felt as a family would have dissipated if we had just been allowed to see the tape. At a later date, much later, another police officer confirmed that we should have been allowed to see the footage.

A few days after Dan's disappearance, a young lady named Amanda reported to us that she saw a man fitting Dan's description walking along the Surf Coast Highway near Torquay the day after he went missing. The clothing, appearance and location all made this sound credible, and yet we were told by Amanda that after she made the report to Crime Stoppers she was never contacted by anyone. We don't know if this report made it to Geelong Police, but we were learning that not all sightings were being followed up, and of course we now know that the police already believed Dan was deceased. Despite Amanda telling us she was never contacted by police after making her report a few days after Dan disappeared, VicPol's response to this was that a call to Crime Stoppers was received on 4 August 2011 and matched the location of the sighting, so they believed the anonymous caller must have been Amanda. So their excuse was that as the caller was anonymous, they couldn't make inquiries.

Within days, we had what we believed to be the first credible sighting of Dan from a man named Les who lived in Colac (75kms from our home). He was certainly sincere. Les reported that he had seen Dan in Colac twice before he knew that Dan was missing. Once he became aware, he notified the police four times and spoke to four different officers. Les left a message for the officer in charge of Dan's case to call, but his calls were never returned.

Les had been able to state the exact colour of footwear Dan left the house in (which wasn't reported in any media), and Les had a good look at this young man and noted that he had very straight teeth. Les mentioned that his "boots were extremely dirty and his teeth were noticeably white." Dan had lovely white teeth, and his Ugg boots were chocolate-brown which would have given the appearance of being dirty when wet. Given these two pieces of information, we felt there could've been merit in Les's observations.

The circumstances added to the plausibility – the young man was seemingly disoriented, walking through the grass alongside the footpath, in the rain. As such, family members spoke with Les on the phone at length, and drove out to Colac on numerous occasions trying to find the man fitting Dan's description. Despite our belief in this possible sighting, it took police 16 weeks to contact Les, with a statement finally being taken three years later.

In Les's statement it says, "I did not see the male's face" and "at no time did I see his face." This isn't what Les told my daughters and me; if he had, we likely would never have pursued the sighting. Understandably, Les could no longer be 100% confident he saw Dan given the passage of time, but this is strikingly different to what he initially told us. In a Law Enforcement

Assistance Program (LEAP) Incident Report dated 23 July 2011, it's recorded that Les called and said in part, "observed to be wearing blue jeans, grey hoodie top and Ugg boots. Boots were extremely dirty, male had facial hair and his teeth were noticeably white." Two different versions – which one is true I don't know, but usually the first account tends to be the most accurate.

My first real searching started in Colac, as there were further reports made to us that a person fitting Dan's description was seen at a café buying chocolate milk (a favourite of Dan's) and drinking it in a park in the town. I visited the café but—unsurprisingly—staff couldn't confirm this, so I wandered the streets looking for any sign of Dan. Another report had him near the local high school, so I went to the school and did a poster drop to the homes in the area. Around this time, we were contacted by a psychic who believed Dan was buried somewhere in Simpson (a small town in the western district of Victoria). The word "pipeline" had some significance. We headed off to Simpson with all sorts of harrowing thoughts running through our minds. We found a road named Pipeline, and there was a small culvert that ran under the main road. I was determined to check it out, but didn't know it was a cattle track and full of cow manure. I was up to my knees in it and glad to get home to the shower; I felt Des found the whole thing rather amusing. From the very beginning and throughout the years, Des was adamant Dan would come home when he was ready – his faith was unwavering.

I'm not sure how it came about (perhaps via the fast-growing Facebook following Loren was harnessing), but we were sent a photo of a young man who looked a lot like Dan. We were able to make contact with this young man's family, who invited me to visit them in Princetown, roughly 30 minutes from Simpson. I headed off on a day trip, eager for any information I could get. I arrived without getting lost to find the mother had set out a lovely afternoon tea for me to enjoy while her son was sleeping. He joined us a few minutes later and I sat in shock, as Brett looked remarkably like Dan. I asked Brett if he had visited the café around the said day or had bought chocolate milk, or had been in the vicinity of Les's shed. He said that he hadn't been in those areas and so couldn't have been the subject of the reported sightings. The mystery continued, as did the public and media attention on and in the Colac region.

My last trip to Colac related to a report from a woman called Cathy who lived in the town. She told me of some clothes she found near Skene's Creek that were half-pushed under a rock, as if hidden. Cathy said she had taken them to the Colac Police Station and wondered if I had been informed. I hadn't, which she said didn't surprise her, as she felt the officer was rather rude and showed no concern or interest in her find.

People trying to help is wonderful—and this should never change—but this phenomenon needs to be understood and accepted for what it is, as it leads to many false leads and crushed hopes. Of course, I now realise the police are expert at identifying this, but where they fail is not explaining their procedures, assessment tools and investigative processes to families (even at a basic level). Desperate families feel the need to follow up on every clue just in case it leads them to their loved one. It is utterly exhausting.

I attended the station and spoke to an officer about the clothes. I felt uncomfortable as the officer checked 'the book', flipping pages back and forth – this went on for some minutes. Another officer entered the station, and the first officer asked him if he knew anything about clothes being handed in. The officer looked perplexed and also began to flick the pages back and forth. I was asked somewhat accusingly how I knew about the clothes, so I told them that Cathy who had found the clothes had contacted me thinking there may be chance the clothes could be Dan's. After what seemed an eternity, the report was found in 'the book' and I asked if I could please see them. A firm, "No." I virtually begged – I'd driven all the way to Colac to have a look. I wasn't allowed to see them because they were in the cupboard. The cupboard was locked and the key was with an officer who was off duty. I asked if they could be sent to the Geelong Police station and the response was, "We don't have a procedure for that." I left almost laughing, feeling as though I'd just left an episode of *Keystone Cops*.

Sometime later I became aware through police that there were many reported sightings of a young man matching Dan's description in the Skenes Creek area, and that an officer had investigated the clothing and it didn't in any way match the clothing Dan was thought to be wearing when he disappeared.

In August, there was a reported sighting of Dan at the Queen Victoria Market – a woman named Robyn had taken a photo and sent it to us. The photograph was from behind and it certainly could have been Dan. Loren went to the market, but after viewing the CCTV footage she knew it was not.

The most significant, most credible sighting of Dan came in January of 2012, six months after his disappearance. We received a phone call (to the dedicated hotline mobile we had for the search), from a woman named Maria who worked as a receptionist at a medical centre in Ipswich in Queensland.

She advised that on 30 November between 7:15pm-7:30pm a man matching Dan's description entered the medical centre after hours. The cleaner had left the front door of the building open, and Maria was in the reception counting the money in the till. The male entered; they both described him as being tall, quite lean, tidy and polite in his mid-20s with short, scruffy, dark brown hair. He was clean-shaven with no beard, and there were no visible distinguishing features such as tattoos, piercings or jewellery. The physical description the medical staff gave matched Dan. They spoke with him face to face at length, even making note of his "perfect teeth." His psychological demeanour was quiet, polite, friendly and non-threatening, which also matched Dan's profile. The staff offered this person money, and he initially refused and only accepted on Maria's insistence – this too matched our knowledge of Dan. Growing up Dan never asked for money, and if it was offered, he often declined.

This man had been "bashed"—he had bruising and swelling to the right side of his face—and his speech was slurred, and from this Maria made the assumption that she believed the man was substance-affected, but she didn't smell any alcohol.

The man requested a glass of water. He reported his name to be "James" (Dan's middle name was James), that he was from Melbourne, and that he had been assaulted for his prescription drugs. James reported that he had sought medical attention including x-rays for his injuries from a local hospital in Brisbane, but he didn't say how long ago this assault took place.

Maria estimated that his bruising to his face may have been one to two weeks old, and was still causing some pain or discomfort as James was rubbing his jaw. Maria noticed that James was an attractive man with very good teeth and that he had some plastic bags with him. She said he was experiencing homelessness, that "that was the way he lived," that he seemed "used to it" and "street wise." James said there was no one that Maria could call for him. He said there was no one in Ipswich that he could stay with, but that he was trying to make his way back to Brisbane as he had friends there. James asked where the closest bus stop or train station was, to get back to Brisbane. Maria said she didn't feel threatened by James and offered him $15 to help him on his way. James initially seemed embarrassed and refused the money, eventually accepting it as a gift and he walked to the bus stop across the road.

The report of this sighting had come about because a couple of weeks later the cleaner of the medical clinic, Joy, saw the story about Dan on Channel 10's popular national nightly news program, *The Project*. Joy called Maria – she was sure the man that came into the clinic a few weeks earlier was this missing man from Victoria. Maria visited our website and agreed that the man known as James was quite likely Daniel O'Keeffe. Joy thought that James was approximately 5'8" or 5'9" and that he was "a lot" thinner than in the pictures shown on TV. Maria immediately reported all of the above information to clinic management, and after management sought legal advice, she reported it to Crime Stoppers a few days later. Maria waited to see if anything had come of her report, and then contacted Crime Stoppers again. By this time, four weeks had elapsed since they saw James, and since both her and Joy were confident it was Dan they decided to contact us directly. Everything she described fitted with what we knew of Dan, but the clincher was that Dan's girlfriend Susie's family lived in Ipswich and her doctor was in the same location as the medical centre where this sighting was made. Dan knew this area, had been to Susie's clinic with her in the past, and had visited her grandmother and knew where she lived. We felt all this combined information, plus two reliable witnesses, added credibility to the sighting. Loren flew immediately to Queensland and attended the medical centre to view the CCTV footage. Since the officer in charge of Dan's case had told us that family members of missing persons weren't allowed to view CCTV footage that may have their loved one captured on it, we purposely kept Loren's visit to the medical centre quiet. After swiftly convincing the manager to show her the footage, Loren soon called to say she believed the young man on the CCTV was Dan. Within hours we were in Queensland, and we all went to the Ipswich Police Station to view the CCTV (as it was now in their control).

This was another occasion I felt strange with a police officer. The officer came out to reception and informed us that we couldn't view the CCTV at the station as she stood with her back to the internal door she had just come through, with her feet and arms crossed as if guarding the door. The officer said she would put it on a USB and we could go to the local library and view it there. We got the USB and hurriedly searched for the library with excitement and hope in our hearts. Finally, we inserted the USB, but to our disappointment it didn't work. Our resident IT guru tried all manner of things, but the USB just would not work. I was devastated and close to tears. Loren called the medical centre and asked if they still had a copy of the CCTV. Fortunately, they did, and warmly welcomed us in to view it.

Maria advised that the CCTV footage from the clinic only showed the man from the back and some slight side profiles, but we were undeterred – we knew we would know if it was Dan. We all watched the footage like hawks. Over and over again. Our joint opinion was that we believed it was Dan – everything about how this person looked and moved screamed Dan. Though concerned about his current state, we were elated to know he was alive. The next task was to find him. We needed a base to coordinate media and searches, and that's when my wonderful, lifelong friend Anne came to our rescue. We stayed in her lovely home for weeks, and set off each day to places we thought Dan may be. We searched parks, city streets, homeless shelters and soup kitchens, all to no avail. Des and I eventually returned home, with Loren staying on in Queensland a bit longer to continue the search. She said she would come home when she found him.

We couldn't find Dan, but I had hope in my heart we would soon be reunited.

EIGHTEEN

The Searching Years

Myself, Dan's father, sisters and partner all saw Dan in the CCTV: his walk, his profile, the shape of his head, the way his hair grew on the back of his neck, the length of his legs, the embarrassed and polite declining of the $15 Marie offered to him. And this in, of all places, his girlfriend's hometown where he had spent time and had very fond memories. I understood that police wouldn't accept this sighting as confirmed, but my family spent six weeks in Queensland searching for Dan. We wouldn't have flown to Brisbane immediately upon reading any reported sighting – we'd had scores of sightings. We were confident the man was Dan, and in our collective opinion at this time the CCTV proved it. For the first time in six months, hope and anticipation was high in our hearts and minds.

The Queensland Police put a picture of this young man on their Facebook page and had two people contact them believing they knew him. The police spoke to the two young men identified as possibly being a match to the image, but neither had been in this medical centre and confirmed they were not the person captured on the CCTV.

Neil and Damien from the Queensland Police Missing Persons Unit had been unbelievably accommodating since we contacted them (they drove Susie and Loren around Ipswich and Brisbane for an entire day). They kept us informed of reports they got from around Queensland that might be of Dan, and they sent Loren stills of CCTV footage from other reports that they were looking into. Their patience, respect and compassion was in such stark contrast to our experience with Victoria Police.

The police officer in charge of our case, who had obviously never met Dan and hadn't even seen the footage, flatly refused to believe it was Dan, despite our whole family's belief it was. It was the only solid lead we had, and yet when the initial report was made to the Geelong Police Station on 22 December 2011, it was immediately discounted. The five-week delay in Marie deciding to contact us directly gave Dan time to move on from the Ipswich/Brisbane region, or so we believed. Over the next couple of years, whenever we had a reported sighting in the greater Brisbane area, Neil would go there and check it out. We have such a deep appreciation to Queensland Police and all the police stations we visited over the years all over the country, who showed us such support and care. My faith in the force was restored.

Although the police manual states that DNA and dental records are to be acquired by police after 28 days, it wasn't until four months later that the police informed me that they would be coming to my home to get these samples from me and my daughter. Loren came home especially for this, as police had informed me that the female strain is predominant. I was hopeful that Dan was still alive, so I was worried that the reason they suddenly wanted DNA samples implied they may have found something.

A local armed robbery arose that afternoon, so the officers were unable to attend and the samples were not obtained. I was told that they would come sometime the following week, but that next week passed, and then the next, without any word from the police. Four days later, as she'd come home especially to give her DNA, Loren attended our local police station to explain she was returning to Melbourne where she lived and wondered if her DNA sample could be taken then and there. Unfortunately, Officer Dale was on the phone and unavailable.

The constable at the counter told her she could attend her local police station and provide the sample there. A few days later she went to her local police station, explained why she was there and waited while the officer called Geelong Police. She was put on the phone to the officer in charge of Dan's case who berated her with, "What on earth made you think you could go into a police station and give a DNA sample?" She explained that she had been told by the constable that she needed to give one and that she could provide the sample at her local station. He said, "If we want your DNA, we will come and get it." Then he told her not to call him because he was on leave for the following two weeks. She asked sincerely, "So who will be taking care of the case while you're away?" and he yelled back, "Don't you dare tell us how to do our job!" and hung up on her.

Sometime later, Loren read about Victoria Police's revered Ron Iddles—'Australia's greatest detective'—who many families with missing loved ones had mentioned as having the skills, determination and heart all families hope cops do. She called Ron and days later met with him at the St Kilda Road Police Headquarters.

During this meeting he reminded Loren that police just think we wanted to *believe* that the man in the footage was Dan. Loren went on to mention to Ron that no DNA samples were taken as yet; he offered to get a DNA sample from her then and there. It took less than a minute, and she could finally rest assured that if Dan's body was found it could be matched against her DNA sample. We'd heard numerous horror stories of families (like the Bibbys) unnecessarily waiting years before DNA samples were tested against unidentified human remains left forgotten in morgues. We had been cooperative from the very beginning, and no one wanted to find Dan more than his family.

Ron Iddles told Loren that VicPol (generally speaking) assumed Dan suicided because he had apparently mentioned suicide to a friend earlier in the year. Loren was confused, because the officer in charge told us the day after Dan disappeared that if he *was* a suicide risk his case would be a priority. Surely this officer was aware of the statistics around suicide; the majority occur within a 1-km radius of the family home. Why wasn't there ever a search by police? Why wasn't our application for an SES search in September approved?

Loren was the closest to Dan, and the two times he vaguely alluded to suicide (put to her as 'going away' and 'leaving everything') he said he wouldn't because he knew how much it would hurt us. I think it's a convenient excuse to immediately assume that a missing person who suffers depression and anxiety has died by suicide. Almost half the population suffers depression at some point in their lives, and in their lowest of lows may fantasise about suicide, but they don't necessarily succumb to it.

Regardless, if VicPol honestly believed Dan had killed himself, the logical place to search for a body would be within the vicinity of his home. We were so disappointed that a search had not been conducted, especially when the SES had offered their services. VicPol had it both ways: to have never conducted a search based on an initial conclusion that Dan *wasn't* a suicide risk, and since the sighting in Queensland deciding Dan *did* die by suicide in Victoria (though it not warranting a search, while simultaneously discounting the mother's, father's and sisters' confirmation of the sighting and not following it up).

Ron Iddles spoke with the officer in charge of Dan's case and asked about his lack of communication with our family. This officer hadn't been in contact with our family in more than six months. My daughter didn't feel comfortable contacting him, since on each occasion he had been aggressive, rude and condescending. Des and I left a number of phone messages and sent emails, but all were left unanswered. The officer told Ron that his lack of communication was due to my family requesting that we only communicate via email. My husband, who was the police contact, had never made such a request. The officer's excuse is completely untrue. Even if there's nothing to report, it would've been helpful for our family to have Geelong Police check in with us every now and again. However, if there had been nothing to inform us of in almost an entire year, why had we been told that Dan's case was more than 1000 pages in length?

Ironically, just after Ron contacted Loren, she received her first email from the officer in charge of the case as a direct result of her liaising with Neil from the Queensland Missing Persons Unit. This officer was only contacted by Neil because VicPol had carriage of the case. Neil and Loren had been corresponding very effectively since we were informed of the Ipswich sighting, and given at this time there were no resources allocated for non-suspicious missing persons cases within Victoria Police, and because we believed Dan was now missing from Ipswich, we wanted to apply for Queensland Police to be given carriage of Dan's investigation.

Over the months since the Queensland sighting, we had asked for Dan's missing person file to be transferred to the Queensland Police Missing Person Unit, as we had rapport with the officers there who couldn't do enough to assist. Neil was especially helpful, and would take off as soon as a sighting came in and investigate and get back to us straight away. If only we had that support from our own officer, the relationship could have been a positive experience (or at least not such a negative one).

Our belief at the time was that Dan had now disappeared from Queensland, so his case could be handled there. Victoria Police refused to accept that the sighting in Queensland was Dan, continuing to consider it an unconfirmed sighting. We all disagreed with this finding, and were of the understanding that

The Searching Years

if Victoria Police confirmed the Queensland sighting, then we may have been able to have the case transferred there. But VicPol wouldn't release Dan's file.

Soon after, we were notified of a possible sighting in Sydney's Bondi Beach. We gave it some merit as apparently this young man who looked very much like Dan was staying in a hostel there and liked to drink lemon, lime and bitters (my drink of choice, which Dan knew of course). Not a typical choice for a young person, especially a young man. I visited the hostel, walked the streets, spoke to young people and attended the local police station where the officers were very kind and helpful. I left feeling the word was out, and was confident NSW police officers would follow up any future sightings.

I again decided to head north, and hopped on a train bound for Newcastle arriving early on a Friday evening. Whilst on the train, I spoke to a train guard who told me that many homeless people travel the overnight train from Sydney to Newcastle as it gave them somewhere warm to sleep safely, and by the time the return train back to Sydney arrived it was morning. I was surprised NSW Rail allowed it, but pleased to see them acting so compassionately. My eyes keenly searched all who boarded on the off-chance Dan might be one of them. Upon my arrival in Newcastle, I contacted the motels in the vicinity of the train station, and—to my disbelief—there were no vacancies. From memory, there was a major sporting event in town – all accommodation was booked. I hadn't thought to book ahead as Newcastle wasn't known as a busy tourist town.

That night, I had a small glimpse of what people experiencing homelessness endure every day – I had nowhere to stay, nowhere to sleep. I went to a park not far from the station, pulled my pillow and a jacket from my luggage and attempted to get comfortable on the freshly mowed grass.

Next to the park was a nightclub with young people coming and going, which gave me a sense of safety. Not long after falling to surface-level sleep, a group of young men approached me and asked if I was okay. I was so touched that young men on a night out cared about an older lady sleeping in the park. I assured them I was okay and they headed towards the nightclub.

Being bitten by angry ants made sleeping impossible. I saw a bench about 20m to my right and headed there. The bench was better than the ants, but I couldn't get comfortable. A few minutes later, a patrol car drove past and checked me out with their torch and I responded with a friendly wave. Still, I had to find somewhere else, so I headed towards the city area looking for anything that may offer some shelter for the night. In the distance I saw that reassuring golden arches and knew I had found my new home with their *24 hours* sign.

I arrived at McDonalds around 1am, the witching hour for young people leaving the nightclubs and bars looking to kick on in the only open establishment in town. The staff were incredibly kind to me, offering to store my luggage for the night and giving me a cubical in which to sleep. Sleep was still impossible though, with a hundred kids all milling around throwing drinks and generally misbehaving until police arrived. Things settled down around early morning and I rested off and on until it was time to leave and find accommodation for the next two nights.

A little out of the main part of town I found a lovely motel, high on a cliff overlooking the ocean with a stunning view. I checked in and then left for my trip to Port Stephens. Dan had visited this area a few times with his girlfriend, as she had family there and so I thought it may be a possible location. I went down to the fishing docks and explained my situation to the workers, suggesting it was possible he could be working on a fishing trawler. They told me they'd be vigilant and make contact if anyone matching Dan's description applied to work there.

The next few years were spent searching. I visited Queensland on numerous occasions, staying with Anne, whose unwavering support I will always cherish. I can remember one occasion, returning to her home on the train after revisiting the usual places of interest, and a lovely young man came up to me and said, "You're Dan's mum, we were just talking about him and I wanted to let you know that we keep a lookout for Dan wherever we go." I was so touched. It took all my strength to not break down into a blubbering mess.

We had another credible sighting in Far North Queensland, just outside of Cairns. I flew there as soon as I could and met two young women who excitedly told me about their experience with a possible Dan. They told me their story over lunch, and it all sounded very positive until—as a side line—they mentioned he was carrying a guitar. I knew instantly it wasn't Dan, but thanked them for their help and headed to Kuranda (about 30kms away). I thought Kuranda could be a place that would appeal to Dan. I visited the local police station, the local hospital and businesses in the area, and finally walked the residential streets, popping Dan's missing person flyers in mailboxes.

Nearby, the town of Mareeba in the Atherton Tablelands attracted all sorts of transient types with plenty of fruit-picking jobs in the area. I figured this

The Searching Years

would be something Dan could do (when someone you love is missing, the possibilities are endless). I visited the local police station—as I did in every town and city I visited—and the officer was very supportive. The guys I spoke to at the pubs were very interested in my story, and said they would keep a lookout for Dan in the farming areas surrounding Mareeba.

A care provider I was still friends with from way back in my Family Day Care days at South Barwon lived in the area, and she very kindly invited me to stay. On another trip of searching Far North Queensland Des and I stayed with Cheryl and Max again, and we will be eternally grateful for their hospitality and compassion.

I had hired a car, so I decided to drive as far north as I could go. Even though I couldn't quite imagine Dan in Port Douglas at this point (a beautiful coastal resort town), I figured I might as well have a look and spread the message as far as I could. My friend Donna had moved to Port Douglas a few years earlier and gave me ideas of where to look, and she too kindly gave me a bed for the night.

The following day, I drove to Cape Tribulation. After taking the barge across the river I stopped to have a look around. I was delighted to see Dan's missing person poster on the riverside noticeboard. Phew – it seemed the fantastic Facebook followers were all over it (by this stage, Loren was imploring a growing following of over 60,000 compassionate strangers who took it upon themselves to print and display posters).

As I drove through the winding roads on my way to the beach hut where I was spending the night, I came to the conclusion that this place was too remote for Dan. I walked into the foyer of my accommodation and started to tell the receptionist about the search for my missing son. She pointed to the wall behind her and there, too, was Dan's poster. I was overwhelmed by the knowledge that—so far away from home—so many people cared enough for my family to display Dan's poster. I went down to the beach and watched the sunset over the picturesque Cape and felt at peace for the first time since he disappeared. I had a solitary night in my little hut and headed back to Cairns the next day, ready for my flight home.

After Dan had been missing for two years, we were invited to the Geelong Police Station for a discussion and review of his case. We arrived on time for our 10am meeting and informed the front desk we were meeting with a particular inspector and subsequent calls were made. By 10:30am, and after the third time front desk had called to check where the inspector was, he eventually came downstairs to greet us. He said he didn't know we were here and he apologised. Having witnessed their struggle to communicate from the front desk to the upstairs of a small station, I was suddenly less surprised by the abominable miscommunication within the investigation into Dan's disappearance.

We discussed our concerns about not having been allowed to see CCTV footage in Victoria and their policy of only showing family footage if it's clear, well-lit and front-on (effectively impossible, given the angles and poor quality of security cameras at the time). The inspector apologised on behalf of the officer in charge of Dan's case for his lack of communication.

The inspector denied it took them 16 weeks to interview Les from Colac, and said the incident report was received on 22 July 2011 and checked on 28 July 2011 by a sergeant. We knew this wasn't true, and immediately dreaded the discrepancies in all the police reports we possessed. The inspector denied that the police manual stated that DNA and dental records should be gained within 28 days of disappearance, and he admitted he didn't know if Dan's dental records were on file.

We discussed the Queensland sighting reported in Ipswich which was sent to Geelong Police on the 22 December 2011. We weren't given an answer as to why (or if) it was looked into. We did know that neither Marie, Joy nor the Medical Clinic itself had been contacted by any police when Loren had arrived on 4 January 2012, which suggests it was not. We were only contacted directly by the centre staff because of their concerns about police inaction.

The inspector said to us, "A sighting is a sighting until it's discounted." We asked the inspector why the Ipswich sighting was discounted, since we had been told the report was in fact sent to Geelong. The entire meeting, he alluded to QPS (Queensland Police Service) and VicPol being able to conclude that the sighting wasn't credible soon after 5 January 2012, when Loren was already in Brisbane following it up. "The evidence suggested it wasn't Dan." The inspector wouldn't tell us what this powerful evidence was until prompted for the umpteenth time. "One person who viewed the footage wasn't 100% sure the man was Daniel." That person was Dan's girlfriend Susie.

Susie had said she wasn't comfortable in the Medical Centre – of course, it was a confronting scenario. It was her hometown, her boyfriend had been missing for six months, and she had never seen Dan like that (none of us had – the man in the footage was completely emaciated). Despite this, she spent a week in Queensland with us, searching for Dan in the middle of the night and doing media. Her discounting the sighting led me to wonder if she knew something we did not (keeping in mind she was the last person to speak to Dan that fateful morning in July).

We asked the inspector why they never searched for Dan, from refusing to deploy constables to doorknock, search dogs or even approving the willing and able SES. He said searches were only conducted for children, the elderly, mentally impaired or when it's a search and rescue operation (based on dangers from the elements). I feel the line between an impairment and severe illness is confusingly blurry (though convenient for them, since they had already concluded Dan had taken his life).

Towards the end of our meeting, the issues with the officer in charge of Dan's case were lightly discussed, with the inspector telling us, "He is one of the best investigators I have, and the case will remain a Victorian one since there is yet to be a credible sighting."

The inspector was pushing to have a brief written to present to the coroner to see if there was sufficient cause to open an inquest. That was the only way we would be able to get any answers into the investigation. The said officer would remain the contact for that process, and the inspector—disappointed the officer had not initiated contact with our family for two years—insisted the officer initiate regular communication with the family (even if there is no news). The general gist of our meeting was that VicPol haven't been able to do anything purely based on the fact there has been no credible sighting. After this meeting in 2012, I don't think we saw an officer again until the day Dan was found, four years later.

Over the following years, Des continued to work and to search. I also continued to search, visiting places already mentioned as well as Lismore, Byron Bay, Casino, Batemans Bay, Kiama, Ballina, Kyogle, Nimbin, Mullumbimby, Gold Coast, Bundaberg, Rainbow Beach, Eumundi, Gympie, Bargara, Gladstone, Rockhampton, Yeppoon, Airlie Beach, Townsville, Innisfail, Cairns, Broome, Darwin, Adelaide, Victor Harbour, Goolwa and many others in between. I travelled many hundreds of kilometres around the back roads of Queensland and New South Wales, with my dear friend Bramani as chauffeur. I had only known Bramani for five years prior to Dan's disappearance, so she was a relatively new friend. We met at a Workplace Bullying Support Group and became close; I respected her immensely, and she was smart, funny and tremendously compassionate. She said she thought the same of me, and our friendship blossomed into a sisterhood. We are now family.

Bramani grew up in the Northern Rivers area of New South Wales and knew her way around. She was a tower of strength to me at this time, and her good humour made a number of our 'getting lost' occasions memorable by saying, "We are here because we are supposed to be here." I was forever hopeful that fate had brought us to where we were because Dan might be there. He never was, but what stood out to me on those travels was how kind and thoughtful people were, and I always left feeling that if Dan came that way he would be cared for.

Des and I travelled to Darwin, not because of a sighting but because we hadn't searched there before and the weather was conducive to someone living a lifestyle we imagined Dan might be. We did our normal routine of visiting the local police station, soup kitchens and homelessness services. The second night we were there, we went to a local park where volunteers were providing free meals from a van, and spoke to the woman who appeared to be in charge. We explained that our son was missing—we were there searching for him—and asked if she had come across a young man matching Dan's description. She ushered us around to the back of the van where the food was dispensed, and pointed. An A3 coloured poster of Dan displayed for all to see. We were taken aback yet again, amazed Dan was well known in faraway Darwin. Tears of gratitude welled, and I let them fall.

NINETEEN

Finding Dan

I remember the day clearly. It was a sunny Monday in March 2016, and I was in the kitchen baking cookies to take to the Missing Persons Advocacy Network (MPAN) board meeting being held that evening in Melbourne. Des, as usual, was pottering around the garden and cleaning out the void at the side of our house. At 102 years of age, his mum had just moved into an aged care facility and we'd inherited a lot of her precious furniture and mementos that the girls wanted us to keep until they had space for them.

I was standing at the sink when I heard a kind of noise I'd never heard before. It sounded like a wounded beast, but worse. I saw Des walking to the front garden so I knew he was okay, but the noise was absolutely chilling. I rushed out to meet him, expecting to see a bloodied hand or missing finger. His face was contorted in shock and I looked at him for answers. Slowly and painfully he said, "I've found Dan." I knew instantly what he meant and collapsed into his arms wailing.

Des is an amazing human being; he still had the presence of mind to call the girls and then the police. It was the longest, most surreal afternoon and evening of our lives. We all waited together while police undertook the necessary tasks, and finally around 11pm I could say my final goodbye. I couldn't touch or hold my son as he was just too fragile – I could only speak tenderly to a black body bag. Words fail to adequately convey the shock, disbelief and grief.

Behind the scenes, Des was a mess. His steadfast faith that Dan would come home when he was ready was shattered in the moment his eyes adjusted in the near pitch black to see his son hanging from a floor truss. I can only imagine it would've taken some seconds for the brain to recognise what it was looking at in the dark crevasse; the terror must have been profound. I am devastated that his father was the one to find Dan, but perhaps that's how it was meant to be – Des was the last one to see him before he disappeared, and the first one to see him when found. There had been no one else in between.

Our nationwide campaign to find Dan had been called *Dan Come Home* – the irony surely lost on no one, and excruciating for Loren in particular (who had devoted her life to it and the search). A police officer came into our kitchen and explained the location Dan was found, and I instantly remembered that there was space behind the walls. (It's important to note here that two relatives had checked this seemingly inaccessible crevasse the day after Dan vanished. There was a lot of stuff jam-packed into the tight space and it seemed undisturbed.) It appeared Dan was still wearing the same clothes he was reported as wearing at the time of his disappearance, and the officer doubted the remains were anyone's but his.

I couldn't comprehend that my beautiful boy, who was so dearly loved and cherished, was gone. Though DNA testing hadn't yet been done, I knew it couldn't have been anyone else. No one knew this space behind the walls of the downstairs area—cut out of a solid limestone hill—existed except for Dan and Loren, who as kids would play under the house before the walls of this room were completed a few years after we'd moved in.

Dan's words from the morning before he left suddenly came back to me: "I want to be where nobody can see me." If my mother-in-law hadn't moved, and the girls hadn't wanted her belongings as mementos, it's not inconceivable that Dan could have been there forever. That we would have continued on that harrowing journey so many others we now know endure, and die never knowing. Fortunately, fate decided it was time for Dan to come home.

My mother-in-law Dot was a remarkable woman, and our bond was more like that of mother–daughter. We'd built our home just around the corner from 'Mum', with the intention of caring for her when she could no longer care for herself. We had a room ready for when the time was right, but she never needed that degree of care. Des visited her every morning, taking care of the garden and whatever else needed attention, and I visited every second day with homemade food and time to take her shopping. She stopped driving at 98 years of age and we were all pleased that she had made this decision for herself rather than having it forced upon her. I happily became her chauffeur.

Dot *loved* shopping. I think it was more about socialising than anything else – living such a long life means a lot of people at the shops recognise you and want to chat. She truly was extraordinary and everybody who knew her adored her.

At 102, and after a number of falls, she decided to move into an aged care facility where she knew a number of the other residents. Once again, we were pleased she had made this decision for herself. Self-determination is immensely important when making decisions about your life; it gives you the power to make your own choices unfettered by others.

Dot was a loving and caring grandmother to my children and very supportive to me, too. She often told me how much she loved me, and how glad she was to have me come into her life. She often told me I was an exceptional mother and that my children were lucky to have me for a mum, and that Des was fortunate to have me as his wife. We shared over 40 years of friendship with never a word of anger or derision; we were all better off for having this incredible woman in our lives, and my girls have the happiest memories of their nana. Plus, it was her decision that ultimately led us to finding Dan.

Would I rather not know, or spend the rest of my years searching and hoping? I honestly don't know. Hope was a comforter that kept me cosy, warm and sane, and then suddenly I had to deal with the unimaginable. But now, with time, I can admit it's a relief to no longer have the desperate need to travel and search. Peering at faces unknown in a crowd and the urge to wake someone sleeping on the street, to see if it's Dan.

As a family we were disappointed with the police inaction in the early days of Dan's disappearance, but we believe they have learned from these errors and that other families will benefit from such in the future. Two major regrets for me were allowing a stranger (the PI) access to my family at a very vulnerable time, and that my husband found his son in the way he did. Des will struggle with this for the rest of his life; it didn't need to be this way. Had any of the actions we requested in the early days been taken, Dan would have been found within 24 hours. Had police resources been available at this time, it would have saved the significant resources expended over nearly five years, by Victoria Police, Queensland Police and our family. "A stitch in time saves nine," my mother used to always say.

Having Dan go missing was horrific, and having the PI make the allegations he did deeply upset me. Nothing could change the fact that our child had died and the pain was monumental. Des and I both knew and understood the circumstances of our child's death, and we didn't feel that anything would be gained by having a full coronial inquest. We were in agreeance with the coroner to make a finding without the need to hold an inquest.

The coronial process wasn't as daunting as I'd anticipated. The staff were pleasant and caring, but given there were numerous and credible others involved in assisting us with our search, I question the evidence that police relied upon to come to the conclusion that it was vital for the PI to give a statement, evidence I have never been told about. His statement was bizarre, and the coroner concluded that there was nothing in his claims that would have assisted the coronial process. I have asked this PI on a number of occasions the reason for his very odd behaviour, and he simply continues to suggest that I know why. My insistence that I do not is always where it rests.

Another thing that caused me concern was some of the reports made to the coroner that were blatantly wrong. I won't go into precise detail, but will mention a few things. A witness statement from a particular police officer contained so many errors I wondered if it was purposeful or just human error. He had said things like, "During this time I requested permission to inspect Dan's bedroom. The family were reluctant to have this occur," and "I subtly suggested that it may be helpful if I were able to walk through the house and Dan's bedroom," and "It is apparent that the family were far from comfortable with the suggestion that I look through the home," and "Missing persons investigation such as this (non-suspicious) matter did not provide for any power of entry or search unless by formal occupier owner consent," and "On that basis I did not have any legislative power of search available to me," and "There is no doubt in my mind that had I pressed the matter of search further, I would have most certainly been refused," and "I spoke with Detective Senior Constable _____ regarding the investigation and house search. Officer _____ stated that it (house search) had not occurred and the family assured him it was not necessary."

This officer was wrong in his assumption that we would have disagreed to a search and would have refused any such request. It would not have "most certainly been refused" – a search of the area is what we had all wanted from the beginning. My family never "assured" police or anyone that it wasn't necessary to search our house; we would have welcomed such an offer.

None of it was true. On this officer's first visit to our home, I asked if he

Finding Dan

would like to see Dan's room. He declined and that was it. As a result, distressed non-resident family members did search our property (as mentioned earlier), and the girls had frantically searched the surrounding parks and reserves surrounding our property but found nothing. Naturally, we believed he must have travelled further away.

When Dan was found, I saw a nationally televised interview with this officer. He stated that when Dan disappeared "an extensive search of the family property was undertaken by police." There was no search of any of the property, let alone an *extensive* search. Again, he seemed to be having it both ways – his media statement completely contradicted his statement to the coroner.

Weeks before Dan was found, a local estate agent was offering 'free' house appraisals in our area, and an agent attended our home. I was busy with friends as we were celebrating a birthday, so Des took him through our home and outside. The agent asked to view the area at the side of the house, but it was packed to the rafters with all the aforementioned stuff (lounge suits, wardrobes, tables, you name it). Understandably, Des was reluctant to show the dark, messy and largely impenetrable space and it didn't consider it necessary for appraisal purposes. After Dan was found, the agent contacted police suddenly suspicious that Des wouldn't let him into the area near where Dan was eventually found, and the police took a statement. There was nothing sinister in Des's refusal to allow him to see this area, but it's innocent instances like these that give grist to the rumour mill. Needless to say, we'll never accept a free market appraisal again.

There are times I wondered if I'd lost touch with reality, for so much of what I read in the various reports was incorrect, and I couldn't understand how. The case was full of emotionally-charged experiences, and I believe that in some cases things were written in such a way as to protect the writer rather than get to the truth. I was interested that the coroner believed some such details important enough to include in his findings, and of course I now realise that part of his role is to consider rumour and innuendo in the off-chance there is a grain of truth sprinkled here and there. But in our case, it was simply, tragically, exactly as it appeared: Dan had decided to end his life, and his illness prevented him from being able to comprehend the repercussions that would be inflicted on his family. I am sure that had he known of the torture we had to endure then his decision may well have been different. All the love in the world couldn't save him, and I honestly believe he thought he was saving us of the burden of him. He wasn't to know that his decision would catapult us all into lifelong grieving.

Organising a funeral befitting our dear Dan and the complex context was exceptionally difficult. We were infinitely fortunate to be guided by Loren's unflappable friend and founder of the Natural Death Advocacy Network (NDAN), Pia Interlandi. She introduced us to the wonderful team at Natural Grace Holistic Funeral Care whose compassion, flexibility, sensitivity and professionalism blew us all away. Between Pia and Libby (the director at Natural Grace), nothing was impossible. The extent of thoughtfulness they demonstrated over that period of time could be a book in itself, so I will just touch on a few details.

Pia planned various activities that allowed the family to have a heartfelt goodbye over the weeks between his discovery and his burial. She brought ink, paint and markers to our home, gently encouraging us to decorate our family's Christmas tablecloth (that I had made myself many years before, when I couldn't find a tablecloth big enough for our dining table). Immediate family members pressed their hands into different colours of ink and firmly placed them onto the spaces we'd ordinarily be seated at for Christmas lunch. It was a beautiful, thick white damask fabric with a silver border, and Dan had spent many a happy Christmas lunch around it. When all handprints were pressed, messages written and illustrations complete, Pia took the tablecloth away – it was to become Dan's burial shroud. She wrapped Dan with all the gentleness and care we could have ever hoped for. It covered him perfectly, and my handprints had happened to rest over his heart.

Pia took plaster casts of every family member's hand (a first for Dot, at 103), and once set they were lovingly placed around Dan as a symbol that we would always be holding him. The evening before our final goodbye, Dan was brought home to be with us and placed in one of his favourite spots: in front of the fireplace where he liked to lay on cold winter nights. We ordered in his favourite Thai takeaway and sat around reminiscing late into the night.

The funeral was held in Geelong's Saint Mary of the Angels Basilica, with our dear family friend James as master of ceremonies. Between eulogies, another very close family friend Steve (an operatic tenor) sang classics like 'Oh, Danny Boy' and 'Bring Him Home' – the entire church was weeping. The whole ceremony was testimony of our love for our son and brother. Media had been formally requested to respect our privacy and the police had kindly offered to cordon off the streets surrounding the church after the service for the procession. The church uncharacteristically, allowed for the grounds to be transformed into a picnic area, where we had coffee caravans, food trucks and drinks supplied by the pub across the road (owned by one of Dan's friends).

Similarly, we wanted something different for Dan's resting place. Dan was too special for something ordinary, and since one of his favourite places on earth was Queenscliff (35kms away with lovely beaches the kids played at in summer holidays) we decided on Queenscliff Cemetery's Mona Walk that was just in the final stages of completion. He was laid to rest in this beautiful bush setting, birds singing and waves crashing in the distance. We visit on special occasions, but his grave makes it all so real and distressing. I still find it very difficult to accept my beautiful boy is really gone.

After our immediate family had lovingly laid Dan to rest, we returned home—where dozens of close family friends awaited—and lit a campfire in his favourite spot, where he spent his last night on earth. We hadn't known what to do with all of his missing person posters (some as big as billboards – leftovers from a national advertising campaign Loren had coordinated)? We weren't comfortable putting anything with his face in the rubbish. However, in many cultures, fire is used for ceremonial cleansing.

My kindergarten friend Anne had come down from Queensland to be with us, and she and I spent the day before the funeral rolling up the posters, tying red ribbon around the bundles and placing them in a basket. Friends and family each took a bundle, reflecting on their own memories with Dan (spoken or silent), placed it in the fire. After all the search collateral had been burned, I placed the brown paper package containing the clothes he was wearing that day into the fire and said, "I love you, Dan" as the flames caressed it until it was gone.

The birth of a child is a wondrous experience and typically creates a bond between the two parents. If the child dies, or suffers severe illness, this bond can sadly be broken. For Des and me, the bond remained intact. I believe this was because neither of us blamed the other; blame is toxic and can destroy a once-loving relationship. Des was a great father, and over Dan's 24 years he shared a caring and loving bond with his son, as he did with me. We never played the blame game – we didn't need to. Our bond couldn't save Dan, which proves how powerful an influence mental illness can be to rational thought. We mourn Dan every day; he is never more than a second away from my thoughts, and he lives peacefully just below my surface.

In Greek mythology, the Trojan War took place between the Greeks and the people of Troy, reportedly over a period of ten years. The Greeks decided it was time to end this war and extended a gift to Troy in the form of a large wooden horse, which Troy took within its walls. When the Trojans were asleep, Greek soldiers sprang out of the horse and killed the guards on the walls and a battle ensued. The Greeks prevailed and so ended the city of Troy. A saying stemming from this myth is, "Beware of Greeks bearing gifts." I forgot the moral of this story and fell for the same strategy, one which bore me such grief I didn't think I would survive.

I mentioned earlier my regret for not doing my due diligence on that PI, letting him into our lives at our most vulnerable. Had I done my homework, below is what I may have found. (It was mid-2011 when he offered his services pro bono, and I didn't do any form of background checking until 2016 – nearly five years after we parted ways. I now feel quite sure that this PI was working under the instruction of someone else – who, I will leave to you to wonder.)

This PI's website depicted a team of nice-looking people, suggesting they were employees. They were stock photos (generic images sourced from the internet) – something people of my generation often aren't so adept at identifying. The website stated, "The collective relationship between Arthur's diverse experience and his hand-picked specialist team of investigators is the core strength of Private Investigators Now." I believe this hand-picked team of specialists consisted only of Arthur and Rachelle, and I would be interested to know what qualifications they've ever held to advertise as specialists, if any.

Their office was listed as being on Little Collins Street, Melbourne – a surprisingly prestigious business address. "You can visit us in person at our Head Office, Level 5, Suite 5.04 365 Little Collins Street Melbourne," it said. However, they actually only had a post office box there; it was a virtual office. I discovered this after trying to visit one day – there was no office, let alone a head office.

I did some reading online and came across the below advice in regards to hiring a private investigator:

"Make sure they have an office. If your private detective only works out of restaurants and over the phone, that is a sign you should get out now. You need to know where to find this person if they don't follow through on their obligations." (From Angie'sList.com.)

Finding Dan

This PI *did* appear to only work out of cafes and by phone. Uh oh.

"Scratch a PI off your list if he conducts business only at restaurants, by phone or through a mailbox address. Once you've handed him a payment, how do you know you'll be able to find him again? An orderly office can also be a window into the degree of his professionalism."

There was a time I offered to meet the PI at his office in Melbourne, and he said, "No, I'll visit you." He met Susie in a restaurant, and now I think I know why.

Another statement on his website said, "email our Accounts Department at: accounts@13004pinow.com.au." I highly doubt he had an Accounts Department, in the manner suggested. His business name was a derivative of a large American firm called PInow, who have an impressive and extensive online presence. Anyone doing a Google search may have thought this was the same firm, or that they were connected in some way. PInow America has confirmed that P.I.NOW was and is not affiliated with their business.

P.I.NOW's website states, "Trusted and Strictly Confidential." Certainly not what I experienced; he betrayed both my trust and his client's confidentiality.

"The team at P.I.NOW will handle your case with the highest regard with an understanding, empathetic & culture sensitive approach to all domestic & corporate matters. If you need to hire a private investigator in Melbourne, turn to us; we are a full-service private investigations firm and we treat each and every single client's circumstance with the respect and it deserves." All the content was fluff that appeared copied and pasted from other websites.

This PI didn't use his real name, but a derivative of his real name; he may have had it changed by deed poll, but clients—especially in such delicate matters—deserve to know who they're dealing with.

What I found really concerning was that this PI appeared to have a number of supportive reviews on his Facebook page. Though I now wonder how many were written by family, friends, himself and the increasingly common 'bots' that infiltrate these spaces. Some may even have been intended for the American firm of PInow, as a few of these came up when I conducted my own search.

The purpose of Facebook's review function is for genuine customers to review the business' services, to better inform potential clients. This PI has 68 reviews, 52 of which allocated a 5-star rating. Only a few gave him 1 star.

The reviews (increasingly flooded with spam bots talking about cryptocurrency) came from California, Texas, Massachusetts, Mississippi, Fort Lauderdale, Florida, Oklahoma, Indonesia, Bakersfield, Utah, Baltimore, Michigan, Canada, Japan, Namibia, the UK, Moscow, India and some places I have never heard of. Surprising for such a small, Melbourne-based team... The PI does state on his website that he has "Global Affiliates." These affiliates may have given him reviews, but of those I have been able to contact, no one actually knows him (surnames removed for their privacy):

Me: "Hi there, I noticed on P.I.NOW Melbourne's Facebook page you gave this person Arthur Athas a highly rated review. This man caused my family immense grief. Did you use his services personally? Are you happy to share your experience with me? Thanks so much, Lori"

Raymond L-T: "I don't even know this person"

Mac F: "lol.. I dnt know him, and never use his services.. u wrong bro..its not my account"

Joel H: "The name doesn't ring a bell..."

Dee P: "I think you have the wrong person. I didn't give anyone by that name a review rating. I don't give anyone a review rating, especially when I don't know them. Never heard that name or that person. Plus, I live in the States. Wouldn't give review for someone in Melbourne. Sorry."

Bob R: "I don't even understand what you are asking me."

I sent a message back to this last person:

"Sorry if I did not make myself clear, Bob. Do you know or have you ever used the services of Arthur Athas of P.I.NOW Melbourne, Australia? You are listed on his FB of making a review. Thanks, Lori"

Bob R: "oh, I have not. Im a private detective from the US and have never procured the services of some one overseas."

Message To: PInow.com – Trusted Network of Investigators (based in the US):

"Hi there, there is a firm of private investigators in Melbourne, Australia, that has the name P.I.NOW – are they related to your organisation?"

Response from PInow: "Greetings, they are not affiliated with us in any way. Best Regards, Debi, Administrative Coordinator"

Lastly, to Bravehearts, a terrific Australian charity protecting children. Their logo is advertised on the PI's website, but I wondered if there was authority to do so. Bravehearts' Community Fundraiser responsibilities state:

"As the Community Fundraiser, you must conduct the event in your club, group or business name and agree to be Bravehearts Inc.'s primary contact for the event. You must ensure that you and your partners, sponsors, associates and volunteers do not claim to represent Bravehearts Inc. nor claim to have any authority to act on behalf of Bravehearts Inc. At no time will any person affiliated with the third-party organiser of the external fundraising activity misleadingly present themselves as a staff member or volunteer of Bravehearts Inc. In addition, an event or activity organised by a third party external to Bravehearts Inc. is not an official Bravehearts Inc. event and must not be promoted as such. If you are raising funds for Bravehearts Inc., you may be required to present a Letter of Consent to Fundraise on behalf of Bravehearts to members of the public during your event or at any point in time during your fundraising journey. Upon approval of your event, you will be issued with a Letter of Consent to Fundraise as part of your Bravehearts Inc. Community Fundraising Kit.

The 'Bravehearts' logo may only be used with our permission for a limited time for the promotion of the event and the logo cannot be provided for placement on clothing, vehicles or other promotional material."

The Bravehearts website stated that this PI was listed in the team section with a goal of raising $5,000. Over two years he had raised $100. I don't believe this gave him continued authority to use Bravehearts' logo.

I want the final chapters of this book to focus on love and positivity, and so I have set out below the birthday wishes sent to Dan on the occasion of his 21st birthday. Loren was overseas at the time, so sent Dan some local artwork from Argentina with words (below) noted on the back.

> Dear kind, generous, honest Daniel,
> What a fantastic man I've had the joy of watching you become. I couldn't be more proud of you.
> Your nature is so endearing to all who are lucky enough to be in your life. I'm so sad I can't be sharing your 21st birthday with you, but i) you were away for mine (so it is only fair), and ii) the world has got to be seen (clearly, you're in agreement).
> I wish you all the very best for your next journey. Please be safe and call me every now and again to tell me how amazing it all is.
> I already miss you – we really must spend some time in the same country when we're older! You're the best little brother anyone could hope for... what a change from how I felt about you just a decade ago!!
> I love you so much. Always remember I will do anything for you. Trust in yourself and please never change who you are.
> Happy birthday from me and Alondra Morales (the artist) here in beautiful Buenos Aires.
> xx
> (This was purchased April 28th on Florida Street, only minutes after I was almost hit and killed by a bus. Always cross at the lights.)

In 2013, Loren established the Missing Persons Advocacy Network (MPAN) – an Australian charity that creates awareness for the individuals as well as the cause, whilst providing both practical and emotional support to those left behind. Since her little brother disappeared, Loren made it her life's work to advocate for other families who have unfortunately experienced the torment of ambiguous loss through 'missingness'. It's often said that something good can be found in loss, and for us this is true. Dan's legacy lives on; through Loren's love for him, he has brought help to many travelling the same road.

Frustrated at the lack of direction, information and resources available to families searching for missing loved ones, and coupled with constant requests for advice from families in a similar predicament, Loren's foundation project for MPAN was the world-first MissingPersonsGuide.com website. It provides a wealth of useful information including templates for media releases and posters, as well as contact databases for every media outlet, hospital, homelessness services (and more) around Australia.

Loren set aside her own career goals and has devoted herself entirely to this growing community issue. Every 10 minutes, someone is reported missing in Australia, and Loren has demonstrated her excellent communication and advocacy skills in successfully navigating the media to get this cause on the agenda. Articulate, passionate, and fiercely committed, she is frequently sought after by media to provide comment on the topic, and gains national and international attention for the work MPAN has done over the past decade. Loren works tirelessly, making herself available to desperate families at all hours. Despite her grief, she feels fortunate to have been given something that provides her with a sense of purpose.

She has made the issue mainstream – not something to be hidden away or ashamed of. Young people are talking about it, interviewing her for university assignments, broadening the narrative from the detrimental confines of the police categorisation it was reduced to before Dan disappeared. I know I'm biased, but Loren truly inspires wherever she goes.

Loren's dedication to finding her brother resulted in the largest social media campaign of its kind in the world (at the time), and that unprecedented public support led to this issue finally gaining the respect and dignified attention it deserves. I am so proud to be her mother.

Kate is another of Dan's very talented sisters. A lifelong thespian, she channelled her experience of Dan's disappearance into writing one-woman shows. First, at the Adelaide Fringe Festival in 2012 with *Life As I Knew It*, which aimed to help spread the word about Dan and share the plight of families of missing people. After Dan was found, Kate said she felt like the theatre was where she could talk about it. In 2017, *Losing You (twice)* premiered in Sydney, telling her story of grief and hope. She wanted to honour Dan and highlight the prevalence of male suicide and felt that writing it down into a play, and sharing that experience, helped her process her grief. Kate hoped her play would help further the conversation around mental illness and depression, and challenge the taboos of missingness, suicide and death.

Of course, as any mother would, I went to every performance of every show and laughed and cried all the way through them both. Kate is a very talented actor, writer and choreographer, and has found her niche in teaching these skills to the next generation. Dan would be very proud of his sisters, as I am.

TWENTY

Lawyers Not Liable

Whilst grieving the loss of Dan and the loss of myself, I needed a powerful distraction to keep me going. Time to take action against my former legal representatives was running out, and with statements made by both Robson and Warren—that any cause of action I may have would be against the lawyers—I initiated my Statement of Claim.

I initially chose my lawyer to represent me based on representations she had made in regard to her professional skills in the assessment of my claim for personal injury. These representations were made verbally by her, as well as in print, including advertising through a promotional card, the Yellow Pages and her business website. These representations, coupled with my lawyer's contribution to a book titled *Bullying in the Workplace*, led me to believe she had the necessary skills and empathy required to conduct my legal matter. On the bottom of her website, was the quote: "The people's good is the highest law."

In the beginning, I liked my lawyer very much, as she did me – there was even an offer of the possibility of my employment with her firm after my legal matters settled. It was an exciting offer, as I had developed an interest in the law and would have loved to be employed in such a field. But as the years rolled by I realised it wasn't going to happen.

In the early years, it was just the lack of contact that concerned me – messages left that were never returned. Over time, I began to feel ill whenever I needed to contact her as I felt like I was a nuisance. Fellow clients of hers told me they felt the same way. Progress reports were non-existent, so I rarely knew what was going on, and for someone like me this was causing unnecessary anxiety. There were so many examples of poor performance – far too many for the purposes of this book.

My first real concerns hit when I read my file in October 2003. Around eight months after the Magistrates' Court hearing, I saw a settlement agreement in my lawyer's file that wasn't signed by me. I hadn't event *seen* the agreement, let alone given her any instructions to settle on those terms. I would not have settled on those terms. The right to pursue compensation for an injury had been excluded, and when I raised this with her, she said that it would be included with my Serious Injury Application before the County Court. But, it wasn't. She hadn't raised this injury in the Serious Injury Application before the court; the judge's decision on this injury was silent. This injury would have met the 10% physical impairment level and would have attracted financial compensation for pain and suffering under the Accident Compensation Act 1984 without the need of a court decision.

For the first seven years, my lawyer and I had a reasonably good relationship, but as the years rolled by—two years, four years—I became restless with the lack of action on my claim. Every step of the process took months, or years, which only worsened my health at a time I wastrying to get my workplace injuries under control. It is a well-known fact that litigation can be one of life's most stressful experiences, and especially so where psychological injury is involved. As an experienced personal injury lawyer, she must have known this. From the time my claim was accepted, it took another five years to have my claim accepted as a work-related serious injury, and then another two years to get to the compensation hearing. By the time the compensation hearing was heard, it had been 10 years since the date of injury.

I recently read a headline in my local paper: 'Woman Allegedly Bashed Waits 18 Months for Court Hearing.' To me, it inferred that having to wait 18 months for justice was alarming. How would readers react to 'Seriously Injured Worker Waits 10 Years for Court Hearing'?

For WorkCover, delay and inaction is the order of the day, every day. An example of this was in June 2006 when I signed a Freedom of Information (FOI) Authority for my lawyer who was requesting documents from WorkCover. The FOI Authority wasn't sent until September 2007 – more than a year later. I once heard a judge say, "Justice is best served hot." In my case, and in many others, it's not served hot, warm or even cool, but frozen. (That's if it's served at all.)

I started to have a number of issues regarding my lawyer's representation of my legal action, which included—but was obviously not limited to—failure to provide a Conditional Costs Agreement for the first seven years of the retainer, and to provide me with progress reports as required under the Legal Professions Act. I formally asked nine times for information regarding costs, but for some unknown reason she would not respond to my requests.

In June 2009, after further and independent legal advice, I decided to change law firms to the one that fought for fair. They said they would take over the running of my case, and it was the first time in many years I felt confident I would have competent legal representation. I felt such relief, but just a week later they changed their mind and I don't know why. They suggested I contact another partner in the original firm and express my concerns at having lost faith and confidence in my lawyer. I contacted this partner and requested he manage my case, but he refused as I was told it would be embarrassing to my lawyer to make such a request. I feel it was at this point that my lawyer and I experienced the irreparable breakdown of our legal relationship. Her lack of communication and the delays in proceedings had caused far too much frustration. It was impacting my already fragile health.

Why didn't I just get another law firm? It was impossible. I tried, but failed to get away from this firm, namely because of the costs already incurred (which would need to be met by any new law firm).

A few weeks after speaking to another partner in the firm, I received a Conditional Costs Agreement, but it remained unsigned because I didn't understand it. I requested a meeting with the partner to discuss the contents, but he declined. I was told by Travis (the firm's junior lawyer) that I had to see her. The last time I had a conference with my principal lawyer was in December 2008 – the last time I ever met with her (except for the few minutes at the end of mediation). I didn't meet with her prior to the Supreme Court hearing in April 2010. So a period of 18 months had passed without seeing my principal lawyer, and after my discussion with another partner, there was no attempt by her to alleviate my concerns. In the end, this didn't matter because my proceedings in the Supreme Court settled on another basis – one that didn't require a Conditional Costs Agreement.

My lawyer caused me to incur unreasonable costs by not taking the legal steps required in a timely manner, sending 1000 photocopies to a medical practitioner, and briefing a barrister to attend a directions hearing on my behalf when I was told that the directions hearing would be 'on the papers', to name a few of my misgivings.

By email, I expressed a desire to attend the June 2009 directions hearing. After the mediation in May 2009, Travis told me that the directions hearing set for June 2009 would be 'on the papers' (so attendance was not required). After the directions hearing, Travis told me a barrister was briefed to represent me at the hearing.

There appeared to me so much unreasonable delay throughout the entirety, despite my lawyer understanding I was eager to have the matter settled as soon as possible due to the way litigation was affecting my health. It was preposterous that she didn't have my case ready for trial in April 2010. It took longer than the two world wars combined to have my compensation case ready for hearing in the Supreme Court. My lawyer did not take action to navigate the legal processes in a timely manner, and I could not understand why no one cared about this. In whose interests was this serving? Certainly not mine.

Delay was very obviously the game plan. In April 2004, I signed a Request for Conciliation that wasn't submitted until five weeks later, missing the deadline by four weeks.

In August 2006, I was told that the next directions hearing for my matter was set down for mid-April 2007. When I asked why so long a wait, I was told that lawyers had no control over the court timetable. Out of interest, I called the County Court Registry and asked how the listing system worked. To my surprise, I was asked if I wanted an earlier directions hearing date. I responded in the affirmative and the date was brought forward to mid-January 2007, stupefying my lawyer.

In a phone conversation in June of 2009, Travis told me that at a June 2009 directions hearing it was requested that a date for hearing not be before November 2009 because Travis stated appointments with "medico-legal" were taking five months. A week or so later I asked one of my treaters—a provider of medico-legal services—if it was taking five months to get appointments with him and/or other services, and his response was "No."

My lawyer's initial timeline to conclusion of my case (as asked in 2003) took far longer than two years, and I do not believe I received the personal care advertised in her promotional material. Over the period of November 2002 to April 2010, five junior lawyers had control of my case; the last one being Travis. An average of almost one lawyer per 18 months, and this would have added to my costs as each lawyer had to familiarise themselves with my case. I understand that this is what lawyers do, but five in seven years was certainly not expected. Whenever there was a change of carriage of my matter I wasn't informed as to who my new lawyer was.

Another delay tactic—and there were many, but I will outline just a few—was in December 2009 when Travis sent an email telling me that he was adjourning my matter set for hearing in the Supreme Court in April 2010 because witness BB would be absent in the first week of my trial. Travis told me that I would be on the stand for one day, so BB had to be there. This was clearly wrong – I was on the stand for seven days. At some point, the dynamics of my case changed from delay to destroy.

Also in December, I was told that Mr Phillip Jewel SC had my case "pencilled in his diary," but he later said he wasn't available after all, yet he *was* available to represent Loiterton whose case started on the same day as mine. The hunt for senior counsel was on again.

The months and years leading up to my hearing in the Supreme Court were distressing for me, as my lawyer wanted to adjourn the case for another seven months because she wasn't ready to proceed to trial because she had failed to brief a barrister. By then I knew "seven months" really meant another year, and I just wasn't prepared to wait another year.

Much later, in 2017, a former client of hers sent me an email which said, "The just and conscionable barristers around Melbourne wouldn't work with her in the end (got that from the horse's mouth) and any decent young solicitors she hired only stayed a few months at CTT and then moved on – got that from one of those young solicitors direct." Whether this was the real problem I don't know, but around 2014 this law firm was sold off and closed down, which didn't surprise me at all. I had no issue with the other two partners, except for their inability to assist her clients when faced with her negligence. Protecting her ego was a higher priority than fiduciary duties owed to clients.

A few days before trial I attended the Supreme Court Registry to file documents terminating the retainer with my lawyer and to proceed as a Self-Represented Litigant, but the Registry refused to file my summons. I feel the Registry informed my lawyer of this and my lawyer then made desperate attempts to get a barrister to represent me. For, if her retainer was terminated because she was not ready to proceed to trial, she may not have been able to claim all her costs.

I visited my lawyer's office to inform her that her services were terminated because of her failure to have my case ready for trial, and while I was sitting in Travis's office ready to say this—as if by magic—a barrister was briefed. Again, *why* Craig Harrison accepted the brief when he was representing Loiterton, and why Mr Jewel who was supposedly representing me represented Loiterton, is unknown.

On the first day of trial, Judge Robson stated that he only received the court book "yesterday." Supposedly, court books need to be filed seven days prior hearing, and the reason I believe this wasn't done is that my lawyer had no intention of conducting my matter on the said day. I believe she informed the court that she would be seeking an adjournment and this is why there was no judge allocated to hear my matter. When it was known that I had intentions of representing myself, a judge was hastily found. Unfortunately for me, this judge had never before conducted a personal injury trial, nor had he conducted a jury trial. This certainly contributed to my claim of an unfair trial, details of which are outlined in previous chapters.

Understandably, my relationship with my senior lawyer had completely broken down by this point, and I believe that's partly why she colluded to 'throw' my case. She did not seem to care about me or my rights and simply wanted out on the best possible terms for her. The power imbalance was truly frightening – I had waited 10 years for my matter to be heard and finally resolved. As she was my advocate, I was completely reliant on my lawyer's professionalism. I was yet to understand that this duty of care is ignored when it suits, and there's nothing that can be done about it.

My lawyer had a copy of a document titled 'FDC Staff Allegation of Harassment' dated 19 April 2001. She knew this document was the cause of great distress for me, and yet she caused this document to be tendered in my hearing. This document is hearsay and contained unsubstantiated allegations against me. This document was clearly prejudicial to my case; had I known my lawyer had plans to tender it, I would have instructed her not to do so. It would have been up to the defendant to have tendered this document in cross-examination, but the defendant *couldn't* have done so, as this document was inadmissible under the hearsay rule. But no matter, the defendant was fortunate that my own legal team tendered into evidence a document beneficial to the defendant. Their 'silver bullet', as I have referred to earlier.

I won't go into further detail regarding the April hearing or the June hearing, as they are extensively covered in previous chapters, but what I do wish to reiterate with strong conviction is that the June hearing was purposely orchestrated to thwart any claim I might bring against my former legal representatives by providing them the opportunity to say derogatory and defamatory remarks without sanction or proof, giving the judge the mantel to repeat these words in his judgement, forever dooming me to a life of the unbelieved, the just disgruntled and simply sour grapes.

I know I have been guilty myself of dismissing a person or situation when these words are trotted out, but now I ask myself why – why was this person disgruntled? The pen can certainly be more powerful than the sword.

Added bonuses to their play was advocate's immunity, witness immunity and proceeding immunity. At the time I wasn't aware of these terms or their significance but I've come to understand that even when perjury is committed it's protected by witness immunity, and most wrongdoing by a judge is protected under proceeding immunity. This is why my former legal team were so willing and prepared to come and be cross-examined by me: they needed it.

Was it all a set up? I will leave that to you to decide. It's my understanding that these immunities fail when breaches of the Legal Professions Act and conspiracy to pervert the course of justice come into play. But even if a litigant can prove this, nothing will happen because your labels of being angry, aggressive and a chronic complainer will protect them. This is exactly why these terms are used (with immunity) and exactly why the judge repeated them.

I already touched on the behaviour of the barristers in previous chapters, so will only add a little. I met Craig Harrison a day before the scheduled five-to-six-week trial. I didn't understand then how easily I was coerced, but can now see it was likely due to a number of relevant factors. I was considerably unwell, I had been on this giddy merry-go-round for 10 years, I had faith in our system of justice, and I trusted comments made in my presence (which I now identify as gaslighting). Like a lamb to the slaughter.

Such comments included those relating to the barrister's grandchildren, particularly the three-year-old who lived with a disability, and his daughter who was ill with multiple sclerosis and unable to care for her children as a result. The barrister had care of his grandchildren while their mother lived in Mildura, and it was his wedding anniversary that day and he spoke so lovingly to his wife on the phone. I didn't need to know about his personal life, but this information certainly led me to believe he was a good person and the right fit for me, so I trusted him implicitly. To this day, I don't know if any of those comments were true or just said as a form of manipulation, as some barristers in the personal injury field are masters of this form of fast-tracked Stockholm syndrome committed on vulnerable clients.

Harrison stated in his evidence in the June 2010 hearing (while being cross-examined by me) that he wanted me to be sure that I wanted to settle because he didn't want me to "sue him." If (as he, Toop and Walsh contend) I willingly wanted to settle the proceedings on that Friday morning then there would be no need for such a response, unless Harrison knew he was doing something I did not want. Why would I sue him if I was happy with the settlement?

I met Matt Walsh two days before the hearing. He seemed nice enough, and I had no preconception to any malice; I genuinely believed he was there to help me. Just before the hearing commenced, Walsh tendered a document titled 'Further Particulars of Claim' dated that day and unsigned. When I later read this amended document, I disagreed with these four new points which would impact my claim of foreseeability and therefore negligence against my former employer, and I was at a loss to understand why he made the changes he did.

I was with Walsh all the previous day and he didn't say anything about changing this document, because if he had, I would have instructed him not to do so. It was basically changing a workplace bullying claim to a physical injury claim using the red herring of Graves' disease.

Walsh had responsibility to brief my witnesses, but it appeared that he didn't brief the witnesses or prepare their statements prior to trial. I now feel he didn't do this as he already knew—from day one of trial—there would be no witnesses but myself. I believe this was why I was on the stand for seven days – it gave the defendant the chance to ask irrelevant questions, and more than enough time to victim-blame. In the hearing of 4 June, Harrison testified under oath that he had a conference with my witness, BB. If this did occur, why hadn't he mentioned it, especially during the days of my trial? Unfortunately, I cannot confirm with BB, as we have lost contact over the years (not an uncommon occurrence in the days before social media).

I was told some time after Christmas 2010 that Tim Tobin had accepted the brief, but a week before trial Travis told me that Mr Tobin could not accept the brief because he had a circuit in three weeks' time and our case had an estimate of five weeks. I'm unsure at what point in time the decision was made that I would be getting a 'Clayton's trial' (nothing more and nothing less), but if I had to guess I would suggest around a year before it commenced.

Walsh said in cross-examination in the June hearing that he recalled being engaged to appear in my case with Mr Tim Tobin, and that he had spoken to Mr Tobin. Walsh thought it would've been on or about the Wednesday of the previous week (one week to trial) while they were both in the environs of the County Court appearing for clients in other matters. Walsh had discussions with Mr Tobin and said that Mr Tobin had said he had conferred with me. I have never met or had any conferences with Mr Tobin, and I cannot understand why Walsh would give such testimony and to what purpose. He must have known that I would know that this was untrue, but I hazard a guess he was confident in spinning the yarn in the court of his family friend and former business partner.

Having no senior counsel to represent me before my trial was extremely distressing; it was the reason I was being ordered to adjourn for another seven months, until November. Had I agreed to the adjournment, I'm confident it would never have gone ahead in November and I would have been told the court couldn't fit a five-to-six-week jury trial in before Christmas.

I felt I experienced numerous breaches of the 'Professional Conduct and Practice Rules 2005', principally that a practitioner must not, in the course of engaging in legal practice, engage in, or assist, conduct which is dishonest or otherwise discreditable to a practitioner and prejudicial to the administration of justice. Practitioners, in all their dealings with the courts, whether those dealings involve the obtaining and presentation of evidence, the preparation and filing of documents, or instructing an advocate or appearing as an advocate, should act with competence, honesty and candour. Practitioners should be frank in their responses and disclosures to the court. 'Should' seems like a free pass – it needs to be 'must'.

The Rules state that a practitioner must not knowingly make a misleading statement to a court, and that a practitioner must take all necessary steps to correct any misleading statement made by the practitioner to a court as soon as possible after the practitioner becomes aware that the statement was misleading.

And further, a practitioner must not seek to invoke the coercive powers of a court or to make allegations or suggestions in court against any person not reasonably justified by the material then available to the practitioner, or made principally in order to harass or embarrass the person. If the factual material available to the practitioner does not provide a proper basis for the allegation, a practitioner must not open as a fact any allegation which the practitioner does not then believe will be capable of support by the evidence which will be available to support the client's case.

A legal practitioner must not suggest criminality, fraud or other serious misconduct against any person in the course of the practitioner's address on the evidence unless the practitioner believes that the evidence in the case provides a proper basis for the suggestion. A practitioner must take all necessary steps to correct any false statement unknowingly made by the practitioner to the opponent as soon as possible after the practitioner becomes aware that the statement was false.

In all of their dealings with other practitioners, practitioners should act with honesty, fairness and courtesy, and adhere faithfully to their undertakings, in order to transact lawfully and competently the business which they undertake for their clients in a manner that is consistent with the public interest.

I believe the public interest is not served when a practitioner remains silent in the court while knowing the court is being deceived (as in my experience).

The Rules say further that a practitioner must not, in any communication with another person on behalf of a client, represent to that person that anything is true which the practitioner knows, or reasonably believes, is untrue; or make any statement that is calculated to mislead or intimidate the other person, and which grossly exceeds the legitimate assertion of the rights or entitlement of the practitioner's client. I believe the defendant was guilty of this on a number of occasions – for example, in the April hearing, the defence barrister made the allegation I had written to the DPP when he knew that I had not, and in the June hearing he gave testimony under oath that he had sought and been given leave of the court to continue my cross-examination.

Also outlined in the Rules is that a practitioner must not engage in conduct, whether in the course of practice or otherwise, which is, dishonest; calculated, or likely to a material degree, to be prejudicial to the administration of justice. I experienced dishonesty and calculated behaviour that was prejudicial, but I have since learnt from my experiences that the "administration of justice" is just a throwaway line to be used to stop disgruntled users of the legal system pursuing claims of an unfair trial. The "administration of justice" is given priority over the legal and human rights of litigants, especially self-represented litigants. There is no way you can fight this, as the 'wagons are circled' and you are outside the perimeter, alone and defenceless.

The Rules go on to state that a practitioner must promptly disclose to RPA (Recognised Professional Associations) and the Legal Practice Board the occurrence of any conduct which is contrary to rule outlined previously and any conduct or event which may reasonably be regarded as adversely prejudicing a practitioner's ability to practise according to these rules. For me, the expectation that a legal practitioner inform on another's misconduct is simply never going to happen. When the defendant barrister gave false testimony, my legal team knew it was false, but it suited their purposes so they decided not to disclose it. I doubt there has ever been an occasion where a legal practitioner has disclosed misconduct in the running of a trial.

Legal practitioners are officers of the court and are bound by strict rules that are rarely enforced; the Rules are window dressing to give the appearance to the community that there are laws in place to keep legal practitioners' behaviour in check. For example, in the June hearing to have the settlement set aside, Toop stated that "there was no evidence of complaint by Mrs O'Keeffe that the stress caused by her work had any detrimental effect on her."

How could this be true? She had access to the many medical reports that stated that the bullying did have a detrimental effect on me, and Judge Misso found I had suffered from harassment and bullying. If Toop held this misguided belief, then why did she represent me for many years, and represent me falsely? Why did she incur costs on a claim she believed would fail? The barrister Walsh accused me of being a "chronic complainer" and yet Toop stated under oath there was no evidence of my making a complaint.

I have highlighted above some of the Rules, and from my reading many other people have also experienced injustice in the court primarily by their own legal representatives – and on occasions also sanctioned by the judge. One only has to google "corrupt courts and judges" and see the hundreds of stories, case studies and reports on this topic to know it is very real and a very real problem.

It is an offence to break these Rules, but good luck with getting anyone to help you – the legal practitioners seem a protected species. Even the brave don't take them on as they know it's a waste of time; the system and judges would never find against a friend. My experiences are testament to that, and I feel no one could have put up a better fight than I attempted to.

For a legal practitioner to have their practising certificate suspended or cancelled, it has to be proved they are no longer a fit and proper person to hold the certificate. This does happen on occasion when tax fraud or stealing from client trust funds occur, but I cannot find a case where a practising certificate was cancelled due to the misconduct of a client's case, which seems far more serious to the "administration of justice" than tax evasion or thievery.

All through my years with my lawyer, and right up and during the trial, I was told so many untruths that—as an honest person—it stunned me. Of course, I wasn't aware of a lot of this until I received my complete lawyer file in 2014. I will set out but a few as an example.

I was told my claim would take two years to resolution, when in fact it took seven years – and no resolution for me, only resolution for my lawyer.

A Memorandum of Advice dated May 2009 stated "for the Plaintiff to anticipate that Counsel will run her trial on a 'no win, no fee' basis is unrealistic." This was not said to me on this day, and if this was indeed correct, I should have already been informed and then I may have no longer been unrealistic. I did not see this memorandum until mid-2014 when I gained access to my legal file, and from past experience I have learned that documents aren't always written on the date stated.

There was a file note dated 12 April 2010 (a day before trial) and a notation on this file note said, "H/C decision in *Colar*." As of that date, this High Court case had not been discussed with me, and I believe if Harrison or Travis were so familiar with this case, since they 'often' discussed it with me, they would know how to spell 'Koehler'. They either didn't know, or they believed *Koehler* wasn't applicable to my case. I feel there were additions to file notes and memorandums written after the stated date in order to provide 'proof' that I was informed in case it became necessary to 'prove'.

I'm no conspiracy theorist, however, I have no doubt—given the evidence I have provided through my story—that I was the victim of a conspiracy perpetrated against me – initially by my own legal team and the defendant legal team, and in the end the judge as well. If the Febriano scenario didn't exist then I might still have some doubt, but as it does exist I am in no doubt. In Fleming's *The Law of Torts* it is stated, "The conspiracy doctrine . . . condemns as actionable any combination by two or more persons to injure the plaintiff, though the means employed be lawful, if its purpose is 'unjustifiable'."

Criminal Law by P. Gillies states "That proof of a conspiracy may be determined 'where the evidence of the alleged co-conspirators' acts and words is such that, when these doings are viewed collectively, no other conclusion is reasonably possible than that a given defendant was united in a conspiracy with these others."

And further, Section 3 of 'Conspiracy to pervert the course of justice' states, "The substantive offence (the essential element of it) does not require that D actually has interfered with the course of justice. It is enough that D's conduct has this tendency or potential."

I briefly read through Archibald's *Criminal Pleadings, Evidence & Facts*, which states, "A conspiracy to obstruct the course of justice . . . (may involve) . . . a conspiracy to fabricate evidence or to keep witnesses away from the court."

After I received my legal file, I found many file notes and memorandums which I don't believe were written on their said dates; one that particularity stands out to me is the memorandum written by Walsh dated 28 April 2010. It consisted of around five pages supposedly outlining difficulties with my case, giving the impression I was informed of these difficulties when I was not. As I was on the stand in court for seven days, not one, and the fact that my witnesses were not interviewed or even met, let alone a signed witness statement taken, leads me to conclude that my witnesses were certainly kept away from the court and kept from giving evidence.

Some other interesting documents I found in my legal file consisted of an email dated January 2009 from a cost advisor asking my lawyer if she wanted to hold off paying the County Court Originating Motion costs of $8,190 (due to the case being adjourned) so she could attempt to negotiate out of the costs orders when negotiating settlement. *When* negotiating settlement, not *if* a settlement is negotiated.

A memorandum dated 23 April 2010 stated, "Conference with Clients in early morning. Craig Harrison and Matt Walsh both have asked the client as with Travis in the presence of Travis Fewster, Lorraine signed an authority authorising us to put $100,000 all-in against Wyndham City Council."

Interestingly, the file details at the bottom of the page reference "30468/d/day 8 file memo 23-4-10.doc - 120510."

Is it possible these last numbers relate to the date the memo was actually written, that being 12 May 2010?

I did not sign any authority authorising my former legal team to put an offer of $100,000 to the defendant. If the evidence of Walsh was to be believed, he confirmed with the defendant barrister Mr Jens the evening prior asking if the $150,000 was still on the table and given this was the settled amount, it appears it was. No such authority for $100,000 was evidenced in my file.

A handwritten file note dated 23 April 2010 stated, "I, Lorraine O'Keefe, hereby authorise my lawyers to put $180,000 all-in to settle my damages claim against Wyndham City Council. Signed by L O'Keeffe."

I remember vividly that morning not wanting to sign anything, and I certainly did not sign any offers to the other side of $100,000 and $180,000, but interestingly my signature appeared on the above file note.

I repeat my comment from above – if the evidence of Walsh was to be believed, he confirmed with defendant barrister Mr Jens the evening prior asking if the $150,000 *was still* on the table, then why was he wasting precious time encouraging me to offer a higher figure? It had been known from before the beginning of the trial that the settlement sum was fixed at $150,000.

I have a vague and distant memory of signing a blank file note after signing the settlement agreement that morning. I had signed blank documents on request from my lawyer over the years. These two offers, supposedly put by me, are not mentioned or referred to in the transcript of the June hearing and there was only the settlement amount that was in the transcript. I can only assess that it was not mentioned as it was known that it could not be proven to be true.

Archibald goes on to state, "If a conspiracy is formed and a person joins it afterwards, he is equally guilty with the original conspirators." Does this mean the appeals processes heard by other judges (who if not believing me must have had some doubts given the evidence presented) are equally guilty? This may account for the Chief Justice of the High Court refusing to look up from the bench to his court and at me.

I am not sure where I first read this, but it was recorded that Hulls did say at one time that "lawyers need to abandon many of their adversarial traditions and join him in a cultural revolution based on an active, problem-solving judiciary."

This must have been said while he was the Attorney-General. Sadly, it seems he didn't have anyone join him in his cultural revolution, and nothing came of these utopian words.

TWENTY-ONE

I Rest My Case

In the June hearing before Judge Robson, he stated in his decision that I "may complain about the conduct of your previous lawyers in whatever forum you wish and that you may have a cause of action against your former solicitors, but that would be a cause of action in negligence or some other such case for bullying you into the settlement, which is really what you have said in your affidavit material." He also said, "The matters that she raises goes to questions that might be dealt with at taxation or in other proceedings that deal with the terms of her retainer with Clark Toop & Taylor. In my view it is unnecessary to me to resolve the matters raised in these proceedings."

He further stated that should I choose to pursue it, "with the opportunity to make allegations and proceed, probably by a separate action, against your former lawyers. It means that the settlement remains binding but you've got your case against your own lawyers and that's your remedy. It leaves you with a cause of action, a right of regress against your former lawyers, that's as far as it goes."

In my Court of Appeal judgement, Chief Justice Warren stated, "Whilst I express no view as to the efficacy or validity of the applicant's allegations with respect to her former solicitors and counsel, her cause of action, if any, lies against those parties and this is not a matter for the Court but a matter taken up elsewhere," and further, "her cause of action, if any, properly lies against her former lawyers."

Given these statements made by the court, it appeared to me that there was some belief that I could well have a cause of action against my former legal representatives, and with this in mind I needed to make a decision that was within time, as I felt an application to extend time would never be granted.

In early 2013, I made a request to Clark Toop & Taylor to release my legal file – of course it should almost go without saying that this was denied. They claimed a "lien" over my file, alleging that I still owed them fees, but I knew this was incorrect as the settlement monies were in full and final payment of all legal fees, and as Harrison said to me on the morning of 23 April 2010, "you will owe us nothing." My former lawyer ignored this, but failed.

I referred this stalemate back to the Supreme Court and my former lawyer was ordered to provide my file to me within 14 days. I received only one folder of documents when I knew my file consisted of 23 boxes, so it was back to court where the order was that I be provided the 23 boxes. The judge admonished my former lawyer for not providing all documents, and it was embarrassing to witness. I liked this judge, shame I wasn't lucky enough to have him hear my case; just sometimes the justice (or injustice) you get is based on luck. Through my experiences and research, I came to the conclusion that there are many good judges in this state and I was just unlucky.

After receiving my complete legal file in mid-2014, it took me many months to review and gather any evidence that may assist in bringing a claim in negligence against my former lawyer. In April 2016, I submitted my Statement of Claim. In my legal file I had found an email from my former lawyer that stated, "We settled her matter for $150,000 all-in on Friday client to get nothing!" To me, the use of an exclamation mark suggested my former lawyer was almost gleeful that her client received nothing. The email went on to say, "so Fiona u can now finalise those costs . . . Can u make sure I get as much as u can." In the June hearing, Travis referred to my case as being a 'dirty nappy' even though the actuary report assessed my case to be worth $745,868, and the barristers and Travis himself stated my claim to be worth around $600,000. My former lawyer received around $240,000 for representing me, while her client, me, received nothing – not bad for a dirty nappy.

I believe what occurred is exactly what happened in the decision in *ACN 131 110 220 PTY LTD v. Lakic*, which stated, "In these circumstances, the solicitors needed to ensure that a client was not advised to accept a settlement offer simply because the law practice believed it would be in its own best interests to withdraw from litigation with a compromise which enabled the solicitor to recover at least part of its costs and disbursements while leaving some limited compensation for the client." The defendant used the tactic of victim-blaming and the possible costs of a five-week trial, so my former lawyer folded. And, as I have said previously, even if the trial *had* run its course and I was successful, I still wouldn't have received any compensation as most funds would have been eaten up in legal fees. It seems this is exactly what WorkCover sets out to do to injured workers – to make the whole process worthless, and to leave the injured worker feeling worthless, as a warning to others.

I won't go into much detail concerning my Statement of Claim other than to say it was well researched and well written, with the assistance of a lawyer. From 2010 to 2015, I had attended the Supreme Court Registry on a number of occasions as a Self-Represented Litigant, and I'll give you an example of my experiences that took place on just one day. (It's important to note that this was the Thursday before the Easter long weekend and my matter was urgent.)

In the late morning, I rang the Registry to speak with A. Her phone rang three times then the line went dead. I rang again and John answered, and he responded that A was not around and he thought she might be at a conference. I asked to be put through to S, but he was with someone. I asked if he could please put me through to M, but his phone doesn't answer and I came back to John, who wanted to know if he could help. I told him that I'd sent—by express post—an envelope that contained a summons and an affidavit the previous evening, and I wanted to be sure they had arrived. John said he would look for me in S's office; he returned to the phone and said that he couldn't see anything that I'd described, but suggested it might come in the afternoon mail.

I asked to be put through to R; John said he thought R was at the same conference as A. I asked John to leave a message for S or M to call me that day, as soon as possible. Mid-afternoon S returned my call, and I asked him if he had received the envelope I'd sent. He said no – it hadn't arrived in today's mail. I asked him if it might arrive that afternoon but he said they only got one mail delivery per day. I informed him that John said it might arrive in the afternoon mail. S said he wasn't aware of a second mail delivery, as he wasn't an expert on the mail delivery system. I asked if I could serve a summons by mail and he referred me to the 'Court Rules on Service Section 6'. I felt he had a copy of these Rules in front of him and so I asked if he could look and let me know. He said "No," and that I would need to read the Rules as they are very complicated and long. (The role of the Self-Represented Litigants Coordinator is to give procedural information only; I believed that asking if I could serve a summons by mail was not asking for legal advice.)

I asked to speak to M, but S said he wasn't in that day. A short time later, I called the Practice Court number. It rang out, then disconnected. I looked at the Daily Listing to see which judge was listed for Practice Court, but none were named. It stated that urgent after-hours matters were to be directed to the associate – but which associate, when the judge isn't named and the Practice Court phone goes unanswered? (As was the case on 4 September 2010, when I called the three urgent phone numbers listed and none of them answered.)

I really needed information, so I next called the Principal Registrar whose phone rang out and disconnected. I tried the Prothonotary and his phone rang out and disconnected. I went back to the General Enquiries number and selected 7 for the Practice Court phone and it rang for five-and-a-half minutes, and then I hung up. I'm not a quitter by nature, and by now I was intrigued as to the failings of their customer service; this would never have happened at my former employer, as we were required to answer a phone within four rings – this was recorded and formed part of our Key Performance Indicators (KPIs).

I love a challenge, so around 3pm I called the Court Liaison Officer's phone, but it rang out and disconnected. Next, I tried the Operations & Improvement Manager – the line was engaged, so it was looking more hopeful as it appeared someone was actually in the office. I would call back if I couldn't get anyone else. A little later, I called the Chief Executive Officer's phone and was pleasantly surprised that it was answered by a staffer named Paul. I explained the difficulties I was having contacting anyone in the Registry, and he said they were "light-on" that day. He made some mention that it must be understood that it was Easter and that people did have the day off. I said I wasn't aware the Thursday was also a public holiday... In my previous employment, I couldn't ever imagine saying something similar to a parent who needed childcare after Easter.

Paul suggested that I ring the General Enquiries line. I told him that I had, and a few others as well. I suggested that phones in the Registry be fitted with answering machines/voicemails so callers would know if someone was away and to leave a message, rather than just have the phone ring out before disconnecting. He explained to me how busy he was and that he couldn't talk, and that he only answered this phone because it was ringing while he was walking past and that he really had to go. I felt that he was fobbing me off and was annoyed for answering it in the first place, but it was the CEO's phone after all.

At last, S called and told me that my express post envelope containing my affidavit and summons had not arrived that afternoon. (I always hand-deliver my documents to the Registry, because in the past documents sent by ordinary post didn't arrive in time.) On this occasion, I didn't want to travel to Melbourne on the eve of a public holiday, so I decided after conversation with my local postmaster that 'Express Post Guaranteed Next Day Delivery' would be the best way to ensure my documents arrived the next day.

I called Australia Post and spoke to a Linda, who explained that the Express Post envelope hadn't been scanned into the system, so they couldn't assist and it wasn't their problem. Linda told me that "Guaranteed does not mean guaranteed." I thought I was going insane. The documents I'd spent all day working on, had sworn by a lawyer so I could post prior to the Easter break, would have arrived *if* I'd sent them by ordinary mail and paid 60 cents instead of $6.10. We're talking central Geelong to central Melbourne (74kms). Australia Post assured me I'd get a refund and told me to have a happy Easter.

I sent A and S an email explaining what had occurred with Australia Post, attaching a copy of my summons and affidavit, and followed this up with a call a few minutes before 5pm to S to ensure they had received my email. The phone wasn't answered and I had to spend the long weekend hoping I met the deadline for filing my documents.

The danger of being a self-represented litigant is that Registry staff will obstruct you as much as possible. I don't necessarily believe it's always intended, but it just seems to stem from the way a self-represented litigant is perceived – they're not respected as a person using the courts who has every right to be there. On a previous visit to the Registry, I decided it would be the last time: I was sitting in the visitor area and saw an elderly gentleman at the Self-Representative Litigant window in discussions with the said Coordinator. My heart went out to this gentleman; he was elderly in age, a little stooped, but I saw a kind, wrinkled face. He was holding an old, tattered briefcase overflowing with paper, which I presumed were documents for his case. He said a friendly, "Goodbye" to the receptionist and slowly walked to the exit, and as he did so the receptionist said something to a colleague and they both laughed. I don't know what prompted the laugh, but it was in that moment I knew I could never go back to that place. I was fortunate enough to have some funds to feed the system, so I made the decision to engage a lawyer to assist me. I preferred to save myself the humiliation, and I needed to be sure my applications were legally sound.

I find it difficult to explain all the legal processes I had to battle my way through to bring my claim to the Common Law Division of the Professional Liability List, but I trust you have an understanding as to what my claims of negligence entailed from previous chapters. I will only briefly outline what they were, and due to the complexity will concentrate on my understanding of it all; I acknowledge that this will only be my understanding of the truth. The lawyer I retained to assist me believed I had a strong case, with a 50/50 chance of success.

In my evidence, I told the court about my lawyer's failure to provide a Conditional Costs Agreement or progress reports as required under the Legal Professions Act. I included evidence regarding the delay of my claim – I was initially told in mid-2003 that the WorkCover legal process would take two years to traverse the required statutory legal steps to conclusion. This was obviously wrong, or purposely misleading, as it ultimately took seven years. Had I been told the claim would potentially take seven years, I might not have continued.

At all times, my lawyer knew I was eager to have the matter settled as soon as possible, due to the effect litigation was having on my health. Ten years after injury, my lawyer still didn't have my case ready for trial. Witnesses weren't ready for trial, and even I—as a witness—wasn't ready. My understanding of court procedure was limited at this time, and I thought that the trial would focus on issues of negligence that led to my injury. I did not expect personal questions that bore no relevance to the matter at hand. I certainly was taken by surprise; the barrister Harrison failed in his duty to me by not objecting to the repetitious, oppressive and/or irrelevant lines of questioning.

Harrison was given a copy of a document (central to my suspension from work in mid-2001) by my lawyer, and I believe my lawyer was in breach of her obligations to work in the best interests of her client. I had given over this document in confidence. I had no reason to believe it would be used for any other purpose than to give my lawyer an understanding as to my distress. They must have known this document was hearsay, and as such WorkCover couldn't rely on it in legal proceedings. This document was prejudicial to my case, so why they made an informed choice to tender it, knowing it would damage my credit unfairly, was unknown at the time. It was only years later that I came to understand that that was precisely the reason why it was tendered. I estimate that even before the trial commenced, the decision was made that my case would settle, and to achieve this I had to be vilified to get the jury off-side in order to support the claim we had to settle because the jury didn't like me. Did a juror really make the comment "Yeah, sure" or was this a possible fabrication to force settlement? I later contacted the judge's associate who supposedly heard this comment and requested that he confirm what he had heard, but unfortunately, he refused to do so. Interestingly, I later found in my legal file an email from Walsh to Harrison dated 22 April at 10.32pm which stated "the Greek juror's response to the Plaintiff's answer was 'Yeah, sure' – I was the only person who heard this as I am closest to the jury."

The following morning, Walsh said to me that he, the lawyer Travis and the judge's associate had heard this comment, and he later included that Mr Jens had heard the comment as well. This was in conflict with his email and testimony he gave in court; whatever the truth is, no doubt it will never be known.

In the same email, Walsh stated that "the defendant has reput 150,000 all-in." I question the 're' prefix, as prior to this date I hadn't been informed of this offer.

In my file, just to complicate matters even further, there was a memorandum titled 'Day 8 on 23-4-2010' which stated, "Conference with Clients in early morning. Craig Harrison and Matt Walsh both have asked the client as with Travis in the presence of Travis Fewster, Lorraine signed an authority authorising us to put $100,000 all-in." Why would they be requesting that I sign an authority for a settlement of $100,000, when according to Walsh's email from the prior evening, "the defendant has reput 150,000 all-in"?

The file name at the bottom of the memorandum references "30468/d/day 8 file memo 23-4-10.doc – 120510". It's possible these last numbers relate to the date the memo was actually written, that being 12 May 2010; I believe this may have been a case of preparation of false documents to be used if proof of settlement negotiations was required – the minor detail of the actual date automatically appearing in the file bar was overlooked. Was this another example of the backdating of documents that I had previously experienced or is it the print date?

There is no doubt in my mind that my former barristers were the masters of gaslighting, attempting to make me doubt my own reality and continually denying they said or did things even though they failed to provide any proof and ignored my proof. A goal of a gaslighter is to turn others against you and to take away your support system while you constantly feel you need to defend your reality. I experienced much of this in my former employment, but didn't realise until it was too late that my former legal representatives were doing it too. A person who has been gaslighted will find themselves collecting proof that things happened so they can reassure themselves. This is exactly what I have done, which has given me the facts I needed to write this book.

I wasn't surprised to see the age-old legal arguments used to support Lansdowne's findings, as I am sure many before have suffered or will suffer the same: that the "administration of justice" and the "finality principle" must be upheld at all costs. Their needs outweigh the rights of a litigant, especially a self-represented litigant, to seek the justice they have a right to seek and even demand protection under the international Declaration of Human Rights (of which Australia is a signatory). My legal and human rights took second place to what the court calls 'justice'.

Given my experiences, I have no doubt that the above legal terms are used to deny a self-represented litigant space to air their case; a good case that has plenty of evidence would undoubtedly cause embarrassment to those that have used court law to hide their unprofessional and illegal conduct. To air a case such as mine would most likely bring the "administration of justice into disrepute." But I believe it brings itself into disrepute; when this occurs, a truly democratic and independent justice system would seek to address a person's rights rather than deny them and hide the truth. Only when the courts themselves expose wrongdoing by officers of the court will they have the respect of the community it serves and the confidence of its customers.

Customers? Yes, customers: the courts are places of business – the so-called justice business. The system has been relegated to a business unit of the government, and even has an ABN.

To seek justice costs lots of money – filing fees alone can cost thousands of dollars, and then there are the daily hearing fees. If you are legally represented . . . well, that's a bottomless pit. You are only represented after careful assessment of how much you have in assets, as those assets may soon become theirs. Only the very poor or the very rich can access justice services. If you don't have your own home and are on a pension or welfare then your fees may well be waived, but as a homeowner you are required to put your home or the equity in your home on the chopping block.

This reminds me of a story I heard many years ago, concerning what might be called the most expensive fence in the state. Ramona's neighbour built a new fence that encroached on her property – by only a foot or so, but it meant she couldn't access the space behind her shed. She wanted the fence moved as it was on her property, and so the games began.

I believe it was a large property in the upmarket suburb of Brighton, so Ramona had substantial assets and was able to enter the justice game. To cut a long story short, the dispute over the fence cost around $600,000 in legal fees (in the currency of the time – about 20 years ago). Being elderly, in order to survive she had to share her home with boarders as a result. Hopefully today, given the Civil Procedure Act 2010, this kind of rorting by lawyers couldn't occur – or could it?

Given the old adage "A fool and their money are soon parted," you are a fool to believe you will have any success against the legal end of town. (When I say the legal end of town, I mean the legal fraternity who practice in Personal Injury law under the Accident Compensation Act.) They seem to stick together more formidably than any other group or profession in history and this is how they get away with the atrocities they commit. They live by the motto 'You look after me, and if the time comes, I will look after you.'

To give the appearance of justice, I believe that one person in every hundred is successful in their claim, but not if that claim is about their legal representation; the statistics of this must be lower again. To be successful, a person must be non-threatening to the establishment. This brings to my mind many heroes of the past, ordinary Australians that tackled injustice and paid the price. I feel in very good company! Thank you to these people for giving so much and getting so little in return. Your integrity goes without saying, and because you are correct in your claims the establishment requires you to stay quiet. If you disobey this edict, they'll send you not to Siberia but to the land of discredit. This destination is far more beneficial to the system: no living costs, no chance of them being seen as martyrs, and no supporters to fight for your release. Discredit is the land where you live from then on, a land where but a few believe a word you say. You are irrelevant, which is a far more successful outcome for the legal fraternity than parting your head from your body, as we are now a civilised society.

Back to my negligence claim against my lawyer: it goes almost without saying that my lawyer had the benefit of her indemnity insurance, so I was up against a mighty insurance company. Predictably, the legal slogan of "abuse of process" was argued, and the defendant made a 'strike out' application.

The bulk of the defendant's arguments centred upon a Magistrates' Court proceeding in 2012, which was a claim by my former lawyer for $7,500 in costs ordered against me in their favour. From memory I had no Costs Order against me and there was no proceeding, just a meeting to settle.

In *State Bank of New South Wales Ltd v. Stenhouse Ltd*, Giles CJ stated that the "guiding considerations" in determining whether re-litigation of an issue in a subsequent proceeding constitutes an abuse of process are "oppression and unfairness to the other party to the litigation and concern for the 'integrity of the system of administration of justice'."

My response to this was that there *was* no "oppression and unfairness to the other party" – I didn't believe the claim was oppressive or unfair on the defendants. The defendants were protected financially by their professional insurance, and by having a law firm act on their behalf. The "concern for the integrity of the system of administration of justice" again appeared to be given more weight than a litigant's right to justice.

On reading this, I came to understand some of the factors to which regard may be had: the importance of the issue in and to the earlier proceedings, including whether it is an evidentiary issue or an ultimate issue; the opportunity available and taken to fully litigate the issue; the terms and finality of the finding as to the issue; the identity between the relevant issues in the two proceedings; and any plea of fresh evidence, including the nature and significance of the evidence and the reason why it was not part of the earlier proceedings.

I argued that the earlier proceedings and the current proceedings had mainly different issues to be decided and had different defendants. There was no opportunity to fully litigate the issues, as the June hearing was only about one issue: whether or not I was pressured into a settlement. Also, the 'finality' only relates to the same single issue: whether or not I was pressured into a settlement. The identity between the relevant issues in the two proceedings are different – the first proceeding was a Workers' Compensation Hearing for damages against my former employer, while the current proceeding was alleging possible negligence, collusion and misconduct against my former legal representatives.

I pleaded 'fresh evidence' that I wasn't aware of at the time of the June hearing, evidence I only became privy to with eventual access to my legal file and the transcript of the April hearing. The April transcript would have been useful for the June hearing, as there were matters of fact presented at the June hearing that were not supported by the April hearing transcript. I had two witness statements of persons who saw me in the Supreme Court ante room on the morning of Friday 23 April, visibly upset and crying with legal counsel standing over me. I also had a witness who would attest that Walsh made a statement to him on the first day of trial that "this case will be settled" or words of similar effect, before the trial had even begun and before the rogue juror had made the supposed comment.

I didn't receive my legal file from my lawyer until August 2014. There were matters of fact presented at the June 2010 hearing that are not supported by the contents of my file. Lawyers and barristers are required to keep detailed file notes of all conferences and phone conversations with clients and others, and these file notes should be dated and identify the author, record of the substance of advice given and the client's response/instructions, and confirm all of the advice in writing to the client.

In the transcript of the June hearing, there are approximately 30 references to: briefs of evidence, memorandums, book records, signed instructions to settle, phone records, handwritten notes, file notes, notes, notes on a blue pad, notes on my phone, extensive advice, written instructions from me, dictated notes, discussion notes and little notes. My file contained only two of the above: the handwritten settlement note on blue paper and the 28 April 2010 memorandum written by Walsh. On page 49 of the June hearing transcript, Walsh states, "I've put this in a memo after the event and before Ms O'Keeffe decided to take this action." I planned to lead evidence at trial that this statement was incorrect, and that this memorandum was written after 28 April 2010 after it was known that I had decided to take action to have the settlement set aside.

In the June hearing, my former legal team stated the *Koehler v. Cerebos HCA 2005* would not augur well for my claim, and yet there are no records prior to my April hearing of me ever being informed of such. The one and only reference to this case was the memorandum of Walsh dated 28 April 2010. There were no records of any kind pertaining to anyone giving such advice over the five years after the High Court decision in 2005.

As stated previously, an important witness for my former employer, my former manager John, went overseas within days of the hearing finishing on 23 April 2010. Obviously, John knew he would be free to travel after 23 April, so I planned to subpoena him for trial. I hoped he would give evidence of how he knew he'd be free to travel after 23 April 2010. I did subpoena his Annual Leave Records for April 2010, and was convinced I would see that he didn't return to work after 23 April, but instead went on leave. The subpoena cost a few hundred dollars, but I considered it worthwhile – to finally to know whether or not he did indeed have annual leave immediately after the trial terminated. The records were provided to the court, but unfortunately, I wasn't allowed to see them. I didn't know that subpoenaed documents could only be viewed with permission of the court. I didn't get that permission and then couldn't argue 'fresh evidence'.

The decision of *Sidhu v. Van Dyke* provides a further salutary lesson that one should not promise what one does not intend to give, and that such promises bind both morally and legally. *Sidhu* is also important because it clarifies what action the promisor may need to take in order to fulfil their promise. The 'doctrine of estoppel' was developed in order to mitigate the harshness of common law. The essence of estoppel is that the promisor will be estopped from resiling from their promise even though the promise is not supported by consideration in circumstances where it would be unfair on the representee to allow the representor to do so.

The concept of keeping one's promise has found expression in the law. In contract law, a promise given for valuable consideration is enforceable. However, the common law refused to enforce mere voluntary promises unless they were found in a deed. In my opinion, briefing a lawyer to run your case and then them accepting to run your case with all skill and due care is a promise they make to you. A number of days after signing the blue note paper, I received the deed, but it was never signed so I wasn't sure whether my 'voluntary' promise was lawful, as it wasn't found in a deed.

In early 2017, the associate justice listed to hear my case was changed to Lansdowne, and it was then that I felt my chances of success fell from 50% to 20%. I had previously experienced hostility from women in positions of power over me, and believed there was a strong possibility that my former lawyer and the associate justice may well be friends. They were of similar age and in same profession, and perhaps even studied law together.

In May, I was ready to put my case, but the evening before I was contacted by the court and informed the court of its own motion had adjourned my hearing for three months. My odds had now fallen to 10%. I felt that three months was needed to give the court time to study my case and find a way to throw it out.

On the 2nd of August, we had the first day of hearing, which only went for an hour or so, with Lansdowne saying from the bench that this might be my only opportunity to put my case and to file all documents I wanted the court to consider. I felt very unsure about this, as giving everything in advance would highlight the actual evidence I had, but what was I to do – I felt I had no choice but to comply.

In my book of evidence, I included references to Griffiths v. Evans, which I believed was very relevant to my case. This case involved dispute between a solicitor and client about the terms of a solicitor's retainer, which all lawyers should be aware of. The decision in this case stated, "On this question of retainer I would observe that where there is a difference between a solicitor and his client, the courts have said for the last 100 years or more that the word of the client is to be preferred to the word of the solicitor, or, at any rate, more weight to be given to it." Further, "the word of the client is to be preferred to the word of the solicitor." This was not my experience and I feel this authority rarely sees the light of day, most judges and lawyers ignore it as it does not suit their agenda of control.

My solicitor's fees were paid for negligently performed work, yet Lansdowne saw no problem with this and obviously wasn't aware of *Abrahams v. Wainwright Brooking* JA (Winneke P and Phillips JJA agreeing), which stated, "Quite apart from negligence, it is a principle of law, or perhaps one should say a consequence of the application of a principle of law, that a solicitor may not recover from the client payment for work that is useless." The decision cited, as establishing the rule with regard to solicitors, the case of *Hill v. Featherstonhaugh*. The court treated the rule about attorneys as "flowing from a more general principle which prevented a bricklayer from charging for a wall which was liable to collapse or a surgeon for an operation which could not in any circumstances have been useful to the patient."

Toop's work—and I say work lightly—was of no use to me whatsoever – in fact it had a detrimental effect on me. Yet this principle of law was ignored in my case, and I believe is ignored in every case where a client brings proceedings against their former lawyer. I have no doubt this principle is only used (if ever) when it suits the court.

The relevant test for an 'abuse of process' claim, in my understanding, includes the following: that proceedings will be an abuse of process where they are foredoomed to fail; that proceedings will generally be an abuse of process where the use of the court's procedures is unjustifiably oppressive to one of the parties; that proceedings may be an abuse of process if they are brought after undue delay; and that if the threshold issue of abuse of process is determined in the applicant's favour then additional discretionary factors may be relevant to the grant of leave.

My case was not foredoomed to fail, as neither the defendant nor Associate Justice Lansdowne found my claim was without merit. I doubted my claim was unjustifiably oppressive, because if it was then so would many other actions be, and actions equal funds for the legal fraternity. I brought my action within the timeframes, so the undue delay was not relevant; discretionary factors always worried me, as a judge's discretion can be whatever they want it to be and isn't appealable. Lansdowne's decision was not a determination following a trial with oral evidence and cross-examination.

My other legal arguments against a 'strike out' application included the doctrine that access to justice for all is central to the Rule of Law, as stated by Carnwath LJ (as Senior President of Tribunals UK at the Commonwealth Law Conference 2011):

> "It should never be forgotten that tribunals exist for users, and not the other way round. No matter how good tribunals may be, they do not fulfil their function unless they are accessible by the people who want to use them and unless the users receive the help they need to prepare and present their cases.
> Only too often the litigant in person is regarded as a problem for judges and for the court system rather that the person for whom the system of justice exists. The true problem is the court system and its procedures which are still too often inaccessible and incomprehensible to ordinary people."

And let us keep it that way.

Nice sentiment, but in my experience, this isn't a sentiment held dear by many in the legal community, including some judges.

The defendant's 'abuse of process' claim was premised on a Magistrates' Court Terms of Settlement made in 2013. My lawyer initiated this action in the Magistrates' Court to retrieve funds she believed were owed to her from an earlier proceeding, even though in the Costs Court, Associate Justice Wood determined no costs were payable. I was so overwhelmed by this time, I just didn't realise or understand that I may have been able to argue this fact and have the 'abuse of process' application defeated because I felt it was possible the Magistrates' Court settlement should never have happened, as it may have been without jurisdiction.

I provided all the correspondence regarding those 'Terms of Settlement' to the court, and it was my argument, backed by evidence, that it was never my intention to settle all matters between my lawyer and myself, and that this action may have related solely to the Costs Court Judicial Registrar Order for $7,500. Most relevantly, the statement I amended read "to this Magistrates' Court Proceeding." I had this reviewed by a lawyer as I wanted to be sure it was 'tight' and only related to *this* proceeding, and his legal opinion was that I had made it clear that this was only a settlement of the Magistrates' Court action brought by my lawyer.

Paragraph 6 of this 'Terms of Settlement' states: "These terms of settlement may be pleaded or tendered by any party to it or by any person having the benefit of it as an absolute bar to any proceedings or claim brought or made in breach of its terms." The words "in breach of its terms" can only relate to a breach in the terms of the Magistrates' Court's 'Terms of Settlement' and the costs claim being resolved by it, or so I believed.

I never expected an 'abuse of process' to be made out on this settlement – it just goes to show how very careful you need to be when settling legal proceedings, even when following legal advice. I believed the lawyer assisting me through all of this was honest and independent, and was as surprised as I was when the 'abuse of process' application was successful based on the Magistrates' Court 'Terms of Settlement'. I just wondered at that time if this 'Terms of Settlement' was written in such a way to enable a wedge for any future legal actions, because at that time my former lawyer knew I was working towards this.

The essential element of the cause of action is fresh facts – it must be shown that there are fresh facts that were not considered by the original trial court and not known to the applicant until after the conclusion of the trial. It must also be established that it was fraud of the party who was successful at the original trial—that was responsible for the fresh facts not being known by the applicant or considered by the court—such that it would be inequitable for the successful party to retain the benefit of the judgement.

Causation is a requirement also – it must be established that the fresh facts are so material such as to make it reasonably probable that, if proven, my case may have succeeded if I had known at the time of the June hearing that there were three references in the April transcript that my former manager would be giving such and such evidence. The barrister for the defendant must have known he was giving these assurances to the court that the manager John would not be available after 23 April, and I felt my own barristers knew this as well.

His Honour Justice Kryou once said:

> "The power to permanently stay a proceeding as an abuse of process is to be exercised sparingly and upon examination of the relevant circumstances of the particular case. In the present case, a consideration of all the circumstances and an overall balancing of justice as between the parties."

It is a well-known principle that only in exceptional circumstances will a civil proceeding be stayed on the ground that it constitutes an abuse of process. As the power to grant a permanent stay is a power to refuse to exercise jurisdiction, the power is exercised sparingly and supposedly with the utmost caution.

As Dixon J said in *Cox v. Journeaux*, "The principle, in general paramount, that a claim honestly made by a suitor for judicial relief must be investigated and decided in the manner appointed, must be observed."

Courts have traditionally refused to erect barriers that would deter citizens from bringing their disputes into court. In *Burton v. Shire of Bairnsdale*, O'Connor J said:

> "*Prima facie*, every litigant has a right to have matters of law as well as of fact decided according to the ordinary rules of procedure, which give him full-time and opportunity for the presentation of his case to the ordinary tribunals, and the inherent jurisdiction of the court to protect its process from abuse by depriving a litigant of these rights and summarily disposing of an action as frivolous and vexatious in point of law will never be exercised unless the plaintiff's claim is so obviously untenable that it cannot possibly succeed."

Section 64 of the Civil Procedure Act permits the court to allow a civil proceeding to go to trial even if satisfied there is no real prospect of success, because it would not be in the interests of justice to summarily dismiss it or the dispute is of such a nature that only a full hearing on the merits is appropriate.

In the decision of *Spencer v. Commonwealth of Australia* 2010 the High Court affirmed the need for great care in determining an application for summary judgment. In Victoria particularly, great care will be needed to observe the requirements of Section 24 of the Charter of Human Rights and Responsibilities Act 2006, which provides that a party to a civil proceeding has the right to have the proceeding decided by a competent, independent and impartial court or tribunal after a fair and public hearing. This all sounds lovely, but rarely actually happens, if at all – my case should have gone to trial. After my experiences, the requirement for an "independent and impartial court" was impossible.

On paper, we appear to have a fair and reasonable system of justice, but in reality, it is anything but. It reminds me of my working days, where my former employer had all the policies and procedures to address the issues but simply chose not use them.

After the hearing in August, I set about presenting all my evidence, and filed two folders of documents. Whilst doing this, I came to realise that it wasn't only my lawyer that I believe committed wrongdoing, but the barristers and Judge Robson as well. Given the detail of the evidence I provided, I was of the opinion that my evidence was not going to be heard in open court. On the next hearing day in December, Associate Justice Lansdowne asked the defendant if they were filing a response to my further application and they responded, "No." The associate judge looked a little surprised. I felt the reason for this to be one of two possibilities, the first being that they couldn't respond because my evidence was true and correct and there was no denying what I had to say, and secondly, they knew their 'strike out' application would be successful, so why go to all the trouble.

The hearing against my former lawyer terminated on 15 December 2017, and the judge asked if I had anything I would like to say before she handed down her decision – a decision likely known from the moment I filed my 'Statement of Claim'.

I stood to give my oral presentation to the court and include the fullness of my words, believing without a doubt in my heart that the defendants would be successful in their 'strike out' application. I said:

"Imagine a perfect world where we all treat each other with respect and dignity and not a means to our own desired ends.
Imagine being a fit, healthy and happy employee, an employee who

was dedicated, committed and competent, an employee who always gave 110% and had an exemplary eight years of employment, with a real can-do work ethic.

Imagine suddenly you are swept into a whirlpool of bullying and harassment which swirls around you unchecked. Your employer condones the behaviour you are subjected to and fails in their duty of care, fails to follow their own policies and procedures and fails you morally, ethically and legally.

Imagine you participate in all actions asked of you, but these requests are designed to fail you. Mediation is compromised and no one comes forward to say this is wrong. The bystander syndrome flourishes and you are on your own, sick, bewildered and devastated, too ill to work.

Imagine you have no choice but to cease the job that you love as you are just too incapacitated. In all innocence and under medical advice you submit a WorkCover claim, but with the intention of returning to work as soon as possible.

Imagine the rejection of your claim opens the floodgates to even more bullying, harassment, discrimination, victimisation and vilification. Your mind fights desperately to make sense of it all, but there is no sense to be found. Your position in the workplace becomes untenable and the wrongdoers are protected.

Imagine receiving no support from your employer as required under law, no Return to Work Plan, no Return to Work Co-ordinator, nothing, zero, zilch.

Imagine making a sincere and courageous attempt to return to full-time work, and on the second day you are suspended and escorted from the building and left standing bewildered on the street. You are horrified by the complaints made against you, complaints that thwart your Work-Cover claim and your return to work.

Imagine the complaints are investigated by an external specialist agency and found to be without foundation, to be exaggeration or blatantly untrue. This is the reason you cannot be terminated from your employment.

Imagine the major players in your suspension suddenly disappear from the workplace after the CEO 'hits the roof' at their behaviour. But you are still not allowed to return to your job because the staff who made the complaints feel uncomfortable having you around.

Imagine your employer still doing nothing to address this injustice. They cannot be seen to be in the wrong as this would support your WorkCover claim – their goal is to thwart it totally and continue in their belief that they are successful workplace leaders.

Imagine having complete faith in all the checks and balances that supposedly exist in a modern Australian workplace, and having them, one by one, fail you; employer, WorkSafe, the legal system.

Imagine Commonwealth, State and employer policies, procedures, guidelines and laws are simply ignored, as they were never intended to really work – they are purely 'window dressing' to convince someone somewhere that we the minions are fairly treated.

Imagine you badly want to keep the job you love, are prepared to forgive the abuses and just get on with it. You offer to drop your Work-Cover claim, as that did nothing to help you but actually made matters worse. Your offer to settle the dispute is the payment of $4,000, mainly made up of medical expenses and a supportive return to work.

Imagine waiting four weeks for a response to your offer and the only counter-offer you receive is that your job is being advertised and has already gone to print without your knowledge.

Imagine someone somewhere did not have the courage to swallow a few crumbs of humble pie while I had the whole pie thrust down my throat. They must be the most expensive crumbs ever crumbled. That offer to settle all-in for $4,000 has now cost someone somewhere nearly a million dollars – and these are only the direct costs. All this paid out to stop an injured worker who just wanted to return to work.

Imagine WorkSafe not abiding by the Model Litigant Guidelines after they have in their possession compelling evidence which proves your claim to be genuine. They still fight you to the bitter end and prefer to pay the legal system funds which could have been used to compensate the injured worker.

Imagine waiting for ten years to be vindicated and validated, and stupidly having faith in the legal system and your legal team, both of which in the end failed you and validated the wrongdoers. The lawyer's needs were paramount to yours; there was no fight by them to protect your legal and human rights against a barrister whose role is to blame the victim and encourage the jury to do the same – a proven, successful strategy.

Imagine your own legal team not informing the judge to alert him of observed conduct which may not be a direct attempt to influence the judge but may nevertheless be aimed at obstructing the course of justice.

Imagine your feelings of intimidation by the presence in court of your major bully, a 'supposed' witness. Your legal team has no plans to protect you. No one calls for 'witnesses out', no question put to the judge regarding this witness being present. Think about the humiliation you would feel when he hears personal details of your life and the effects of your injury over seven hearing days. Appropriate steps to protect such a witness are not inconsistent with judicial impartiality, but your legal team fails to raise this with the court.

Imagine having your compensation hearing 'thrown' by your own legal representatives, and realising the validation and vindication you need is never going to come because you are just collateral damage, a pawn in the game of law.

Imagine every time you fight to protect a legal or human right that another is taken from you. Your right to privacy is well and truly out the window, your medical records since the dawn of time and as recent as yesterday are regularly subpoenaed and pored over by someone somewhere – by strangers. That thing you told your doctor 20 years ago is now on the internet. You are innocent, have been through very trying times, but you are labelled a chronic complainer, a difficult personality and someone exhibiting bizarre conduct. The victim is now the perpetrator, the perpetrator is now the victim, the desired cycle is now complete.

Imagine the above labelling and legal processes were purely an avenue to offer and support, witness immunity, proceedings immunity, as advocates immunity alone will not be sufficient to protect the lawyers. Imagine your biggest crime was guilty of being innocent. I have paid a huge price for the bad behaviour of others.

Imagine your reputation is as important as a celebrity's reputation, and your livelihood also depends on it. But you are not a celebrity, just an ordinary everyday person who fights for what she believes in without help or assistance from anyone anywhere.

Imagine you have the power to right some of this wrong. No, you do not need to imagine, you do have the power. I implore Your Honour to

use your discretion and allow my case a full hearing on its merit, according to the Civil Procedure Act 2010's Section 64.
Court may allow a matter to proceed to trial, and despite anything to the contrary in this part or any rules of court, a court may order that a civil proceeding proceed to trial if the court is satisfied that, despite there being no real prospect of success, the civil proceeding should not be disposed of summarily because it is not in the interests of justice to do so, or the dispute is of such a nature that only a full hearing on the merits is appropriate. My case is deserving of a full hearing on its merits."

If you can only imagine all the above then you are indeed fortunate. I do not need to imagine any of it, as I lived it.
Lysaght Building Solutions Pty Ltd v. Blanalko Pty Ltd, Warren CJ and Nettle JA:

"The test for summary judgment under the Civil Procedure Act 2010 is whether the respondent to the application for summary judgment has a 'real' as opposed to a 'fanciful' chance of success; and at the same time, it must be borne in mind that the power to terminate proceedings summarily should be exercised with caution and thus should not be exercised unless it is clear that there is no real question to be tried; and that is so regardless of whether the application for summary judgment is made on the basis that the pleadings fail to disclose a reasonable cause of action (and the defect cannot be cured by amendment) or on the basis that the action is frivolous or vexatious or an abuse of process or where the application is supported by evidence."

There were many "authorities" referred to in Associate Lansdowne's decision, and I have now come to learn that authorities or precedents can be made to fit any occasion, with judge's associates or lawyers searching through the piles now available on the internet until they find one or two or many that suit their agenda. Remember there is always a 'yin' to every 'yang.' It of course goes without saying that none of the authorities I provided were considered.

Given the stated position, I didn't believe my case against my lawyer was "fanciful," "frivolous" or did not disclose a cause of action, and I believe that it was actually a strong case that had to be disposed of arbitrarily as it may have well brought the "administration of justice into disrepute." As was said in the joint reasons in *Coulton v. Holcombe*, "it is fundamental to the due administration of justice that the substantial issues between the parties are ordinarily settled at the trial."

My claim should have been settled at trial, but Lansdowne appeared not to follow any of the above stated legal principles. She did not "exercise sparingly with the utmost caution," and she should not have summarily disposed of my action. She made no decision as to whether my action was frivolous or vexatious, and as a point of law, these must never be exercised unless the claim is so obviously untenable that it cannot possibly succeed. Lansdowne nor the defendant raised these in their 'abuse of process' application, and neither attacked the merits of my case, so given this it is my opinion that it was not in the interests of justice to grant the application. The dispute was of such a nature that only a full hearing on the merits was appropriate.

I considered Lansdowne's judgement to be harsh and felt she could have (and probably should have) found for me on a least one of the above points, particularly given it was a summary dismissal application. Keeping in mind her revised judgement at paragraph 37: "The defendants do not seek a determination that the plaintiff has no real prospect of success on the basis of the case that she wishes to bring."

I read this as the defendant thought my case had merit, and given this, Lansdowne had a choice to use some discretion in my favour, but she chose not to. Really, could I have expected anything else? Lansdowne said very little or made little finding regarding the defendant's defence where I proved it to be false, and my claims which I proved to be true, as it wasn't necessary in a 'strike out' application to canvass these facts.

I should add here that the defendant's lawyers Landers & Rogers were lovely to deal with, and I felt that I was treated with respect and dignity. I have a strong feeling that they were as surprised as I was that their 'strike out' application had been successful. I believe they considered my claims legitimate, but they were just doing their job on behalf of their client, the insurer. Someone showed compassion, either Landers & Rogers or the insurer, as they did not pursue their costs as ordered by the court. I should mention that I was offered $50,000 to settle before the case commenced, but sadly again money was not my motivator. My motivator was truth, but had I known at the time that my truth was never going to be heard and Lansdowne and the court would effectively shut me out on a technicality, then I may have accepted their offer. I have no doubt that the Court's own motion adjournment of my case for three months was used to find the 'silver bullet' to dispense with my claim.

A year after my case had concluded, I received from Associate Lansdowne a package containing a lot of the evidence and exhibits I had presented in my case, stating she didn't require it to be retained on file as my matter was finalised. She said in her letter, "Please find exhibits and confidential documents enclosed. I advise these documents are no longer required."

This is odd, given the Supreme Court Guidelines for Inspecting a Court File state, "Court Files contain important records and are regularly required in Court and by members of the Judiciary and Court Files and all documents contained within must never be removed from the premises."

I found it strange that these court records were no longer part of the court record, and the returned documents were labelled 'confidential'. I never requested confidentiality, and given these documents were discussed or referred to in open court and form part of the transcript, they should have remained with the court, and certainly did not attract any confidentiality.

It appeared to me that the court was in effect restricting access to this evidence, and I felt that as this evidence was true and accurate, it wasn't wanted to be retained on file in case a future journalist, law student or interested person might seek access to such file, see such evidence and have it known that I was telling the truth. But maybe there has been a change in the rule of law or legislation I don't know about that gives this move legitimacy. I remember a statement I once read: "All the evidence in the world is useless when there is nowhere to take it." Well, I took it to where it belonged, but it was returned unwanted. It was truth, and truth is always the first casualty of war.

At the conclusion of the negligence hearing, a barrister not involved with my case stated to me that the outcome was "practically inevitable," and I now understand that even with all the rhetoric, the supposed justice/legal system is not for people like me; it is inevitable that we will fail because we don't matter, and if we do matter it is only for a short time while they convince us we need their services and they need our money.

I recently read the book by Evan Whitton titled *Our Corrupt Legal System: Why Everyone is a Victim (Except Rich Criminals)*, and can say unequivocally —based on my experience—what the author has written is absolutely correct. I recommend this book, especially for those contemplating entering the ring – it can be read for free online.

After reading Whitton's book, I wondered if we really do have a cartel of lawyers and judges running the system as a business, and whether this system doesn't seek the truth, as trial lawyers (trained liars) are in charge of the evidence and judges are untrained former trial lawyers. The consequences of this, says Whitton, is that too many innocent people go to prison, too many criminals get off, and—very relevant to me—is that civil hearings take too long.

I feel such empathy for anyone entering our civil legal system, because even if you win, you will lose, and this is the story for most litigants. If you do win, was it worth the pain, years of misery, the pyrrhic victory? I know it wasn't about the dollars for you, but something far more important: the principle of justice. Sadly, your principle was lost, and it all becomes about money to your lawyer. I doubt the system will change anytime soon, if ever, as it is too entrenched. Thirty-six years ago, Chief Justice Burger of the American Supreme Court said, "Trials by the adversarial contest must in time go by the way of ancient trial by battle and blood. Our system is too costly, too painful, too destructive, and too inefficient for a truly civilised people."

I fought for justice with all I had in me. Did I fail? I don't believe so – failing would be if all things were equal in the fight, and when accessing the law, all things are certainly not equal. I may have had some success if I was David fighting the Goliath, but I was Davina fighting a hundred Goliaths.

A 2007 paper by Benjamin Barton, a Professor of Law at the University of Tennessee, titled 'Do Judges Systematically Favour the Interests of the Legal Profession?' may have been written a number of years ago, but to me, it is still relevant today. The paper includes what has become known as the Barton Hypothesis, which says, "judge hypothesis in a nut shell: many legal outcomes can be explained, and future cases predicted, by asking a very simple question: is there a plausible legal result in this case that will significantly affect the interests of the legal profession (positively or negatively)? If so, the case will be decided in the way that offers the best result for the legal profession."

I rest my case.

TWENTY-TWO

Occasional Integrity

"The Public trust concept is foundational to integrity in government and public administration."
—Peter M Hall KC, former judge of the Supreme Court of NSW.

Initially, I wasn't planning to write this following chapter, but given the outcome I thought it was important to try and understand how our integrity bodies work or don't work.

It is timely that those in powerful positions are these days being held more accountable for their alleged wrongdoing, but there is still one bastion that enjoys much immunity: the legal profession and the judiciary.

Given this profession's perceived and actual power, many who have been damaged by it are fearful of speaking out, and I feel others who are in the position to create change may also experience the same fear. It takes great courage to hold a judge accountable, far more courage than holding the Attorney-General accountable for perceived wrongdoing. Yet these days, we have a conundrum of the highest legal officer in the land being held to account, but not a judge. The only reason I can fathom as to why this is so, is that the Attorney-General is politically elected and answerable to the public, while a judge is not. Also, the judge's allies 'circle the wagons' to protect their own. In this day and age, there cannot be any more 'circling of the wagons' in the political area, for it's too dangerous to the political lives of other politicians.

Times are changing; you only need to google "corrupt judges" or "corruption in the legal profession" to see countless examples of such alleged wrongdoing.

The Prime Minister recently stated that if you have suffered abuse, you should report it to the police, not the media. From my experience, a complaint from a powerless victim against a powerful wrongdoer usually leads to nowhere except a cover-up. Nowadays, it seems media exposure is often the only way that brave whistleblowers and the occasional public integrity body can finally hold alleged perpetrators of wrongdoing to account.

Over many years, I have attempted to have my concerns addressed. Alas, I am insignificant while the wrongdoers hold positions of significance; it was never a level playing field.

In July 2020, the Victorian Ombudsman appeared on the ABC's *Four Corners* TV program supporting a formal review into complex compensation claims for the injured workers of Victoria. At long last, someone understood the immoral and unethical behaviour of the workers compensation system. I can only attest to its accuracy from my experience – I have been vilified, labelled and punished because of my fight to have a fair hearing of my compensation claim. I made a submission to this review and look forward to the outcome.

It isn't just the WorkCover process that causes immense pain, but also the second stage of the process – litigation. It may well be more than 10 years since my Supreme Court action and 20 years since the cause of injury, but it's all only yesterday to me. When you're abused and vilified by those who supposedly have your best interests at heart, it takes a long time to process it. And it takes even longer to try and have it addressed when you're up against such power imbalances. WorkCover abiding by the Model Litigant Guidelines would drastically lessen the negative impact on injured workers entering litigation.

It seems ironic to me now, but back in 2013 Justice Heydon made the comment, "Those judges who advocate or choose the course of concealment rather than revelation constitute the most insidious of threats to judicial independence, the enemy within." I certainly met the enemy within and have paid a high price for their bad behaviour.

Prior to my own experience, I had heard stories of judicial misconduct and brushed them off as aggrieved or disgruntled litigants. I've since learned there are truths to these stories and many probably have every right to feel let down by the judicial process, which often violates their human right to a fair trial. I stated all of the above in a letter to the Ombudsman thanking her for her support of injured workers. I received a sincere reply from the Ombudsman's office, with the suggestion that if I had any concerns regarding the judicial officer who heard my case, I had the option of raising it with the Judicial Commission of Victoria.

This Commission was formed in 2016 and was tasked with investigating complaints against the judges of this state. I read about the Commission a few years after its inception, but felt given my experiences a complaint would be futile. There has been much community outrage regarding police investigating police, but we have lawyers investigating lawyers and doctors investigating doctors with no apparent community outrage. I don't know the answer to this conundrum, as only lawyers understand the legalities of other lawyers' crimes, like only doctors can understand the significance of another doctor's negligence. The most transparent option I see is that statutory authorities involve laypersons in their decisions whether to investigate or not – community-minded laypersons who are experienced in the field of transparency and who do not align with any side or any interested party, but instead simply search for the truth.

The Judicial Commission appears to have such laypersons on their board, with six members being judicial officers and four being non-judicial and appointed by the Governor in Council. I don't know the role of the non-judicial members – it may purely be for administrative and governance purposes and they may not play any actual part in a decision to investigate a complaint or not. I imagine it would be a difficult task to disagree with a judicial officer's decision and to advocate for a complaint to be investigated, if that is indeed part of their role. These judicial officers are powerful people and would be intimidating to most of us, but do these non-judicial officers do what is right, or do what is wanted by the establishment that actually put them in the position they hold? Where do their loyalties lie – is self-preservation part of their persona? Is it a career stepping stone to other government appointments in the future?

By now, you've probably gathered that I love a challenge. So, given making a complaint to this body was suggested to me by another statutory body, I decided to give it a go, even with my reservations. I didn't want to publish my book and then have someone say that I should have made a complaint to the Judicial Commission – that it was unfair of me not to do so and a compliant would allow the judge to explain himself. I may well be wrong in regards to the case of 'Febriano', but certainly not wrong when it comes to the judge ignoring false testimony.

The Judicial Commission Board Chairperson is the Chief Justice of the Supreme Court of Victoria, who just happens to be the wife of the judge who presided in the Practice Court who referred my case back to Justice Robson. I wasn't sure if this judge's purpose was benign or if it was designed to allow Judge Robson the opportunity to destroy my credibility; this could well have been a case of when they can't kill your potential, they simply go after your character. Whether this fact would play any part in a decision by the Commission to ignore any complaint by me is unknown.

In September 2020, I wrote to the Commission outlining my complaint (certainly living up to one of my labels!), which outlined my concerns, which were: that my case was prejudged; the failure of judicial oath; some issues outside of jurisdiction; that I was denied procedural fairness; bias; the reasonable apprehension of bias; lack of impartiality; and lack of independence. I provided evidence to support each argument I made, and felt quite sure at least one of these arguments would be made out if indeed truth and transparency were valued by the Commission.

Much of the information I provided to the Commission is outlined in previous chapters, but I'll briefly include parts of it below so you know the information the Commission relied on to come to their decision. If you feel you have a good understanding of what the complaint to the Commission entailed, you may want to skip the next few pages.

I told the Commission of my experiences, and that even though they were a number of years ago, a decade in the law calendar is not too remote a time, and many injured workers through no fault of our own are often forced to wait ten years or more for the hearing of our claims. It appeared that it's now accepted that historical allegations of sexual harassment are finally being investigated, and I requested that my experience of legal abuse be given the same standing.

I believed that while a judge is performing judicial functions they may enjoy immunity, but I allege that the denial of my legal and human rights is absolutely not a judicial function and conflicts with any definition of a judicial function, and as such is an individual act, an act which represents the judge's own bias, lack of impartiality and independence. I feel this was done to advantage Judge Robson's friends and colleagues, my former legal team and the barrister acting for the defendant.

My former legal team's desired and purposeful narrative was that I was aggressive, unreasonable, a chronic complainer and exhibited bizarre conduct, but gave little to no evidence that this was true – it was just their necessary position to justify why I was forced to settle. My former legal team purposely conveyed these words, giving the judge the legal opportunity to defame and discredit, as he then had the mantra to repeat them in his judgement thereby fulfilling their desired narrative.

These were the necessary labels required to exonerate his legal brothers and sisters from their wrongdoings. As I've said, I have no doubt these experienced legal professionals would be worried about a disenchanted client who was "strong, independent, competent, capable and possess a strong character" as being a potential threat down the track, so the track had to be deep and unforgiving.

It wasn't until writing this chapter that I came to realise why these words were needed to be said. I had to be "strong, independent, competent, capable and possess a strong character" to relieve the judge of any responsibility he would have had under the Victorian Charter of Human Rights and Responsibilities Act 2006. Under the Act, I was a vulnerable Self-Represented Litigant, and as such the judge was required to take *more* care, not less.

As Judge O'Neill of the County Court determined in *Briggs v. Victorian WorkCover Authority*:

> "Where the risk to the vulnerable is high, the level of care required is raised.
> His Honour's reference to the use of court procedures as being unjustifiably oppressive to one party or that they would bring the administration of justice into disrepute.
>
> 20 Section 8 of the Act provides that a court must give effect to the overarching purpose in the exercise of its powers, or in the interpretation of those powers."

The Judicial Commission states that particular care should be taken to avoid causing unnecessary hurt in the exercise of judicial function. This includes observations made in reasons for judgement. As Gleeson CJ stated in his monograph of 2004, "A judge should never cause unnecessary hurt."

I do not believe I experienced judicial independence or the observance of the principles of natural justice or the right to an unbiased adjudicator. Everyone who comes before the court should be treated in a manner that respects their dignity.

To blame the victim of abuse for that abuse is unconscionable, and to label a victim of workplace bullying (when extensive evidence exists that the bullying did indeed take place) as not having been bullied is unconscionable. Given my former employer and the WorkCover authority have expended more than $1,000,000 on my claim, my claim cannot possibly be without merit.

In my opinion, Judge Robson did in fact cause unnecessary hurt, and my former legal team attempted to exert influence over the judge's exercise of judicial function and this attempt was successful. Their protection was dependent upon my credibility being destroyed.

Had I known at the time of the personal relationship between Judge Robson, Walsh and Jens, I would have requested he recuse himself from the hearing. I highly doubt their mateship would pass the 'ordinary, reasonable person test' that I had a fair trial not tainted by bias. I feel these personal relationships of the judge compromised his capacity to objectively evaluate the evidence or evaluate my evidence.

Given what I had stated, it was incumbent on this judge to recuse himself; why he didn't do so leads me to feel he had decided to assist these legal personnel in their quest to shut me down and shut me out of a full and fair hearing on the merits of my case, and to rid the court of a potentially difficult self-represented litigant.

I believed the judgement was to elicit the 'Febriano affect' due to the personal dagger-in-the-heart comments which were unnecessary to the matter at hand; the matter was simply: was I put under duress to settle? Had he stayed with the matter in dispute without all the erroneous decisions he made, I might not have felt so wronged.

I informed the Commission it would be necessary to read the judgement and transcript in unison to gain an understanding of what I was alleging, and to seek evidence from the judge's associate regarding whether or not the reported comment from a juror actually occurred.

I went on to tell the Commission that I believed I didn't receive a fair hearing as afforded under legal and human rights provisions.

The judge in the Practice Court adjourned the hearing to consider my response to my former lawyer's request to have the settlements funds paid directly to them. He returned around 15 minutes later and requested that I return to the court the next day in front of Robson and conduct cross-examination of my former legal team.

As stated earlier, I did not believe this was a fair hearing given I had less than one day's notice and so had little time to prepare, and none of the usual legal steps were undertaken. I couldn't possibly do justice to my case with one day's notice. The judge should have considered conducting a directions hearing instead of the substantiative hearing as it turned out to be, and as such I was denied procedural fairness.

With little opportunity to prepare a case, I did the best I could to present my claims against my former legal team. Given the outcome of the June hearing, I don't believe this opportunity was legitimate; it provided the scene for a self-represented litigant to be shut down and shut out with a judgement that was purposely designed to denigrate and humiliate.

The judge failed to ensure I had the transcript for the April hearing which would have assisted me in the June hearing, and as such I felt I was again denied procedural fairness. Later, after a number of requests, WorkCover reluctantly gave me a copy on 22 July 2010, too late to be of assistance. Contained in that transcript was the evidence of the false testimony given by the defendant barrister regarding his supposed leave of the court to continue cross-examination, and three references that his witness John Circosta would be giving evidence regarding certain matters. The defendant barrister must have known at this time that his witness would not be giving such evidence, as Circosta supposedly went overseas on the weekend following the case terminating on 23 April. Therefore, I contend that it was known well before 23 April that the case would be terminating on this day. I attached three pages of transcript where Mr Jens made reference to Circosta giving evidence.

The judge made purposely erroneous decisions and false findings of fact which were not open to him on the evidence. He recorded that my history of complaints against a number of organisations equated to "bizarre conduct." He was attempting to give fodder to the "chronic complainer" label that was to be used to discredit and to denigrate.

He either ignored the evidence or didn't avail himself to read and consider the evidence or ask me for a response. Had he, I would have attested that my WorkCover claim was accepted, my discrimination claim successful, my privacy complaint upheld by the Victorian Privacy Commissioner, and the County Court issued a serious injury certificate. Also, the insurer accepted liability for all my injuries and illnesses and various medical practitioners have all been supportive of my claim. Had I been informed that the judge would be making such a determination on whether or not I was bullied, I would have had the opportunity to give evidence, including: the numerous medical reports both from treaters and Independent Medical Examiners; the insurer who accepted liability; the report of human resource expert Bailey Shaw; the statements of other judicial officers that I was "genuine and sincere" and that "It is clear when a comparison is made between what the plaintiff says occurred and what the various deponents and makers of statements say occurred that there is quite a dramatic conflict in evidence," and "I believe what Mrs O'Keeffe said happened did happen," and "In the circumstances, I accept the plaintiff's evidence that the events she describes did occur and that her work was a significant contributing factor to the onset of injury."

This accords with Dr Benjamin's assessment, when he stated to me, "What you think is happening is happening."

All these specialist opinions were ignored by the judge who was determined to support the barrister's false narrative.

The judge erroneously found my submission of a WorkCover claim to be supportive of a 'chronic complainer' label. He decided that my response to complaints from co-workers equated to me making complaints against them, rather than understanding they were simply my responses to their complaints and the false allegations that were made. The judge stated this (me responding to these issues) to be unusual to say the least; they were susceptible to an interpretation that I was particularly aggressive and unreasonable. Was the judge suggesting I had no right of reply? I don't understand how a right of reply is considered aggressive and unreasonable; even during this difficult time my behaviour was impeccable – absolutely no evidence existed of me being aggressive, because if I *had* been aggressive in any way, my employer would have used it to terminate my employment.

Under cross-examination, Walsh stated in his evidence that my pursuit of these actions displayed a personality which was unreasonable – the judge used these words in his judgement. It is not unreasonable to pursue your legal rights when they are violated, and the judge must've known this, but he purposely ignored this fact in order to support Walsh in his denigration. The judge ignored the fact that it was neither aggressive nor unreasonable to use the law to fight for your legal and human rights.

The transcript clearly showed on a number of occasions how flustered the witnesses were in answering my questions, and especially so for Harrison, who as an experienced barrister admitted he didn't check his diary each day – not believable by any stretch of the imagination. But the judge purposely believed it, even though his body language spoke to his true beliefs when he placed his elbows on the bench with his arms upright and his head in his hands.

The judge found that Harrison had advised me that the evidence was pretty clear that there was no basis upon which my former employer would have had knowledge of my particular psychological susceptibility, but there was no evidence that this was 'pretty clear', and no evidence that Harrison advised me of this. Had the judge availed himself of the evidence in the court books rather than just accept false testimony then he would have known this to be untrue.

Judge Robson just kept agreeing with the barristers, making their stories officially true by ignoring the evidence that didn't fit the story spun to him by them.

The judge stated that Walsh claimed I didn't say I had my chequebook in my handbag. According to the transcript, both Harrison and Toop testified I did say I had my chequebook in my handbag, and yet the judge made no mention of the false testimony of Walsh.

The judge ignored the evidence of Walsh, who stated under oath that he did not leave my presence in the court ante room until he had my agreement to accept the $150,000, and Walsh replied "That's correct."

The judge knew this to be untrue, as I was in the court ante room for more than four hours, and Walsh did leave my presence on a number of occasions to be present in the judge's court. The judge could have viewed the court surveillance cameras which are situated just outside the door to the room which would've proved Mr Walsh's testimony false, but he had no desire to find fault with any of my former legal representative's evidence, only fault with my evidence.

At paragraph 90 (of the judgement), Judge Robson stated that Toop referred to the evidence that I had not reported to my superiors that I was suffering from Graves' disease until the mediation on 25 October 2000. The County Court had already made the determination that the Graves' disease was a red herring. It was not this disease that necessitated the submission of a WorkCover Claim. This statement by Toop wasn't recorded in the transcript, so the judge was making judgement on issues not raised in court, thereby denying me procedural fairness.

The judge further stated after hearing the evidence that had been elicited to that date (which was only oral false evidence) that he wasn't surprised the case ended as it did – he, of course, still had a *completely* open mind at that stage. The pathway of the judge's reasoning to this decision was inadequate; having an open mind means you will give fair consideration to all possibilities, especially where independent evidence exists.

His decision failed to consider that any one of those five lawyers could have even remotely given an untrue answer; even when lies were elicited in evidence the judge explained it away, made excuses for it or utterly ignored the discrepancy. He stated that it wasn't necessary for him to comment on any other matters I raised, yet he then made comment on matters not raised. My matters were significant; he would not allow me to raise issues of credit, which in the situation we found ourselves were extremely relevant, even when issues of my creditability were extensively recorded in his decision.

I went on to say that in my belief the Evidence Act stated that the court may disallow an improper question or improper questioning put to a witness in cross-examination, or inform the witness that it need not be answered. My legal team failed to do this, but the court failed as well. This occurred all through my cross-examination and the court remained silent. I was never informed that I did not have to answer irrelevant questions.

The judge stated that he carefully observed Mr Jen's cross-examination and that in his view his questioning was proper, but he gave no pathway to his decision that the cross-examination was proper, simply because he chose not to. In what way can the question regarding the kind of car I drove be in any way relevant to a personal injury claim relating to workplace bullying and harassment? And how was it okay to ask the same question four times after it had been answered or to seek leave to continue cross-examination supposedly just to ask where I met a friend years after the workplace injury occurred?

I further stated that the judge ignored false testimony. Towards the end of my questioning of the defendant's barrister, I put to him that on the morning of 23 April 2010 at approximately 8:30am, I was informed by my former legal representatives that he had requested leave of the court to continue with his cross-examination and such leave was given. The transcript records, "But you asked for leave to continue cross-examination on that Friday morning? Mr Jens replied, "M'mm, and leave was granted."

Months later I received a copy of the April hearing transcript, and there was no record in the transcript of the defendant's barrister seeking leave of the court to continue cross-examination and no mention that the judge gave such leave. My former barrister had told me this at 8:30am on the morning of 23 April, but court wasn't in session until 10:30am, so when exactly had Mr Jens sought this leave and when had the judge granted it? I attached two pages of the transcript to my submission to the Commission which showed no record of the asking for leave or leave being granted.

There was no evidence in the transcript on either the Thursday 22 April or Friday 23 April that proved the seeking and granting of leave, and yet the defendant barrister under oath stated, "M'mm, and leave was granted and the case ended shortly after."

Barristers have a duty as an officer of the court not to mislead the court, but if the transcript was correct then he ignored his duty to the court and advanced his client's case based on a lie. This was done to support the untruth fed to me by my former barristers, and in doing so, he swore under oath to something he knew to be untrue.

I stated that he did not seek this leave at all, that it was a designed tactic by my former barristers to force me to settle, and thereby Mr Jens was complicit in this behaviour.

Had Mr Jens attested he did not seek leave of the court to continue cross-examination, I would then have proof my legal team had lied and I may have had a chance to have my case reopened and heard as a cause.

There can be no doubt the judge knew that Mr Jens testified under oath to something which was not true – the judge knew he didn't give leave but ignored this false evidence.

The judge talked about when a settlement is binding between the defendant and the plaintiff, but in my understanding any evidence that proves a defendant was complicit null and voids that principle.

I told the Commission that the judge failed to ensure relevant documents were tendered to the court. In the transcript there are a number of references to notes, written instructions, file notes and memorandums supposedly made by legal counsel, and yet none were tendered to the court, nor have I seen them, nor were they in my file. It's one thing to write a note you know to be untrue, but another altogether to put your name to it and have it tendered in court. The judge ignored the very real possibility that these documents did not exist, but were a fabrication by my former legal team.

I didn't understand the tendering process, and this was where the judge should have ensured he protected the rights of an unrepresented litigant, as he had a duty to do so, but he failed in his duty and I was denied procedural fairness.

I further stated to the Commission that the judge committed unnecessary acts of cruelness. The judge stated that my "complaints of bullying were baseless" – this comment flew in the face of all the evidence, which he obviously chose to ignore.

The judge purposely found that the entire 20 professionals and his judicial comrades were all wrong and that he was right, because denigration of the victim was the primary method to protect the positions of his legal friends. No reasonable judge free of malice could have come to such a conclusion based on the available evidence.

In my legal file (held by my former lawyers until years later), I found some pages of the transcript from the April hearing of my cross-examination. On these pages were notations made by my barrister – I didn't know which one as I didn't know their handwriting. The notations on page 44 stated "deliberate bullying," page 51 "bullying," and page 63 "more bullying by John" – coupled with the above, this proved that my barristers knew that my complaints of bullying were not baseless.

The judge made decisions on issues not raised in this trial, so I had no right of reply or any chance to give evidence in my own defence. During the trial he stated—and it is in the transcript—that this hearing was only about one issue and one issue only: was I overborne in giving my consent to the settlement. There was no mention in this hearing transcript of any discussions or evidence around the staff complaint of April 2001, and yet he stated that my complaints arose primarily because some of my own staff had indicated that they did not wish to work with me, and this was simply untrue.

This fact was wrong, and had the judge read the court book he would have known that my WorkCover claim was lodged in November 2000 and didn't involve any issues or problems with my staff – it arose *before* the staff complaint.

An independent investigator found the complaints were baseless, and had the judge told me he would be making a ruling on whether I was bullied or not then I could have provided my evidence. The judge wrongly stated that my response to the staff complaint was a complaint, when it really was a response to their complaint, my right of reply.

The judge denied me the right of natural justice because he was on the trail to prove all the labels directed at me, and was making assumptions not based on fact. He had no intention of addressing his errors because he didn't think it appropriate to make any observations about whether these points were well founded; if he believed this then in all fairness, he should not have included it in his decision. The judge made an accusation but did not give a balanced view or allow me to respond in my own defence.

The judge purposely and unnecessarily made a finding not based on the available evidence, to my detriment; he blamed the victim for being assaulted, and by this time he knew of my psychological susceptibility, and so in total disregard for my welfare made findings designed to further cause me harm.

The judge ignored my right to natural justice by not informing me that he would be making such findings after he had already stated in court that the only point he was adjudicating was whether I was overborne or under duress during the settlement process.

As stated in *Jones v. National Coal Board* (1957), "There is one thing to which everyone in this country is entitled and that is a fair trial at which he can put his case properly before the judge. No cause is lost until the judge has found it so, and he cannot find it without a fair trial."

Lastly, I gave evidence pertaining to *Febriano v. State of Victoria*. I won't go into the full circumstances pertaining to this case, as it's been extensively covered in earlier chapters.

I received a reply from the Commission a few weeks later, stating that I would receive a response to my complaint by no later than the 17th of December 2020. Today, as I write this sentence, it's the 17th of December 2020, and I haven't heard anything as yet. I don't expect anything to come of my contact with the Commission, but I am very interested to see how two of the issues I raised are dealt with: firstly, the case of 'Mrs Febriano', and secondly, Mr Jens giving evidence in court that he and the judge both knew was false. I am guessing it won't be dealt with at all. I can almost hear the buckets of whitewash being stirred.

"Every step toward the goal of justice requires sacrifice, suffering, and struggle; the tireless exertions and passionate concern of dedicated individuals." —Martin Luther King.

On Christmas Eve, I received an email from the Judicial Commission and decided I wouldn't read it until after Christmas, as I was convinced it wouldn't be good news. On Boxing Day, I opened the email and it simply said that more time was required to investigate my complaint. This sounded promising—more time to investigate—but I know not to feel overly positive when dealing with the establishment. I wondered if the Commission was waiting until July 2021, when Judge Robson retired and they'd no longer have jurisdiction to investigate or that any investigation would be moot. Conveniently, a judge isn't accountable for their wrongdoing once retired.

Finally, in late July 2021, a week after the judge had retired from the bench, I received the outcome: my complaint had been dismissed by the Commission. I wasn't surprised.

Human rights and the rule of law are supposedly based on fairness. It is disappointing that the Commission did not have jurisdiction to prove validity of complaints; I believe this is a fundamental problem with the Judicial Commission Act. The Commission appears to rely on a litigant's right to appeal a decision, but it is my understanding that an appeal may only be lodged on an 'error of law', and many of the examples I have provided do not fulfil the criteria of 'errors of law' – they are, in my opinion, errors of conduct.

It appears to me that there must be many occasions when the Commission relies on the catch-all claim that "the Commission does not have jurisdiction to investigate complaints which relate to the merits or lawfulness of a decision" – even when actual wrongdoing is proved. In effect, this may mean that misconduct outside of the actual decision will not be investigated because it appears the Commission has lumped the misconduct as a part of the decision and therefore this misconduct is not open to investigation.

I responded to the Commission and asked a few questions in regards to the dismissal, namely that some areas of my complaint weren't considered in the Commission's determination.

I believe that justice is based on fact and whether a fair investigation has taken place. The major fact of my hearing is that someone said something, not whether that something was true. I understand the Commission's hesitancy, given I've been seen as a threat by some, and so for this I had to be discredited. All that was needed to prove what I said to be true was reviewing even just one piece of the evidence – the audio of the trial, or the trial transcript, or the judge's personnel records.

I further stated that Judge Robson made purposely erroneous decisions and false findings of fact that were not open on the evidence, that he failed to rule out false testimony, and the statement that my "complaints of bullying were baseless."

It is my understanding a judge's ruling must be based on facts that are proven at trial; his ruling that my complaints of bullying were baseless was not factually supported.

The judge's ruling that the complaint to the DPP was "bizarre conduct" was not based on fact, given the sworn evidence I gave in court that I had not written to the DPP.

These are just two examples where the judge made findings of fact which were not fact.

The Commission stated that counsel in my case (Walsh) referred to the matter of *Febriano v. State of Victoria*, even though I hadn't ever been able to find any information on this case.

The Commission stated, "During the 3 June Proceeding, the Complainant's former counsel referred to the matter of *Febriano v. State of Victoria*. The Complainant appears to suggest that this was a coded message from counsel to the Officer as "fabriano" is a Latin word from which the word "fabricate" is derived. The reference was made by counsel. Even if it could possibly be given the meaning the Complainant alleges there is no conduct by the Officer relevant to this complaint." I believe the judgement was the conduct.

There were occasions during trial that irrelevant statements were made that were out of context, which lead me to wonder if there were indeed messages being conveyed.

The reference to the *Febriano* decision made by counsel is possibly another—in the Commission's words—"coded message." To make this irrelevant and out of context statement, I felt counsel may have thought the judge would understand what he was stating, otherwise why make such an oblique statement in the first place?

The Commission found that even "if it could possibly be given the meaning I allege that there is no conduct by the Officer relevant to this complaint." I disagreed with this statement because there was conduct related to this: firstly, the writing of a judgement not based on fact; secondly, the unnecessary findings which caused hurt; thirdly, the fact that the judge did not respond to this statement in any way or seek clarification tells me he may have known what counsel was inferring; fourthly, the length and detail of the ruling in comparison to a number of other cases; and fifthly, the taking of leave right after the judgement was given when the judge had just returned from leave six weeks prior.

I requested the Commission direct me to where I may find *Febriano v.*

State of Victoria, because I was happy to be proven incorrect in my reasonable suspicion. There was no response to my request, and given this I now firmly believe that no such case has ever existed.

I raised the fact that another case heard well after mine was handed down before mine. I believe the Commission was attempting to give legitimacy as to why the judge gave his decision in *Shirreff* before mine by stating, "It is not uncommon for judges to work towards a goal of handing down outstanding decisions before they go on leave. This is not for any malicious reason but rather to prevent parties from waiting even longer for a decision."

I waited longer than *Shirreff,* and as my case ran for about seven hours and *Shirreff* ran for ten days, and given the Commission's response, my ruling could have been handed down before the judge went on leave in July.

The Commission stated, "That another matter that was heard later received a decision earlier is also not evidence of any improper conduct directed at the Complainant. Necessarily each matter must be considered on their merits. As such, some matters may take less time to consider than others."

I agree that this is not necessarily evidence of wrongdoing on its own, but when coupled with other allegations it can take on more relevance. My seven hours of hearing was only to consider one point: was I placed under undue influence to settle. My Ruling appeared to have considerably more "merit" as it took much longer than *Shirreff*'s ten days of hearing, where a number of witnesses and medical evidence needed to be untangled.

I believe for reasons unknown to me that my decision needed to be handed down late on the Thursday, instead of on the previous day (Wednesday) like *Shirreff*. This reminds me of another occasion when I was asked to meet late at work on a Thursday afternoon, when it must have been known that the advertisement of my position was already set for print. I took from this that print deadlines for the weekend closed late on Thursday afternoons.

The Commission's statement said, "some matters may take less time to consider than others." Given my case ran for seven hours, the ruling for my case should have taken much less time than a case which ran for ten days. From the date of hearing, conclusion to judgement in my case took 89 days, while *Shirreff* took just 22 days, and this I believe supports my contention that my decision should have been delivered prior to *Shirreff*.

My seven hours of hearing generated 46 pages of judgement, while the ten-day *Shirreff* hearing generated just 52 pages of judgement. More time was taken on my judgement because of the need to cover every contingency to protect the judge's legal brethren and ensure his decision was not open to appeal.

Interestingly, it appeared the judge keenly wanted *Shirreff* to be successful and awarded over a million dollars in compensation. I believe the judge needed *Shirreff* to be successful, as this case was the only other Workers Compensation case he presided over between the months of June to September 2010. He seemingly had no choice but to use *Shirreff* to prove my earlier statement that if you're going to do something bad, first do something good so your badness isn't questioned because of your goodness.

On my reading of *Shirreff*, there was one important question to be answered—and in reality, a very simple question—which was whether the plaintiff in *Shirreff* was deemed an employee under the Workers Compensation Act. Judge Robson got this simple question wrong (or was he wrong on purpose?) – Shirreff was not an employee, but a contractor. It's common knowledge that if a worker is paid annual leave, sick leave, long service leave and superannuation then the worker is an employee; if they are not paid for these provisions and an invoice is tendered for payment then the worker is a contractor.

Given this, the plaintiff in *Shirreff* lost on appeal. It appears the defendant took issue with two of Judge Robson's findings of fact and that he had 'erred' on around ten findings of fact. For example, the defendant submitted that Judge Robson's reference to a lift shaft being "pitch black" was not supported by the evidence concerning the state of the lighting at the relevant time. Not supported by the evidence? It appears to me that the judge made lots of findings of fact in my case that were not supported by any evidence other than what my former legal team said on the stand.

The Judicial Commission went on to state that they "dismissed this part of the Complaint under section 13(2) (c) of the Act on the grounds that section 16(4) (c) of the Act applies. Section 16(4) (c) of the Act states that the Commission may dismiss a complaint if it is satisfied having regard to all the circumstances of the case, investigation or further investigation of the complaint is unnecessary or unjustified."

Given the information I had provided of my experiences, it was disappointing that the Commission was satisfied that having regard to all the circumstances of the case, investigation or further investigation of the complaint was unnecessary or unjustified. It appeared to me that the Commission had only considered one circumstance—the judgement—and nothing more. Other evidence, such as the trial transcript, had not been part of the investigation – I was told that reading a transcript takes too long. I felt perplexed as to what was required before a complete investigation could take place. I stated that only when a full investigation takes place can the truth be known; an investigation that considered all the evidence and interviewed witnesses, and not just consider one document written by the alleged wrongdoer.

I believe an investigation to be a systematic, minute and thorough attempt to learn the facts about something complex or hidden. The purpose of an investigation is to establish relevant facts to prove or disprove allegations of fraud and corruption. It is a legally established fact-finding process conducted in an impartial and objective manner, with the aim to establish the relevant facts and make recommendations in response. One of the most important virtues of a professional investigator is integrity, and I am not convinced the investigation of my complaint fulfilled any of this criteria.

The Commission further stated that "it has dismissed the remainder of the Complaint pursuant to section 13(2)(c) of the Act on the grounds that section 16(4)(a) of the Act applies. Section 16(4)(a) of the Act provides that the Commission may dismiss a complaint in whole or in part if it is satisfied the complaint has not been substantiated."

The Commission made no reference to the allegation I made about the false testimony of Mr Jens regarding the seeking of leave. The Commission ignored this part of my complaint and remained silent. This part of my complaint had been substantiated by the trial transcript, but the Commission was saying it was unsubstantiated, I find this was at odds with the evidence.

The Commission appeared to be ignoring this false evidence.

In its determination, the Commission made no reference to the allegation that the judge failed to ensure relevant documents were tendered to the court. The judge ignored the very real possibility that these documents did not exist, and given this I believe he had displayed a lack of impartiality and independence, and yet the Commission had made no mention of this lack of procedural fairness.

The Commission also made no reference to the 'unnecessary acts of cruelness' in its determination.

The judge ignored my right to procedural fairness by not informing me that he would be making such finding after he had already stated in court "that the only point he was adjudicating was whether I was overborne or under duress during the settlement process."

The judge went much further than just deciding whether I was overborne or under duress in the settlement process. In my opinion, this was a perfect example of an unnecessary act of cruelness, but I understand that Gleeson CJ's statement "A judge should never cause unnecessary hurt" was just his opinion, and that inflicting psychological pain is not illegal, just immoral.

Finally, the Commission made no determination as to whether the judge should have recused himself from hearing the matter due to his long term personal and professional relationship with Matt Walsh. I believe this amounted to the heightened possibility of bias, or at the least the reasonable apprehension of bias.

An investigation is a search for the truth, to discover truth and to prove certain facts, and I feel the Commission failed in this regard by not conducting initial interviews with me, the judge, or possible witnesses such as the judge's associate. The collection of evidence was limited to just the written judgement.

The leave applications for the judge were not considered – at least the date and time of the judge's leave application should've been verified. This would've been a very easy task for the Commission: if this leave was planned at a much earlier time than 2 September 2010 or there was a health emergency, then there may well be no connection to the *Febriano* evidence given by Walsh. I had no doubt that the judge's associate knew the truth of this and that his evidence was vital. Sadly, a decision which may lack transparency appears to have been made not to interview him or access the audio or any video of the trial.

How can a proper investigation be undertaken and a decision made on such little evidence, when much of my evidence could actually be verified? An investigation involves the discovery of both facts and the examination of those facts to discover the truth. How can this be achieved on one document when that document is not factual?

Arthur Conan Doyle said, "It is a capital mistake to theorise before you have all the evidence. It biases the judgement." Conan Doyle would be rolling in his grave.

I recently read the article 'Brown Political Review: Institutional Gaslighting; Investigations to Silence the Victim and Protect the Perp' written by Michaela Kennedy-Cuomo, and I finally came to understand how the system works against people seeking justice. I've highlighted parts of this paper below in an attempt to offer you a better insight to what I was subjected to in my journey over the past twenty years.

Interestingly, the paper says that when personal injustice, discrimination, harassment or assault is perpetrated within the context of an institution such as a workplace or school—and I would add government organisations such as the police, courts and the legal system generally—the institution often responds – and I would add nearly always responds with action intended not to understand the transgression, but rather to protect itself by silencing the victim or survivor, all while the individual is already vulnerable due to the precipitating harm of "institutional betrayal," which often causes the victim to feel doubted and unsupported.

It goes on to say that the betrayal is uniquely poignant because it's often committed by a team of esteemed people who are framed as the arbiters of justice. In reality, that respected team is intended to protect its institution. In effect, the goal of those who investigate the wrongdoing is not always to decipher the truth or dole the consequences, but rather to silence the victim, consequently enabling the predator. (This is what I had experienced all through my attempts to set the record straight, as you've read.)

Kennedy-Cuomo further states when a group of respected people within an institution are posed as investigating on the victim's behalf, but in actuality act to belittle or deny the reality of the harm committed in order to protect the institution's reputation, the institution can cause the victim to question their own perceptions or reality, feelings, instincts and even sanity. When an authority figure incites self-doubt in the victim, they're employing a tactic of emotional abuse referred to as 'gaslighting'. Perpetrators, whether they be individuals or institutions, use gaslighting to get want they want, typically without ever taking responsibility for their actions. This is certainly what I experienced by some of those involved in the judicial process.

The paper goes on to say that when an institution gaslights a victim in order to protect its own reputation, the institutional betrayal silences, invalidates and harms survivors in their most vulnerable state.

The more shameful the transgressions are, the more likely an institution is gaslighting the victim to silence and bury the issue. This paper included some interesting tactics that are used to cause the victim to question their own perceptions; two of these tactics I experienced while dealing with the Commission were: 'withholding', which occurs when the abuser refuses to listen to the victim – this is demonstrated by the failure to undertake an investigation; and secondly, 'denial', when the abuser pretends that they're not aware of what actually occurred, and this is evidenced by the failure to respond to particular areas of complaint in its determination. All throughout my quest for justice, I found the strategy of 'ignoring' to be tremendously frustrating, as to ignore it suggested it did not happen and thus no incriminating explanation was required.

Institutions commonly betray the victim through their use of gaslighting to inspire doubt, disbelief and dismissal. These abusive tactics culminate, beginning with the first steps after an interpersonal injustice is realised, and this is most certainly my experience. The institution trivialises the survivor's pain while simultaneously dehumanising the survivor. When the institution works to bury cases of harassment instead of working to understand the story, the institution degrades the vulnerable, and this is what happened in most of the institutions in which I found myself, including my former workplace.

I was gaslighted because of my expectation to trust the judgement of the institution, but the institution betrayed justice. When this occurs, it significantly harms the healing of the victim, and proves that one can perpetrate harm without being held accountable for the offense. When a survivor in the wake of injustice stands up and tells their truth, it propels the journey towards justice. I hope this is my journey.

Judge Robson violated my human right to a fair trial, and the Commission violated my right to a fair investigation. Unfortunately, the Commission did not investigate all of my complaint, as it was not within the jurisdiction of the Judicial Commission Act 2016.

Human rights violations by all government departments, boards, commissions, public authorities in the state of Victoria come under the jurisdiction of the Charter of Human Rights and Responsibilities Act 2006, which is governed by the Victorian Ombudsman.

I asked the Commission if they were a "public authority," and their response was: "Apologies for the confusion regarding the question about whether the Commission is a public authority. It can be a bit confusing, and for that reason, I am not able to provide legal advice." I do not believe the simple question of whether the Commission, a taxpayer-funded body, is a public authority warrants legal advice.

I found it laughable that no one in government knew the answer as to whether the Judicial Commission is a 'public authority'. As it's funded with public money, I believe it is a public authority.

Surprisingly, the Ombudsman Act which has the jurisdiction to investigate breaches of the Charter, doesn't have jurisdiction in regards to the Judicial Commission, as the Commission is an exempt body. It appears the Commission is totally unaccountable.

The Ombudsman referred me to the Judicial Commission, the Commission referred me to the Victorian Equal Opportunity and Human Rights Commission, and they referred me to the Ombudsman. This is typical of how our integrity bodies are hamstrung by the law; given the laws are written by lawyers, is it any surprise the laws protect members of arguably the biggest scammers in town, the legal fraternity? I travelled full circle and, the simple question "Is the Judicial Commission a public authority?" remained unanswered. As the Judicial Commission referred me to the Attorney-General, I made contact, asking for the answer to this simple question. Eventually, the Attorney-General's office confirmed that the Commission *is* a public authority.

The need for change is clearly articulated in the following statement of principle by McHugh, J. in the 1994 case of *Stephens*:

> "In the last decade of the twentieth century, the quality of life and the freedom of the ordinary individual in Australia are highly dependent on the exercise of functions and powers vested in public representatives and officials by a vast legal and bureaucratic apparatus funded by public monies. How, when, why and where those functions and powers are or are not exercised are matters that are of real and legitimate interest to every member of the community. Information concerning the exercise of those functions and powers is of vital concern to the community. So is the performance of the public representatives and officials who are invested with them. It follows in my opinion that the general public has a legitimate interest in receiving information concerning matters relevant to the exercise of public functions and powers vested in public representatives and officials.
> Moreover, a narrow view should not be taken of the matters about which the general public has an interest in receiving information. With the increasing integration of the social, economic and political life of Australia, it is difficult to contend, (that the exercise or failure to exercise public functions or powers at any particular level of government or administration, or in any part of the country), is not of relevant interest to the public of Australia generally."

Occasional Integrity

In the *Commonwealth of Australia v. Griffiths 2007*, which was an application for special leave to appeal to the High Court, which I can completely relate to, it was said:

> "Why is it that a judge who disgraces his office, and speaks from the bench words of defamation, falsely and maliciously, and without reasonable or probable cause, is not liable to an action? Is not such conduct of the worst description, and does it not produce great injury to the person affected by it? Why should a witness be able to avail himself of his position in the box and to make without fear of civil consequences a false statement, which in many cases is perjury, and which is malicious and affects the character of another?"

Has anything changed over these years? I fear the philosophy of not bringing "the administration of justice into disrepute so public confidence is maintained" was a powerful consideration for the Commission. My belief is that when the administration of justice brings itself into disrepute, or when there is abuse of the judicial process, it needs to be transparently investigated. I was hopeful that would have occurred.

The Commission expressed to me that I should feel some validation as the judge would be informed of the decision to dismiss. The judge never knew about my submission until the decision to dismiss – an investigation without even talking to the alleged wrong doer, is not an investigation. I felt no validation or joy, and it reminded me when Harrison said I should be happy that WorkCover had to pay out $150,000 in compensation.

The Universal Declaration of Human Rights 1948, which I believe is relevant to my situation, says that no one shall be subjected to torture or to cruel, inhuman or degrading treatment or punishment, that everyone has the right to recognition everywhere as a person before the law, that all are equal before the law and are entitled without any discrimination to equal protection of the law, that all are entitled to equal protection against any discrimination in violation of this Declaration and against any incitement to such discrimination, and that no one shall be subjected to arbitrary interference with his privacy, family, home or correspondence, or to attacks upon his honour and reputation. Everyone has the right to the protection of the law against such interference or attacks.

From the Commission's response, I understand that they cannot conduct a more thorough investigation because the areas of my concerns are not covered by the Judicial Commission Act, therefore they don't have jurisdiction. If this is true, then I believe that this Act is incompatible with the Charter of Human Rights and Responsibilities Act 2006. Or, alternatively, as there appears to be no cause of action for Charter breaches or any oversight of the Commission by another integrity body, they're essentially free to do whatever they like!

If it is correct that the Commission had no jurisdiction to consider all my areas of concern then I feel that a declaration of inconsistent interpretation needs to be made, by whom I do not know, and I'm unable to find out.

In June 2020, the United Nations Human Rights Office through its Special Rapporteur on the Independence of Judges and Lawyers sought international comment for its report 'Disciplinary Measures Against Judges 2020.'

The response from the Judicial Conference of Australia, based in Melbourne, stated:

"We respond to the request from the UN Special Rapporteur as follows:

1. That information is not available. No judges were removed from office.
2. No.
3. No.
4. Constitutional and legislative guarantees of independence have been in place for over a century.

Kind Regards,
Secretary
Judicial Conference of Australia"

According to Transparency International, since 2012 Australia has dropped 8 points, down to 77 in the Corruption Perceptions Index – this is considered a significant decline. Our neighbour, New Zealand, scores much better than Australia. We must improve or it won't be long before we are on a par with many developing countries. What's needed is a National Integrity Commission, that along with state integrity bodies considers all areas of corruption, big and small. Because small can become big.

Judicial Commission of Victoria, Annual Report 2020

"Transparency in the process is critical to achieve the function of instilling public confidence in courts and tribunals." I'm not confident.

Judicial Commission of Victoria, Annual Report 2021

"The Commission provides the officer, the relevant heads of jurisdiction, and the complainant a full report of the outcome, including investigation processes and responses by each party. This is an important element to support transparency of the Commission's complaint procedures. Each party is made aware of outcomes and the rationale behind decisions. This level of clarity and transparency enables the Commission to meet its core aim of maintaining public trust in the courts." Not in my experience.

"The Commission received its 970th complaint since its inception in 2017." Almost 1000 Complaints and not one Judge dismissed. A couple were spoken to, and one or two referred for counselling. It doesn't seem like good value for the millions of dollars in funding the Commission has received and the employment of around 11 highly-paid staff. There must be a better way – 970 people can't all be wrong.

Complaints in the current Annual Report include; failure to give fair hearing (67), denial of due process (55), bias (31), failure to act in judicial manner (29), corruption (13), prejudice (9), conflict of interest (7), and apprehension of bias (6). This totals 217 such complaints and yet it appears only one or two were substantiated. Given this, do we really need a Judicial Commission costing millions where 99% of judges are as pure as the driven snow?

I am no longer of the belief we are all equal under law. Some are more equal than others.

I no longer believe in the Rule of Law or the separation of powers, this separation of powers allows those who hold the ultimate power to be unaccountable. The law is whatever these people want it to be.

In August 2022, Labor MP Gary Maas stated publicly, "The committee work is critically important, because no agency is beyond scrutiny, especially in matters that relate to the welfare of Victorians." He is incorrect – there are some agencies beyond scrutiny and, in my opinion, the Judicial Commission is one such agency.

I followed procedure and referred my concerns to the current Attorney-

General, Jaclyn Symes and am still awaiting acknowledgment more than six months on.

A few years ago, I read on the 'Kangaroo Court of Australia' website (I won't use the author's name): "The most notorious belligerent liars are Lawyers, Barristers and Judges of whom without their blatant misconduct and disregard for truth and justice we might otherwise not have a need for such a Commission."

In late 2022, someone else wrote: "Each generation comes along believing in the political party they support. Some will continue to follow their choice to the end, some will let the scales fall from their eyes but do naught; some will campaign against the corruption that infects politics in Australia. Unfortunately, the latter will always be a minority. At least we try against the entrenched power of the Establishment. But mere ranting will never work. It takes the guts of whistleblowers to point the way. Even if little comes of their efforts, the example of courage should inspire us."

"Conscious bias is one of the hardest things to get at."
Ruth Bader Ginsburg.

Epilogue

Bullying isn't just one or two isolated incidents of physical or mental abuse, but a sustained pattern of negative behaviour directed at you over a prolonged period of time, designed to cause you harm. When bullying is physical, we go to the police or the headmaster or Mum and Dad, and action against the bullying can take place. But when the bullying is psychological, it's more difficult to understand what is happening to you. You question your own mind; your own sanity. Trying to explain what's happening to someone may well end with them believing you're becoming unhinged. Younger targets sadly might not even have the language to describe it.

Why is bullying so effective on diminishing the target's wellbeing? There are a myriad of reasons, but fundamentally, it's because humans are hard-wired to need to be part of the group/clan/village for our physical protection from outside threats.

Bullying obstructs our innate need to belong and to feel valued. This leaves many targets in a state of despair; some will never recover, some will have long-term health issues, and some will end their suffering, with very few reaching their full potential.

A line in a medical report from my then-General Practitioner in 2004 says, "She has continued to suffer as a result of the bullying and subsequent skulduggery used to silence her claim." The skulduggery at my workplace was bad, but the skulduggery of some of those in the legal profession and the judiciary was beyond anything my doctor could have fathomed. I suspect only those who've endured it themselves can imagine. To be accused of wrongdoing and punished, whilst your innocence is known, is surely one of the greatest methods of torture.

In 2012, I participated in the Parliament of the 'Representatives Standing Committee on Education and Employment into Workplace Bullying', and made a submission to the Committee. Part of my submission was included in their report.

When a number of targets of workplace bullying (including myself) made submissions to the Standing Committee, we requested that our names be published. Submissions made by the legal fraternity, the medical fraternity and academics were published with the writers' names, but our names were anonymised, as they were in the final report. Already feeling marginalised, it felt as it our voices were being stifled, to once again protect the reputations of the guilty.

I also attended a forum which allowed those present to make a verbal statement. I quickly wrote down a few notes on how I felt about my experiences, and as difficult as it was, I took the floor. (These notes formed the basis of the oral presentation I gave the court in front of Associate Lansdowne.) After giving my oral presentation to the forum, a man approached me who I came to know as Dr Doug from Heathcote, telling me he found my presentation quite powerful and added, "You're not a harridan." I knew it wasn't a complimentary term but looked it up in the dictionary to be sure – harridan: a strict, bossy or belligerent old woman. Dictionary.com adds: "When you see the word harridan, think of the Wicked Witch of the West." Dr Doug appeared to have come to an earlier conclusion that I *was* a harridan because he had heard of me; I was correct that my reputation had indeed been purposely sullied to protect the guilty. As a fan of *The Wizard of Oz* (from which the term used as the title of this book originates) as well as the musical *Wicked*, I wasn't particularly offended by his comment, especially since he had retracted it.

In order for a bully or bullies to be successful in the workplace, the employer must condone a climate of acceptance and/or ignorance, both equally abhorrent scenarios. In my opinion, far worse than any boss in denial is when others at the workplace, who through their inaction, allow this behaviour. In many organisations, people who call-out wrongdoing are the 'canaries down the coal mine' and should be thanked for giving the organisation an opportunity for improvement. Unfortunately, they usually become scapegoats. Scapegoats for raising organisational failings.

I now tend to feel that everything that happened to me was my own fault, and blame my naivety for believing people are inherently good. Most people are, that is, until they're called out or cornered with a lie or bad behaviour – then self-preservation steps in. I rubbed some people the wrong way by asking questions they didn't want to answer. In actor Denzel Washington's words, "Some people will never like you because your spirit irritates their demons."

I was too trusting, and have paid dearly for this trust, this ingenuousness. Perhaps writing of my experiences is yet another act of trust, but it's something I needed to do. In the words of Karen Salmansohn, "Sometimes you just need to talk about something, not to get sympathy or help, but just to kill its power by allowing the truth of things to hit the air."

I am now wondering if seeking justice was a hindrance to moving on from such an experience, and whether just forgetting and moving on is in the end the right thing to do. The answer will be different for everyone who has suffered abuse of one kind or another. There can be no doubt that the pursuit of justice can bring great unhappiness.

In 'Beyond Reasonable Doubt' (2021), Sawyer wrote, "Injustice does not have a discount rate. Injustice sixty years ago is as important as today," and, "Injustice is not corrected by moving on. Injustice must be redressed to prevent future injustice."

I couldn't agree more. The Nuremburg Trials are an excellent example of 'old' injustices still being relevant today, with war criminals being held to account decades after their offences. Holocaust survivor Elie Wiesel wrote, "What hurts the victim the most is not the cruelty of the oppressor but the silence of the bystander." Wiesel may or may not be aware of similar historical quotes by Napolean Bonaparte, "The world suffers a lot. Not because the violence of bad people. But the silence of good people". And, lastly Roman Emperor and philosopher Marcus Aurelius (121 AD - 180 AD), "You can also commit injustice by doing nothing." And yet here we are, in the civilised 21st century.

I believe that if you've suffered an injustice, the suffering continues until the scales have been rebalanced. The Commission into Institutional Child Abuse has now recognised that it can take a survivor of child sexual abuse up to 33 years to come forward to tell their story. We now know many of these stories, and the effect of long-term injustices assists us as a society to work towards preventing future injustice to vulnerable children. My hope is that these learnings extend to all those who have been abused, through work, through family and through the courts.

I asked my counsellor one day how he would feel if a patient made unfounded allegations against him and then his regulatory board suspended him from practising and then took a couple of years to make a finding. I asked him if he would accept this, and he replied, "No." I then asked him if those who find themselves in this situation should simply ignore this affront to their integrity and just accept their reputation is permanently damaged and move on to some other career? Or should they stand up for themselves? It was then that he understood where I was coming from.

I don't believe that all those named in my book are inherently bad; some just made a bad decision without considering the consequences or their obligations, either personally or professionally.

I'm intrigued by the term 'integrity', and unequivocally believe that many I have mentioned in this book believe that they are people of integrity. Yet their actions don't exemplify integrity or fit my interpretation of the meaning: "Integrity is doing the right thing or making the right decision even if it personally disadvantages you."

In my working life, I had to make decisions I didn't want to make because I knew I would be personally and/or professionally disadvantaged, but I made the decision anyway because it was the right thing to do. I feel this made me enemies, and I now wonder if working to be popular would have been a better option. But a better option for whom? I had to stay true to myself and do the right thing; I couldn't be any other way.

I didn't do anything wrong; I don't have to accept the blame I don't deserve. Slander is toxic—a recognised civil wrong—and it's just *one* aspect of what I have suffered.

It has been my decision and my self-determination driving me to right the wrong. If I didn't go to such lengths, I genuinely believe the toll of not standing up for myself would have been even more damaging to my self-esteem, and to my health, too. I still feel battered and bruised, but in the words of Winston Churchill, "If you're going through hell, keep going."

I travelled three journeys: one path to expose the bullying, one to clear my name and one to obtain justice. I came to understand that the system only seems concerned with how much money it can make out of you and your pain. If you complain, then worse is to come.

Epilogue

I would like to see many changes, beginning with a change to the system that allows this behaviour without chastisement. It's a system that allows an employee to be treated cruelly without intervention, despite clearly suffering, even after raising a concern; a system that allows those in power to turn a blind eye to the behaviour without reprimanding the wrongdoer. And in my case, further victimisation for the submission of a WorkCover claim. It's a system that allows innocent injured workers to have their whole life investigated and paraded in court, despite its relevance being questionable, ultimately resulting in complete unaccountability for the perpetrators – and in the extreme (as in my case), the perpetrators being validated and vindicated.

Whether real change will happen within workplaces is debatable, especially when insurance companies cover the cost of personal injury claims. In the scheme of things, is an increase in premiums really a penalty to a large employer?

Real change in the legal system is what is needed, as said by Chris Graham in his essay "Defending The Indefensible: The Case For Reforming A Justice System That Fails Half The Population." This essay deals mainly with rape survivors, but I feel it relates to all forms of physical and psychological violence against women.

"Our legal system reflects how we really feel about women. A woman's life is not as important as a man's reputation. That must change." And, "It's so important for people to own their own story, their own narrative and to take back control of who they are. And it's so important that survivors know that it's not their fault and to have support of the community and the support of the law."

In the essay, Chris asks a survivor how any woman could trust a system that so routinely and comprehensively fails them. Her reply was, "When you go to court, not only do you have to get past the fact that you feel vulnerable, shameful about your own rape, but you're entering into a process that tells you it's your fault, aggressively accuses you of lying and you've got to prove you're telling the truth." Even though my case was different, I feel that women bullied in the workplace suffer the same fate. To prove you are telling the truth is incredibly difficult when those in power don't want to hear it.

It's over simplistic to suggest we simply need more women in positions of power to balance the male perspective, as there are women in positions of power who could help their struggling sisters, but don't. Some women who gain these lofty positions unfortunately develop the same characteristics of their male counterparts and this fits well with my experiences. Whilst gender equality is something every society should be striving for, the key ingredient—especially in such significant roles—is *integrity*.

In the words of Jo (a bullied worker), "Walking away will only cement what the bully said, what the managers/HR/employers failed to do. If you can move on and live with that, do so, it is less damaging. But for some, living with that is damaging in itself – you will remember that for the rest of your life. Not standing up for your principles and values, no chance to forget, no chance to stop the bully from doing it again, no chance to stop managers turning blind eyes to the mistreatment of employees etc. If you were murdered, would you not want it to be investigated, to never get justice for the loss? Would you want the murderer to be free to do it again and never learn that it is wrong, never to pay? Why should bullying be any different? Some of us lose our lives, physically or near physically and quite often psychologically."

I have a commitment to ethics, which is a commitment to a life of questioning what everybody does. There are occasions where I feel out of step with the rest of the world. When experiencing my first bout of discrimination, I asked Denise, a trusted work colleague, if there was something wrong with me, as it couldn't be the rest of the world. Her response was, "Lori, it's the rest of the world." In moments of self-doubt, I remind myself of Denise's words.

On 11 November 2011, I received the below email from a friend that made me realise that I'm not alone, and never have been – I am in the best of company even though I don't know their names nor they mine.

> "Today in Australia there are many freedom fighters. Some are on the road to changing legislation, some are attempting to gain apologies for past atrocities, some are offering a helping hand at meals on wheels, some are working for changes in the legal system, some trying to protect other living, feeling species, some are helping their neighbours when there is nothing in it for them. They are not giving their lives, but part of their lives in an endeavour to seek a better life including justice for themselves and others.
> However, they are doing this in a country where self-interest, bullying and corrupt conduct appear to rule the day, where few when faced with the mistreatment or unfairness to others are willing to speak up.
> They are doing this when some people are positioning themselves to benefit from impending changes but won't offer an iota of support to

those who have sacrificed years to bring those changes about. So, fellow freedom fighters, if you're being ignored by those in authority, or being thrown out of the Office of the Attorney-General, or wondering why your fight for justice is such a lonely one, you may want to remind those who are creating obstacles, turning a blind eye or waiting for some other sucker to do all the work, of the freedom fighters of long ago, who now sleep in Flanders Fields where poppies grow."

I salute those who have given their life—or who have had their life so changed that they no longer reflect the life they once had—in their action to keep our country and our democracy safe. I thank the unknown heroes who walk among us, forever relegated to the unacknowledged and unappreciated.

Whatever you may think of me and my personality type, ask yourself this question: if your way of life and liberty were threatened, would you want people like me who are persistent, who fight with fairness and never give up, on your side, or would you prefer the bystanders of our world to protect you?

I used to feel privileged to have been born and raised in a democratic country and have my sense of fairness related to my sense of democracy. I have since learnt that our democracy is for the greater good, and individuals such as me, who question authority, experience derision and ostracism.

Though I like to consider myself a forgiving person, over the years, I've struggled with the concept of forgiveness. Small slights or petty actions I can forgive, and do forgive, but what I was subjected to by all those in my story go well beyond the ambit of slight or petty; the impact on me was serious. I read somewhere that in order to forgive someone, they have to first apologise. "If your bully hasn't apologised to you, you do not owe them anything." Not one of the bullies, mobbers or manipulators named in this book has apologised, and I expect no apology from them, as they know not—or do not accept—what they have done. I can live without this forgiveness, as my greatest hurdle is to forgive myself for my naivety; for making foolish mistakes in my search for justice.

The body's physiological response to severe danger is hardwired, and commonly known as the 'fight or flight' response. I believe there's a third response—'freeze'—which traps the victim on the spot. I oscillated between fight and freeze, I fought hard for many years, and the freeze response was my way of allowing myself psychological support and rest. I perfected this strategy; when required I was able to freeze my emotions, which assisted me to survive.

I believe my experiences demonstrate a model of collusive behaviour commonly found in corporate settings, especially government. I never did any wrong or broke any law, and was honest at all times. How I was manipulated into being the perpetual wrongdoer is complex, but I will make one last attempt to explain it with the following analogy.

A (Workplace), B (WorkCover), C (the legal system) and D (Police High Command) perceive that it is in their interests to collude to exclude Z (me). So what needs to be unravelled is why it is in the interest of these four parties for them to collude. The answer to that is usually a combination of reasons such as: if they support Z rather than A, they may have to admit some liability of their own. Plus there's the risk of other liability (i.e. to other parties), and it may be too costly to support Z.

A, B C and D each do an implicit cost-benefit analysis and arrive at the conclusion that it is less costly and less risky to support A, B C and D rather than Z, as Z is powerless and can't do anything about it anyway.

In simple terms, you are falsely accused of being angry and aggressive, you fight, and then another level of accusation that relies on the first accusation to add weight to allegations is made. You fight, and another level of accusations is made which rely on the previous accusations to support their accusations as being true. The innocent becomes the guilty as there are now too many accusations for them not to be true.

Booker T. Washington said, "A lie doesn't become truth, wrong doesn't become right and evil doesn't become good just because it is accepted by a majority."

I have never at any time displayed anger or aggressive behaviour in the workplace – or any place, for that matter. I'm a "chronic complainer" but am a respondent to allegations made against me, and because of this, the label "bizarre conduct" was attached. I admit there were occasions when my behaviour verged on the bizarre, but these occasions were actually months after the label was attached. Given all that I'd experienced, I was fortunate to not have totally lost my mind.

> "It actually doesn't take much to be considered a difficult woman, that's why there are so many of us." — Jane Goodall

Epilogue

You've read about me challenging the narcissists I met on this journey—possessing their carefully constructed delusional world of power—with the truth I possessed about their characters. It's what set me up to be a target of a massive smear campaign, where I was fought against with a psychopathy I didn't know existed. I did not allow these narcissists to lie, denigrate and disrespect me without a fight, and so they called me difficult. To make smear campaigns more believable, abusers of this ilk gang up against victims to feel empowered, to oppress their targets, and to victim-blame. It is unbelievable to me that so many did this – but more unbelievable to me is that, in this enlightened world, they actually got away with it.

If I could give three pieces of advice, here's what they'd be. One: if you're feeling bullied at work, leave, as nothing will change, as once targeted your job is gone. Do not expect that laws, regulations and guidelines will save you – they won't! No job is worth your physical and mental health. I know this is difficult, as you've done no wrong, but that doesn't matter – you are guilty of being innocent, and the bullies cannot stand that and will make sure you're guilty of *something*.

If resigning isn't your first option, I've recommended to others to take your record of bullying and a lawyer to a visit with the CEO (or whoever is the top of the tree at your workplace). Often these people don't know what's going on and have only been briefed by the perpetrators.

Make an offer of settlement to the CEO, and if this person is wise, they should offer you some financial compensation to tide you over until a new job is found.

If you see the CEO *without* a lawyer it may be viewed as blackmail, and could be used against you, and your employment may be terminated. As you will understand, I am certainly not a supporter of most in the legal profession, but they do play a role here, one that may save you your sanity and your life.

The second piece of advice is somewhat oxymoronic: never engage with the legal profession. Most are sharks and you are nothing but a minnow. Justice can be a game, one you are not allowed to play, and if you think you have 'right' on your side please reread my chapters on the legal profession. A common saying goes, "The courts are littered with the remains of people who thought they mattered." And I love this quote from George Bernard Shaw, "I learned long ago, never to wrestle with pigs. You get dirty, and besides the pig likes it."

And thirdly, be kind – to yourself, and to others who come your way. Or in the words of Anne Lamott, "You own everything that happened to you. Tell your stories. If people wanted you to write warmly about them, they should have behaved better." Every person has a story worth telling, tell yours before it is too late – the future may need it.

Everything I have written in this book is true. There are people out there who know this, but will never come forward, at least not until self-preservation no longer rules their lives. If you witness wrongdoing, please stand by her or him – don't be a bystander.

I fought hard believing the system was broken and that somehow I could fix it—and that I actually had a responsibility to try and fix it—but after some reading, critical thinking, soul-searching and putting my story into words, I now understand that the system isn't broken: it's working the way it's supposed to.

Every now and then I receive an email that fills me with a sense of validation, like this one:

> The way you have performed in your fight for justice is just amazing.
> I am so proud to know you.
> You are my hero.

Since I began writing this book, presidents, princes, premiers, cardinals and attorney-generals are now being held accountable for their bad behaviour. I can only hope that one day those who see themselves above the law—because they *are* the law—will be held similarly accountable for the wrongs they have committed.

> "When the law doesn't apply to the lawmakers you're not being governed: you're being ruled." Author Unknown

I am apprehensive that writing my experiences will make me some enemies, but the truth should not be hidden because of fear, and I want to face my fear head-on. It will not be said at my funeral that "she was such a lovely lady who didn't have an enemy in the world" – I'd much rather it be said that "she had prominent enemies because she stood up for what she believed in and was fearless in the face of adversity."

Robert Green, an enlightened 1500s English playwright, once said, "Reputation is the cornerstone of power. Through reputation alone you can

Epilogue

intimidate and win; once it slips, however, you are vulnerable, and will be attacked on all sides. Make your reputation unassailable." I worked hard to ensure I had a positive personal and professional reputation, but I now understand the need of the bullies to attack this to strip me of my power. I have learned through my experiences that it takes years to build trust, but it only takes the most minor of suspicion, not proof, to destroy all you have worked for.

Adapted from Cherie White's blog:

"Once your reputation is gone, you're defenceless and extremely vulnerable to attack. Bullies can then freely attack you from all directions. Even worse, you're at the mercy of virtually everyone around you. Bullies know they can poke holes in your reputation; they won't have to work so hard to bring you down because now they have public opinion on their side. They can stand back and watch with glee as widely held perceptions of you finish you off. The bullies start by planting seeds of doubt about your character in the minds of others. Doubt is a powerful tool, coupled with the rumours and lies they spread."

I understand this strategy all too well, and find it quite chilling that my former barrister and the judge possibly colluded in encouraging me to end my life, so I would no longer be a problem for them or the Court. They failed, and I survive in spite of them.

It must be remembered that it is common for workplace bullies and narcissists to claim to be victims of bullying themselves. DARVO offers an explanation.

DARVO is a concept developed by psychology professor Jennifer Freyd and:

"Refers to a reaction perpetrators of wrongdoing, particularly sexual offenders, may display in response to being held accountable for their behaviour. DARVO stands for "Deny, Attack, and Reverse Victim and Offender. The perpetrator or offender may Deny the behaviour, Attack the individual doing the confronting, and Reverse the roles of Victim and Offender such that the perpetrator assumes the victim role and turns the true victim, or the whistleblower, into an alleged offender. This occurs, for instance, when a guilty perpetrator assumes the role of "falsely accused" and attacks the accuser's credibility and blames the accuser of being the perpetrator of a false accusation.

And, not surprisingly there is institutional DARVO which occurs when the DARVO is committed by an institution (or with institutional complicity) as when police charge rape victims with lying. Institutional DARVO is a pernicious form of institutional betrayal."

As someone who has experienced multiple manifestations of DARVO, I feel I have a profound understanding of the devastating impact it can have on one's psychological health.

The best way to describe how it is to live with trauma is this quote from a mental health discussion blog: "We live through a traumatic event and people think we should get over it, because it's the past. The thing they don't realise is we are reliving it over and over again in our heads. In our minds there is no past, it's always present."

This is what I have been living with now for many years, trauma upon trauma upon trauma. It is always there, playing softly in the background, dulled by the noise of daily life, becoming loud each night when my head seeks solace in sleep.

It is liberating when you're no longer afraid of what people think of you, and even more liberating when you no longer fear death. Death will come to us all – some early and some later. Death is the one thing we all have in common, and no amount of money or power can change your destiny, so live your best life. And if you can leave this world a better place for having you in it then your life has had meaning and purpose.

I haven't written this book believing that it would be a bestseller or even a seller at all – I wrote it for my own self. To put words down on paper and out of my head, so that I may live the remaining years of my life in some peace. If my story helps just one person, that's a bonus.

Hannah Gadsby wrote in *Ten Steps to Nanette*:

> "As I watch people walk away when it gets too hard, as I find myself defeated and wanting to return to my performed self, I think of Adrienne Rich: 'When a woman tells the truth she creates the possibility of more truth around her.' What I would have done to have heard a story like mine. Not for blame. Not for reputation, not for money, not for power. But to feel less alone. To feel connected. I want my story heard."

Epilogue

"Every time I addressed something that bothered me, I became the problem." I believe the truth sets us free.

I am fortunate to have many friends who understand me and support me without question. I have loved and lost, have family that cares for me and a warm and loving home. I am truly blessed, I am resilient and I am a survivor.
I feel Dan would be proud of his Ma.

"Every time we turn our heads the other way when we see the law flouted, when we tolerate what we know to be wrong, when we close our eyes and ears to the corrupt because we are too busy or too frightened to speak up and speak out, we strike a blow against freedom, decency and justice." Robert F Kennedy

Please feel free to say hello, share your feedback and/or your own experience with me at loriokeeffe@gmail.com

www.ingramcontent.com/pod-product-compliance
Lightning Source LLC
Chambersburg PA
CBHW050257010526
44107CB00055B/2080